THE HISTORY OF CALIFORNA CENTRAL SECTION WRESTLING
(and more)

2007-2020

Compiled and Edited by
MIKE STRICKER

JANAWAY PUBLISHING
Santa Maria, California

The History of California
Central Section Wrestling (and More)
2007-2020

Copyright © 2020 by Mike Stricker

ALL RIGHTS RESERVED.
No part of this publication may be reproduced, stored in a retrieval
system, or transmitted in any form or by any
means whatsoever, whether electronic, mechanical,
magnetic recording, or photocopying, without the
prior written approval of the Copyright holder
or Publisher, excepting brief quotations
for inclusion in book reviews.

Compiled and Edited by: Mike Stricker

Published by:

Janaway Publishing, Inc.
James J. Skidmore
732 Kelsey Ct.
Santa Maria, California 93454
(805) 925-1952
www.janawaygenealogy.com

2020

ISBN: 978-1-59641-457-0

Made in the United States of America

INTRODUCTION / DEDICATION

Over the years, I have spent countless hours researching the history of the San Joaquin Valley Wrestling. In this book I have compiled the results both Central Section qualifiers, beginning with the Yosemite Championships and the Sierra-Sequoia Championships. In addition, this book documents the results of the South Yosemite League, Southeast Yosemite League, Southwest Yosemite, South Sequoia League and the Division I, II, III, IV, V Championships.

My research of the Central Section, or "Valley" has allowed me to share the rich wrestling history and bring forth the proud tradition of this area in the sport of wrestling. The Central Section is noted for its wrestling prowess through the state of California and across the nation. The Central Section produced NCAA wrestling champions and numerous wrestlers who have competed and captured victories at the highest level of competition.

This book is dedicated to these four outstanding educators and coaches who 60 years ago jump-started high school wrestling in the Bakersfield and Kern County area.

Mike Stricker
Bakersfield, California
2020

Leon Tedder
Math Teacher/Coach
East Bakersfield High School

Win "Boot" Boatman History
Teacher/Coach North
Bakersfield High School

Bruce Pfutzenreuter History
Teacher/Coach South
Bakersfield High School

Olan Polite
History Teacher/Coach
Bakersfield High School

—Californian Photo

PREP GRAPPLING COACHES-Responsible for a tremendous increase in schoolboy wrestling interest and participation in Bakersfield have been coaches (left to right) Leon Tedder, East High; Win Boatman, North High; Bruce Pfutzenreuter, South High, and Olan Polite, Bakersfield High.

The History of Central Section Wrestling (and more) 1952-2020

Compiled and Edited by Mike Stricker
First Edition 2007 Mike Stricker
Second Edition 2020 Mike Stricker

Credits:
  The Bakersfield Californian
  The Fresno Bee
  Selma Enterprise
  Tech-Fall.com   John Sachs
  Santa Maria Times
  Visalia Times Delta
  Clovis Independent
  Amateur Wrestling News
  USA Wrestler
  Wrestling International News Magazine
  Cal-Hi Sports   Dennis Bardsley
  The California Wrestler   Al Fontes
  The Mat.com   David Gardner
  Sinai Enterprises   Gary Pederson
  Rhonda Moore
  Driller Wrestling
  Clovis Wrestling
  Porterville Wrestling
  Dinuba Wrestling
  Nick Ellis
  Sylvia Lomas
  Armand Guerrero
  Javier Valdes
  Ray Hammond

Special thanks to the numerous people in The valley who took time to look in high school yearbooks for first names of wrestlers and Coaches.

Funding for the printing of this book
Generously provided by:
Harry and Ethel West Foundation
Bakersfield, California
Coyote Club Armature Wrestling
P.O. Box 9865
Bakersfield, CA. 93389

Please send corrections and/or additions:
Mike Stricker c/o The Coyote Club
P.O. Box 9865 Bakersfield, CA. 93389
Or e-mail mikestricker@sbcglobal.net

Disclaimer: The accuracy of the information Here is limited to the accuracy of the sources and to the recording of the sources.

About the author

Mike Stricker has made numerous contributions to the sport of Wrestling through his life. As a founding executive board member and CEO of the Coyote Club, an amateur wrestling support group established in 1986, Stricker has led the organization in raising more the $3 million during the last 34 years in support of "the world's oldest sport." In addition, he serves on various committees and associations, including the committees responsible for having his hometown of Bakersfield the home of state wrestling championships. Stricker was a founding member and officer of Kern County Wrestling Association from 1974 to 1984. He is an inductee of the California Wrestling Hall of Fame, the California Chapter of the National Wrestling Hall of Fame, and the South Bakersfield High Hall of Fame. Stricker has been a wrestling competitor as a youth in high school and college, a referee, and youth, high school and college coach, and continues to support the sport as a fan, booster and fundraiser. In 2000, Stricker was honored with the prestigious Irv Olinger Award by the California Wrestling Coaches Association at the state wrestling championships in Stockton. His 30-year career began at Chico State under coaching legend Dick Trimmer. Stricker went on to coach with some of the finest coaches in the history of the Central Section, including Joe Seay, Art Chavez, Bob Lathrop, Eugene Walker and his sons Ty Stricker wrestled at South Bakersfield High and Bakersfield College, and son Tad wrestled at South Bakersfield High and Oklahoma State University. Stricker resides in Bakersfield with his wife Lynn, and is immensely proud of his two sons, Ty (former head coach at West Bakersfield High and North Bakersfield High) and Tad (former head coach at Loara High in Anaheim and currently an assistant wrestling coach at Servite High School) Stricker is current a board member of the California Hall of Fame and an Ad Hoc committee member of the California Chapter of the National Hall of Fame.

Cover photo: Jake Varner, Bakersfield High School, Iowa State and Olympic Champion

CONTENTS

Section I: Central Section
South Yosemite League 2011-2020 2
Southeast Yosemite League 2007-2020 16
Southwest Yosemite League 2007-2020 40
South Yosemite Conference 2019-2020 63
South Sequoia League 2007-2020 66
Yosemite Divisional 2007-2018 90
Sierra-Sequoia Divisional 2007-2018 124
Central Section Team Champions and Most Outstanding Wrestlers 152
Division Championships 1,2,3,4,5, 2019-2020 156
Central Section Masters 2000-2020 178
California State Championships 2007-2020 218

Section II: National High School
National High School Wrestling Coaches Association Championships
1990-2019 Senior, Junior, Sophomore, Freshman 238
Amateur Wrestling News All-Americans 243
Wrestling USA Magazine All-Americans 245
Asica High School All-Americans 247
Junior USA National Championships 249
Cadet USA National Championships 251
Flo Nationals 254
Folkstyle Nationals Junior 255
Folkstyle Nationals Cadet 256
USWF Nationals, National AAU, Junior National AAU, FILA Junior Nationals
FILA Cadet Nationals, FILA Junior World, Cadet World 257
Young Wrestler, Inter-Mat, USA Today,Open-Mat All-American Teams 259
Clinch Gear, Pittsburg Post Classic, FILA Cadet, UWW Cadet, FILA World Cadet 260

Section III: Collegiate Wrestling
NCAA Division I 262
NCAA Division II 264
NCAA Division III and National Association Intercollegiate Athletics 266
Midlands Championships 267
National Wrestling Coaches All-Star Classic 268

Section IV: National and International Wrestling
USA Senior National Freestyle and GrecoRoman Championships 270
AAU National Freestyle and Greco Roman Championships, USWF National Freestyle
and Greco Roman Championships, National YMCA Championships, Goodwill Games
FILA World University World Games 271
Olympic Games, World Championships, World Cup, Pan-American Games 272
FILA Junior Nationals, U-23 Worlds, UWW, Espoir Nationals, Espoir FILA Juniors
Tbilsi Russia, U.S. Olympic Festival 273
USA Wrestling National UniversityChampionships 275

Section V:
Kern County Coaching Staffs 278
Coach and Wrestlers Profiles 318

SOUTH YOSEMITE LEAGUE

2007-2020

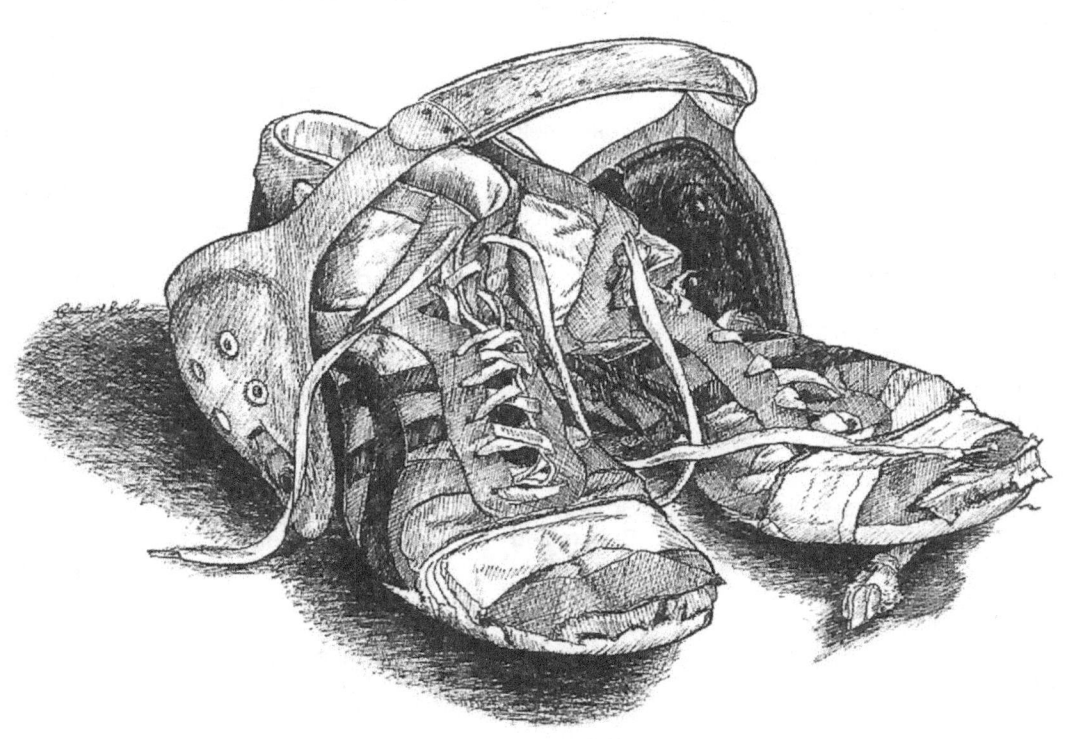

SOUTH YOSEMITE LEAGUE
TEAM CHAMPIONS

Date	Location	Dual Champion	Tournament Champion	Overall Champion	Coach
1/30/1957	Bakersfield	Bakersfield 5-1	East	Bakersfield	Paul Briggs
2/08/1958	North	Bakersfield 6-0	East	Bakersfield	Paul Briggs
2/13/1959	East	Bakersfield 8-1-1	East	Bakersfield	Paul Briggs
2/13/1960	Arvin	South 7-0-1	South	South	B. Pfutzeneuter
2/11/1961	North	East 8-0	East	East	Leon Tedder
2/10/1962	South	East 7-0	Bakersfield	East	Leon Tedder
2/09/1963	East	East 10-0	Bakersfield	East	Leon Tedder
2/15/1964	Bakersfield	South 9-0-1	Bakersfield	South	B. Pfutzeneuter
2/2019/65	Foothill	South 9-0-1	South	South	Joe Seay
2/19/1966	North	South 7-1	South	South	Joe Seay
2/11/1967	Bakersfield	South/North 6-2	South	South	Joe Seay
2/10/1968	East	South 8-1-1	Bakersfield	South	Joe Seay
2/15/1969	Bakersfield	South 10-0	South	South	Joe Seay
2/14/1970	Foothill	Bakersfield 10-0	Bakersfield	Bakersfield	Olan Polite
2/12/1971	West	Bakersfield 8-2	Bakersfield	Bakersfield	Olan Polite
2/19/1972	Bakersfield	Bakersfield 11-1	Bakersfield	Bakersfield	Olan Polite
2/10/1973	South	Bakersfield 11-1	Bakersfield	Bakersfield	Olin Polite
2/09/1974	Highland	West 6-0	Highland	Highland	Joe Barton
2/15/1975	Foothill	Highland/West 10-2	Highland	Highland	Joe Barton
2/14/1976	Foothill	Highland 5-1	Highland	Highland	Joe Barton
2/11/1977	Foothill	Bakersfield 6-0	Bakersfield	Bakersfield	Steve Varner
2/15/1978	Foothill	North 6-0	Bakersfield	Bakersfield	Steve Varner
2/10/1979	Foothill	Bakersfield/North/South 5-1	South	South	Eugene Walker
2/16/1980	Foothill	Bakersfield 7-0	Bakersfield	Bakersfield	Steve Varner
2/12/1981	Foothill	South 7-0	South	South	Eugene Walker
2/12/1982	Foothill	Bakersfield 7-0	South	Bakersfield South	S.Varner E.Walker
2/11/1983	Foothill	Foothill 7-0	Foothill	Foothill	Seymour Nerove
2/11/1984	Foothill	Arvin 7-0	Foothill	Foothill	Seymour Nerove
2/09/1985	Foothill	Foothill 7-0	Foothill	Foothill	Seymour Nerove
2/15/1986	Foothill	South 7-0	South	South	Eugene Walker
2/14/1987	Foothill	South 7-0	South	South	Eugene Walker
2/1219/88	Foothill	Arvin 7-0	Arvin	Arvin	Ruben Ramirez
2/11/1989	Foothill	Bakersfield 7-0	Bakersfield	Bakersfield	David East
2/10/1990	Foothill	Bakersfield 7-0	Bakersfield	Bakersfield	David East
2/09/1991	Foothill	Bakersfield 7-0	Bakersfield	Bakersfield	David East
2/08/1992	East	North 6-0	Bakersfield	Bakersfield North	David East Rick McKinney
2/13/1998	East	Bakersfield 7-0	Bakersfield	Bakersfield	David East
2/12/1994	East	Bakersfield 7-0	Bakersfield	Bakersfield	David East
2/12/2011	South	West 3-1	West	West	James Herrera
2/11/2012	South	South 4-0	South	South	Brian Henderson
2/08/2013	Mira Monte	Golden Valley 4-0	South	South Golden Valley	Brian Henderson Aaron Wherry
2/14/2014	Mira Monte	Golden Valley 4-0	South	Golden Valley	Aaron Wherry
2/15/2015	East	Golden Valley 5-0	Golden Valley	Golden Valley	Aaron Wherry
2/10/2016	East	Golden Valley 4-1	Golden Valley	Golden Valley	Aaron Wherry
2/09/2017	East	Golden Valley 5-0	Golden Valley	Golden Valley	Aaron Wherry
2/07/2018	East	Ridgeview 5-0	Golden Valley	Golden Valley Ridgeview	Aaron Wherry Aaron Garza
2019		Golden Valley 5-0	No Tournament		Aaron Wherry
2020		No dual Champion		Ridgeview	Aaron Garza

SOUTH YOSEMITE LEAGUE
MOST OUTSTANDING WRESTLERS

Year	Name	School
1959	Larry Carpenter	East
1971	Gary Mayberry	Foothill
1972	Ed Valdes	South
1973		
1974	Ray Garza	East
1975	Paul Felez	South
1976		
1977	Jeff Fahy	West
1978		
1979		

Year	Lower Weight		Upper Weight	
1980	Joe Bisig	South	Flint Pulskamp	Highland
1981	Richie Sinnott	Highland	Dan Mayberry	Foothill
1982				
1983				
1984				
1985	Mike Dallas	Foothill	Ben Lizama	Foothill
1986				
1987	Troy Beavers	Highland	Chris Olinger	South
1988				
1989	Parris Whitley	South	Jassen Frohlich	Bakersfield
1990	Parris Whitley	South	Tad Stricker	South
1991	Jeff Heberle	North	Paul Carrillo	South
1992	Mario Gonzales	South	Romel Green	Highland
1993	Chad Hobbs	North	Willie Herron	Highland
1994	Kelly Miller	Bakersfield	Jeremy Karle	Highland
2011	Francisco Gomez	Ridgeview	Tyson-Lee Hodges	South
2012	Abel Mejio	Golden Valley	Adam Morrison	Ridgeview
2013	Jovan Carrillo	South	Gabriel Rosas	Ridgeview
2014	Jose Beltran	Mira Monte	Nimrod Quintanilla	Golden Valley
2015	Daniel Uranday	East	Christian Montano	West
2016	Esteban Corona	Independence	Gilbert Varela	Independence
2017	Marcus Hutcherson	West	Albert Urias	Ridgeview
2018	Vincent Carrillo	Independence	Valentin Sanchez	Ridgeview
2019	Jayven Rojas	Golden Valley	Nathan Enriques	Independence
2020	Sabastian Lara	Ridgeview	Dominic Leon	Golden Valley

Starting in 1985, the Coyote Club Membership sponsored the awards

Parris Whitley - South High School
Lorenzo Neal – Lemoore High School

SOUTH YOSEMITE LEAGUE - South
February 12, 2011

103
Castaneda, Victor	West, Fall 1:52
Roberto, Carlos	South

112
Gomez, Francisco	Ridgeview, 12-9
Medina, Jesus	Golden Valley
Nava, Sal	South, Fall 1:27
Cruz, Alex	West

119
Leandro, Jose,	Golden Valley, TF 16-0
Hernandez, Martin	West
Torres, Dakota	South, Fall 1:01
Macias, Sergio	Mira Monte

128
Sanchez, Joshua	Ridgeview, 2-1
Toro, James	West
Nava, Carlos	South

130
Fuentes, Adam	Ridgeview, Fall 3:17
Rueda, Miguel	Mira Monte
Barboza, Chris	South

135
Gutierrez, Jeffery	Golden Valley, Fall 3:49
Valdez, Bryan	Ridgeview
Nolbert, Malcom	South, Fall 1:16
Hahn, Leonard	West
Gutierrez, Andrew	Mira Monte

140
Trejo, Miguel	West, Major 23-9
Andrade, Eric	Mira Monte
Banducci, Kendall	Golden Valley, 10-5
Ruiz-Haods, David	South
Talan, Adam	Ridgeview

145
Ortiz, Able	Golden Valley, Fall 1:48
Garcia, Phillip	West
Mota, Felipe	?

152
Chavez, Victor	West, 11-6
Daniels, Dale	South
Pearson, Fashawn	Golden Valley, 10-5
Sanchez, Alejandro	Mira Monte

160
Luna, Cesar	West, Fall 3:35
Morrison, Aaron	Ridgeview
Loera, Felipe	Mira Monte

170
Spears, Jacob	Ridgeview, Fall 4:55
Hernandez, Jorge	West
Schultz, Jeffery	South, Fall 1:31
Perez, Mark	Mira Monte
Corona, William	Golden Valley

189
Williams, Chantz	South, Fall 4:34
Carrillo, Andres	West
Rodriguez, Fernando	Ridgeview, Fall 1:27
Garcia, Omar	Golden Valley

215
Webber, Jay	South, Major 15-4
Delgado, Noe	Ridgeview
Romero, Edwin	Golden Valley, 4-3
Lainez, Oscar	Mira Monte

285
Hodges, Tyshon-Lee	South, Fall :28
Rosas, Salvador	Ridgeview
Navieras, Pedro	Golden Valley, Fall 1:58
Villanueva, Angel	Mira Monte
Chavez, Roman	West

Most Outstanding Wrestlers

Lower Weight: Francisco Gomez, Ridgeview
Upper Weight: Tyson-Lee Hodges, South

TOURNAMENT
West	176.5
Ridgeview	155
South	153
Golden Valley	111
Mira Monte	64

DUAL	LEAGUE	SEASON
West	3-1	3-7
Ridgeview	3-1	4-2
South	3-1	3-2
Golden Valley	1-3	10-3
Mira Monte	0-4	0-5

SOUTH YOSEMITE LEAGUE – Mira Monte
February 11, 2012

106
Mejia, Abel	Golden Valley, Fall: 55
Salas, Xavier	Mira Monte
Romero, Carlos	South, Fall 3:27
Gonzalez, Gilbert	Ridgeview

113
Castaneda, Victor	West, Fall 3:24
Daniels, Jovan	South
Nieto, Carlos	Mira Monte

120
Gomez, Franco	Ridgeview, 8-1
Echeveria, Emmanuel	South
Gonzalez, Roman	West, 13-12
Hord, Charles	Golden Valley
Stidman, John	Mira Monte

126
Nava, Sal	South, 14-4
Villanueva, Able	Mira Monte
Griego, Michael	Ridgeview

132
Torres, Dakota	South, 10-2
Garcia, Phillip	West
Gonzalez, Eduardo	Golden Valley, Fall 3:41
Magno, Brandon	Ridgeview

138
Andrade, Eric	Mira Monte, Fall 4:20
Saenz, Christian	South
Franco, Phillip	West, Fall 1:10
Gonzales, Christian	Ridgeview

145
Toro, James	West, TF 28-12
Lopez, Eddie	Golden Valley
Mota, Felipe	South, Fall 1:32
Spainhoward, Josh	Ridgeview
Soto, Felipe	Mira Monte

152
Trejo, Miguel	West, TF 5:20
Alfaro, Silvester	South
Fuentes, Julio	Golden Valley, Fall 1:31
Harelston, Paul	Mira Monte

160
Pearson, Fashawn	Golden Valley, Decision
Daniel, Dale	South

170
Morrison, Aaron	Ridgeview, Fall 3:40
Lugo, Eric	Golden Valley
Flores, Mark	West, Fall 1:57
Thomas, Troy	Mira Monte
Rodriguez, Edwin	South

182
Pineda, Richard	South, 8-2
Ortiz, Los	Ridgeview
Carrillo, Andres	West, Fall 1:06
Gamino, Edward	Golden Valley
Moreno, Edward	Mira Monte

195
Lopez, Jacob	Ridgeview, 8-5
Gutierrez, Greg	South
Miniz, Juan	Golden Valley, 8-4
Garcia, Gustavo	Mira Monte

220
Delgado, Noe	Ridgeview, Fall 1:23
Webber, Jay	South
Hernandez, Rene	Golden Valley, Fall 1:51
Alvarez, Diego	Mira Monte
Hernandez, Andrew	West

285
Hodges, Tyshon	South, Fall :52
Hernandez, Jose	Golden Valley
Rosas, Gabriel	Ridgeview, Fall :37
Alaron, Miguel	Mira Monte

Most Outstanding Wrestlers

Lower Weight:	Abel Mejia, Golden Valley
Upper Weight:	Aaron Morrison, Ridgeview

TOURNAMENT
South	206.5
Golden Valley	151
Ridgeview	132.5
West	125.5
Mira Monte	93

DUAL	LEAGUE	SEASON
South	4-0	4-1
Golden Valley	2-2	7-4
Ridgeview	2-2	3-4
West	1-3	1-3
Mira Monte	1-3	1-3

SOUTH YOSEMITE LEAGUE – Mira Monte
February 8, 2013

106
Cruz, Joseph	West, Fall 1:42
Hernandez, Daniel	Golden Valley
Romero, Carlos	South, 13-11
Nunez, Rudy	Mira Monte

113
Daniel, Jovan	South, 8-1
Salas, Xavier	Mira Monte
Butler, William	West, DQ
Linthicum, Edward	Golden Valley

120
Cordona, Daniel	Golden Valley, Fall 3:55
Vasquez, Christian	West
Nieto, Carlos	Mira Monte

126
Kyle, Simon	South, 8-7
Medina, Jesus	Golden Valley
Castaneda, Victor	West, 2-0
Villanueva, Abel	Mira Monte, 12-1
Gonzalez, Gilbert	Ridgeview

132
Carrillo, Javan	South, 18-4
Hord, Charles	Golden Valley
Saldana, Francisco	Mira Monte, Fall 1:17
Cruz, Alex	West

138
Alcala, Eric	Mira Monte, 13-10
Jones, Phelan	South
Stainaker, Braxton	Golden Valley, 8-2
Navarro, Robert	Ridgeview, Fall :58
Jaramillo, Joseph	West

145
Alfaro, Silvester	South, 10-2
Gonzalez, Edward	Golden Valley
Beltran, Jose	Mira Monte, Fall 1:34
Terrazas, James	Ridgeview, Fall 1:00
Salazar, Christian	West

152
Lopez, Eddie	Golden Valley, Fall 5:52
Mara, Jose	South
Segura, Anthony	Mira Monte

160
Fuentes, Julio	Golden Valley, 13-2
Garcia, Chris	South
Munoz, Christian	West

170
Mireles, Isaiah	South, Fall 3:09
Romero, Issek	Golden Valley
Lugo, Matthew	West, Fall 1:33
Castillo, Daniel	Mira Monte

182
Bustamante, Brando	West, Fall 1:47
Dhanna, Manvir	Golden Valley
Reice, Rubin	South, Fall 4:41
Gonzales, Rogelio	Mira Monte, Forfeit
Ortiz, Los	Ridgeview

195
Lopez, Jacob	Ridgeview, 11-4
Castro, Jonathan	Golden Valley
Martinez, Diego	South, Fall 1:27
Quiroz, Michael	West

220
Delgado, Noe	Ridgeview, Fall 4:42
Oganista, Miguel	South
Mendez, Aaron	Golden Valley

285
Rosas, Gabriel	Ridgeview, 5-0
Harris, Dartanyan	South
Quintonilla, Nimrod	Golden Valley, Fall :25
Romo, Jose	Mira Monte

Most Outstanding Wrestlers

Lower Weight: Jovan Carrillo   South
Upper Weight: Gabriel Rosas   Ridgeview

TOURNAMENT
South	205
Golden Valley	196
West	116
Ridgeview	97
Mira Monte	97

DUAL	LEAGUE	SEASON
Golden Valley	4-0	8-1
South	3-1	3-2
Ridgeview	2-2	4-4
Mira Monte	1-3	1-4
West	0-4	0-8

SOUTH YOSEMITE LEAGUE – Mira Monte
February 14, 2014

106
Garcia, Levi-Chevy	South, Fall :44
Hutcherson, Marcus	West
Nunuez, Rudy	Mira Monte, 10-2
Salazar, Bobby	Golden Valley

113
Cruz, Joseph	West, Fall 1:20
Gautan, Karam	South
Aubrey, Lawrence	Mira Monte, Fall 1:35
Silva, Irving	Golden Valley

120
Butler, William	West, Fall 5:39
Daniels, Jovan	South
Nieto, Carlos	Mira Monte, Fall 3:50
Bishop, Austin	Golden Valley

126
Hord, Charles	Golden Valley, 10-3
Gueymock, Anthony	South
Chairez, Jacob	West, 15-10
Villanueva, Able	Mira Monte

132
Stainaker, Braxton	Golden Valley, Major 11-3
Macias, Martin	South
Gonzalez, Gilbert	Ridgeview, Fall 1:23
Marquez, Johnny	West

138
Alcala, Erik	Mira Monte, 11-3
Simental, Saul	Golden Valley
Moreno, Dominic	Ridgeview, Fall 5:23
Gonzalez, Carlos	South
Martinez, Diego	West

145
Beltran, Jose	Mira Monte, Fall 4:47
Guerrero, Ronnie	Ridgeview
Barahona, Jose	South, Fall 5:12
Johnson, Jared	Golden Valley
Ochoa, Victor	West

152
Fonseca, Brandon	West, 8-5
Jones, Phelan	South
Romero, Issek	Golden Valley, Fall 3:30
Becerra, Daniel	Ridgeview
Segura, Gerardo	Mira Monte

160
Fuentes, Julio	Golden Valley, Fall 1:23
Torres, Montana	South
Salazar, Christopher	West

170
Wilson, Chris	Ridgeview, Fall 1:21
Dhanoa, Manvir	Golden Valley
Contreras, Eduardo	South, Fall 3:23
Munoz, Christian	West
Morales, Edward	Mira Monte

182
Mireles, Isaiah	South, Fall 3:23
Lugo, Matthew	West
Fuentes, Kevin	Golden Valley, 6-2
Robles, Fortino	Mira Monte

195
Lopez, Jacob	Ridgeview, TF 17-1
Chavez, Miguel	West
Munoz, Johnathan	South, Fall 3:07
Ortiz, Angel	Golden Valley
Castello, Jose	Mira Monte

220
Jaramillo, Ricardo	Golden Valley, Fall 5:40
Cabral, Freddie	Ridgeview
Olmedo, Jesse	Mira Monte, Fall 3:22
Duran, Rafael	South
Sanders, Durea	West

285
Quintanillo, Ricardo	Golden Valley, Fall 3:41
Organista, Victor	South
Bravo, Alfonso	Mira Monte, Fall 3:00
Boykin, Cedric	West

Most Outstanding Wrestlers

Lower Weight: Jose Beltran   Mira Monte
Upper Weight: Nimrod Quintanilla Golden Valley

TOURNAMENT
South	211.5
Golden Valley	177
West	155
Ridgeview	117.5
Mira Monte	114

DUAL	LEAGUE	SEASON
Golden Valley	4-0	4-0
West	3-1	3-3
South	2-2	2-3
Mira Monte	1-3	1-4
Ridgeview	0-4	0-7

SOUTH YOSEMITE LEAGUE - East
February 15, 2015

106
Salazar, Bobby — Golden Valley, 15-4
Wan, Aaron — East
Palos, Brandon — Tehachapi, Forfeit
Medina, Anthony — Ridgeview

113
Cruz, Joseph — Ridgeview, 7-4
Hutcherson, Marcus — West
Perez, Brian — Golden Valley, Fall :48
Cruz, Jose — East

120
Gonzalez, Nick — East, 4-1
Silva, Irving — Golden Valley
Rodriguez, Robert — West, Fall 1:50
Meza, Arturo — Tehachapi

126
Stainaker, Braxton — Golden Valley, Fall 2:43
Butler, William — West
Becas, Ken — East

132
Corona, Peter — Independence, 7-1
Guey-Mock, Andrew — East
Hernandez, Gustavo — Golden Valley, 7-5
Quintana, Abraham — Ridgeview

138
Corona, Esteban — Independence, Fall 1:10
Urias, Albert — Ridgeview
Chairez, Jacob — West, Fall 2:15
Perez, Javier — Golden Valley
Garcia, Alfonso — East

145
Navarro, Robert — Ridgeview, Fall 4:50
Simental, Saul — Golden Valley
Bell, Tyler — Independence, Fall 3:05
Carroll, Brett — Tehachapi
Perales, Josh — West

152
Duran, Thomas — Tehachapi, 11-3
Ponce, Eric — Golden Valley
Beccera, Daniel — Ridgeview, Fall 5:25
Serna, Matthew — East

160
Villa, Gabe — Ridgeview, Fall 4:30
Napier, Thomas — Independence
Lindsey, Andrew — Tehachapi, TF 2:40
Lemus, Andres — East

Thompson, Tyler — Golden Valley

170
Hunter, Jonathan — Golden Valley, Fall :39
Glass, Anthony — Ridgeview
Hoisington, Dean — Tehachapi, Fall 5:48
Amaya, Angel — East

182
Fuentes, Julio — Golden Valley, Fall 2:46
Roberson, Zavion — Ridgeview
Lugo, Matthew — West, 7-3
Herrera, Raymond — East

195
Fuentes, Kevin — Golden Valley, Fall :56
Taylor, Robert — West
Guey-Mock, Anthony — East, Fall 1:01
Sepulveda, Gabe — Ridgeview
Hurtado, Jonathon — Tehachapi

220
Lopez, Jacob — Ridgeview, 9-7 OT
Jaramillo, Ricardo — Golden Valley
Quiroz, Michael — West, 7-1
Basulto, Chris — East

285
Quintanilla, Nimrod — Golden Valley, 6-2
Varela, Gilbert — Independence
Smith, Wyatt — Tehachapi, Fall 1:34
Sanders, Dubrea — West
Garza, Brian — Ridgeview

Most Outstanding Wrestlers

Lower Weight: Esteban Corona — Independence
Upper Weight: Julio Fuentes — Golden Valley

TOURNAMENT
Golden Valley — 232
Ridgeview — 174.5
East — 130
West — 109
Tehachapi — 97.5
Independence — 90

DUAL	LEAGUE	SEASON
Golden Valley	5-0	5-0
Ridgeview	4-1	4-1
West	3-3	3-4
Independence	1-4	1-5
Tehachapi	0-5	0-7

SOUTH YOSEMITE LEAGUE - East
February 10, 2016

106
- Salazar, Bobby — Golden Valley, Fall :46
- Salcido, Zayne — Tehachapi
- Montoya, Miguel — Independence, Fall 4:16
- Guey-Mock, Isaiah — East

113
- Hucherson, Marcus — West, 15-8
- Machado, Ernie — Golden Valley
- Wan, Aaron — East, Fall 4:33
- Carrillo, Vincent — Independence

120
- Estrada, Keithan — East, Fall 4:37
- Ramirez, Pedro — Ridgeview
- Tabarez, Vincent — West, Fall 4:41
- Mendez, Diego — Golden Valley

126
- Corona, Peter — Independence, Fall 3:45
- Valdovinos, Christopher — Golden Valley
- Becas, Kenneth — East, 8-4
- Genel, Anthony — Ridgeview
- Meza, Arturo — Tehachapi

132
- Guey-Mock, Andrew — East, Fall :25
- Cardie,l Joseph — Golden Valley, 8-3
- Martinez, Anthony — Ridgeview

138
- Corona, Esteban — Independence, Fall 5:31
- Chairez, Jacob — West
- Quiroz, Josiah — East, Fall 1:45
- Biakuse, Larry — Golden Valley
- Rodriguez, Eduardo — Ridgeview

145
- Bell, Tyler — Independence, 4-2
- Urias, Albert — Ridgeview
- Carriere, Christian — East, 9-8
- Meek, Jacob — Tehachapi

152
- Ponce, Eric — Golden Valley, Fall 1:36
- Cisneros, Aldo — Independence
- Quintana, Abraham — Ridgeview, Fall 1:51
- Lindsey, Andrew — Tehachapi

160
- Hunter, Jonathan — Golden Valley, Fall 4:26
- Villa, Gabe — Ridgeview, Fall 4:12
- Lemus, Andres — East

170
- Hoisington, Dean — Tehachapi, Fall 3:03
- Thompson, Tyler — Golden Valley
- Mirelas, Alexis — Independence, Fall 1:44
- Beccera, Daniel — Ridgeview
- Vasquez, Eric — East

182
- Bordon, John — Ridgeview, 4-1
- Otriz, Manuel — East
- Magana, Axel — Golden Valley, Fall 3:47
- Faleafine, Dominic — Independence

195
- Roberson, Zavion — Ridgeview, Fall 1:45
- Chavez, Miguel — West
- Mendoza, Ismael — Golden Valley, Fall :45
- Enriquez, Nathan — Independence

220
- Jimenez, Issac — Ridgeview, 9-3
- Basulto, Christopher — East
- Medina, Fernando — Golden Valley, Fall 5:34
- Enriquez, Nick — Independence

285
- Varela, Gilbert — Independence, 7-0
- Jaramillo, Ricardo — Golden Valley, 8-0
- Rodriguez, Jose — East

Most Outstanding Wrestlers

Lower Weight: Esteban Corona — Independence
Upper Weight: Gilbert Varela — Independence

TOURNAMENT
Team	Points
Golden Valley	228
East	186
Independence	182
Ridgeview	176
West	73
Tehachapi	67

DUAL	LEAGUE	SEASON
Golden Valley	4-1	4-1
Independence	4-1	4-2
Ridgeview	4-1	4-1
East	2-3	4-4
West	1-4	1-4
Tehachapi	0-5	1-5

SOUTH YOSEMITE LEAGUE - East
February 9, 2017

106
Rojas, Jayven	Golden Valley, Fall 1:25
Gutierrez, Elijh	Ridgeview
Guey-Mock, Elijah	East, Fall 3:13
Saldana, Devin	Independence
Dobbins, Zach	Tehachapi

113
Salazar, Bobby	Golden Valley, Fall 1:54
Sanchez, Gerardo	Ridgeview
Castro, Jesse	Independence

120
Hutcherson, Marcus	West, 2-1
Ramirez, Pedro	Ridgeview
Machado, Ernie	Golden Valley, 8-3
Estrada, Keihan	East

126
Silver, Irving	Golden Valley, 7-5
Guerrero, Rudy	Ridgeview
Meza, Arturo	Tehachapi, Fall 1:35
Carrillo, Vincent	Independence
Giron, Jonathan	East

132
Guey-Mock, Andrew	East, TF 17-0
Chairez, Brandon	West
Gonzalez, P. J.	Golden Valley, Fall 3:28
Palos, Brandon	Tehachapi
Solozano, Francisco	Ridgeview

138
Cardiel, Joseph	Golden Valley, Fall 1:58
Hawkins, Vincent	East
Gonzalez, Anthony	Ridgeview, Fall :27
Zomora, Zachary	Independence

145
Bell, Tyler	Independence, Fall 5:28
Martinez, Anthony	Ridgeview
Quiroz, Josiah	East, Fall 1:49
Estrada, Anthony	Golden Valley

152
Urias, Albert	Ridgeview, Fall 1:37
Chairez, Jacob	West
Cisneros, Aldo	Independence, Fall 2:41
Nash, Adam	East
Biakuse, Larry	Golden Valley, Fall 2:39
Meek, Jacob	Tehachapi

160
Eaton, Ricardo	East, Fall 1:12
Lindsey, Caleb	Tehachapi
Kim, Cedric	Golden Valley, Fall :31
Jimenez, Michael	Independence
Gonzalez, Gabe	Ridgeview

170
Ponce, Eric	Golden Valley, Fall 1:16
Amaya, Angel	Ridgeview
Palmer, Hayden	Tehachapi

182
Bordon, John	Ridgeview, Major 13-4
Shaw, Masial	East
Enriquez, Nathan	Independence, Fall 3:49
Abdulla, Ben	Golden Valley

195
Mendoza, Ismael	Golden Valley, Fall 1:17
Sepulveda, Gabe	Ridgeview
Santella, Jesus	East

220
Castillo, Jacinto	Ridgeview, 6-5
Medina, Fernando	Golden Valley

285
Butler, Steven	Golden Valley, Fall 3:13
Almendariez, Angel	Independence
Zalvala, Jacob,	Ridgeview

Most Outstanding Wrestlers

Lower Weight: Marcus Hutcherson   West
Upper Weight: Albert Urias   Ridgeview

TOURNAMENT
Golden Valley	231.5
Ridgeview	222
East	144
Independence	113.5
Tehachapi	77
West	56

DUAL	LEAGUE	SEASON
Golden Valley	5-0	5-0
Ridgeview	4-1	7-2
Independent	3-2	4-2
East	2-3	2-3
Tehachapi	1-4	1-4
West	0-5	0-6

SOUTH YOSEMITE LEAGUE - East
February 7, 2018

106
Carrillo, Vincent — Independence, Fall 4:50
Gutierrez, Elijah — Ridgeview
Alonzo, Marcos — Golden Valley, 16-11
Marquez, Aiden — East

113
Martinez, Xavier — Golden Valley, Fall 2:36
Maradiaga, Jacob — Ridgeview

120
Rojas, Jayven — Golden Valley, Fall 3:01
Sanchez, Gerado — Ridgeview
Saldana, Devin — Independence, Fall 1:01
Soto, Roberto — Tehachapi

126
Rueda, Everardo — Golden Valley, Fall 2:46
Salcido, Zayne — Tehachapi
Hall, Zion — Ridgeview

132
Leon, Dominic — Golden Valley, Fall 1:48
Vasquez, David — Independence
Lota, Mike — Ridgeview

138
Machado, Ernesto — Golden Valley 15-14
Becerra, Alex — Ridgeview
Quiroz, Josiah — East

145
Guerrero, Rudy — Ridgeview, Fall 1:55
Mejia, Mario — Golden Valley
Lewis, Josh — Independence

152
Cisneros, Aldo — Independence, Fall 3:59
Spainhoward, Justin — Ridgeview
Hernandez, Luis — Golden Valley

160
Urias, Albert — Ridgeview, Fall 1:31
Ali, Mohammed — Golden Valley
Galvan, Martin — Independence

170
Eaton, Ricardo — East 8-6
Sepulveda, Gabe — Ridgeview
Biaskuse, Larry — Golden Valley

182
Bordon, John — Ridgeview, Fall 1:25
Tejeda, Enrique — Golden Valley
Alwaseen, Mohamed — West

195
Sanchez, Valentin — Ridgeview, Fall 4:30
Enriquez, Nathan — Independence
Perez, Alejandro — Golden Valley, Fall 2:13
Sanders, Zach — Tehachapi

220
Medina, Fernando — Golden Valley, Fall :16
Perez, Nate — Ridgeview
Chavez, Angel — Independence

285
Zavala, Jacob — Ridgeview, Fall :56
Singh, Alex — Independence
Briseno, Juan — Golden Valley, Forfeit
Martinez, Elijah — West

Most Outstanding Wrestlers
Lower Weight: Vincent Carrillo, Independence
Upper Weight: Valentin Sanchez, Ridgeview

TOURNAMENT
Team	Points
Golden Valley	255
Ridgeview	254
Independence	160
East	59.5
Tehachapi	36
West	27

DUAL	LEAGUE	SEASON
Ridgeview	5-0	5-0
Golden Valley	4-1	4-1
Independence	3-2	3-2
East	2-3	2-3
Tehachapi	1-4	1-4
West	0-5	0-5

SOUTH YOSEMITE LEAGUE - 2019

Most Outstanding Wrestlers

Lower Weight: Javan Rojas   Golden West
Upper Weight: Nathan Enriques   Independence

DUAL	LEAGUE	SEASON
Golden Valley	5-0	5-1
Ridgeview	4-1	9-1
Independence	3-2	4-3
Tehachapi	0-5	0-5
West	0-5	0-5
Bakersfield Christian	0-0	0-5

* No League Tournament was held

Coaching Greats: Olan Polite (Bakersfield High School), Win Bootman (North High School), Joe Seay (South High School), Ray Juhl (West High School)

SOUTH YOSEMITE LEAGUE – Independence
January 29, 2020

106
Jara, Sabastian	Ridgeview, Fall
Galindo, Christian	Independence
Vargas, Christian	Golden Valley

113
Medina, Josh	Ridgeview, Fall
Soto, Augustine	Tehachapi

120
Rojas, Jayven	Golden Valley, Fall
Ochoa, Jesus	Ridgeview
Castaneda, Matthew	West, Fall
Schuler, Brian	Bakersfield Christian, 8-4
Wilcox, Nasir	Independence

126
Saldana, Devin	Golden Valley, TF 17-2
Croften, Curtis	West
Aldana, Christian	Ridgeview, Fall
Santiago, Felix	Independence

132
Rueda, Everardo	Golden Valley, Fall
Verdin, Ismael	Ridgeview
Heimburger, Jonah	Independence

138
Lewis, Josh	Independence, 5-1
Arias, Malichi	Ridgeview
Saldana, Rafael	Golden Valley

145
Ramirez, Arturo	Ridgeview, Fall
Zabatta, John	Independence
Arias, Angel	Golden Valley, Fall
Brasuell, Enrique	West

152
Stansbury, Dylan	Ridgeview, Fall
Cambers, Zachary	Golden Valley
Lopez, Jeremiah	Independence

160
Leon, Dominic	Golden Valley, Fall
Graves, Elijah	Tehachapi
Jara, Sergio	Ridgeview, 14-9
Galvan, Martin	Independence

170
Zavala, Juan	Ridgeview, Fall
Romero, ?	Golden Valley
Morales, ?	Ridgeview, Fall
Burger, Dawson	Bakersfield Christian

182
Spainhoward, Justin	Ridgeview, TF 22-6
Galvan, Javre	Independence
Montelongo, Nestor	Golden Valley

195
Deval, Nathaniel	Independence, Fall
Sanders, Jason	West
Bell, ?	Tehachapi
Enciso, Alfonso	Ridgeview
Gonzalez, Isaiah	Golden Valley

220
Schuler, Brian	Bakersfield Christian, 8-4
Romero, Michael	Independence
Reyes, Daniel	West
Morales, Esteban	Ridgeview
Medina, ?	Tehachapi

285
Sanchez, Andrew	West, Fall
Kopp, Luke	Ridgeview
Chavez, ?	Golden Valley, Fall
Grewal, Jaskaran	Independence

Most Outstanding Wrestlers
Lower Weight: Sabastian Jara Ridgeview
Upper Weight: Dominic Leon   Golden Valley

TOURNAMENT
Ridgeview	83
Golden Valley	63
Independence	58
West	30
Tehachapi	16
Bakersfield Christian	12

DUAL	LEAGUE	SEASON
Golden Valley	1-0	2-1
Independence	1-0	2-0
West	1-1	3-3
Ridgeview	0-1	2-2
Tehachapi	0-0	2-0
Bakersfield Christian	0-0	0-0

SOUTHEAST YOSEMITE LEAGUE

2007-2020

SOUTHEAST YOSEMITE LEAGUE CHAMPIONSHIP TEAMS

Date	Location	Dual Champion	Tournament	Overall Champion	Coach
2/04/1995	Highland	Bakersfield 4-0	Bakersfield	Bakersfield	David East
2/03/1996	Highland	Bakersfield 4-0	Bakersfield	Bakersfield	David East
2/08/1997	East	Bakersfield 4-0	Foothill	Bakersfield/Foothill	Alan Paradise, David East
2/13/1998	East	Bakersfield 4-0	Foothill	Bakersfield/Foothill	Alan Paradise, David East
2/13/1999	East	Bakersfield 4-0	Bakersfield	Bakersfield	David East
2/12/2000	East	East 4-0	Bakersfield	Bakersfield/East	Joe Triggs, David East
2/10/2001	East	Bakersfield 4-0	Bakersfield	Bakersfield	David East
2/09/2002	East	Bakersfield 4-0	Bakersfield	Bakersfield	David East
2/15/2003	East	Bakersfield 5-0	Bakersfield	Bakersfield	Andy Varner
2/14/2004	East	Bakersfield 5-0	Bakersfield	Bakersfield	Andy Varner
2/12/2005	East	Bakersfield 5-0	Bakersfield	Bakersfield	Andy Varner
2/11/2006	East	Foothill 4-0	Bakersfield	Bakersfield	Andy Varner
2/10/2007	East	Bakersfield 5-0	Bakersfield	Bakersfield	Andy Varner
2/09/2008	East	Bakersfield 5-0	Bakersfield	Bakersfield	Andy Varner
2/14/2009	East	Bakersfield 5-0	Bakersfield	Bakersfield	Andy Varner
2/10/2010	East	Bakersfield 5-0	Bakersfield	Bakersfield	Andy Varner
2/11/2011	East	Foothill 3-0	Foothill	Foothill	Brad Hull
2/12/2012	East	Foothill 3-0	Foothill	Foothill	Brad Hull
2/08/2013	East	Foothill 4-0	Foothill	Foothill	Brad Hull
2/14/2014	East	Foothill 4-0	Foothill	Foothill	Brad Hull
2/13/2015	South	Foothill/South 3-1	Foothill	Foothill	Brad Hull
2/12/2016	Mira Monte	Foothill 4-0	South	Foothill/South	Addison Hay, Manuel Vasquez
2/09/2017	Mira Monte	North 4-0	North	North	Brady Garner
2/09/2018	North	Highland 4-0	Highland	Highland	Joe Kuntz
2019		North/South 4-1	No Tournament		Brady Garner, Manuel Vasquez
1/29/2020	North	North			Brady Garner

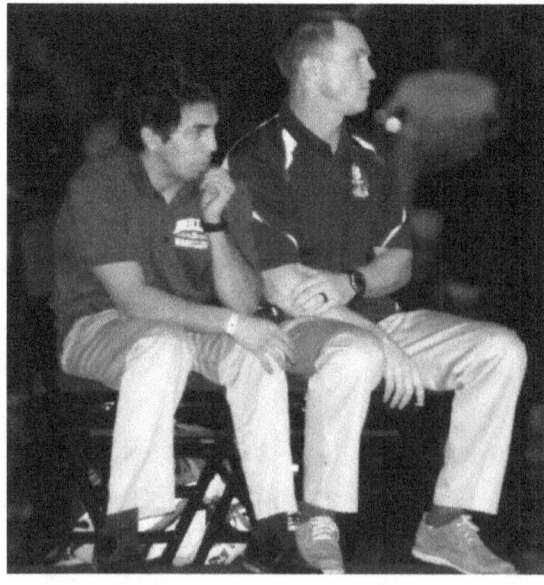

Frank Lomas and Andy Varner
Bakersfield High School

SOUTHEAST YOSEMITE LEAGUE
MOST OUTSTANDING WRESTLERS

Lower Weight

Year	Name	School
1995	Juan Lopez	Highland
1996	Anthony Adame	Foothill
1997	Chris Ressequie	East
1998	Chris Felix	East
1999	Andrew Spradlin	Bakersfield
2000	Tony Franco	Foothill
2001	Anthony Marquez	Foothill
2002		Bakersfield High Team
2003	Mike Marquez	East
2004	Nathan Morgan	Bakersfield
2005	Addison Hay	Foothill
2006	David Chaidez	Foothill
2007	Marc Collier	East
2008	Pete Gonzalez	East
2009	Natrelle Demison	Bakersfield
2010	Jose Leandro	Golden Valley
2011	Julio Gonzalez	East
2012	Candido Pena	East
2013	Nick Marquez	Foothill
2014	Marco Velasquez	Foothill
2015	Mark Baker	North
2016	Ralph Suarez	Foothill
2017	Emmit Kuntz	Highland
2018	Brian Worshim	South
2019	Shane Corona	Foothill
2020	Anthony Ruvalcava	South

Upper Weight

Year	Name	School
1995	Fred Ashley	Bakersfield
1996	Jose Galarza	East
1997	Ryan McWilliams	Foothill
1998	Kirk Moore	Foothill
1999	Sam Burk	Ridgeview
2000	Britt Mooney	East
2001	Carlos Gonzalez	East
2003	Jake Varner	Bakersfield
2004	Kev Koy	Highland
2005	Jake Varner	Bakersfield
2006	Matt Peralta	Foothill
2007	Eric Dela Rosa	Foothill
2008	David Travis	Foothill
2009	Tony Hernandez	East
2010	Colman Hammond	Bakersfield
2011	Jarred Roark	North
2012	Jordan Olgin	Foothill
2013	Dillion Harroun	Tehachapi
2014	David Bautista	Foothill
2015	Phelan Jones	South
2016	Phelan Jones	South
2017	Adrian Godinez	Foothill
2018	Aventino Gonzalez	Highland
2019	Nevada Torres	South
2020	Cesar Cuevas	East

*Awards sponsored by The Coyote Club

SOUTHEAST YOSEMITE LEAGUE - East
February 10, 2007

103
Collier, Marc	East, Fall 4:37
Rizo, Derk	Foothill
Delfin, Paul	Bakersfield, 11-4
Lenier, Jeff	Liberty
Silva, Brandon	Golden Valley

112
Demison, Nektoe	Bakersfield, 9-1
Gonzalez, Peter	East
Bohannan, Scott	Liberty

119
Lomas, Frank	Bakersfield, 16-2
Tarkington, Richard	Highland
Miani, Keith	Liberty, 5-3
Berianga, Ryan	Golden Valley

125
Kapler, Greg	Liberty, Fall 3:09
Morgan, Jacob	Bakersfield
Ramirez, Richie	Highland, Fall
Florez, Miguel	East

130
Gonzalez, Freddy	East, 12-8
Franco, Steve	Highland
Olmos, Juan	Golden Valley, 17-2
Bryan, Jordan	Liberty
Gurlani, Andrew	Bakersfield

135
Cruz, Jonah	Bakersfield, Fall 1:59
New, Mark	Foothill
Rivera, Vince	Liberty, Fall (time?)
Gutierrez, Markey	Golden Valley
Bermudez, Jose	East

140
Miller, Justin	East, 8-1
Box, Anthony	Bakersfield
Rios, Robert	Liberty, 4-2
Matthews, Robert	Golden Valley
Sandoval, Marcos	Foothill, 19-18
Valdez, Marc	Highland

145
Rasmussen, Travis	Bakersfield, 7-4
Christensen, Colton	Liberty
Mudheneke, Aaron	Golden Valley, 8-4
Gordillo, Derek	East
Torres, Victor	Highland, 19-8
Wren, Nathan	Foothill

152
Rodriguez, Jamie	Bakersfield, 7-4
Lopez, Martin	East
Custer, Dylan	Liberty, 8-0
Marsh, Jeff	Highland
Hernandez, Jesus	Golden Valley

160
Delarosa, Eric	Foothill, 3-2
Rogers, Kail	Liberty
Hernandez, Cruz	East, 5-1
Arriaga, Ruben	Bakersfield
Gutierrez, Ivan	Golden Valley, Fall 5:27
Martinez, Miguel	Highland

171
Carls, Brad	Bakersfield, 17-0
Thomas, Tim	Foothill
Nistory, Geoff	Liberty, 17-8
Pena, Michael	East
Burnett, Josh	Highland, Fall (time?)
Rodriguez, David	Golden Valley

189
Travis, David	Foothill, Fall 4:34
Schoene, Brian	Bakersfield
Avena, Xzayium	Fall (time?)
Wilson, Laramie	Highland
Pienado, Delfino	East

215
Cummings, Eddie	East, Fall 1:57
Daniel, Cristen	Bakersfield
Chavez, Armando	Foothill, 7-5
Goldberg, Trevor	Liberty

285
Alvarez, Lamar	Bakersfield, 4-2
Cisneros, Efren	Golden Valley
Hernandez, Antonio	East, Fall (time?)
Anders, Tamir	Liberty

Most Outstanding Wrestlers
Lower Weight: Marc Collier   East
Upper Weight: Eric Delarosa   Foothill

TOURNAMENT
Bakersfield	274
East	216
Liberty	194.5
Foothill	127
Golden Valley	106
Highland	104

SOUTHEAST YOSEMITE LEAGUE - East
February 10, 2007

DUAL	LEAGUE	SEASON
Bakersfield	5-0	6-0
East	3-2	7-5
Liberty	3-2	10-3
Foothill	3-2	5-2
Golden Valley	1-4	2-7
Highland	N/A	N/A

Frank Lomas and Andy Varner
Bakersfield High School - 2007

SOUTHEAST YOSEMITE LEAGUE - East
February 9, 2008

103
Collier, Marc	East, Fall :17
Silva, Brandon	Golden Valley
Mercado, Alex	Highland, Fall :39
Nickell, Ian	Bakersfield

112
Gonzalez, Pete	East, Major 18-1
Lanier, Jeff	Liberty
Torres, Hector	Highland, 10-5
Torres, Jonathan	Golden Valley

119
Rizo, Derik	Foothill, 4-1
Gonzalez, Nick	East
Delfin, Paul	Bakersfield, 6-2
Bohannan, Scott	Liberty
Alvarez, Gibran	Golden Valley
Burnett, Justin	Highland

125
Box, Timmy	Bakersfield, 6-1
Mioni, Keith	Liberty
Berlanga, Ryan	Golden Valley, Fall 3:01
Torres, Conrad	East
Ramos, Gabe	Foothill

130
Rivera, Vince	Liberty, 7-0
Marquez, Ernie	Foothill
Galaviz, John	East, Fall 4:53
Rivera, Eric	Highland
Giulani, Andrew	Bakersfield
Castro, German	Golden Valley

135
Kapler, Greg	Liberty
Valdez, Marc	Highland
New, Mark	Foothill
Neri, Robert	East
Torres, ?	Bakersfield
Mathews, Melelik	Golden Valley

140
Cruz, Jonah	Bakersfield
Sanchez, Machi	Foothill
Bridges, Sam	Highland
Rueda, Frank	Golden Valley
Valaderez, Luis	East

145
Rasmussen, Travis	Bakersfield, 7-4
Rios, Robert	Liberty
Loera, Jerry	Highland
Rasmussen, Nick	Golden Valley
Wren, Nathan	Foothill
Carrillo, Anthony	East

152
Hammond, Bryce	Bakersfield
Childers, Nick	Liberty
Marsh, Jeff	Highland
Servin, Benny	East
Salgado, Jessy	Foothill
Gamino, David	Golden Valley

160
Ramirez, Jose	Bakersfield
Cueto, Martin	Liberty
Villareal, Josh	East
Burnett, Josh	Highland
Rubacaldo, Juan	Foothill

171
Carls, Brad	Bakersfield, 9-3
Berlango, Daniel	Foothill
Campos, Jesse	East, Fall 4:24
Ruiz, Frank	Highland
Tjepkema, Luke	Liberty
Rodriguez, David	Golden Valley

189
Valasquez, Dakota	Bakersfield, 8-3
Thomas, Terry	Highland
Thomas, Nick	Foothill, Fall 2:58
Abundez, Sergio	Golden Valley
Angulo, Brian	East
Arambula, Hector	Liberty

215
Travis, David	Foothill, Fall 1:00
Schoene, Brian	Bakersfield
Angulo, Juan	East, Fall :58
Childers, Mike	Liberty
Tovar, Geo	Highland

285
Hernandez, Antonio	East, Fall 3:46
Posadas, Angel	Foothill
Padilla, Anthony	Bakersfield, Fall :19
Sizemore, Chris	Liberty
Hernandez, Richard	Highland

*Some scores weren't given

SOUTHEAST YOSEMITE LEAGUE - East
February 9, 2008

Most Outstanding Wrestlers

Lower Weight: Pete Gonzalez	East
Upper Weight: David Travis	Foothill

TOURNAMENT

Bakersfield	241.5
East	201
Liberty	194
Foothill	182
Highland	151.5
Golden Valley	98.5

DUAL	LEAGUE	SEASON
Bakersfield	5-0	6-1
East	3-2	3-2
Liberty	3-2	4-2
Foothill	3-2	9-2
Golden Valley	1-4	2-4
Highland	0-5	1-5

SOUTHEAST YOSEMITE LEAGE – East
February 14, 2009

103
Gonzalez, Julio	East, 13-2
Nickell, Ian	Bakersfield
Silva, Brandon	Golden Valley, Fall 4:58
Rizo, Eric	Foothill
Hartsfield, Tyler	Liberty

112
Demison, Natrelle	Bakersfield, 10-4
Collier, Marc	East
McKinzie, Josh	Highland, 7-2
Leandro, Jose	Golden Valley
Manriquez, Patrick	Foothill

119
Gonzalez, Peter	East, 13-1
Cruz, Micah	Bakersfield
Lanier, Jeff	Liberty Fall (time?)
Palafox, Chris	Foothill
Gutierrez, Jeff	Golden Valley

125
Ramirez, Maxx	Bakersfield, 9-0
Gonzalez, Nick	East
Moncada, Sammie	Foothill Fall, 4:28
Delatorre, Jesse	Golden Valley

130
Box, Timmy	Bakersfield, 8-3
Rizo, Derik	Foothill
Martin, Sean	Liberty, Fall 5:48
Matthews, Melelik	Golden Valley
Elizondo, Jorge	East, Fall 5:53
Hurtado, Ariel	Highland

135
Kapler, Greg	Liberty, TF 16-0
Nacita, Silas	Bakersfield
Sanchez, Machi	Foothill, 11-2
Gibson, Mike	Golden Valley
Diaz, Jose	Highland

140
Cruz, Jonah	Bakersfield, Fall 3:18
Rueda, Frank	Golden Valley
Sandoval, Marcos	Foothill, 3-0
George, Nic	Liberty
Burnett, Justin	Highland, 12-7
Recio, James	East

145
Fierro, Adam	Bakersfield, TF 5:26
Cueto, Martin	Liberty
Bridges, Sam	Highland, 11-1
Matthews, Richard	Golden Valley
Solorio, Anthony	Foothill, Fall 3:13
Molitor, Justin	East

152
Hammond, Bryce	Bakersfield, Fall 1:26
Stiebler, Ryan	Liberty
Rubalcado, Juan	Foothill, Fall 1:26
Gaminino, David	Golden Valley
Alconaz, Rafael	Highland, Fall 1:47
Soto, Hector	East

160
Ramirez, Jose	Bakersfield, TF 18-2
Rubalcado, Jesse	Foothill
Alvardo, Collin	Liberty, 11-2
Orozco, Anastacio	East

171
Buffington, Levi	Liberty, Fall 1:30
Enderton, D.J.	Foothill
Moore, Darien	Bakersfield, TF 15-0
Phillips, James	Highland
Angulo, Bryan	East Default
Abundes, Sergio	Golden Valley

189
Palafox, Jon	Foothill, 6-3
Angulo, Juan	Foothill
Dunwoody, Joseph	Highland, Default
Saldana, Jesus	Golden Valley

215
Schoene, Brian	Bakersfield, Fall 1:16
Gutierrez, Oscar	Foothill
Hurtado, Frankie	Liberty, Fall (time?)
Ambriz, Rene	East

285
Hernandez, Tony	East, 4-2OT
Posadas, Angel	Foothill
Jaramillo, Jose	Golden Valley, Fall (time?)
Saldana, Eric	Bakersfield
Hernandez, Richard	Highland

Most Outstanding Wrestlers
Lower Weight: Netrelle Demison Bakersfield
Upper Weight: Tony Hernandez East

TOURNAMENT
Bakersfield	266.5
Foothill	214
East	177
Liberty	163.5
Golden Valley	138.5
Highland	83

SOUTHEAST YOSEMITE LEAGE – East
February 14, 2009

DUAL	LEAGUE	SEASON
Bakersfield	5-0	11-0
Foothill	4-1	7-1
East	3-2	3-2
Golden Valley	2-3	5-6
Highland	1-4	2-4
Liberty	0-5	0-5

L-R Anthony Box, Andy Varner and Frank Lomas Bakersfield High School

SOUTHEAST YOSEMITE LEAGUE - East
February 10, 2010

103
- Gonzalez, Julio — East, 6-2
- Nickell, Ian — Bakersfield
- Vela, Jon — Foothill
- Selz Lane — Liberty

112
- Leandro, Jose — Golden Valley, 8-3
- Hartsfield, Tyler — Liberty
- Marquez, Nic — Foothill, Fall 5:21
- Castro, Alberto — East

119
- Cruz, Micah — Bakersfield, Fall 5:11
- Gonzalez, Nick — East
- Travis, Chris — Foothill, 7-5
- Torres, Jonathan — Golden Valley
- George, Ryan — Liberty, Fall 3:52
- Mercado, Juan — Highland

125
- Lanier, Jeff — Bakersfield, Fall 1:19
- Shumway, Randy — Foothill
- Plyer, Jacob — Liberty, TF 16-1
- Hernandez, Chris — Golden Valley

130
- Demison, Netrelle — Bakersfield, TF 15-0
- Palafox, Cris — Foothill
- Gutierrez, Jeff — Golden Valley, Major 20-7
- Rudnick, Lucas — Liberty, Fall 2:32
- Dye, Sean — Highland

135
- Ramirez, Maxx — Bakersfield, Major 14-1
- Steiber, Ryan — Liberty
- Corona, Oscar — Foothill, 7-6 OT
- Gibson, Mike — Golden Valley
- McGraw, Brian — East, 7-3
- Haycock, Austin — Highland

140
- Box, Timmy — Bakersfield, TF 16-1
- Sanders, Hudson — Liberty
- Gamino, David — Golden Valley, 7-0
- Recid, John — East
- Avila, Robert — Foothill

145
- Hammond, Coleman — Bakersfield, 8-4
- Rizo, Derik — Foothill
- George, Nick — Liberty, 4-1
- Rueda, Frank — Golden Valley
- Lopez, Emmanuel — Highland

152
- Fierro, Adam — Bakersfield, TF 17-2
- Greynolds, Clayton — Liberty
- Rodriguez, Nathan — East, 4-3
- Marquez, Ernie — Foothill
- Ahmed, Ali — Highland, Default
- Banducci, Kendell — Golden Valley

160
- Hammond, Bryce — Bakersfield, TF 20-4
- Greynolds, Joseph — Liberty
- Hannible, Dandy — East, Major 10-0
- Pearson, Fashawn — Golden Valley
- Varela, Paul — Foothill

171
- Nacita, Silas — Bakersfield, Fall 3:46
- Buffington, Levi — Liberty
- Fainter, Curtis — Foothill, Fall (time?)
- Manzano, Juan — Golden Valley
- Cook, Timothy — East

189
- Mendoza, Daniel — Liberty, Fall :34
- Romero, Edwin — Golden Valley
- Velasquez, Dakota — Bakersfield, Fall :11
- Gutierrez, Marisol — Foothill
- Angulo, Juan — East

215
- Schoene, Brian — Bakersfield, Fall 1:17
- Sizemore, Chris — Liberty
- Amaya, Rudy — Foothill, Default

285
- Hurtado, Frankie — Liberty, Fall 1:17
- Silva, Adrian — Bakersfield
- Adame, Vincent — East, Fall 3:41
- Cervantes, Mario — Golden Valley
- Pfeifle, Kaleb — Foothill, Fall 2:19
- Jano, Taylor — Highland

Most Outstanding Wrestlers

Lower Weight: Jose Leandro, Golden Valley
Upper Weight: Coleman Hammond, Bakersfield

TOURNAMENT
Bakersfield	291.5
Liberty	221
Foothill	194.5
East	147
Golden Valley	143.5
Highland	29.5

SOUTHEAST YOSEMITE LEAGUE - East
February 10, 2010

DUAL	LEAGUE	SEASON
Bakersfield	5-0	9-2
Liberty	3-2	3-2
Foothill	3-2	3-2
East	2-3	2-3
Golden Valley	2-3	7-3
Highland	0-5	0-6

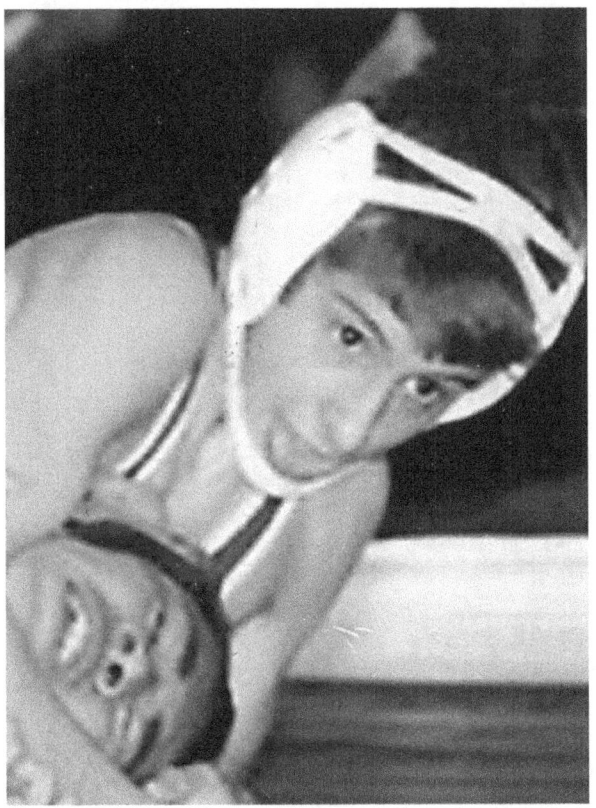

Ian Nickell – Bakersfield High School 2011

SOUTHEAST YOSEMITE LEAGUE - East
February 11, 2011

103
Velasquez, Marco	Foothill, Fall :40	
Nebre, Peter	Highland	

112
Gonzalez, Julio	East, 6-1	
Marquez, Nick	Foothill	
Cardoza, Sonny	Highland	

119
Gonzalez, Nick	East, 6-2	
Saavedra, Willyam	Foothill	
Lenander, Zackary	North, 5-4	
Logan, Cody	Highland	

125
Onsurez, Adrian	East, 3-2	
Aguirre, Cesar	Foothill	
Royal, Isaiah	North, 15-9	
Robles, Larenz	Foothill	

130
Guardo, Alan	North, Fall 5:31	
Shumway, Randy	Foothill	

135
Collins, Conner	Foothill, 17-14	
Mello, John	North	

140
Palafox, Brandon	Foothill, 5-3	
Randel, Nicholas	North	
Recio, John	East, 11-8	
Haycock, Austin	Highland	

145
Corona, Oscar	Foothill, TF17-0	
Lopez, Emmanuel	Highland	
Alvardo, Bryan	East, 8-5	
Mattson, Jeffery	North	

152
Avila, Roberto	Foothill, Fall 3:58	
Gomez, Keno	North	
Flores, Ivan	East	

160
Travis, Steven	Foothill, Fall 4:40	
Delacruz, Alex	Highland	
Fisher, Jacob	North	

171
Ahmed, Ali	Highland, 5-0	
McBride, Tim	North	
Fainter, Curtis	Foothill	

189
Rubalcado, Jess	Foothill, Fall 1:14	
Welsh, Josh	North	
Mora, Daniel	Highland	

215
Amaya, Rudy	Foothill, Default	
Ringer, Joshua	North	
Juarez, Joseph	Highland	

285
Roark, Jarred	North, 5-2	
Olgin, Jordan	Foothill	
Toavalu, Anthony	Highland	

Most Outstanding Wrestlers

Lower Weight: Julio Gonzalez   East
Upper Weight: Jarred Roark   North

TOURNAMENT
Foothill	259.5
North	164.5
Highland	110
East	88

DUAL	LEAGUE	SEASON
Foothill	3-0	7-0
North	2-1	11-4
East	1-2	1-2
Highland	N/A	N/A

SOUTHEAST YOSEMITE LEAGUE - East
February 10, 2012

106
Valasquez, Marco	Foothill, Fall 3:08
Gonzalez, Niko	East
Nebre, Peter	Highland, Fall 1:10
Ringer, Aaron	North

113
Marquez, Nick	Foothill, TF19-1
Munoz, Andy	North
Davila, Samuel	Highland, Fall 1:29
Turney, Jason	East

120
Aguirre, Cesar	Foothill, 5-2
Onsurez, Adrian	East
Cardoza, Sonny	Highland, Forfeit
Stubblefield, A.J.	North

126
Saavedra, Willyam	Foothill, Fall 1:05
Logan, Cody	Highland
Amiama, J.C.	East

132
Pena, Candido	East, Fall 5:37
Guardado, Allan	North
Hinojosa, Abraham	Foothill, Fall :21
Robles, Larenz	Highland

138
Gomez, Keno	North, 9-2
Enciso, Jose	Foothill
Cruz, Juan	East

145
Corona, Oscar	Foothill, 11-4
Randel, Nick	North
Mosely, William	Highland, Fall 2:40
Hernandez, Brandon	East

152
Mello, John	North, 8-7
Palafox, Brandon	Foothill
Silva, Brandon	East

160
Ahmed, Ali	Highland, Fall 3:50
Amiama, Lucas	East
Bayard, Garrett	North, Decision?
Collins, Conner	Foothill

170
Avila, Michael	East, Fall 3:53
Gonzalez, Joseph	Foothill
Mata, Isaac	Highland, 12-0
Zavala, Joey	North

182
McWilliams, Cody	North, Fall 5:08
Lopez, Diego	Foothill

195
Juarez, Joseph	Highland, Fall 5:08
Helston, Andrew	Foothill
Franco, John	North, Fall :32
Garcia, Elijah	East

220
Olgin, Jordan	Foothill, Fall 1:14
Heath, A.J.	North
Pena, Joel	East

285
Amaya, Rudy	Foothill, 10-4
Roark, Jarrod	North
Bueno, Chris	East

Most Outstanding Wrestlers

Lower Weight: Candido Pena — East
Upper Weight: Jordan Olgin — Foothill

TOURNAMENT
Foothill	235.4
North	164
East	143
Highland	103

DUAL	LEAGUE	SEASON
Foothill	3-0	9-1
North	2-1	9-3
East	1-2	1-2
Highland	0-3	0-3

SOUTHEAST YOSEMITE LEAGUE - East
February 8, 2013

106
Perez, Fern — Foothill, 20-5
Bracamonte, Matthew — East
Davila, Sammy — Highland, 16-8
Garrett, Janney — Tehachapi, Default
Davidson, Jonathan — North

113
Velasquez, Mario — Foothill, Fall 5:10
Nebre, Peter — Highland
Gonzalez, Niko — East, Fall :24
Hall, Joey — North

120
Marquez, Nick — Foothill, Fall 2:59
Jacinto, Issak — East
Morgret, Zachary — North, 9-2
Hernandez, Angel — ?

126
Bracamonte, Adam — East, 10-7
Fletcher, Allen — Tehachapi
Lopez, Juan — Foothill, Fall 3:51
Pelham, Daniel — North

132
Duxbury, Klayton — Tehachapi, Fall 3:21
Robles, Larenz — Highland
Rodriquez, Julio — North, Fall 3:30
Turney, Jason — East, Fall 1:40
Villela, Oscar — Foothill

138
Gamble, Jason — Tehachapi, Fall 4:51
Tootle, Jacob — Foothill
Cruz, Juan — East, Fall 5:01
Menendez, Nicholas — Highland, Fall 2:17
Turner, Jeremy — North

145
Palafox, Brandon — Foothill, 1:07
Mattson, Jason — North
Carrillo, Josh — East, Fall 1:05
Patino, Irvin — Highland
Minton, Zachary — Tehachapi

152
Corona, Oscar — Foothill, Fall :56
Duran, Thomas — Tehachapi
Silva, Brandon — East, Fall 4:42
Heath, Matthew — North, Fall :12
Miranda, Michael — Highland

160
Allen, Zachary — Tehachapi, Fall 5:04
Torres, Rolando — Foothill
Lemus, Ruben — East, Fall 1:49
Binger, Andrew — North
Martinez, Paul — Highland

170
Lora, Pedro — Foothill, 9-8
Horton, Rodney — North
Chavez, Alex — East, Fall 1:33
Leon, Isaac — Highland

182
Harroun, Dillion — Tehachapi, Fall 2:42
Gonzalez, Joseph — Foothill
Avila, Michael — East, Fall 2:20
Lucas, Jacob — North

195
Mello, Kevin — North, 5-2
Garcia, Elijah — East

220
Guillen, Chris — Foothill, 6-1
Garcia, Christian — Highland, 11-10
Earwood, Dylan — North

285
Guerrero, Mark — North, Fall 2:42
Garza, Richard — Foothill
Braswell, Andrew — East

Most Outstanding Wrestlers

Lower Weight: Nick Marquez — Foothill
Upper Weight: Dillion Harroun — Tehachapi

TOURNAMENT
Foothill — 233.5
East — 178
North — 146
Tehachapi — 141
Highland — 91

	DUAL	LEAGUE	SEASON
Foothill	4-0		10-0
East	3-1		3-1
Tehachapi	2-2		2-2
North	1-3		6-5
Highland	0-4		1-4

SOUTHEAST YOSEMITE LEAGUE - East
February 14, 2014

106
- Bracamonte, Matthew — East, Fall 1:08
- Kuntz, Emmett — Highland
- Stovall, Kennith — Foothill

113
- Perez, Fern — Foothill, Fall 1:19
- Davila, Sammy — Highland
- Gonzalez, Niko — East, 5-1
- Meza, Arturo — Tehachapi

120
- Velasquez, Marco — Foothill, Fall 3:41
- Janney, Garrett — Tehachapi
- Rios, Marc Anthony — Highland, Fall 3:45
- Becas, Kenny — East

126
- Morgret, Zach — North, 4-1
- Cardoza, Sonny — Highland
- Escalera, Albert — Foothill

132
- Allen, Fletcher — Tehachapi, 4-0
- Baker, Mark — North
- Zozaya, Miguel — Highland, Fall 5:05
- Martinez, Angel — Foothill

138
- Rodriguez, Julio — North, Fall 1:42
- Perez, Antonio — Highland
- Marin, Chris — Foothill, Fall 2:27
- Arevalo, Kevin — Tehachapi

145
- Toole, Jacob — Foothill, 10-5
- Lemus, Ruben — East
- Turner, Jeremy — North, Fall 3:13
- Arreola, Jesus — Highland

152
- Chocoteco, Juan — Foothill, Fall 1:37
- Menendez, Nico — Highland
- Mattison, Jacob — North

160
- Duran, Thomas — Tehachapi, Fall 2:49
- Martinez, P.J. — Highland
- Velasquez, Mark — North, Fall 3:19
- Cisneros, Alberto — Foothill

170
- Binger, Andrew — North, Fall 1:53
- Snella, Eian — Highland
- Grimaldo, Jose — Foothill, 8-4
- Hoisington, Dean — Tehachapi

182
- Lora, Petie — Foothill, Fall 3:18
- Deleon, Chris — Highland
- Kline, James — North

195
- Lucas, Jacob — North, 13-6
- Saavedra, Eric — Highland
- Bermudez, David — East, Fall 3:23
- Barrena, Alan — North

220
- Gonzalez, Joseph — Foothill, Fall 2:23
- Garcia, Chris — Highland
- Hattfield, Tristan — North

285
- Bautista, David — Foothill, 7-4
- Guerrero, Mark — North
- Bueno, Chris — East, Fall 2:04
- Akroush, Faris — Highland

Most Outstanding Wrestlers

Lower Weight: Marco Velasquez — Foothill
Upper Weight: David Bautista — Foothill

TOURNAMENT

Foothill	173
Highland	159
North	155
East	63
Tehachapi	55

DUAL	LEAGUE	SEASON
Foothill	4-0	12-1
Highland	3-1	6-1
North	2-2	9-4
Tehachapi	2-2	3-7
East	0-4	0-4

SOUTHEAST YOSEMITE LEAGUE – South
February 13, 2015

108
Kuntz, Emmett	Highland, Fall, 1:45
Jimenez, Ruben	Foothill,
Romero, Pete	South, TF?
Mullins, Sean	North
Herrera, Jesus	Mira, Monte

115
Davila, Sammy	Highland, Decision?
Ornelas, Nick	South
Stovall, Kenneth	Foothill, Major?
Hieneman, Blake	North

122
Chevy-Garcia, Levi	South, Fall, 1:00
Delacruz, Matt	Mira, Monte
Gonzales, Paul	Highland, Fall, 1:47
Rodamer, Anthony	Foothill

128
Perez, Fern	Foothill, Fall, 1:30
Morgret, Zach	North
Dye, Hayden	Highland, Decision?
Zeferino, Miguel	South
Sanchez, Ernesto	Mira, Monte

134
Sanchez, Mike	Highland, Decision?
Nieto, Carlos	Mira, Monte
Mosqueda, Emilio	South, Decision?
Pelham, Daniel	North
Espinoza, Sergio	Foothill

140
Baker, Mark	North, Fall, 3:15
Escalera, Alberto	Foothill
Perez, Antonio	Highland, Decision?
Barahona, Jose	South
Acosta, Brandon	Mira, Monte

147
Rodriguez, Julio	North, Decision?
Suarez, Ralphy	Foothill
Green, Jerome	South
Bookout, Nate	Highland

154
Mattson, Jacob	North, Fall?
Menendez, Nico	Highland
Marin, Chris	Foothill, Decision?
Perez, Michael	South
Orozco, Angel	Mira, Monte

162
Jones, Phelan	South, Fall, 3:00
Chocoteco, Juan	Foothill
Reed, Matt	North, Fall, 5:18
Martines, Jose	Mira, Monte
Carbajal, Eric	Highland

172
Godinez, Adrian	Foothill, TF?
Binger, Andrew	North
Mireles, Isiah	South, Fall, 5:00
Esqueda, Matt	Highland
Morales, Edward	Mira, Monte

184
Velasquez, Mark	North, Fall, 2:28
Grimaldo, Josse	Foothill
Martinez, Paul	Highland, Fall, 1:30
Castaneda, Oscar	South
Castillo, Jose	Mira, Monte

197
Saavedra, Eric	Highland, Decision?
Torres, Montana	South
Johnson, Ronnie	Foothill, Fall, 1:29
Reyes, Daniel	Mira, Monte

222
Bocanegra, De, Marco	Highland, Decision?
Mello, Kevin	North
Olmedo, Jesse	South, Fall, 1:45
Duran, Rafael	Mira, Monte
Daugherty, Victor	Foothill

287
Organista, Victor	South, Decision?
VanTassell, Ian	Foothill
Creel, Logan	North, Fall, 5:00
Saucedo, Antony	Highland

* Some scores weren't given

Most Outstanding Wrestlers
Lower Weight: Mark Baker   North
Upper Weight: Phelan Jones South

TOURNAMENT
Foothill	201.5
North	197
South	192.5
Highland	192
Mira, Monte	87

SOUTHEAST YOSEMITE LEAGUE – South
February 13, 2015

DUAL	LEAGUE	SEASON
Foothill	3-1	3-2
North	2-2	9-3
South	1-3	1-3
Highland	2-2	6-2
Mira Monte	0-4	2-4

Jerome Green – South High School

SOUTHEAST YOSEMITE LEAGUE – Mira Monte
February 12, 2016

108
Jimenez, Ruben — Foothill, Fall, 3:39
Romero, Petie — South

115
Mullins, Sean — North, Fall, 5:20
Perez, Felipe — South

122
Bracamonte, Matt — Foothill, Fall, 4:42
Mendoza, Julio — South
Lucero, Isaiah — North

128
Kuntz, Emmett — Highland, Fall, 2:43
Garcia, Levi — South
Hieineman, Blake — North, 10-8
Delacruz, Mathew — Mira Monte

134
Jacinto, Issak — Foothill, Major, 14-3
Zeferino, Miguel — South
Flores, Aaron — Highland, Fall, 1:34
Wade, Steven — North

140
Acosta, Brandon — Mira Monte, 10-3
Armstrong, Eric — North
Cordero, Kristian — South, Fall, 5:16
Martinez, Angel — Foothill
Dye, Hayden — Highland

147
Suarez, Ralphy — Foothill, TF15-0
Perez, Antonio — Highland
Torres, Nevada — South, Fall, 3:54
Garcia, Sergio — Mira Monte
Fenton, Ethan — North

154
Green, Jarome — South, 4-1
Kelley, Trevor — Highland
Stovall, Eric — Foothill, Fall, 3:32
Sevilla, Luis — North

162
Reed, Matt — North, Fall, 1:25
Reyes, Gabe — Highland
Gallegos, Justin — Foothill, Fall, 3:07
Perez, Michael — South

172
Jones, Phelan — South, Fall, 5:19
Chocoteco, Juan — Foothill
Krasky, Daniel — North

184
Castillo, Juan — South, 9-2
Grimaldo, Jose — Foothill
Whiteby, Connor — North, Fall, 4:12
Morales, Edward — Mira Monte
Garcia, Ricardo — Highland

197
Godinez, Adrian — Foothill, Fall, 3:07
Castaneda, Oscar — South,
Kline, James — North, Fall, 1:30
Hubbard, Issah — Highland
Torres, Juan — Mira Monte

222
Torres, Montana — South, 4-3
Mello, Kevin — North
Salinas, Alejandro — Highland, 5-4
Santana, Hugo — Foothill

287
Organista, Victor — South, 3-0
VanTassel, Ian — Foothill
Abernathy, Kaleb — North, Fall, 5:15
Flores, Pedro — Highland

Most Outstanding Wrestlers

Lower Weight: Ralphy Suarez — Foothill
Upper Weight: Phelan Jones — South

TOURNAMENT

South	215.5
Foothill	186.5
North	141
Highland	96.5
Mira Monte	35

DUAL,	LEAGUE	SEASON
Foothill	4-0	12-2
South	3-1	12-2
Highland	2-2	3-3
North	1-3	5-5
Mira Monte	N/A	N/A

SOUTHEAST YOSEMITE LEAGUE – Mira Monte
February 9, 2017

106
Jimenez, Ruben	Foothill, Fall
Fugazzi, Dante	North
Weldon, Richie	Highland

113
Worsham, Bryan	South, Fall
Gibson, Michael	North
Casmiro, Christian	Foothill

120
Romero, Pete	South, Fall
Duarte, Daniel	North

126
Ocampo, Javier	North, Fall
Cordero, Kristian	South
Patino, Aries	Highland

132
Ceferino, Miguel	South, Decision
Hieneman, Blake	North
Flores, Aaron	Highland, Decision
Perez, Eduardo	Mira Monte
Rodamer, Anthony	Foothill

138
Kuntz, Emmit	Highland, Fall
Garcia, Levi	South
Gomez, Andrew	Mira Monte, Decision
Camacho, Julio	Foothill
Grisdale, Caden	North

145
Torres, Nevada	South, Decision
Stovall, Eric	Foothill
Miner, Shawn	North, Fall
Allen, Tyler	Highland
Reyes, Harvey	Mira Monte

152
Mayall, Julius	North, Fall
Delarosa, J.R.	Foothill
Rubalcava, Martin	South

160
Reed, Matt	North, Decision
Kelly, Trevor	Highland
Gallegos, Justin	Foothill, Fall
Loza, Josh	South

170
Castillo, Juan	South, Decision
Bojorquez, Michael	Highland
Whitby, Connor	North, Major, Decision
Herrera, Abel	Foothill

182
Quintana, Antonio	Foothill, Fall
Krasky, Daniel	North
Aguirre, Michael	Highland, Fall
Gomez, Eduardo	South
Inzunza, Jorge	Mira Monte

195
Godinez, Adrian	Foothill, Fall
Thomas, James	North
Vasquez, Vlad	South, Decision
Diaz, Jesus	Highland

220
Graham, Dakota	North, Fall
Garcia, Ricardo	Highland
Bonilla, Milton	South, Decision
Manriquez, Juan	Foothill

285
Oliver, Billy	North, Decision
Saucedo, Anthony	Highland
Canfield, Gabriel	South, Decision
Florez, Oscar	Foothill

*Fall times and scores not provided

Most Outstanding Wrestlers

Lower Weight: Emmitt Kuntz   Highland
Upper Weight: Adrian Godinez Foothill

TOURNAMENT
North	227
South	184
Foothill	152
Highland	142.5
Mira, Monte	33

DUAL	LEAGUE	SEASON
North	4-0	9-3
Foothill	3-1	3-2
Highland	2-2	9-3
South	1-3	1-3
Mira Monte	0-4	0-5

SOUTHEAST YOSEMITE LEAGUE - North
February 9, 2018

106
Corona, Shane	Foothill, Fall
Ornales, Daniel	North
Cardenas, Eli	Highland

113
Casmiro, Angel	Foothill
Lopez, Kalob	North, Major, Decision
Oregon, Julian	Highland

120
Romero, Pete	South, Decision
Patino, Kaileb	Highland
Fugazzi, Dante	North, T-Fall
Ochoa, Angel	Foothill

126
Worsham, Brian	South, Fall
Rios, Isaiah	Highland
Vargas, Alvaro	Foothill, T-Fall
Mendez, Andrew	Mira Monte
Toro, Joziah	North

132
Ocampo, Javier	North, Decision
Lopez, Carlos	Highland
Job, Amador	South

138
Perez, Edwardo	Mira Monte, Decision
Griffin, Matthew	North
McCabe, Brendon	Foothill, Fall
Ramirez, Heaven	Highland
Mora, Matt	South

145
Torres, Raymond	South, Major, Decision
Reyes, Xaiver	Mira Monte
Corona, Anthony	North, Decision
Roquemore, Alex	Highland
Hernandez, Christian	Foothill

152
Gallegos, Justin	Foothill, Decision
Mayall, Julias	North
Kindred, Howard	Highland, Decision
Villatoro, Brandon	South

160
Stovall, Eric	Foothill, Decision
Hernandez, Christian	Highland
Palmer, Jacob	North
Rubalcava, Martin	South

170
Whitby, Connor	North, Decision
Hill, Tyler	Foothill
Aguirre, Michael	Highland, Fall
Rivera, Adrian	South

182
Gonzalez, Aventino	Highland, Major, Decision
Buyard, Elijah	South
Marquez, Alejandro	North, Fall
Sandoval, Santiago	Foothill

195
Martinez, Bryce	Highland, Decision
Herrera, Abraham	Foothill
Reyes, Luis, North	Forfeit
Mendoza, Lorenzo	South
Rueda, Adrian	Mira Monte

220
Sega, Paul	Highland, Fall
Gonzales, Edward	South
Backman, Zion	North

285
Bonilla, Milton	South, Fall
Gonzales, Benny	Highland
Pepper, Ned	North, Fall
Rosales, Jiobany	Foothill

Most Outstanding Wrestlers

Lower Weight: Brian Worshim   South
Upper Weight: Aventino Gonzalez Highland

TOURNAMENT
Highland	164
North	157
South	135
Foothill	131.5
Mira Monte	47.6

DUAL	LEAGUE	SEASON
Highland	4-0	7-0
North	3-1	5-1
Foothill	2-2	3-4
South	1-3	3-7
Mira Monte	0-4	0-4

SOUTHEAST YOSEMITE LEAGUE 2019
No Southeast Tournament was held – The coaches selected an All-League Team from the dual results.

106
Mays, Eric — Foothill
Sital, Stevie — North

113
Corona, Shane — Foothill
Ornelz, Daniel — North

120
Bailey, Royal — South
Casimro, Angel — Foothill

126
Ochoa, Angel — Foothill
Errecalde, Morgan — Highland

132
Job, Amador — South
Ramos, Michael — Highland

138
Ocampo, Javier — Mira Monte
Vejar, Victor — Highland

145
Reyes, Xavie — Mira Monte
Corona, Anthony — North

152
Torres, Nevada — South
Perez, Eduardo — Mira Monte

160
Hernandez, Christian — Highland
Mayall, Julius — North

170
Easton, Ricardo — East
Rivera, Adrian — South

182
Buyard, Elijah — South
Rushing, Blain — North

195
Valahakis, Yiannia — Mira Monte
Martinez, Bryce — Highland

220
Gonzalez, Edward — South
Chucca, Zion — North

285
Aqaerez, Fernando — South
Whitby, Trey — North

Most Outstanding Wrestlers

Lower Weight: Shane Corona — Foothill
Upper Weight: Nevada Torres — South

DUAL	LEAGUE	SEASON
North	4-1	12-4
South	4-1	6-1
Highland	3-2	8-4
Foothill	3-2	3-2
Mira Monte	1-4	2-4
East	0-4	0-5

Zion Chuca, North High School (01/30/2020)
Photo courtesy of Rod Thornburg

SOUTHEAST YOSEMITE LEAGUE - North
January 29, 2020

106
Jackson, Nathaniel	North, Fall, 1:30
Casas, Andrew	Foothill
Mesa, Andrew	Highland

113
Ornelas, Andrew	North, Fall, :37
Trevino, Elias	Foothill
Guzman, Jose	Highland

120
Corona, Shane	Foothill, 7-2
Lopez, Kaleb	North
Martinez, Jose	East, 8-0
Nunez, Christian	Highland

126
Ornelas, Anthony	North, 13-4
Casmiro, Angel	Foothill
Kuntz, Lee	Highland, 9-3
Perez, Erick	South
Azurdia, Christian	East

132
Ruvalcava, Anthony	South, 12-10
Yelland, Martin	North
Gallegos, Evan	Foothill, Fall, 1:51
Hernandez, Israel	East
Truskoki, ?	Highland

138
Ochoa, Angel	Foothill, Fall, 3:29
Erracalde, Angel	Highland
Gonzalez, Mario	North
Amador, Job	South
Martinez, Jesus	East

145
Ocampo, Javier	North, 7-5
Amaya, Luis	Foothill
Gomez, Johnathan	Mira Monte, 6-5
Nunez, Tony	South
Gonzalez, Abe	Highland

152
Garcia, Richard	Fall, 4:33
Hernandez, Christian	Foothill
Renteria, Jose	North, 7-2
Wadsworth, Taj	Highland

160
Reyes, Xavier	Mira Monte, 17-5
McBride, Drew	North
Helm, Jeremy	South, 10-5
Fuentez, A.J.	Highland
Rios, Andrew	Foothill

170
Eaton, Ricardo	East, 10-3
Thomas, Drake	Highland
Ciccio, Angel	Mira Monte, 8-2
Aguilar, Jose	South
Marquez, Carlos	Foothill
Duarte, Daniel	North

182
Patino, Jonathan	East, Fall, 3:03
Marquez, George	Mira Monte
Buyard, Elijah	South, Fall, 1:07
Martinez, Caleb	Highland
Cisneros, Christian	Foothill, Default
Marquez, Alejandro	North

195
Chuca, Zion	North, 4-2
Perez, Gerado	Mira Monte
Ortiz, Lucas	Highland, Fall, :48

220
Barajas, Freddy	South, 3-2
Gonzalez, Benny	Highland
Elisa, Isiah, Foothill	Fall, 2:51
Montez, Steven	Mira, Monte
Whitbey, Trey	North

285
Cuevas, Cesar	East, Fall, 3:30
Nicholson, Leroy	North
Hernandez, Gabriel	South, Default
Saucedo, John	Highland

SOUTHEAST YOSEMITE LEAGUE - North
January 29, 2020

Most Outstanding Wrestlers

Lower Weight: Anthony Ruvalcava   South
Upper Weight: Cesar Cuevas   East

TOURNAMENT
North	215
Foothill	180
South	157
Highland	144
East	102
Mira Monte	88.5

DUAL	LEAGUE	SEASON
North	2-1	5-3
Foothill	2-1	7-2
South	2-1	12-4
Highland	2-1	5-3
East	0-1	0-1
Mira Monte	0-1	0-1

SOUTHWEST YOSEMITE LEAGUE

2007-2020

SOUTHWEST YOSEMITE LEAGUE CHAMPIONSHIP TEAMS

Date	Location	Dual Champion		Tournament Champion	Overall Champion	Coach
2/04/1995	Stockdale	Stockdale	4-0	Stockdale	Stockdale	Craig Schoene
2/03/1996	Stockdale	South	4-0	South	South	Brian Henderson
2/08/1997	Centennial	South	4-0	Centennial	South	Brian Henderson
					Centennial	Paul Olejnik
2/13/1998	Centennial	Centennial	4-0	Centennial	Centennial	Paul Olejnik
2/13/1999	Centennial	Centennial	4-0	Centennial	Centennial	Paul Olejnik
2/12/2000	Centennial	Centennial	4-0	Centennial	Centennial	Paul Olejnik
2/10/2001	Centennial	Centennial	4-0	Centennial	Centennial	Paul Olejnik
2/09/2002	Centennial	Centennial	4-0	Centennial	Centennial	Paul Olejnik
2/15/2003	Centennial	Centennial	3-1	Stockdale	Centennial	Paul Olejnik
		South	3-1			
2/14/2004	Centennial	Centennial	3-1	Stockdale	Stockdale	Paul Garcia
		Stockdale	3-1			
		South	3-1			
2/12/2005	Centennial	Centennial	4-1	Centennial	Centennial	Mike Hicks
		South	4-1			
2/11/2006	Centennial	South	5-0	Centennial	South	Brian Henderson
					Centennial	Mike Hicks
2/10/2007	Centennial	Centennial	5-0	Centennial	Centennial	Mike Hicks
2/09/2008	Centennial	Frontier	6-0	Frontier	Frontier	Kirk Moore
2/14/2009	Centennial	Frontier	6-0	Frontier	Frontier	Kirk Moore
2/13/2010	Frontier	Frontier	6-0	Frontier	Frontier	Kirk Moore
2/12/2011	Frontier	Bakersfield	5-0	Bakersfield	Bakersfield	Andy Varner
2/11/2012	Frontier	Bakersfield	5-0	Bakersfield	Bakersfield	Andy Varner
2/09/2013	Frontier	Bakersfield	5-0	Bakersfield	Bakersfield	Andy Varner
2/15/2014	Frontier	Bakersfield	5-0	Bakersfield	Bakersfield	Andy Varner
						Anthony Box
2/14/2015	Frontier	Bakersfield	4-0	Bakersfield	Bakersfield	Andy Varner
						Anthony Box
2/11/2016	Frontier	Bakersfield	4-0	Bakersfield	Bakersfield	Andy Varner
						Anthony Box
2/10/2017	Frontier	Bakersfield	4-0	Bakersfield	Bakersfield	Andy Varner
						Frank Lomas
2/08/2018	Frontier	Bakersfield	5-0	Frontier	Bakersfield	Andy Varner
						Frank Lomas
					Frontier	Carlo Franciotti
2019		Frontier	5-0	No Tournament		Carlo Franciotti
2020	Frontier	No Dual Champion		Bakersfield		Andy Varner
						Frank Lomas

SOUTHWEST YOSEMITE LEAGUE
MOST OUTSTANDING WRESTLERS

Year	Lower Weight		Upper Weight	
1995	Tom Aguirre	North	Rocky East	North
1996	Frank Lara	South	Peter Ghitty	South
1997	Brian Leonard	South	Juan Jimenez	South
1998	Joel Goings	West	Josh Naus	Centennial
1999	Sean Sheets	Centennial	Marcos Rivera	South
2000				
2001	Jason Matthews	Stockdale	Colin Shields	South
2002	Derrick Hunter	North	Jeff Baker	Centennial
2003	Rolland Parli	West	Jeff Baker	Centennial
2004	Joe Kuntz	North	Rolland Parli	West
2005	Freddie Vigil	South	Bryce Horton	Centennial
2006	Eric Matthews	Stockdale	Bryce Horton	Centennial
2007	Vince Hamey	Stockdale	Chris Smith	West
2008	Derek Tallit	Centennial	Eric Matthews	Stockdale
2009	Seth Hicks	Centennial	Roman Flores	Stockdale
2010	Vincent Gomez	Frontier	Eric Schoenborn	Centennial
2011	Josh Lopez	Frontier	Sean Hendrix	Independence
2012	Tyler Hartfield	Liberty	John Popek	Frontier
2013	Sean Nickell	Bakersfield	Shag Garrett	Bakersfield
2014	Brock Welton	Frontier	Carlos Montejo	Frontier
2015	Jonathan Garcia	Frontier	Jeremy Mass	Liberty
2016	Ryan Morphis	Frontier	Noah Rodriguez	Bakersfield
2017	Andrew Bloemhof	Bakersfield	Dillon Cravens	Bakersfield
2018	Garrett Fletcher	Frontier	Josiah Hill	Bakersfield
2019	Andrew Bloemhof	Bakersfield	Trent Tracy	Frontier
2020	Lake Combs	Frontier	Josiah Hill	Bakersfield

*Awards sponsored by the Coyote Club Membership

Josiah Hill - Bakersfield High School

Trent Tracy – Frontier High School

SOUTHWEST YOSEMITE LEAGUE - Centennial
February 10, 2007

103
Hamey, Vince	Stockdale, Fall, :29
Ramirez, Jesus	Ridgeview
McKee, Nick	Centennial, Fall, 2:42
Cardenas, Dallas	South

112
Tablit, Derek	Centennial, Fall, 2:11
Cerna, Marcus	North
Aguilar, Chris	Stockdale

119
Hurtado, Aaron	Centennial, Fall, 5:26
Magno, Jon	Ridgeview,
Perry, Ryan	Stockdale, Decision
Hernandez, Mike	North
Estrada, Ruben	South

125
Magno, Bryan	Ridgeview, Fall, 5:42
Staffero, Adam	Centennial
Romero, Dominic	South, Fall, 4:54
Deleon, Demetrio	North

130
Hicks, Seth	Centennial, Fall, 1:56
Fuentes, Phillip	South
Myer, Chris	Stockdale, Decision
Lozano, Jesse	Ridgeview

135
Ballard, Austin	Centennial, 5-0
Gonzalez, Nathan	North
Cavazos, Kyle	Ridgeview, Decision
Pinuelas, Johnny	West
Martinez, David	South
Payne, Jordan	Stockdale

140
Tacket, Jack	Centennial, 11-9
Garcia, Rene	Ridgeview
Ryther, Nathan	Stockdale, Fall, 1:41
Cordova, Josh	North
Moreno, Alex	South

145
Ends, Dalton	Centennial, 10-2
Mathews, Eric	Stockdale
Arguello, Miguel	Ridgeview, Fall, 1:04
Jones, David	North

152
Smith, Chris	West, 14-5
Harrison, Alex	North
Beardsely, Tyler	Centennial, Decision
Nevarez, Mark	Ridgeview
Nipper, Lance	South

160
Sotelo, Nick	West, 4-2
Payne, Joel	Stockdale
Velasquez, Jose	South, Forfeit
Pence, Bobby	Centennial
Farley, Dan	North

171
Thomason, Joey	North, Fall, 1:52
Sotelo, Matt	West
Handy, Zak	Centennial, 11-6
Aceves, Pedro	South

189
Ryder, Glenn	Centennial, Fall, 1:49
Maricich, Corban	North
Parea, Manuel	West, Decision
Gutierrez, Herman	South

215
Terrell, Lake	North, 14-4
Castillo, Michael	Centennial
Mitchell, Aaron	Stockdale, Fall, 5:13
Davenport, Chris	South
Hinojosa, Andrew	Ridgeview

285
Wills, Brent	North, Fall, 2:18
Hinojosa, Steven	Centennial
McGill, Andrew	South, Fall, 2:26
Martinez, Alex	West

Most Outstanding Wrestlers
Lower Weight: Vince Hamey   Stockdale
Upper Weight: Chris Smith   West

TOURNAMENT
Centennial	247
North	180
Ridgeview	119
Stockdale	118.5
South	109
West	N/A

DUAL	LEAGUE	SEASON
Centennial	5-0	6-0
North	3-2	3-2
Ridgeview	3-2	3-3
Stockdale	3-2	6-6
South	2-3	3-4
West	0-5	1-6

SOUTHWEST YOSEMITE LEAGUE - Centennial
February 9, 2008

103
Gomez, Alexandrea (F)	Frontier, 5-4, *30-7
DeGough, Scotty	Centennial
Sanchez, Josh	Ridgeview, 15-1
Cardenas, Isaiah	South
Ruiz, Michael	West

112
Casper, Torrey	Frontier, Fall, 5:05
Aguilar, Chris	Stockdale
Cera, Marcus, North	Fall, 3:38
Ramirez, Jesus	Ridgeview
Castro, Rudy	South

119
Talbit, Derek	Centennial, Fall, 1:07
Lopez, Josh	Frontier
Mendez, Oscar	North

125
Whitby, Jacob	Frontier, Fall, :46
Perry, Ryan	Stockdale
Staffero, Adam	Centennial, Fall, 2:40
Vidalez, Gabe	South

130
Magno, Bryan	Ridgeview, 13-4
Shoemaker, Codi	Stockdale
An, Andre	Frontier, 12-3
Deleon, Demetrio	North

135
Garcia, Rene	Ridgeview, 15-2
Ballard, Austin	Centennial
Barton, Nick	Frontier, Fall, 4:01
Haidze, Josh	Stockdale
Espinoza, Ali	South, 7-5
Steed, Cody	North

140
Hicks, Seth	Centennial, Fall, 5:18
Payne, Jordan	Stockdale
Mearse, Nolan	Frontier, Fall, 3:14
Fuentes, Phillip	South
Singh, Ranjit	Ridgeview, Fall, 2:04
Patterson, Ryan	North

145
Myer, Chris	Stockdale, Fall, 3:05
Bishop, Ryan	Frontier
Singh, Gil	Ridgeview, 11-4
Schoenborn, Eric	Centennial
Onsure, Albert	West

152
Matthews, Eric	Stockdale, 6-5
Castaneda, Lance	Frontier
Harrison, Alex	North
Nunez, Rickey	Centennial
Mercado, Fabian	South, Fall, 2:04
Turner, Chris	West

160
Narvaez, Mark	Ridgeview, 10-5
Nipper, Lance	South
Delfino, Santino	Frontier, Fall, :44
Gonzales, Fernando	Stockdale
McCaffrey, Mike	Centennial, TF, 17-1
Galindo, Brian	West

171
Musquez, John	Centennial, Fall, 2:36
Liggett, Kenny	North
Cerreon, Rene	South
Baca, Tim	Frontier
Ryther, Nathan	Stockdale

189
Ryder, Glen	Centennial, 5-4
Thompson, Joey	North
Walker, Blake	Frontier, Fall, :58
Samano, Ray	West

215
Castillo, Michael	Centennial, Fall, 3:28
Whitesell, Nick	Frontier
Fisher, Josh	North, 6-4
Davenport, Christopher	South
Myers, Anthony	West

275
Wills, Bret	North, 7-1
Quinterro, Pedro	Centennial
Davis, Josh	Frontier, Fall, 2:59
Gutierrez, Arnold	South
Hinojosa, Andrew	Ridgeview

SOUTHWEST YOSEMITE LEAGUE - Centennial
February 9, 2008

Most Outstanding Wrestlers

Lower Weight: Derek Talbit   Centennial
Upper Weight: Eric Matthews Stockdale

TOURNAMENT
Frontier	222
Centennial	186.5
Stockdale	125.5
North	106
Ridgeview	96.5
South	56
West	4

DUAL	LEAGUE	SEASON
Frontier	6-0	17-3
Centennial	5-1	12-1
Stockdale	3-3	10-6
North	3-3	3-3
South	3-3	3-4
Ridgeview	2-4	3-4
West	0-6	0-7

* Season, record
F = Female

Kirk Moore and Carlo Franciotti - Frontier High School

SOUTHWEST YOSEMITE LEAGUE - Centennial
February 14, 2009

103
Gomez, Alexandrea(F)	Frontier, 3-1, *27-9
Magno, Brandon	Ridgeview
Armijo, Jason	Centennial, Fall, 2:39
Johnson, Cole	West
Corona, Alberto	South
Leanander, Zack	North

112
Hamey, Vince	Stockdale, 4-2
Cardenas, Dallas	South
Sanchez, Josh	Ridgeview, Default
Lopez, Josh	Frontier
Ruiz, Michael	West

119
Casper, Torrey	Frontier, Fall, 3:36
DeGough, Scotty	Centennial
Ramirez, Jesus	Ridgeview, Default
Aguilar, Chris	Stockdale
Castro, Rudy	South
Melendez, Oscar	North

125
Tablit, Derek	Centennial, Fall, 1:29
Blood, Cody	Frontier
Lozano, Jesse	Ridgeview, Fall, 1:26
Cortez, Josh	South
Hernandez, Raphael	West
Hulbert, Nick	North

130
Sanchez, Eric	Centennial, Fall, 1:36
Contreras, Andrew	Frontier
Pineda, Edgar	South, 4-1
Dahlquist, Cameron	Stockdale
Randall, ?	North

135
Hicks, Seth	Centennial, Fall, 2:34
Shoemaker, Cadi	Stockdale
Espinoza, Alex	South, Default
Barton, Nick	Frontier
Mello, John	North

140
Sanchez, Javier	Ridgeview, Fall, 2:34
Bullard, Austin	Centennial
Mearse, Nolan	Frontier, 7-0
Hibler, Austin	Stockdale
Ybanez, ?	South

145
Castaneda, Lance	Frontier, Fall, 2:33
Diaz, Matt	Stockdale
Roberts, Chris	Centennial, 5-4
Bellamy, Devon	North
Wilcox, Robert	South

152
Bishop, Ryan	Frontier, 7-4
Haidze, Jeremy	Stockdale
Steed, Cody	North, Fall, 5:43
McCaffrey, Mike	Centennial

160
Flores, Roman	Stockdale, 5-2
Endes, Dalton	Centennial
Delfino, Santino	Frontier, Fall, 1:12
Meek, Jason	West
Priest, Tyler	North

171
Baca, Tim	Frontier, Fall, 3:56
Carreon, Rene	South
Schoenborn, Erik	Centennial, Fall, 3:30
Branson, Sam	Stockdale
Santos, Jose	West

189
Walker, Chace	Centennial, Fall, 2:50
Davenport, Christopher	South
Ellis, Shane	Frontier, Default
McBride, Tim	North
Fletes, Sergio	Ridgeview,
Marquez, Alex	West

215
Oropeza, Diego	Frontier, Fall, :38
Gutierrez, Bravilo	Ridgeview
Crawford, Carson	Centennial, Fall, 4:48
Escelera, Phillip	South
Hale, Shelton	North

275
Davis, Josh	Frontier, Fall, 3:36
Regla, Julio	South
Melson, Tanner	North

SOUTHWEST YOSEMITE LEAGUE - Centennial
February 14, 2009

Most Outstanding Wrestlers

Lower Weight: Seth Hicks   Centennial
Upper Weight: Roman Flores   Stockdale

TOURNAMENT
Frontier	226.5
Centennial	159
Stockdale	117.5
South	114
Ridgeview	102
North	28
West	27

DUAL	LEAGUE	SEASON
Frontier	6-0	14-0
Centennial	5-1	10-2
Stockdale	4-2	10-4
South	3-3	3-3
Ridgeview	1-5	1-6
West	1-5	2-4
North	0-6	0-6

* Season record

Roman Flores – Stockdale High School

SOUTHWEST YOSEMITE LEAGUE - Frontier
February 13, 2010

103
Gomez, Vincent	Frontier, Fall, 1:11
Gomez, Frank	Ridgeview
Stublefield, A. J.	North, 8-5
Nova, Sal	South

112
Paregien, Montana	Frontier, Fall, :53
Melandez, Oscar	North
Newton, Derek	Stockdale, 8-7
Echaverria, Emmanuel	South,
Hernandez, Martin	West

119
Lopez, Josh	Frontier, 9-3
Fiddler, Chase	Centennial
Aguilar, Chris	Stockdale, TF, 16-1
Holmes, Garrett	North
Nava, Carlos	South, Fall, 5:42
Singh, Mani	Ridgeview

125
DeGough, Scotty	Centennial, 9-2
Wahl, Tommy	Frontier
Ramirez, Jesus	Ridgeview, 10-3
Hernandez, Rafael	West
Lotter, D. J.	Stockdale, TF, 5:00
Guardado, Alan	North

130
Blood, Cody	Frontier, Fall, 3:53
Sanchez, Josh	Ridgeview
Castro, Rudy	South, Fall, ?
Armijo, Jason	Centennial
Pate, Brad	Stockdale

135
An, Andre	Frontier, 7-2
Tablet, Derek	Centennial
Mello, John	North, 9-6
Dahlquist, Cameron	Stockdale
Gray, Steven	South, 11-9
Fuentes, Adam	Ridgeview

140
Villalobos, Jovan	Centennial
Mariscal, Frankie	Stockdale
Paregien, Dakota	Frontier, Fall, :29
Gomez, Keno	North
Butler, John	North

145
Sotomayer, Eric	Centennial, 9-3
Herring, Shawn	Stockdale
Barton, Nick	Frontier, Fall, 1:10
Green, Gage	South

152
Castaneda, Lance	Frontier, Fall, 1:17
Diaz, Matt	Stockdale
Steed, Cody	North, 7-4
Ballard, Billy	Centennial
Schultz, Jeff	South

160
Haidze, Jeremy	Stockdale, Fall, 4:43
Schoenborn, Aaron	Centennial
Spears, Jacob	Ridgeview, Major
Romero, Alonso	Frontier
Vasquez, Chris	West, Fall
Henry, D, J.	North

171
Schoenborn, Eric	Centennial, Fall, 5:17
Flores, Roman	Stockdale
Carreon, Rene	South, Default
Delfino, Santino	Frontier
Marrison, Aaron	Ridgeview, TF
Woods, Ryan	North

189
Ellis, Shane	Frontier, TF, 20-5
Williams, Chantz	South
McBride, Tim	North, Decision
Gonzales, Fernando	Stockdale
Zubia, Alex	Centennial

215
Huych, Adam	Frontier, 7-2
Branson, Sam	South
Ringes, Josh	North, Decision
Ortiz, Rene	Centennial
Vega, Johnny	Ridgeview

285
Davis, Josh	Frontier, Fall, 3:30
Regla, Julio	South
Nelson, Tanner	North, 7-5
Crawford, Carson	Centennial
Tinco, Adam	Ridgeview

SOUTHWEST YOSEMITE LEAGUE - Frontier
February 13, 2010

Most Outstanding Wrestlers

Lowe Weight: Vincent Gomez Frontier
Upper Weight: Eric Schoenborn Centennial

TOURAMENT
Frontier	290.5
Centennial	208.5
Stockdale	194
South	134.5
North	127
Ridgeview	103.5
West	51

DUAL	LEAGUE	SEASON
Frontier	6-0	6-0
Stockdale	5-1	7-5
Centennial	4-2	6-2
South	3-3	3-3
North	2-4	2-4
West	1-5	1-5
Ridgeview	0-6	0-6

Vincent Gomez, Frontier High School (02/28/2013)
Photographer: Felix Adamo, Bakersfield Californian

SOUTHWEST YOSEMITE LEAGUE - Frontier
February 12, 2011

103
- Onsurez, Arik — Bakersfield, TF 16-1
- Bettis, Devin — Independence
- Triberg, Alex — Centennial, Major, 11-3
- Cisternia, Jason — Frontier

112
- Nickell, Ian — Bakersfield, 11-4
- Gomez, Vincent — Frontier
- Hamey, Vito — Stockdale, 4-0
- Kellogg, Gage — Centennial
- Carter, Nick — Liberty, Decision
- Powell, Sean — Independence

119
- Martin, Bryce — BHS, Fall, 3:28 *34-11
- Weaver, Preston — Frontier
- Sanchez, Omar — Independence, 5-1
- Armijo, Jason — Centennial

125
- Lopez, Josh — Frontier, 2-1
- Cruz, Micah — Bakersfield
- Hartsfield, Tyler — Liberty, 5-2
- Cotter, D, J. — Stockdale
- Weeks, Kyle — Independence, Dec.
- Worthen, Holden — Centennial

130
- Demison, Natrelle — Bakersfield, Fall, 1:25
- Paregien, Dakota — Frontier
- Dominguez, Alex — Centennial
- Colometes, Fernando — Stockdale

135
- Box, Timmy — Bakersfield, Fall, 3:14
- Ozuna, Isaiah — Frontier
- Pate, Brad — Stockdale, Fall, 3:30
- Lee, Andrew — Centennial
- McGune, Tyler — Liberty

140
- Ramirez, Maxx — Bakersfield, TF, 17-2
- Fambrough, Jawayn — Independence
- Ballard, Billy — Centennial, 12-8
- Rodriguez, Brandon — Frontier
- Thomas, Jacob — Liberty

145
- Hammonds, Colman — Bakersfield, Fall, 3:05
- Sotomayer, Brandon — Centennial
- Mass, Jacob — Liberty, 11-8
- Stillion, Michael — Frontier
- Carrillo, James — Independence

152
- Fierro, Adam — Bakersfield, TF, 18-2
- Castillo, Mason — Centennial
- Shepherd, Kyle — Frontier, Fall, 5:00
- Dahlquist, Cameron — Stockdale

160
- Hammond, Bryce — Bakersfield, Fall, 3:03
- Worth, Andrew — Stockdale
- Schoenborn, Aaron — Centennial, Fall, :30
- Heinsohn, Jacob — Liberty
- Honea, Andrew — Frontier

171
- Nacita, Silas — Bakersfield, Fall, 1:11
- Altanour, Ahmad — Stockdale
- Linderman, Jason — Independence, 9-5
- Guevara, Victor — Centennial

189
- Murphy, Jack — Frontier, 5-3
- Sizemore, Chris — Liberty
- Branson, Sam — Stockdale, Default
- Pope, Kyle — Bakersfield
- Saverdra, Chris — Independence

215
- Hendrix, Sean — Independence, Fall, 5:15
- Swainston, Nathan — Liberty
- Cameron, Gage — Bakersfield, Fall, 2:40
- Ortiz, Rene — Centennial
- Rivera, Greg — Frontier

285
- Hurtado, Frankie — Liberty, Fall, 5:15
- Popek, John — Frontier
- Crawford, Carson — Centennial, 7-1
- Gamez, Steven — Independence
- Silva, Adrian — Bakersfield

Most Outstanding Wrestlers
Lower Weight: Josh Lopez — Frontier
Upper Weight: Sean Hendrix — Independence

TOURNAMENT
- Bakersfield 276
- Frontier 193
- Centennial 158
- Stockdale 138.5
- Liberty 131.5
- Independence 129.5

SOUTHWEST YOSEMITE LEAGUE - Frontier
February 12, 2011

DUAL	LEAGUE	SEASON
Bakersfield	5-0	6-0
Frontier	4-1	9-2
Centennial	3-2	3-2
Stockdale	2-3	7-16
Independence	1-4	1-4
Liberty	0-5	0-5

Bryce Hammond – Bakersfield High School

SOUTHWEST YOSEMITE LEAGUE - Frontier
February 11, 2012

106
Herrera, Carlos	Bakersfield, 7-1
Armijo, Etienne	Centennial
Cisterna, Jason	Frontier, Fall, 3:55
Meek, Bryson	Stockdale
Pineda, Joseph	Liberty
Castello, ?	Independence

113
Onsurez, Airk	Bakersfield, 21-8
Spears, Cole	Stockdale
Valenzuela, Andrew	Independence, Fall
Carter, Nick	Liberty
Shepherd, Chandler	Frontier

120
Marin, Oscar	Bakersfield, TF, 18-3
Pizano, Izaiah	Stockdale
Weaver, Preston	Frontier, 15-9
Kellogg, Gage	Centennial
George, Ryan	Liberty
Bettis, Davin	Independence

126
Martin, Bryce	Bakersfield, Fall, 3:18
Ozuna, Izaiah	Frontier
Treiberg, Alex	Centennial, Fall, 3:59
Ibarra, Anthony	Stockdale
Connelly, Keith	Liberty

132
Cruz, Micah	Bakersfield, TF
Cotter, D, J.	Stockdale
Armijo, Jason	Centennial, 9-7
Gamboa, Austin	Frontier
Briseno, Anthony	Liberty
Ochoa, Ben	Independence

138
Demison, Natrelle	Bakersfield, Fall, 1:07
Gomez, Aaron	Frontier
Dominguez, Alex	Centennial, 8-1
Saldana, Ray	Stockdale
Carrillo, James	Independence
Rojas, Felipe	Liberty

145
Hartsfield, Tyler	Liberty, 9-7
Ramirez, Maxx	Bakersfield
Fiddler, Chase	Centennial, Fall, 1:35
Orozco, Jose	Independence
Stillion, Michael	Liberty
Turner, Keyon	Stockdale

152
Hammond, Colman	Bakersfield, TF, 23-6
Ryder, Ryan	Centennial
Montejo, Carlos	Frontier, Fall, 1:48
Robles, Richey	Independence
Trevino, Junior	Liberty
Rodriguez, Johnny	Stockdale

160
Fierro, A, J.	Bakersfield, 5-1
Castillo, Mason	Centennial
Shepard, Kyle	Frontier, 5-1
Worth, Andrew	Stockdale
Swank, Tyler	Independence
Thomas, Jacob	Liberty

170
Nacita, Silas	Bakersfield, TF, 18-3
Bailey, Josh	Frontier
Holmes, Ryan	Stockdale
Schoenborn, Aaron	Centennial
Webb, Landyn	Independence
Heinsohn, Jacob	Liberty

182
Pope, Kyle	Bakersfield, TF, 20-5
Honea, Andrew	Frontier
Linderman, Jason	Independence, Fall, :46
Guevara, Victor	Centennial
Quintero, Daniel	Liberty

195
Murphy, Jack	Frontier, Fall, 4:46,
Willis, Cameron	Liberty
East, Jake	Bakersfield, Fall, 2:19
Herring, Jkell	Independence

220
Swainston, Nathan	Liberty, Fall, 4:32
Sunquist, Chase	Bakersfield
Sipe, Mitch, Frontier	Fall, 3:28
Alderidge, Nick	Centennial

285
Popek, John	Frontier
Crawford, Carson	Centennial
Mata, Jorge	Bakersfield, Fall, 3:00
Guerra, Ruben	Liberty

SOUTHWEST YOSEMITE LEAGUE - Frontier
February 11, 2012

No fifth place matches were held

Most Outstanding Wrestlers

Lower Weight: Tyler Hartsfield Liberty
Upper Weight: John Popek Frontier

TOURNAMENT
Bakersfield	301.5
Frontier	222.5
Centennial	199
Stockdale	95
Liberty	88
Independence	53

DUAL	LEAGUE	SEASON
Bakersfield	5-0	6-0
Frontier	4-1	9-1
Centennial	3-2	7-3
Liberty	1-4	3-4
Independence	1-4	1-4
Stockdale	0-5	2-9

Darryl Pope, Kyle Pope and Andy Varner – Bakersfield High School

SOUTHWEST YOSEMITE LEAGUE - Frontier
February 9, 2013

106
Herrera, Carlos — Bakersfield, Fall, 5:17
Morphis, Calloway — Frontier
Rodriguez, Ivan — Liberty
Shephard, Kyle — Frontier
Mass, Jacob — Liberty, Major, 17-7
Lee, Andrew — Centennial

113
Nickell, Sean — Bakersfield, 12-11
Cisterna, Jason — Frontier
Patoc, Jordan — Liberty, Fall, :35
Castillo, Isai — Independence

120
Onsurez, Arik — Bakersfield, 6-1
Armijo, Etienne — Centennial
Weldon, Brock — Frontier, Fall, 4:33
Subia, Elijah — Stockdale

126
Gomez, Vincent — Frontier, Fall, 1:29
Amaya, Melvin — Bakersfield
Kellogg, Gage — Centennial, 10-8
Cotter, Nathan — Stockdale

132
Ozuna, Izaiah — Frontier, 10-5
Gutierrez, Antonio — Bakersfield
Treiberg, Alex — Centennial, 8-7
Wright, Logan — Stockdale
Carter, Nick — Liberty

138
Santore, Johnny — Liberty, 12-6
Cotter, D, J — Stockdale
Gamboa, Austin — Frontier, Fall, :50
Braughton, Tristan — Centennial
Cristea, Kevin — Bakersfield, Fall, 2:21
Ochoa, Ben — Independence

145
Fierro, A, J. — Bakersfield, Fall, 1:25
White, Levi — Centennial
Gomez, Aaron — Frontier, Fall, 1:02
Beaumont, Scott — Stockdale
Bingham, Jason — Liberty

152
Hammond, Coleman — Bakersfield, Fall, 3:05
Saldana, Ray — Stockdale
Ryder, Ryan — Centennial, Fall
Garten, Parker — Frontier
Trevino, J. R. — Liberty

160
Hodges, Hunter — Bakersfield, 8-2

170
Martin, Bryce — Bakersfield, Major, 18-4
Komin, Mike — Frontier
Arguello, Marco — Independence, Default
Holmes, Ryan — Stockdale

182
Pope, Kyle — Bakersfield, Major, 14-6
Montejo, Carlos — Frontier
Webb, Landyn — Independence, Fall, 3:02
Thomas, Jacob — Liberty
Graves, T.J. — Stockdale

195
Bailey, Josh — Frontier, 8-3
Kidd, Nick — Bakersfield
Heinsohn, Jacob — Liberty, Fall, 1:18
Rodriguez, Johnny — Stockdale

220
Alcantar, Augie — Frontier, Fall, :56
Song, Troy — Stockdale
Ellebrachi, Travis — Bakersfield, 8-5
Hall, Jacob — Independence

285
Garrett, Shag — Bakersfield, Fall, :14
Watts, Cody — Independence,
Ramos, Isaac — Stockdale, Fall, 1:05
Flippo, Gabe — Liberty

Most Outstanding Wrestlers
Lower Weight: Sean Nickell — Bakersfield
Upper, Weight: Shag Garrett — Bakersfield

TOURNAMENT

Team	Points
Bakersfield	281
Frontier	247
Stockdale	163
Liberty	150
Centennial	128.5
Independence	90

DUAL	LEAGUE	SEASON
Bakersfield	5-0	6-0
Frontier	4-1	8-1
Centennial	3-2	3-2
Liberty	2-3	2-3
Stockdale	1-4	5-3
Independence	0-5	0-5

SOUTHWEST YOSEMITE LEAGUE - Frontier
February 15, 2014

106
Demision, Natreelle	Bakersfield, Fall, :30
Mares, Juan	Frontier
Rodriguez, Nick	Liberty

113
Figueroa, J J	Bakersfield, Fall, 2:56
Potoc, Jordan	Liberty
Meyers, Brandon	Stockdale, 3-2
Saradia, Pedro	Frontier

120
Weldon, Brock	Frontier, Fall, 5:31
Herrera, Carlos	Bakersfield
Rodriguez, Ivan	Liberty, 10-3
Masqueda, Emilio	Stockdale
Aguirre, Sam	Independence, Fall 3:51
Compos, Drew	Centennial

126
Nickell, Sean	Bakersfield
Martin, Josef	Stockdale
Morphis, Calloway	Frontier, 2-1
Corona, Peter	Independence
Rojas, Santana	Liberty, 14-7
Burgoni, Cameron	Centennial

132
Garcia, Jonathan	Frontier, Major, 15-2
Osurez, Arik	Bakersfield
Armijo, Etienne	Centennial, Fall, :42
Wright, Logan	Stockdale
Connelly, Keith	Liberty, Decision
Ruiz, Alex	Independence

138
Treiberg, Alex	Centennial, 2-1
Santore-Tovar, Johnny	Liberty
Annis, Josh	Bakersfield, Fall, 3:33
Corona, Estabon	Independence
Cotter, Nathan	Stockdale, Major, 14-3
Valdez, Joe	Frontier

145
Gutierrez, Antonio	Bakersfield, Major, 9-1
Castillo, Cody	Stockdale
Garten, Parker	Frontier, Fall, 3:45
Manzo, Armando	Liberty
Braughton, Tristan	Centennial, Forfeit
Salazar, Logan	Independence

152
Lee, Andrew	Centennial, 9-4
Gonzalez, Ricardo	Bakersfield
Gamboa, Austin	Frontier, Fall, 3:45
Trevino, J.R.	Liberty
Moreno, Adrian	Stockdale, Fall, 3:05
Ochoa, Ben	Independence

160
Lopez, Sam	Bakersfield, 8-7
Mass, Jake	Liberty
White, Levi	Centennial, Fall, 3:52
Komin, Mike	Frontier

170
Martin, Bryce	Bakersfield, Fall, 1:27
Mass, Jeremy	Liberty
Robles, Ricardo	Independence, 9-6
Byrd, Ethan	Frontier
Reed, Brandon	Stockdale

182
Montego, Carlos	Frontier, 4-3, OT
Rosales, Elias	Bakersfield
Thomas, Jacob	Liberty

195
Bailey, Josh	Frontier, Fall, :19
Amaya, Frank	Bakersfield
Mitchell, Zack	Liberty, 8-5
Griffith, Daniel	Independence

220
Yarbrough, Travis	Bakersfield, 3-2
Hall, Jacob	Independence
Song, Henry	Stockdale, Forfeit
Goodwin, Andrew	Frontier

285
Snyder, Jarrod	Frontier, Fall, 3:19
Schoene, Daniel	Bakersfield
Sanchez, Marcos	Liberty, 6-0
Garris, Maxx	Centennial
Chavez, Rafael	Independence

SOUTHWEST YOSEMITE LEAGUE - Frontier
February 15, 2014

Most Outstanding Wrestlers

Lower Weight: Brock Walton   Frontier
Upper Weight: Carlos Montejo Frontier

TOURNAMENT
Bakersfield	273.5
Frontier	227
Liberty	186
Centennial,	141.5
Stockdale	141
Independence,	125

DUAL	LEAGUE	SEASON
Bakersfield	5-0	10-1
Frontier	4-1	9-1
Liberty	3-2	3-2
Centennial	2-3	6-6
Independence	1-4	1-4
Stockdale	0-5	0-5

Sean Nickell – Bakersfield High School

SOUTHWEST YOSEMITE LEAGUE - Frontier
February 14, 2015

108
Olejnik, Izzek — Bakersfield, 5-3
Sarabia, Pedro — Frontier, Major, 10-2
Rodriguez, Nick — Liberty

115
Arenas, Anthony — Bakersfield, Fall, 3:54
Maldonado, Johnny — Liberty
Mares, J, J, Frontier — Fall, :41
Martinez, Aid — Centennial

122
Demison, Navonte — Bakersfield, Fall, 1:24
Acala, Justin — Frontier
Myer, Brandon — Stockdale, Fall, :49
Trevino, Elijah — Liberty

128
Figueroa, J.J. — Bakersfield, 4-3
Ozuna, Elijah — Frontier
Patoc, Jordon — Liberty, Default
Vandoom, Dylan — Centennial
Terronez, Jason — Stockdale

134
Herrera, Carlos — Bakersfield, 10-0
Armijo, Etienne — Centennial
Marquez, Hondo — Liberty, Fall, 2:20
Mendoza, David — Stockdale

140
Garcia, Johnathan — Fall, 5:39
Rodriguez, Mark — Bakersfield
Rojas, Santana — Liberty, 6-3
Hartsfield, Chris — Centennial, 8-5
Browen, Justin — Stockdale

147
Annis, Josh — Bakersfield, 1-0
Morphis, Calloway — Frontier
Castillo, Cody — Stockdale, Default
Manzo, Amando — Liberty
McQuin, Brandon — Centennial

154
Gonzales, Ricky — Bakersfield, Fall, 5:26
Gamboa, Austin — Frontier
Reyes, Eric — Liberty, Fall, 2:56
Gaver, Matt — Centennial
Burkhart, Noah — Stockdale

162
Loera, Sam — Bakersfield, TF, 26-11
Harper, Brady — Centennial
Hernandez, Luis — Liberty

172
Mass, Jeremy — Liberty, Fall, 1:53
Gutierrez, Antonio — Bakersfield
Maiden, Nic — Stockdale, Fall, 1:23
Redmond, Tyler — Frontier

184
Rodriguez, Noah — Bakersfield, Fall, 4:51
Montejo, Ed — Frontier
Lopez, Andy — Liberty, Fall, 4:32
Rojas, Nathan — Centennial

197
Rosales, Elias — Bakersfield, Fall, 3:16
Reed, Jeff — Frontier, Fall, ?
Dyer, Nate — Centennial

220
Song, Henry — Stockdale, 6-3, OT
Guillermo, Dyllan — Bakersfield

285
Snyder, Jarrod — Frontier, Fall, 1:54
Barnes, Payton — Centennial
Delatorre, Angel — Bakersfield, 5-0
Saindon, J.P. — Stockdale
Ramirez, Pablo — Liberty

Most Outstanding Wrestlers

Lower Weight: Jonathan Garcia — Frontier
Upper Weight: Jeremy Mass — Liberty

TOURNAMENT
Bakersfield   292.5
Frontier   223.5
Liberty   174
Centennial   145
Stockdale   138

DUAL	LEAGUE	SEASON
Bakersfield	4-0	8-0
Frontier	3-1	7-1
Liberty	2-2	4-2
Centennial	2-2	2-2
Stockdale	2-2	2-6

SOUTHWEST YOSEMITE LEAGUE - Frontier
February 11, 2016

108
Olenik, Izzak — Bakersfield, 2-1
Reyes, Cole — Frontier
Hinkle, Blake — Centennial

115
Morphis, Ryan — Frontier, 5-4
Navarro, Elijah — Bakersfield, Major, 10-0
Martinez, Aiden — Centennial

122
Abas, Jaren — Frontier, TF, 16-1
Myers, Brandon — Stockdale
Maldonado, Johnny — Liberty, Fall, 5:50
Briseno, Andrew — Bakersfield

128
Gonzalez, Adrian — Bakersfield, 7-6
Patoc, Jordan — Liberty
Tracy, Trent — Frontier, TF, 15-0
Willis, Zack — Centennial
Mendoza, Daniel — Stockdale

134
Figueroa, J.J. — Bakersfield, Fall, 1:50
Aguirre, Polly — Frontier
Riley, Brayden — Centennial, Fall, 2:55
Terronez, Jason — Stockdale

140
Demison, Navonte — Bakersfield, Fall, 3:15
Rojas, Santana — Liberty
Aguirre, Max — Frontier, SV, 13-11
Vandoom, Dylan — Centennial, Fall, 1:27
Mendoza, David — Stockdale

147
Cravens, Dillion — Bakersfield, Fall, 3:40
Reyes, Erik — Liberty
Weir, Marco — Centennial, Fall, 3:57
Burkhart, Noah — Stockdale

154
Garcia, Jonathan — Frontier, 2-0
Gonzalez, Rickey — Bakersfield
Harper, Bradley — Centennial, 11-4
Lucas, Anthony — Centennial

160
Loera, Sam — Bakersfield, Major, 15-4
Manzo, Armando — Liberty
Komin, Blaine — Frontier, Fall, 1:58
Domingo, Noel — Centennial

172
Deboer, Willem — Frontier, 8-6
Gutierrez, Antonio — Bakersfield
Maiden, Nic — Stockdale, Fall, 5:00
Wirowek, Chance — Liberty

184
Rodriguez, Noah — Bakersfield, TF, 22-7
Mass, Jeremy — Liberty
Cabrales, Alberto — Centennial, 7-4
Myers, Marc — Frontier

197
Rosales, Elias — Bakersfield, 5-4
Torres, Andrew — Frontier
Lopez, Andy — Liberty, Forfeit
Brown, Isaac — Centennial

222
Abbott, Brian — Stockdale, 7-2
Valle, Antonio — Centennial
Barrientos, A.J. — Bakersfield, 5-1
Hernandez, Matt — Frontier

285
Snyder, Jarrod — Frontier, Fall, 3:00
Delatorre, Angel — Bakersfield
Ramirez, Pablo — Liberty, 7-2
Ramirez, Gio — Stockdale

Most Outstanding Wrestlers

Lower Weight: Ryan Morphis — Frontier
Upper Weight: Noah Rodriguez — Bakersfield

TOURNAMENT
Bakersfield 269
Frontier 231
Liberty 160.5
Centennial 140
Stockdale 96

DUAL	LEAGUE	SEASON
Bakersfield	4-0	9-0
Frontier	3-1	8-1
Liberty	2-2	2-2
Centennial	2-2	5-8
Stockdale	1-3	3-8

SOUTHWEST YOSEMITE LEAGUE - Frontier
February 10, 2017

108
Reyes, Cole — Frontier, Fall, 1:27
Flores, Mosses — Bakersfield
Bonilla, Chris — Centennial

115
Navarro, Elijah — Bakersfield, TF, 17-2
Cota, Cross — Frontier
Kittredge, Jacob — Centennial, Fall
Deleon, Aaron — Stockdale

122
Bloemhof, Andrew — Bakersfield, SV, 6-4
Morphis, Ryan — Frontier
Maldonado, Johnny — Liberty, TF, 18-3
Hinkle, William — Centennial
Andriaano, Brian — Centennial

128
Olejnik, Izzak — Bakersfield, 5-1
Fletcher, Garrett — Frontier,
Lopez, David — Stockdale, 14-9
Magana, Anthony — Centennial

134
Ozuna, Eligah — Frontier, Fall, 5:33
Gonzalez, Adrian — Bakersfield
Willis, Zachary — Centennial, Fall
Marquez, Hondo — Liberty
Broome, Logan — Stockdale

140
Figueroa, J.J. — Bakersfield, Major, 12-3
Hernandez, Marco — Frontier
Riley, Brayden — Centennial, Fall
Mendoza, Daniel — Stockdale

147
Demison, Navonte — Bakersfield, Fall, 1:45
Tracy, Trent — Frontier
Rojas, Santana — Liberty, SV, 5-3
Olejnik, Lucas — Centennial
Terronez, Jason — Stockdale

154
Cravens, Dillion — Bakersfield, 5-3
Garcia, Jonathan — Frontier
Harper, Bradley — Centennial, Fall
Ramirez, Jesse — Liberty
Santamaria, Anibal — Stockdale

160
Gonzalez, Ricky — Bakersfield, 7-3
Aguirre, Max — Frontier
Wirowek, Chance — Liberty, Fall
Weir, Matt — Centennial
Burkart, Noah — Stockdale

172
Mass, Jeremy — Liberty, Major, 9-1
Swall, Ben — Bakersfield
Carter, Andrea — Frontier, Major, 8-0
Ortega, Anthony — Centennial
Castro, Jesus — Stockdale

184
Loera, Sam — Bakersfield, 4-3
DeBoer, Willem — Frontier
Maiden, Nic — Stockdale, Fall
Jennings, Jonathan — Centennial
Berry, Dylan — Liberty

197
Lopez, Andy — Liberty, 8-2
Clark, James — Centennial
Budak, Kobie — Frontier, 4-2
Dorado, Jacob — Bakersfield

222
Abbot, Brian — Stockdale, Major, 13-3
Vasquez, Jake — Bakersfield
Gonzales, Jon — Liberty, 11-5
Valle, Antonio — Centennial
Hernandez, Matt — Frontier

285
Bryant, Grant — Frontier, Fall, 1:41
Bass, Ogden — Liberty
Ramirez, Walter — Stockdale, Fall
Posadas, Ivan — Bakersfield
Chambers, Richard — Centennial

SOUTHWEST YOSEMITE LEAGUE - Frontier
February 10, 2017

Most Outstanding Wrestlers

Lower Weight: Andrew Bloemhof   Bakersfield
Upper Weight: Dillion Cravens   Bakersfield

TOURNAMENT
Bakersfield	266.5
Frontier	234
Centennial	158
Liberty	133.5
Stockdale	90

DUAL	LEAGUE	SEASON
Bakersfield	5-0	8-1
Frontier	4-1	7-2
Centennial	3-2	5-3
Liberty	2-3	5-3
Stockdale	1-3	4-5
Garces	0-5	2-8

Garrett Fletcher – Frontier High School

Kirk Moore – Frontier High School

SOUTHWEST YOSEMITE LEAGUE - Frontier
February 8, 2018

108
Acala, Josh — Frontier, 7-1
Flores, Moses — Bakersfield

115
Ozuna, Noah — Bakersfield, Fall, :39
Ludwig, Mark — Centennial
Howington, Kehmanni — Bakersfield

122
Reyes, Cole — Frontier, 4-1
Lucio, Cade — Bakersfield
Segura, Jacob — Centennial, Fall
Deleon, Aaron — Stockdale

128
Rosales, Angel — Bakersfield, 6-3
Maldonado, Johnny — Liberty
Landin, Jose — Frontier, Fall
Lara, Logan — Stockdale
Donath, Noah — Centennial

134
Fletcher, Garrett — Frontier, 6-4
Bloemhof, Andrew — Bakersfield
Marquez, Alejandro — Liberty, Fall
Cooper, Jordan — Garces
Broom, Logan — Stockdale

140
Morphis, Ryan — Frontier, 7-3
Marin, Valentin — Bakersfield
Willis, Zach — Centennial, Major, Dec
Trevino, Elijah — Liberty

147
Olejnik, Izzak — Bakersfield, 4-2
Landin, Christian — Frontier
Lucas, Anthony — Liberty, Fall
Aceves, Andrew — Stockdale

154
Gonzalez, Adrian — Bakersfield, 5-3
Carter, Andrew — Frontier
Olejnik, Andrew — Centennial, Fall
Grey, Will — Liberty

162
Aguirre, Max — Frontier, 3-1, SV1
Priest, Jared — Bakersfield
Ortega, Anthony — Centennial

172
Tracy, Trent — Frontier, 5-1
Annis, Jordan — Bakersfield
Pantoja, Bryan — Garces, Fall
Ramirez, Jesse — Liberty

184
Maiden, Nic — Stockdale, 9-3
Lopez, Anthony — Bakersfield
Pafford, Jack — Frontier, Decision
Cueto, Andre — Centennial

197
Shepherd, Ty — Frontier, 8-6, SV1
Gonzalez, Jonathan — Liberty
Dorado, Jacob — Bakersfield, Forfeit
Smith, Jalen — Garces

222
Darter, Justin — Bakersfield, 5-3
Martin, Isaiah — Garces
Hernandez, Matt — Frontier, Decision
Valle, Antonio — Centennial

287
Hill, Josiah — Bakersfield, T-Fall, 21-4
Abernathy, Kaleb — Centennial
Bryant, Grant — Frontier, Fall
Carvajal, Rafael — Garces
Howarden, Maximus — Stockdale
Spittler, Ryan — Liberty

Most Outstanding Wrestlers

Lower Weight: Garrett Fletcher Frontier
Upper Weight: Josiah Hill Bakersfield

TOURNAMENT
Frontier 277
Bakersfield 263
Centennial 139
Liberty 108
Stockdale 69
Garces 67

DUAL	LEAGUE	SEASON
Bakersfield	5-0	6-0
Frontier	4-1	4-1
Centennial	3-2	3-2
Liberty	2-3	4-3
Stockdale	1-4	1-6
Garces	0-5	0-5

SOUTHWEST YOSEMITE LEAGUE
2019

* No league tournament was held

Most Outstanding Wrestlers
Lower Weight: Andrew Bloemhof   Bakersfield
Upper Weight: Trent Tracy   Frontier

DUAL	LEAGUE	SEASON
Frontier	5-0	7-1
Bakersfield	4-1	5-2
Centennial	3-2	4-2
Liberty	2-3	5-5
Garces	1-4	1-4
Stockdale	0-5	0-5

Andrew Bloemhof – Bakersfield High

Trent Tracy – Frontier High School

SOUTHWEST YOSEMITE LEAGUE - Frontier
January 31, 2020

108
- Woods, Jonathan — Bakersfield, Fall
- Nagatani, Jacob — Liberty

115
- Alcantar, Derek — Frontier, Fall
- Gacad. Binon — Liberty
- Cordero, Xavier — Bakersfield

122
- McEloy, Carson — Bakersfield, Decision
- Wiles, Chase — Frontier
- Contreras, Isaiah — Centennial, Decision
- Solano, Wes — Liberty
- Doyle, Cooper — Stockdale

128
- Appleton, Jonny — Frontier, Decision
- Hunt, Colton — Liberty
- Regalado, Gabe — Bakersfield, Fall
- Pitcher, William — Centennial

134
- Bingham, Kyden — Frontier, Decision
- Segura, Jacob — Centennial
- Solano, Jimenez Jacob — Stockdale, Fall
- Green, Donovan — Liberty, Fall
- Carrillo, Sean — Bakersfield

140
- Juarez, Adrian — Bakersfield, Fall
- Bayaca, Christian — Stockdale
- Muana, Kevin — Centennial, Decision
- Jimenez, Ernesto — Liberty

147
- Combs, Luke — Frontier, Fall
- Elcano, Luke — Centennial
- Medding, Jaden — Stockdale, Decision
- Ramirez, Dakota — Bakersfield

154
- Weimer, D.J. — Bakersfield, Major
- Aceves, Andrew — Stockdale
- Branam, Baily — Centennial

162
- Sanchez, Jaden — Bakersfield, Decision
- Barajas, Jeremiah — Frontier
- Olejnik, Lucas — Centennial

172
- Lobos, Daniel — Bakersfield, Decision
- Sullivan, Keenan — Centennial
- Churchman, Landon — Liberty

184
- Trujillo, Pedro — Bakersfield, Decision
- Shepard, Jake — Frontier
- Sanchez, Simon — Liberty, Fall
- Valle, Alex — Centennial

197
- Trujillo, Chente — Bakersfield, Fall
- Garcia, Sonny — Liberty
- Hernandez, Kaden — Frontier, Fall
- Barron, Andrew — Stockdale
- Felix, Alex — Centennial

222
- Shepard, Ty — Frontier, Fall
- Denz, Efren — Bakersfield
- West, Jacob — Centennial, Fall
- Bradford, Kaiden — Stockdale

287
- Hill, Josiah — Bakersfield, Fall
- Andrews, Jake — Frontier
- Garcia, Marco — Stockdale, Major
- Ramer, Carl — Centennial
- Westbrook, Blake — Liberty

Most Outstanding Wrestlers

Lower Weight: Luke Combs — Frontier
Upper Weight: Josiah Hill — Bakersfield

TOURNAMENT
Bakersfield	282
Frontier	232
Centennial	197
Liberty	172
Stockdale	154
Garce	42

DUAL	LEAGUE	SEASON
Bakersfield	1-0	6-3
Frontier	1-1	5-3-1
Centennial	1-1	5-2
Liberty	1-0	3-0
Stockdale	0-1	0-1
Garces	0-0	0-0

SOUTH YOSEMITE CONFERENCE – North

2019

106
Sital, Shane — North

113
Corona, Shane — Foothill

120
Gutierrez, Elijah — Ridgeview

126
Martinez, Xavier — Golden Valley

132
Rueda, Everardo — Golden Valley

138
Leon, Dominic — Golden Valley

145
Wills, Zach — Centennial

152
Guerrero, Rudy — Ridgeview

160
Mayall, Julius — North

170
Spainhoward, Justin — Ridgeview

182
Tracy, Trent — Frontier

195
Martinez, Brice — Highland

220
Pafford, Jack — Frontier

285
Castro, Emmanuel — Garces

Most Outstanding Wrestlers

Lower Weight: Shane Corona Foothill
Upper Weight: Trent Tracy Frontier

2020

106
Jara, Sebastian — Ridgeview, 6-4, OT
Nagatani, Jacob — Liberty

113
Alcantar, Derrek — Frontier, 12-10
Ornelaz, Daniel — North

120
Corona, Shane — Foothill, TF
McElroy, Carson — Bakersfield

126
Ornelaz, Anthony — North, 12-11
Appleton, Johnny — Frontier

132
Rueda, Everardo — Golden, Valley, TF, 21-6
Bingham, Kayden — Frontier

138
Juarez, Adrian — Bakersfield, 7-2
Lewis, Josh — Independence

145
Ocampo, Javier — North, Fall, 2:54
Amaya, Luis — Foothill

152
Weimer, D, J — Bakersfield, Fall, :21
Stansbury, Dylan — Ridgeview

160
Sanchez, Jaden — Bakersfield, 6-5
Leon, Dominic — Golden, Valley

170
Lobos, Daniel — Bakersfield, 3-2
Zavala, Juan — Ridgeview

182
Spainhoward, Justin — Ridgeview, 6-5
Trujillo, Pedro — Bakersfield

195
Trujillo, Chente — Bakersfield, Fall, 2:43
Chuca, Zion — North

220
Shepard, Ty — Frontier, Fall, :56
Romero, Michael — Independence

285
Hill, Josiah — Bakersfield, 13-3
Andrews, Jake — Frontier

SOUTH SEQUOIA LEAGUE

2007-2020

SOUTH SEQUOIA LEAGUE CHAMPIONSHIP TEAMS

Date	Location	Dual Champion	Tournament Champion	Overall Champion	Coach
2-11-1966	West	Arvin 8-1	Arvin	Arvin	John Burton
2-11-1967	Shafter	West 6-0	West	West	Ray Juhl
2-10-1968	Shafter		Arvin		
2-15-1969	Wasco	Wasco/Shafter	Arvin	Wasco	Ted Hammack
2-14-1970	Shafter	Shafter 8-0	Shafter	Shafter	Darrell Fletcher
2-11-1971	Taft		Highland		
2-19-1972	Shafter	Arvin 6-0	Arvin	Arvin	Phil McIntyre
2-09-1973	Wasco	Shafter 5-0-1	Shafter	Shafter	Darrell Fletcher
2-09-1974	Coalinga	Wasco 8-0	Wasco	Wasco	Gerald Brandon
2-15-1975	Shafter	Wasco 8-0	Wasco	Wasco	Gerald Brandon
2-14-1976	Corcoran	Wasco 8-0	Wasco	Wasco	Gerald Brandon
2-12-1977	McFarland	Shafter 8-0	Shafter	Shafter	Darrell Fletcher
2-15-1978	Wasco	Shafter 6-0	Shafter	Shafter	Darrell Fletcher
2-10-1979	Corcoran	Shafter/Wasco	Shafter	Shafter	Don Burns
2-15-1980	Shafter	Shafter 6-0	Shafter	Shafter	Lisle Gates
2-11-1981	Shafter	Shafter 6-0	Shafter	Shafter	Lisle Gates
2-11-1982	Shafter		Shafter		
2-10-1983	Coalinga	Shafter 2-0	Shafter	Shafter	Joe Lopez
2-11-1984	Wasco	Woodlake	Woodlake	Woodlake	Ron Barkley
2-09-1985	Woodlake		Caruthers		
2-13-1986	McFarland	Wasco/Undefeated	Wasco	Wasco	Phil Sullivan
2-12-1987	Coalinga	Shafter 4-0			
2-12-1988	Shafter	McFarland 4-0	Shafter	McFarland	Ed Levenson
2-09-1989	Wasco		Corcoran		
2-08-1990	McFarland	Corcoran	McFarland	Corcoran	
2-08-1991	Arvin	Wasco	Arvin	Arvin	Ruben Ramirez
2-14-1992	Shafter		Wasco		
2-11-1993	Wasco	Tehachapi 4-0	Tehachapi	Tehachapi	John Caminiti
2-11-1994	Stockdale	Wasco 6-0	Wasco	Wasco	Brett Clark
2-10-1995	Centennial	Wasco	Wasco	Wasco	Brett Clark
2-10-1996	Centennial	Centennial 5-0	Centennial	Centennial	Paul Olejnik
2-15-1997	Shafter	Tehachapi	Wasco	Wasco/Tehachapi	Brett Clark/ John Caminiti
2-12-1998	Tehachapi		Shafter		
2-12-1999	Tehachapi	Shafter 5-0	Shafter	Shafter	Gary Pederson
2-12-2000			Tehachapi		
2-09-2001	Shafter	Shafter 5-0	Shafter	Shafter	Gary Pederson
2-09-2002	Wasco	Shafter 5-0	Liberty	Liberty/ Shafter	Joe Vega/ Gary Pederson
2-14-2003	McFarland	Shafter 4-0	Shafter	Shafter	Gary Pederson
2-13-2004	Tehachapi	Shafter 4-0	Shafter	Shafter	Gary Pederson
2-11-2005	Arvin	Arvin	Arvin	Arvin	Miguel Sanchez
2-10-2006	Shafter	Tehachapi 5-0	Tehachapi	Tehachapi	Tony Keller
2-09-2007	McFarland	Tehachapi 5-0	Arvin	Arvin/ Tehachapi	Miguel Sanchez/ Tony Keller
2-07-2008	Bak. Christian	Tehachapi 5-0	Tehachapi	Tehachapi	Tony Keller
2-09-2009	Bak. Christian	Tehachapi 5-0	Arvin	Tehachapi	Desi Levenguth
2-11-2010	Shafter	Wasco 5-0	Tehachapi	Wasco/ Tehachapi	J. Gallardo/ D. Levenguth
2-12-2011	Wasco	Wasco 5-0	Wasco	Wasco	Juan Gallardo
2-11-2012	Tehachapi	Wasco 5-0	Wasco	Wasco	Juan Gallardo

SOUTH SEQUOIA LEAGUE CHAMPIONSHIP TEAMS

Date	Location	Dual Champion	Tournament Champion	Overall Champion	Coach
2-08-2013	Shafter	Wasco 6-0	Wasco	Wasco	Juan Gallardo
2-14-2014	Wasco	Wasco 6-0	Wasco	Wasco	Juan Gallardo
2-15-2015	McFarland	Wasco 6-0	Wasco	Wasco	Juan Gallardo
2-11-2016	Cesar Chavez	R F Kennedy 5-1	R F Kennedy	R F Kennedy	Miguel Sanchez
2-09-2017	Wasco	Shafter 6-0	Shafter	Shafter	Rick Gabin
2-09-2018	Wasco	Shafter 6-0	Shafter	Shafter	Rick Gabin
2019		Arvin/ R F Kennedy 4-1	No Tournament was held		Jose Marin, Miguel Sanchez
2020		Wasco 5-0	No Tournament was Held		Garth Wara

SOUTH SEQUIA LEAGUE
MOST OUTSTANDING WRESTLERS

Year	Name	School
1966	John Lowe	Wasco
1967	Mike Garcia	West
1968	Mike Terry	Wasco
1969	Manuel Machado	McFarland
1970	Frank Ramos	Arvin
1971	Mike Machado	McFarland
1992		
1973	Mike Johnson	Wasco

Year	Lower Weight	School	Upper Weight	School
1993	Aaron Rodriguez	Wasco	Tony Keller	Tehachapi
1994	Jeremy Roper	Shafter	Dennis Clark	Wasco
1995	Eric Serda	Wasco	Kevin Cierley	Centennial
1996	Jeremy Roper	Shafter	Eli Espercueta	Shafter
1997	Sam Jameson	Wasco	Rodney Leisley	Ridgeview
1998	Tony Madrigal	Shafter	Narcy Martinez	Wasco
1999	Nick Rosales	Arvin	Narcy Martinez	Wasco
2000				
2001	Matt Maldonado	Shafter	Patrick Acosta	Wasco
2002	Antonio Hernandez	Liberty	Jarred Ghilarducci	Liberty
2003	Rudy Tabada	Arvin	Jedd Ingram	Tehachapi
2004	Dustin Cruz	Shafter	Orlando Landois	Wasco
2005	Vincent Navarro	Shafter	Marvin Statler	Shafter
2006	Frank Castillo	Arvin	Zack Johnson	Wasco
2007	Efrain Sanchez	Arvin	Rene Medina	Shafter
2008	Edgar Diaz	Arvin	James Funk	Bakersfield Christian
2009	Jared Steinbach	Tehachapi	Jason Hail	Tehachapi
2010	Justin Solorio	Wasco	Jacob Fulce	Bakersfield Christian
2011	Anthony Lopez	McFarland	Michael Martinez	Wasco
2012	Michael Martinez	Wasco	Garrett Johnson	Wasco
2013	D J Lopez	McFarland	Eric Torres	Shafter
2014	Alvaro Tomato	Arvin	Casper Lopez	Wasco
2015	Tommy Ortiz	R F Kennedy	Ramiro Macias	R F Kennedy
2016	Mario Hernandez	R F Kennedy	Brett Schuler	Bakersfield Christian
2017	Mario Birreta	Wasco	Eric Campos	R F Kennedy
2018	Anthony Perez	Shafter	Anthony Banuelos	Shafter
2019	Valentin Marin	Arvin	Gerardo Aispuro	McFarland
2020	Anthony Bartoiome	Cesar Chavez	Juan Alonso	R F Kennedy

Awards sponsored by the Coyote Club Membership starting in 1993

SOUTH SEQUOIA LEAGUE - McFarland
February 9, 2007

103
Diaz, Edger	Arvin, Fall, 2:13
Messier, Colton	Tehachapi
Sanchez, Eric	Wasco, 8-1
Wahl, Tommy	Frontier

112
Steinbach, Jarrad	Tehachapi, Fall, :32
Casper, Torry	Frontier

119
Tamayo, Luis	Arvin, Default
Martinez, Sergio	Tehachapi
Blanco, Jose	Wasco, 6-4
Miller, Brandon	Frontier
Burt, Jordan	Shafter

125
Sanchez, Efrain	Arvin, Fall, 5:09
Reyes, Josh	McFarland
Ramos, Rickey	Wasco, 9-3
Moreno, Adam	Tehachapi

130
Castillo, Frankie	Arvin, Fall, :38
Martin, Chance	Frontier
Raya, Sal	Wasco

135
Solorio, Phillip	Wasco, 12-9
Hall, Jason	Tehachapi
Campos, Cesar	Arvin, Fall, :47
Bishop, Steven	Frontier
Parrish, Clinton	Shafter

140
Varela, Abel	Arvin, Fall, 1:53
Gonzalez, Jacob	Shafter
Romero, Bean	Wasco, 18-9
Bishop, Ryan	Frontier
Sheahan, Ben	Tehachapi

145
Rojo, Adolfo	Arvin 15-5
Montoya, Manury	Wasco
Jimenez, Martin	McFarland, 12-1
Rocha, Austin	Frontier
St. John, James	Tehachapi

152
Molina, Guillermo	Arvin, 12-4
Mulligan, Oliver	Shafter
Hack, Joey	Tehachapi, Fall, :14
Tomayo, Jose	Arvin
Thompson, Jacob	Shafter

160
Ames, Joseph	Shafter, Fall, 5:58
Wehurst, Jerry	Tehachapi
Delfino, Santino	Frontier, Default
Bowman, Chris	McFarland

171
Medina, Rene	Shafter, 6-4
Hack, Tyler	Tehachapi
Karr, Cody	Bakersfield Christian Fall, 2:39
Walker, Blake	Frontier
Alvarez, Jose	Arvin, Default
Delfin, Tommy	?

189
Abarquez, Marquez	Tehachapi, Fall, 1:13
Doyle, Curtis	Bakersfield, Christian
Hodges, Jeyy	Arvin, 9-4
Oropeza, Diego	Frontier

215
McBride, Evan	Tehachapi, Fall, 2:26
Funk, James	Bakersfield, Christian
Cantu, Felipe	Wasco, 7-1
Whitesell, Nick	Frontier
Velazquez, Senaido	Arvin

285
Hood, Cameron	Tehachapi, Fall, 2:26
Rodriguez, Edgar	Wasco
Rodriguez, Gildardoa	Arvin, Fall, :29
Urrea, Jesus	McFarland
Davis, Joshua	Frontier

Most Outstanding Wrestlers

Lower Weight: Efrain Sanchez   Arvin
Upper Weight: Rene Medina   Shafter

TOURNAMENT
Arvin	208.5
Tehachapi	205
Wasco	133
Shafter	64
Bakersfield Christian	63
McFarland	50
Frontier	?

DUAL	LEAGUE	SEASON
Tehachapi	5-0	5-0
Arvin	4-1	6-2
Frontier	4-2	10-2-1
Wasco	3-2	3-3
Shafter	3-3	5-3
McFarland	1-5	2-8
Bak Christian	0-5	0-5

SOUTH SEQUOIA LEAGUE – Bakersfield Christian
February 7, 2008

103
Diaz, Edgar — Arvin, Fall, 1:30
Sanchez, Eric — Wasco
Dezubiria, Ernesto — Tehachapi

112
Steinbach, Jared — Tehachapi, Fall, :49
Solano, Justin — Wasco
Hough, Tyler — Bakersfield Christian

119
Martinez, Sergio — Tehachapi, 14-11
Hallmark, Michael — Wasco
Ozuna, Ruben — McFarland

125
Garcia, Spencer — McFarland, Fall, 3:02
Blanko, Jose — Wasco
Moreno, Adam — Tehachapi, 6-5
Barron, Juan — Shafter

130
Stone, Luke — Tehachapi, Fall, :39
Marroquin, Alex — McFarland
Veemer, Jake — Bakersfield Christian

135
Hail, Jason — Tehachapi, Fall, 2:44
Romero, Beau — Wasco
Bugambelia, Francisco — Arvin, Fall, 1:19
Parrish, Clinton — Shafter
Nelson, Alex — Bakersfield Christian

140
St., John, Jamie — Tehachapi, Fall, 3:20
Morse, Michael — Wasco
Rodriguez, Rudy — McFarland, Fall, 4:27
Fulce, Jacob — Bakersfield Christian
Villalobos, Mario — Shafter

145
Harroan, Eric — Tehachapi, 10-4
Gafner, Grey — Shafter
Wedel, Jeff — Bakersfield Christian, 18-6
Marquez, Eric — McFarland

152
Montoya, Manury — Wasco, 15-7
Henry, Matt — Tehachapi
Ramirez, Jose — McFarland, 6-2
Thompson, Jacob — Bakersfield Christian,
Mulligan, Oliver — Shafter, ?
Alvarez, Jose — Arvin

160
Hack, Tyler — Tehachapi, 8-7
Medina, Rene — Shafter
Escobar, Jordon — Bakersfield Christian

171
Ames, Joseph — Shafter, Fall, 5:40
Wehurst, Jerry — McFarland
McNaughton, Bradford — Bakersfield Christian, Forfeit
Valdovinos, Jesus — McFarland

189
Arbarquez, Marcus — Tehachapi, Fall, 1:59
Wilson, Wyatt — Shafter
Moreno, Edgar — Arvin, Forfeit
Doyle, Curtis — Bakersfield Christian

215
Funk, James — Bakersfield Christian, Fall, 1:02
Fowlks, Nick — Tehachapi
Seymour, Jesse — Shafter

275
Hood, Cameron — Tehachapi, Fall, 1:03
Rodriguez, Edgar — Wasco
Urea, Jesus — McFarland, Fall, 5:19
Guillen, Ricky — Arvin
Lopez, Andres — Shafter

Most Outstanding Wrestlers

Lower Weight: Edgar Diaz   Arvin
Upper Weight: James Funk   Bakersfield Christian

TOURNAMENT
Tehachapi	215
Wasco	116
McFarland	79
Shafter	78
Bakersfield Christian	76
Arvin	50

DUAL	LEAGUE	SEASON
Tehachapi	5-0	14-0
Shafter	4-1	5-2
Arvin	3-2	3-2
Bakersfield Christian	2-4	3-4
Wasco	1-6	1-6

SOUTH SEQUOIA LEAGUE – Bakersfield Christian
February 12, 2009

103
- Morfin, Gabe — Bakersfield, Christian Fall, :52
- Ibarra, Javier — Shafter
- Zavala, Brenda — Arvin, Female

112
- Marin, Oscar — Arvin, 12-3
- Sanchez, Eric — Wasco
- Chavez, Ryan — McFarland, 12-7
- Cronin, Paul — Tehachapi
- Viss, Perter — Shafter

119
- Rodas, Mario — Shafter, Fall, 4:46
- Hough, Tyler — Bakersfield, Christian
- Reed, Trever — Tehachapi, Fall, 1:33
- Ramos, Pedro — Arvin
- Lara, Ivan — McFarland

125
- Steinbach, Jared — Tehachapi, Fall, :14
- Acosta, Victor — McFarland
- Parra, Omar — Arvin, Fall, 1:16
- Lara, Ron — Shafter

130
- Tamayo, Luis — Arvin, 4-2
- Solorio, Justin — Wasco
- Moreno, Adam — Tehachapi, Fall, 1:16
- Ozuna, Ruben — McFarland
- Siemans, Michael — Shafter

135
- Barron, Juan — Shafter, Fall, 3:27
- Acevedo, Armando — Arvin
- Newman, Ryker — Tehachapi, Fall, 1:42
- Marquez, Adam — McFarland

140
- Martinez, Michael — Wasco, 6-1
- Bugambilia, Francisco — Arvin
- Parrish, Clinton — Shafter, 8-6
- Stone, Luke — Tehachapi
- Reed, Kevin — Bakersfield Christian, Default
- Arana, ? — McFarland

145
- Feemster, James — Shafter, Fall, 2:57
- Fulce, Jacob — Bakersfield Christian
- Garner, Trent — Tehachapi, 11-6
- Rivera, Neftali — Arvin

152
- Mirales, Rosendo — Arvin, 2:57
- Escobar, Jordon — Bakersfield, Christian
- Marquez, Eric — McFarland, 11-4
- Gomez, Rogelio — Shafter
- Ramos, Ricky — Wasco

160
- St., John, James — Tehachapi, Fall, :34
- Aguilera, Luis — Arvin
- Velasquez, Victor — Shafter, Fall, 3:36
- Acevedo, Eric — Wasco

171
- Hail, Jason — Tehachapi, Fall, 4:48
- Medina, Rene — Shafter
- McNaughton, Brad — Bakersfield Christian, Fall, :44
- Moreno, Edgar — Arvin
- Solian, Pedro — McFarland

189
- Machado, Michael — Arvin, 7-4
- Wilson, Wyatt — Shafter
- Avery, William — Tehachapi, Fall, 1:16
- Moreno, Armando — McFarland

215
- Urrea, Jesus — McFarland, 9-6
- Beltran, Rogelio — Shafter
- Crosby, Zach — Tehachapi, 9-5
- Aguilera, Mariano — Arvin

285
- Taliulu, Niko — Tehachapi, Fall, 2:16
- Miller, Tyler — Bakersfield, Christian
- Maldonado, Christian — Fall, 5:01
- Zamudio, Juan — Arvin
- Portillo, George — Shafter

Most Outstanding Wrestlers

Lower Weight: Jared Steinbach Tehachapi
Upper Weight: Jason Hail   Tehachapi

TOURNAMENT

Arvin	197
Tehachapi	187
Shafter	177
McFarland	112
Bakersfield Christian	105
Wasco	63

SOUTH SEQUOIA LEAGUE – Bakersfield Christian
February 12, 2009

DUAL	LEAGUE	SEASON
Tehachapi	5-0	5-0
Shafter	4-1	4-1
Arvin	3-2	3-2
Bakersfield Christian	3-2	5-2
Wasco	N/A	N/A
McFarland	N/A	N/A

Rene Medina (Shafter) and Brad McNaughton (BCHS) (02/13/2009)
Photographer: Casey Christie, Bakersfield Californian

SOUTH SEQUOIA LEAGUE - Shafter
February 11, 2010

103
Marin, Oscar	Arvin, 11-4
Ibarra, Javier	Shafter
Salgado, Antonio	Wasco
Gardner, Trent	Tehachapi
Salas, Juan	Shafter
Rodriguez, Rudy	McFarland

112
Madera, Noe	Tehachapi, 14-3
Gutierrez, Francisco	Shafter
Nava, Frescoed	McFarland, Fall, 5:59
Ramirez, Eduardo	Wasco
Morfin, Gabe	Bakersfield, Christian

119
Rodas, Mario	Shafter, 17-2
Olvera, Jorge	Arvin
Chavez, Ryan	McFarland, 7-3
Duxbury, Klayton	Tehachapi
Moore, Cody	Wasco

125
Barron, Juan	Shafter, 7-1
Sanchez, Eric	Wasco
Reed, Trevor	Tehachapi, Fall, 4:25
Nunez, Raul	Wasco

130
Blanco, Jose	Wasco, 6-5
Dezubiria, Ernesto	Tehachapi
Lara, Ivan	McFarland, Fall, 2:46
Beckemeyer, Dustin	Shafter

135
Solorio, Justin	Wasco, TF, 15-0
Cronin, Paul	Tehachapi
Ozuna, Ruben	McFarland, Fall, 1:27
Coyle, Ben	Shafter
Parra, Omar	Arvin
Stewart, Grayson	Bakersfield, Christian

140
Newman, Ryker	Tehachapi, Fall, 1:00
Torres, Eric	Shafter
Marquez, Adam	McFarland

145
Martinez, Michael	Wasco, Fall, 3:10
Gamble, Jacob	Tehachapi
Lopez, D.J.	McFarland, 17-2
Dominguez, Luis	Shafter

152
Fulce, Jacob	Bak. Christian, 6-4
Machado, Michael	Arvin
Aispuro, Josh	Wasco, Fall, 1:24

160
Mireles, Rosendo	Arvin, 7-2
Aguirre, Celso	Shafter
Harroun, Dillon	Tehachapi, 5-4
Marquez, Eric	McFarland
Cheatman, Quentin	Wasco

171
Medina, Rene	Wasco, 11-1
McNaughton, Brad	Bakersfield, Christian
Valdovinos, Jesus	McFarland, Fall, 2:47
Escutia, Froylan	Arvin
Brown, Steven	Shafter

189
Avery, Will	Tehachapi, Fall, 1:05
Munoz, Joseph	Shafter
Robledo, Michael	Wasco, Fall, :52
Medina, Armando	McFarland

215
Medley, Sean	Wasco, 3-1
Wilson, Wyatt	Shafter
Porter, John	Tehachapi, 9-1
Aguilera, Mariano	Arvin
Hernandez, Oscar	McFarland

285
Taliulu, Niko	Tehachapi, Fall, 3:00
Portillo, George	Shafter
Johnson, Garrett	Wasco, 6-2
Ortiz, Eric	McFarland
Miller, Tyler	Bakersfield, Christian

Most Outstanding Wrestlers

Lower Weight: Justin Soloria — Wasco
Upper Weight: Jacob Fulce — Bak Christian

TOURNAMENT

Tehachapi	166
Wasco	158.5
Shafter	143.5
McFarland	95.5
Arvin	82
Bakersfield Christian	36

SOUTH SEQUOIA LEAGUE - Shafter
February 11, 2010

DUAL	LEAGUE	SEASON
Wasco	5-0	5-0
Tehachapi	4-1	4-2
Shafter	4-1	4-1
McFarland	2-3	2-3
Arvin	1-4	1-4
Bakersfield Christian	0-5	0-5

Michael Machado - Arvin
Jacob Fulce - Bakersfield Christian High School

SOUTH SEQUOIA LEAGUE - Wasco
February 12, 2011

103
Fletcher, Allen	Tehachapi, 10-6
Ibarra, Javier	Shafter
Moita, Alberto	Wasco, Fall
Velasquez, Susana	Arvin, Female

112
Lopez, Anthony	McFarland, Fall
Ramirez, Joe	Shafter
Salgado, Antonio	Wasco

119
Madera, Noe	Tehachapi, Fall
Morfin, Gabe	Bakersfield, Christian
Perez, Jesus	Shafter, Fall
Diaz, Jacob	Wasco

125
Olvera, Jorge	Arvin, 9-3
Diaz, Javier	Wasco
Martinez, Gerado	Shafter, Fall
Moreno, Adrian	Tehachapi

130
Rodas, Mario	Shafter, Major, 9-0
Ramirez, Norberto	Arvin
Lara, Ivan	McFarland, Fall
Jaramillo, Peter	Wasco

135
Lopez, D.J.	McFarland, 5-3
Lopez, Casper	Wasco
Newman, Ryker	Tehachapi, Fall
Beach, Brian	Shafter

140
Aispuro, Josh	Wasco, Fall
Gomez, Gustavo	Shafter
Marquez, Adam	McFarland, Fall
Hayden, Ryan	Bakersfield, Christian

145
Solorio, Justin	Wasco, 6-2
Fulce, Jack	Bakersfield, Christian
Gamble, Jacob	Tehachapi, 6-3
Garcia, Efrain	Shafter

152
Martinez, Michael	Wasco, Fall, *31-7, 26 Falls
Stone, Luke	Tehachapi
Rodriguez, Rudy	McFarland, 5-4
Reed, Kevin	Bakersfield, Christian

160
Gardner, Trent	Tehachapi, 8-2
Marquez, Eric	McFarland
Deval, Loel	Wasco, Fall
Portillo, Ramon	Arvin

171
Harroun, Dillon	Tehachapi, 7-5
Valdovinos, Jesus	McFarland
Aguirre, Celso	Shafter
Robledo, Jose	Wasco

189
Robledo, Michael	Wasco, Fall
Munoz, Joseph	Shafter
Garcia, Robert	Bakersfield, Christian, 11-5
Hernandez, Oscar	McFarland

215
Medley, Sean	Wasco, Default
Valdovinos, Raul	McFarland
Porter, John	Tehachapi, 6-2
Barton, Bryson	Shafter

285
Taliulu, Niko	Tehachapi, Major, 10-0
Johnson, Garrett	Wasco
Garcia, Dan	Shafter
Ramirez, Joey	Bakersfield, Christian

Most Outstanding Wrestlers

Lower Weight: Anthony Lopez   McFarland
Upper Weight: Michael Martinez   Wasco

Fall times were not given
* Season record

TOURNAMENT
Wasco	198
Tehachapi	147
Shafter	136
McFarland	120
Bakersfield Christian	58.5
Arvin	55

DUAL	LEAGUE	SEASON
Wasco	5-0	5-0
Tehachapi	4-1	4-1
Shafter	3-2	7-4
McFarland	2-3	6-6
Bakersfield Christian	1-4	1-4
Arvin	0-5	0-5

SOUTH SEQUOIA LEAGUE - Tehachapi
February 11, 2012

106
Hokit, Isaiah — Wasco, Fall, 5:42
Ibarra, Javier — Shafter
Espinoza, Jamie — Arvin

113
Salgado, Antonio — Wasco, Fall, 3:46
Lara, Joe — Shafter
Felix, Alex — McFarland

120
Fletcher, Allen — Tehachapi, 8-2
Ramirez, Joe — Shafter
Diaz, Jacob — Wasco, 8-0
Torres, Carlos — McFarland

126
Macias, Isaac — Wasco, 14-10
Gutierrez, Frankie — Shafter
Duxbury, Kayton — Tehachapi, Fall, 3:32
Morfin, Gabe — Bakersfield Christian
Lopez, Alex — McFarland

132
Lara, Ivan — McFarland, Fall, 3:18
Dominguez, Miguel — Shafter
Rivera, Samuel — Arvin

138
Lopez, Casper — Wasco, Fall, 3:42
Gamble, Jacob — Tehachapi
Quintero, Josh — Shafter, Fall, 1:02

145
Martinez, Michael — Wasco, Fall, 1:03
Nunez, Raul — McFarland
Gallardo, Luis — Arvin, Fall, :27
Duran, Thomas — Tehachapi
Munoz, Willie — Shafter

152
Ritualo, Chris — Wasco, Fall, 2:48
Coyle, Ben — Shafter
Satelo, Alvaro — Arvin, Forfeit
Rynders, Cole — Tehachapi

160
Harroun, Dillion — Tehachapi, 10-7
Robledo, Jose — Wasco
Velasquez, Herman — Arvin, Fall, 5:14
Nunez, Josh — Shafter

170
Ramirez, Mike — Shafter, Fall, 3:00
Saldana, Armando — Wasco
Stewart, Grayson — Bakersfield Christian

182
Robledo, Michael — Wasco, Fall, :38
Mendoza, Robert — Arvin
Valenzuela, Alex — Shafter

195
Torres, Eric — Shafter, Fall, :38
Acevedo, Eric — Wasco

220
Medley, Sean — Wasco, Fall, 1:37
Taboado, Berardo — Arvin

285
Johnson, Garrett — Wasco, Fall, 1:37
Valdovinos, Raul — McFarland
Wilson, Wade — (School?) Fall, 2:22
Diaz, Sergio — Arvin

Most Outstanding Wrestlers

Lower Weight: Michael Martinez — Wasco
Upper Weight: Garrett Johnson — Wasco
*Michael Martinez 4X SSL Champion

TOURNAMENT
Wasco — 226
Shafter — 153
Arvin — 73
Tehachapi — 68
McFarland — 58
Bakersfield Christian — 11

DUAL	LEAGUE	SEASON
Wasco	5-0	5-0
Shafter	4-1	7-7
Arvin	2-3	2-3
Tehachapi	2-3	2-4
McFarland	2-3	3-12
Bakersfield Christian	0-5	0-5

SOUTH SEQUOIA LEAGUE - Shafter
February 8, 2013

106
Gutierrez, Juan	Wasco, Default
Ortiz, Tommy	Kennedy

113
Hokit, Isaiah	Wasco, Fall, 3:48
Valdez, Israel	Shafter
Tamayo, Alvaro	Arvin, Fall
Ayon, Abron	McFarland

120
Macias, Michael	Wasco, 7-3
Munoz, Eric	Shafter
Beltran, Ricardo	Arvin, Fall
Pimentel, Silvester	McFarland

126
Hokit, Joshua	Wasco, TF, 18-3
Duran, Thomas	Kennedy
Villa, Chris	Shafter

132
Diaz, Jacob	Wasco, TF, 18-3
Lopez, Alex	McFarland, Fall
Pineda, Jose	Shafter

138
Lopez, D.J.	McFarland, Fall, 3:05
Dominguez, Miguel	Shafter
Loza, Daniel	Wasco, Fall
Mendoza, Nicholas	Arvin

145
Reyes, Trinidad	Shafter, Fall, :52
Perez, Andrew	Kennedy
Aranda, Christian	Wasco, Fall
Nieto, Ivan	McFarland

152
Lopez, Casper	Wasco, Fall, 4:17
Villa, David	Shafter, 16-8
Castulo, Rodolfo	Kennedy

160
Coyle, Ben	Shafter, Default
Martinez, Roel	Wasco
Mireles, Angel	Arvin

170
Hernandez, Adrian	Kennedy, Major, 14-2
Saldana, Armondo	Wasco
Nunez, Josh	Shafter, Fall
Sanchez, Santos	?

182
Robledo, Jose	Wasco, Fall, 4:48
Santoyo, Juan	Kennedy
Valenzulela, Alex	Shafter, Fall
Morales, Isai	Arvin
Ozuma, Roman	McFarland

195
Torres, Eric	Shafter, Fall, 3:22
Dibble, Jason	Wasco
Soto, Daniel	Kennedy, Fall
Hernandez, Filipe	McFarland

220
Medley, Sean	Wasco, Fall, 3:12
Rosiquez, Raul	Cesar, Chavez
Alfaro, Alejandro	McFarland, Fall
Mondrajon, Jovanny	Shafter

285
Johnson, Garrett	Wasco, Fall, :36
Gutierrez, Eric	Shafter
Macias, Romero	Kennedy, Fall
Zermeno, Gerard	McFarland

Not all fall times were given.

Most Outstanding Wrestlers

Lower Weight: D. J. Lopez   McFarland
Upper Weight: Eric Torres   Shafter

TOURNAMENT
Wasco	252.5
Shafter	191
R F Kennedy	112
McFarland	99
Arvin	47
Cesar Chavez	14
Bakersfield Christian	0

DUAL	LEAGUE	SEASON
Wasco	6-0	12-1
Shafter	4-2	4-2
R F Kennedy	4-2	7-3
McFarland	3-3	9-5
Cesar Chavez	3-3	3-3
Arvin	1-5	1-5
Bakersfield Christian	0-6	0-6

SOUTH SEQUOIA LEAGUE - Wasco
February 14, 2014

106
Ortiz, Tommy	R F Kennedy Fall, 1:28
Sierra, Juan	Arvin
Villa, Nicholas	Shafter, Fall
Hinojosa, Ezequiel	Wasco

113
Birrueta, Marin	Wasco, Fall, :47
Fuentes, Lucio	Arvin

120
Tomayo, Alvaro	Arvin, Fall, 1:15
Pena, Roger	Cesar Chavez
Villa, Chris	Shafter
Crumm, Michael	McFarland
Perez, Alberto	R F Kennedy
Sullivan, Zach	Wasco

126
Gutierrez, Juan	Wasco, 7-6
Gamboa, Manuel	Cesar Chavez
Munoz, Eric	Shafter, Decision
Ayon, Abron	McFarland
Coss, Jorge	Arvin

132
Jaramilla, Peter	Wasco, Fall, 2:51
Gutierrez, Carlos	McFarland
Deandra, Adrian	Cesar Chavez, Major Decision
Gonzalez, Marcos	Arvin
Perez, David	Shafter

138
Villa, David	Shafter, 7-5
Lopez, Alex	McFarland
Amador, Frankie	Arvin, Fall
Martin, Esquivel	Cesar Chavez
Garza, Damian	Wasco

145
Macias, Michael	Wasco, Default
Averndano, Marco	Shafter
Leyva, Christian	Arvin, Decision
Lemus, Juan	Cesar Chavez
Nieto, Ivan	McFarland, Fall
Garcia, Isaac	R F Kennedy

152
Lopez, Casper	Wasco, Default
Dominguez, Miguel	Shafter
Cisneros, Homer	Cesar Chavez, TF
Boetger, Austin	Arvin

160
Loza, Daniel	Wasco, 5-3, OT
Castulo, Rodolfo	R F Kennedy
Medrano, Victor	Arvin, Forfeit
Delarosa, Christian	Shafter
Estrella, Julio	McFarland

170
Nunez, Joshua	Shafter, TF, 21-6
Sanchez, Santos	McFarland
Couch, Brandon	Wasco, Fall
Mazone, Hayden	Bakersfield Christian

182
Robledo, Jose	Wasco, Fall, 1:57
Lua, Julian	Shafter

195
Darden, Marcus	Wasco, Fall, 2:52
Schuler, Brent	Bakersfield Christian
Marin, Issac	R F Kennedy, Fall
Gonzalez, Armondo	Shafter
Hernandez	Felipe, McFarland

220
Macias, Ramiro	Kennedy, Fall, 3:20
Alfaro, Alejandro	McFarland
Dibble, Jason	Wasco, Fall
Barrios, Marcos	Cesar Chavez,
Barraza, Juan	Shafter

285
Martinez, Rodney	Wasco, 7-3
Guerra, Jesus	R F Kennedy
Avendano, Javier	Shafter, Fall
Campos, Luis	McFarland

*All the times weren't given.

Most Outstanding Wrestlers

Lower Weight: Alvaro Tomayo   Arvin
Upper Weight: Casper Lopez   Wasco

TOURNAMENT
Wasco	225
Shafter	171.5
Arvin	118
McFarland	116
R F Kennedy	98
Cesar Chavez	89.5
Bakersfield Christian	25

SOUTH SEQUOIA LEAGUE - Wasco
February 14, 2014

DUAL	LEAGUE	SEASON
Wasco	6-0	9-2
Shafter	5-1	11-10
R F Kennedy	4-2	7-3
Cesar Chavez	4-2	4-2
Arvin	2-4	2-6
McFarland	2-4	2-8
Bakersfield Christian	0-6	0-6

Tommy Ortiz (RFK) and Juan Sierra (Arvin)
02/14/2014 Photo courtesy of Bakersfield.com

SOUTH SEQUOIA LEAGUE – McFarland
February 12, 2015

106
Fulce, James — Bakersfield Christian, 2-0
Ayon, Brandon — Shafter
Acuna, Leonardo — Wasco, 4-2
Sanchez, Angel — R F Kennedy

113
Ortiz, Tommy — R F Kennedy, TF, 20-4
Terrigues, Joseph — Cesar Chavez
Hinojosa, Ezaquiel — Wasco, 5-3
Villa, Nick — Shafter

120
Hernandez, Marco — R FKennedy, Major 13-2
Birrueter, Mario — Wasco
Pena, Roger — Cesar Chavez, Fall
Crumm, Michael — McFarland

126
Ramos, Ethan — Shafter, Fall
Sierra, Juan — Arvin
Rodriguez, Daniel — Cesar Chavez, 9-1
Anrelland, Anselmo — Wasco

132
Villa, Chris — Shafter, 9-2
Esquivel, Martin — Cesar Chavez
Figueroa, Raymond — McFarland, 10-8
Gomes, Eduardo — Arvin

138
Tamayo, Alvaro — Arvin, 8-2
Gamboa, Manuel — Cesar Chavez
Torres, Carlos — McFarland, 8-3
Gutierrez, Juan — Wasco

145
Macias, Michael — Wasco, Fall
Deanda, Adrian — Cesar Chavez
Gonzalez, Marcos — Arvin, Fall
Garduno, Chaz — Shafter

152
Deboer, Willem — Bakersfield Christian, Fall
Lemus, Juan — Cesar Chavez
Bernaedino, Arturo — Wasco, 12-6
Lopez, Alex — McFarland

160
Loza, Daniel — Wasco, Fall
Rosigue, Matthew — Cesar Chaves
Watson, Weston — Shafter, Fall
Estrella, Julio — McFarland

170
Soto, Daniel — R F Kennedy, Fall
Leyva, Cristian — Arvin
Gonzalez, Armando — Shafter, 3-2
Chase, Brenden — Bakersfield Christian

182
Castulo, Rodolfo — R F Kennedy, 7-5
Ramirez, Jose — Wasco
Rodriquez, Anthony — Bakersfield Christian, Fall
Cisneros, Noel — Arvin

195
Darden, Marcus — Wasco, 3-0
Nunez, Josh — Shafter
Velez, Christopher — R F Kennedy, 5-2
Gauthier, Jason — Bakersfield Christian

220
Macias, Ramiro — R F Kennedy, Fall
Schuler, Brett — Bakersfield Christian
Espinoza, Angel — Cesar Chavez, Major 13-4
Romero, Angel — Wasco

285
Marin, Isaac — R F Kennedy, 2-1
Martinez, Rodney — Wasco
Camacho, Sergio — Shafter, Fall
Gomez, Javier — McFarland

Most Outstanding Wrestlers

Lower Weight: Tommy Ortiz   R F Kennedy
Upper Weight: Ramiro Macias R F Kennedy

TOURNAMENT

Team	Points
Wasco	181
R F Kennedy	156
Shafter	144
Cesar Chavez	139
Bakersfield Christian	101
Arvin	92
McFarland	71

DUAL	LEAGUE	SEASON
Wasco	6-0	13-3
Shafter	5-1	9-2
Cesar Chavez	4-2	13-8
R F Kennedy	3-3	8-4
Arvin	3-3	3-3
McFarland	1-5	3-8
Bakersfield Christian	0-6	0-6

SOUTH SEQUOIA LEAGUE – Cesar Chavez
February 11, 2016

106
Nunez, Isaac	Shafter, 6-0
Villa, Luis	R F Kennedy

113
Birrueta, Mario	Wasco, Major, 10-0
Ortiz, Adam	R F Kennedy
Arriaza, Wilfredo	Arvin, 9-6
Delacruz, Juan	Shafter
Iglesias, Gerardo	Cesar Chavez

120
Terriquez, Joseph	Cesar Chavez, 8-3
Arrellano, Anselmo	Wasco
Villa, Nick	Shafter, Fall, 1:28
Desantiago, Ezekiel	R F Kennedy

126
Villa, Chris	Wasco, 7-5
Soto, Manuel	R F Kennedy
Crumm, Michael	McFarland, Fall, 1:11
Fulce, James	Bakersfield, Christian
Perez, Anthony	Shafter, Forfeit
Gonzalez, Angel	Wasco

132
Hernandez, Marco	R F Kennedy, 5-1
Ramos, Ethan	Shafter
Rodriguez, Daniel	Cesar Chavez, Fall, 3:11
Sierra, Juan	Arvin
Horton, Justin	Wasco

138
Gamboa, Manuel	Cesar Chavez, 9-3
Mendoza, Alberto	Wasco
Flores, Jonathan	R F Kennedy, 7-5
Estrella, Nathan	McFarland
Garcia, Xavier	Shafter, Major, 14-1
Fuentes, Lucio	Arvin

145
Tamayo, Alvaro	Arvin, 4-3
De, Anda, Adrian	Cesar Chavez,
Prieto, Cezar	Wasco, Fall, 1:49
Brown, Seth	Bakersfield, Christian
Coon, George	Shafter, Default
Figueroa, Raymond	McFarland

152
Zumudio, Rafael	Shafter, Fall, 4:41
Zaragoza, Jamie	R F Kennedy
Sanchez, Jose	Arvin, 12-11
Lemus, J., J.	Cesar Chavez
Magana, David	Wasco

160
Leyva, Christian	Arvin, Fall, 1:38
Enciso, Enrique	R F Kennedy
Chase, Brenden	Bakersfield, Christian, Fall, 1:25
Valdez, Elias	Shafter
Melgar, Josh	Wasco, Fall, 1:55
Macias, Ivan	Cesar Chaves

170
Hernandez, Felipe	McFarland, Fall, 5:38
Tapia, Anthony	Wasco
Ruiz, Brian	R F Kennedy, Fall, 1:58
Figueroa, Alexis	Cesar Chavez
Raya, Adrian	Shafter

182
Castulo, Rodolfo	R F Kennedy, 4-2, OT
Sandoval, Juan	Cesar Chavez
Ayala, Edwin	Shafter, 2-1
Martinez, Vince	Wasco

195
Garcia, Javier	McFarland, 8-6
Velez, Christian	R F Kennedy
Gauthier, Jason	Bakersfield, Christian, Fall, 5:32
Garza, Damian	Wasco
Banuelos, Anthonie	Shafter

220
Macias, Ramiro	R F Kennedy, Fall, 1:58
Sanchez, Enrique	Shafter
Acuna, John	Cesar Chavez, Fall, 1:12
Romero, Angel	Wasco

285
Schuler, Brett	Bakersfield, Christian, Fall, 1:26
Guerra, Jesus	R F Kennedy
Camacho, Sergio	Shafter, Fall, 1:08
Torres, Lawrence	Cesar Chavez
Gomez, Javier	McFarland

Most Outstanding Wrestlers

Lower Weight: Marco Hernandez, R F Kennedy
Upper Weight: Brett Schuler, Bakersfield Christian

SOUTH SEQUOIA LEAGUE – Cesar Chavez
February 11, 2016

TOURNAMENT

R F Kennedy	248
Shafter	207
Wasco	195
Arvin	98
McFarland	93
Bakersfield Christian	88
Cesar Chavez	N/A

DUAL	LEAGUE	SEASON
R F Kennedy	5-1	10-2
Shafter	3-2	3-2
Wasco	3-2	9-3
Arvin	2-4	3-4
Bakersfield Christian	0-5	0-5
Cesar Chavez	N/A	N/A
McFarland	N/A	N/A

Marco Hernandez (Frontier High School) and JJ Figueroa (Bakersfield High School) (03/02/2017) Photo courtesy of Bakersfield.com

SOUTH SEQUIOA LEAGUE - Wasco
February 9, 2017

106
Bartolome, Daniel	Cesar Chavez, Fall
Vidal, Ethan	Bakersfield Christian
Isaiah, Contreras	Wasco, Fall
Diaz, Johnathan	McFarland
Olivas, Tino	Shafter, 4-3
Villa, Luis	R F Kennedy

113
Landin, Jose	Wasco, Major, 11-2
Nunez, Isaac	Shafter
Gamboa, Eric	R F Kennedy, Fall
Fernandez, William	Cesar Chavez

120
Birrueta, Mario	Wasco, Fall
Perez, Tony	Shafter
Ortiz, Adam	R F Kennedy, Fall
Bartolme, Anthony	Cesar Chavez
Arriaza, Wilfredo	Arvin

126
Garcia, Xavier	Shafter, Fall
Sullivan, Cody	Wasco

132
Arellano, Anselmo	Wasco, 7-3
Soto, Manuel	R F Kennedy
Fulce, James	Bakersfield Christian, 12-4
Pompa, Andrew	Shafter
Ayala, Jose	Arvin, Fall
Esquivel, Sergio	Cesar Chavez

138
Gamboa, Manuel	Cesar Chavez, 8-0
Portillo, Caleb	Bakersfield Christian
Brown, Aaron	Shafter, Fall
Fuentes, Lucio	Arvin
Ortiz, Renato	R F Kennedy, 6-0
Estrella, Nathan	McFarland

145
Valdez, Elias	Shafter, Fall
Nunez, Ezequel	Wasco
Mendez, Adrian	Arvin, Fall
Reyes, Ivan	R F Kennedy

152
Santoyo, Eduardo	R F Kennedy, 2-1
Prieto, Cezar	Wasco
Gonzalez, Nathan	Shafter

160
Zaragoza, Jaime	R F Kennedy, Fall
Rivera, Angle	Shafter
Sanchez, Jose	Arvin, Fall
Ramirez, Roman	Wasco

170
Zamudio, Rafael	Shafter, 4-2
Brendan, Chase	Bakersfield Christian
Perez, Oscar	R F Kennedy, Fall
Gambro, Carlos	Wasco

182
Sandoval, Juan	Cesar Chavez, 3-1,
Banuelos, Anthonie	Shafter
Alcaraz, Adrian	R F Kennedy, Fall
Myer, Ethan	Bakersfield Christian,
Neto, Raul	Wasco

195
Valdez, Christian	R F Kennedy, 6-0, (*35-14)
Ayala, Edwin	Shafter
Aispuro, Gerardo	McFarland, Fall
Schuler, Brian	Bakersfield Christian
Muro, Aldo	Cesar Chavez, Disqualified
Garza, Damian	Wasco

220
Campos, Eric	R F Kennedy, 5-2
Sanchez, Enrique	Shafter
Taboer, Nylainder	Bakersfield Christian, Fall
Ocampo, Ivan	Wasco

285
Schuler, Brett	Bakersfield Christian, Fall
Contreras, Enrique	Wasco
Gustavo, Roberto	R F Kennedy, 5-3
Alexander, Tyler	Shafter
Ruezga, Gerardo	Arvin, Fall
Ramos, Pedro	Cesar Chavez

*Record

Most Outstanding Wrestlers

Upper, Weight: Eric Campos   R F Kennedy
Lower, Weight: Mario Birrueta   Wasco

SOUTH SEQUIOA LEAGUE - Wasco
February 9, 2017

TOURNAMENT

Shafter	209
RF Kennedy	176
Wasco	171
Bakersfield Christian	108
Cesar Chavez	105
Arvin	55
McFarland	42

DUAL	LEAGUE	SEASON
Shafter	6-0	10-2
Wasco	5-1	9-1
R F Kennedy	4-2	5-5
Cesar Chavez	3-3	4-3
Bakersfield Christian	3-3	3-3
Arvin	1-5	1-6
McFarland	0-6	0-7

SOUTH SEQUOIA LEAGUE - Wasco
February 9, 2018

106
Macias, Jimmy	Cesar Chavez, 4-2
Olivas, Florentino	Shafter
Macias, Ruben	Wasco, Fall, 3:54
Garcia, Steven	McFarland

113
Vasquez, Keith	Shafter, Fall
Bartolome, Daniel	Cesar Chavez,
Contreras, Isaiah	Wasco, Fall
Vidial, Ethann	Bakersfield Christian
Diaz, Jonathan	McFarland

120
Garza, Christian	Shafter, 8-5
Ortiz, Adam, R, F	R F Kennedy
Guerra, Joel	McFarland, Fall
Macia, Alisian	Wasco

126
Perez, Anthony	Shafter, Fall, *30-6, 77-17
Bartolme, Anthony	Cesar Chavez,
Gamboa, Eric, R, F	R F Kennedy, Default
Padilla, Juan	McFarland

132
Gonzales, Eli	Shafter, Fall
Herrera, Juvenal	R F Kennedy
Rivera, Mario	Wasco, 11-7
Ochoa, Jesus	Cesar Chavez
Garcia, Alllan	McFarland

138
Fulce, James	Bakersfield Christian, Fall
Colmenanares, Oscar	Cesar Chavez,
Martin, Jonathan	Wasco, Fall, 3:06
Castellanos, Angel	R F Kennedy
Montgomery, Sebastian	Shafter

145
Carranza, Mike	Shafter, Fall
Enciso, Xavier	R F Kennedy,
Patino, Alex	McFarland, Fall
Esquivel, Sergio	Cesar Chavez
Epperly, Joshua	Bakersfield Christian

152
Santoyo, Eduardo	R F Kennedy, 3-1
Pompa, Andrew	Shafter
Arredondo, Ulices	Cesar Chavez, Fall
Quinones, Jesue	Arvin
Holguin, Jacob	McFarland

160
Gonzales, Nathaniel	Shafter, 4-1
Ruiz, Joncarlo	Wasco
Orozco, Angel	McFarland, 13-8
Gorospe, Kenneth	Cesar Chavez

170
Zumudio, Rafael	Shafter, Fall
Ruiz, Alex	McFarland,
Servin, Fernando	R F Kennedy

182
Banuelos, Anthonie	Shafter, Fall
Osuna, Anthony	Cesar Chavez
Meyers, Ethan	Bakersfield Christian, Fall
Robledo, Matthew	Wasco
Chaidez, Daniel	McFarland

195
Schuler, Brian	Bakersfield Christian, 4-2
Gonzales, Adrin	Shafter
Vega, Juan	Wasco

220
Aispuro, Gerardo	McFarland, 6-1
Campos, Eric, R, F	R F Kennedy
Ruezga, Gerardo	Arvin, Fall
Steele, David	Bakersfield Christian
Valera, Jonathan	Wasco

285
Amaya, Jesus	McFarland, 2-1
Guzman, Roberto	R F Kennedy
Valdivia, Geronimo	Wasco, Fall
Garduno, Chaz	Shafter,
Ceja, Anthony	Bakersfield Christian

Fall times not given
*Season and Career record

Most Outstanding Wrestlers

Lower Weight: Anthony Banuelos   Shafter
Upper Weight: Anthony Perez   Shafter

TOURNAMENT
Shafter	233
R F Kennedy	134
Cesar Chavez	131
Wasco	110
McFarland	106
B. Christian	84
Arvin	28

SOUTH SEQUOIA LEAGUE - Wasco
February 9, 2018

DUAL	LEAGUE	SEASON
Shafter	6-0	11-2
R F Kennedy	5-1	5-4
Cesar Chavez	4-2	4-3
Wasco	3-3	7-3
McFarland	2-4	2-4
B. Christian	1-5	1-5
Arvin	1-5	1-5

SOUTH SEQUOIA LEAGUE

2019

DUAL	LEAGUE	SEASON
Arvin	4-1	5-2
R F Kennedy	4-1	5-3
Shafter	4-1	4-2
Cesar Chavez	3-2	3-4
McFarland	1-4	1-4

Most Outstanding Wrestlers
Lower Weight: Valentin Marin — Arvin
Upper Weight: Gerardo Aispuro — McFarland

*No league tournament was held

Cole Reyes - Frontier 2019

2020 All South Sequoia League Team

108
Bartolome, Daniel — Cesar Chavez

115
Vasquez, Thomas — Wasco

122
Macias, Jimmy — Cesar Chavez

128
Bartolome, Anthony — Cesar Chavez

134
Guzman, Elijah — Cesar Chavez

140
Rojas, Ivan — Arvin

147
Martinez, Carlos — Shafter

154
Navarro, Angel — Wasco

162
Pesina, Avian — R F Kennedy

172
Enciso, Xavier — R F Kennedy

184
Alonso, Juan — R F Kennedy

197
Millian, Pascual — Wasco

222
Ramirez, Deny — Cesar Chavez

287
Valdivia, Geronimo — Wasco

Most Outstanding Wrestlers

Lower Weight: Anthony Bartolome — Cesar Chavez
Upper Weight: Juan Alonso — R F Kennedy

*No league tournament was held
Coaches selected the wrestlers in the weights

DUAL	LEAGUE	SEASON
Wasco	5-0	13-2
Cesar Chavez	4-1	5-1
Shafter	3-2	6-13
McFarland	1-4	1-4
Arvin	1-4	1-4
R F Kennedy	1-4	1-4

Daniel Long, Coach Wright and Noah Cortez

YOSEMITE DIVISIONAL

2007-2018

YOSEMITE DIVISIONALS CHAMPIONSHIP TEAMS

Date	Champion	Coach	Location
2-18-1967	McLane	Vern McCoy	Northern Division/Roosevelt
2-18-1967			Central Division
2-18-1967	South	Joe Seay	Southern Division/ North
2-17-1968	McLane	Vern McCoy	Northern Division/Dos Palos
2-17-1968	Bakersfield	Olan Polite	Southern Division/South
2-21-1969	Madera	Al Kiddy	Yosemite Division/McLane
2-21-1970	Madera	Al Kiddy	Mt. Whitney Visalia
1-20-1971	South	Joe Seay	South Bakersfield
2-26-1972	Bakersfield	Olan Polite	Bakersfield College
2-17-1973	Clovis	Dennis Deliddo	Hanford
2-16-1974	Clovis	Dennis Deliddo	Clovis
2-21-1975	Clovis	Dennis Deliddo	Fresno High
2-21-1976	Clovis	Dennis Deliddo	Hanford
2-19-1977	Clovis	Dennis Deliddo	Hanford
2-18-1978	Highland/Monache	Joe Barton/D. Williams	Clovis
2-17-1979	South	Eugene Walker	Tulare Western
2-23-1980	Clovis	Rodney Balch	Bakersfield College
2-21-1981	Monache	Drew Williams	Clovis
2-20-1982	Clovis West	Lennis Cowell	Hanford
2-19-1983	Clovis West	Lennis Cowell	Tulare Western
2-18-1984	Clovis West	Lennis Cowell	Arvin
2-16-1985	Clovis	Rodney Balch	Tulare Western
2-22-1986	Clovis	Rodney Balch	Bullard/Fresno
2-21-1987	South	Eugene Walker	Mt. Whitney/Visalia
2-20-1988	Clovis West	Joe Faria	Arvin
2-18-1989	Clovis West	Joe Faria	Hanford
2-17-1990	Clovis	Rodney Balch	Clovis
2-16-1991	Clovis	Rodney Balch	East Bakersfield
2-22-1992	Clovis	Rodney Balch	Tulare Western
2-20-1993	Madera	Corky Napier	Bullard/Fresno
2-19-1994	Monache	Drew Williams	Arvin
2-18-1995	Bakersfield	David East	Mt. Whitney/Visalia
2-17-1996	Buchanan	Chris Hansen	Buchanan
2-22-1997	Clovis West	Brad Zimmer	East Bakersfield
2-21-1998	Buchanan	Buchanan	Mt. Whitney/Visalia
2-20-1999	Clovis	Steve Tirapelle	Clovis
2-18,19-2000	Buchanan	Dustin Riley	East Bakersfield
2-16,17-2001	Clovis	Steve Tirapelle	Clovis
2-15,16-2002	Bakersfield	David East	East Bakersfield
2-21,22-2003	Clovis	Steve Tirapelle	Lemoore
2-20,21-2004	Bakersfield	Andy Varner	Buchanan
2-18,19-2005	Bakersfield	Andy Varner	East Bakersfield
2-17,18-2006	Buchanan	Dusty Riley	Lemoore
2-16,17-2007	Buchanan	Dustin Riley	Clovis West
2-15,16-2008	Clovis	Steve Tirapelle	East Bakersfield
2-20,21-2009	Buchanan	Chris Hansen	Lemoore
2-19,20-2010	Clovis	Steve Tirapelle	Buchanan
2-18, 19-2011	Clovis	Steve Tirapelle	East Bakersfield
2-17,18-2012	Clovis	Steve Tirepelle	Lemoore
2-15,16-2013	Buchanan	Troy Tirapelle	Madera South
2-21,22-2014	Clovis	Steve Tirapelle	East Bakersfield
		Ben Holscher	

YOSEMITE DIVISIONALS
CHAMPIONSHIP TEAMS

Date	Champion	Coach	Location
2-20,21-2015	Buchanan	Troy Tirapelle	Lemoore
2-19,20-2016	Buchanan	Troy Tirapelle	Clovis
2-17,18-2017	Buchanan	Troy Tirapelle	East Bakersfield
2-16,17-2018	Buchanan	Troy Tirapelle	Lemoore

Giano Petrucelli – Clovis
Joseph Martin - Buchanan

Kirk Moore and Carlo Franciotti - Frontier 2016

YOSEMITE DIVISIONAL
MOST OUTSTANDING WRESTLERS

Year	Name	School
1967	Joe Nigos	Delano
1968	Cecil Crowder	Foothill
1971	Dennis Burnett	North
1992	Mario Gonzales	South
1996	Jaime Garza	Selma
	Adam Tirapelle	Buchanan
	Telly Sanders	Buchanan
	Victor Leyva	Monache
1997	Jaime Garza	Selma
	Telly Sanders	Buchanan
	Grant Harrington	Redwood
1998	Ben Martinez	Tulare Union
	Josh Naus	Centennial
1999	Ben Martinez	Tulare Union
	Max Odom	Foothill
2000	Darrell Vasquez	Bakersfield
	Chris Pendleton	Lemoore
2001	Gerard Contreras	Buchanan
	Miguel Gutierrez	Foothill
2002	Darrell Vasquez	Bakersfield
	Jacob Weaver	Sanger
2003	Chris Mendez	Hanford
	Jake Varner	Bakersfield
2004	Nathan Morgan	Bakersfield
	Josh Marquez	Bakersfield
2005	Mark Anderson	Lemoore
	Jake Varner	Bakersfield
2006	Alfonso Sanchez	McLane
	Tony Webber	Bakersfield
2007	John Rios	Madera
	Jacob Maxon	Redwood
2008	Randall Watts	El Diamante
	Andrew Balch	Buchanan
2009	Nicholas Sierra	Lemoore
	Stephen West	Buchanan
2010	Zach Zimmer	Clovis West
	James Cook	Madera
2011	Shane Yacata	Porterville
	Bryce Hammond	Bakersfield
2012	Michael Knoblauch	Clovis West
	Zach Nevills	Clovis
2013	Michael Knoblauch	Clovis West
	Kyle Perreault	Clovis East
2014	Mason Pengilly	Porterville
	Nick Nevills	Clovis
2015	Khristian Olivas	Clovis
	Zackary Levatino	Buchanan
2016	Gary Joint	Lemoore
	Seth Nevills	Clovis
2017	Chris Deloza	Clovis North
	Seth Nevills	Clovis
2018	Ryan Franco	Clovis North
	Seth Nevills	Clovis

Bryce Hammond - Bakersfield 2011

*Starting in 1992 awards were sponsored by the Coyote Club

YOSEMITE DIVISIONAL – Covis
East February 16-17, 2007

103
Done, Chris	Buchanan, 6-4
Collier, Marc	East
Zimmer, Zach	Covis West, 13-4
Diaz, Chris	Sanger
Ban, Jason	Sunnyside, 5-2
Jordan, Elmer	Redwood
Gomez, Eric	Madera, 5-2
Omata, Ben	Clovis

112
Demison, Nektoe	Bakersfield, 6-3
Fitzgerald, Steven	Covis East
Jaramillo, A. J.	Lemoore, 2-0
Gonzalez, Peter	East
Everwine, Chase	Covis West, Fall, 1:37
Roberts, Nathan	Buchanan,
Perez, Miguel	Madera, 4-1
Uribe, Victor	Hanford, West

119
Lomas, Frank	Bakersfield, 5-0,
Weimer, Steve	Clovis
Waters, Anthony	Buchanan, 10-2
Rocha, Brandon	Lemoore
Tarkington, Richard	Highland, Default
Nam, Chantra	Sunnyside,
Masuta, Armajit	Madera, Default
Magno, Jon	Ridgeview

125
Arredondo, Justin	Buchanan, 3-1
Ramos, Chris	Bullard
Fisher, Nick	Covis West, 12-0
Pered, Julian	Lemoore
Chatman, Charles	Edison, Fall, 4:48
Williams, Galen	Tulare, Western
Morgan, Jacob	Bakersfield, 8-7
Valle, Ramiro	Redwood

130
Roman-Marin, Sean	Lemoore, 10-3
Kelley, Cameron	Clovis
Gutierrez, Isidro	Buchanan, Fall, 3:44
Hicks, Seth	Centennial
Gonzalez, Freddy	East, 9-3
Franco, Steve	Highland
Lugan, Brian	Clovis West, 6-4
Pavone, Ryan	Porterville

135
Rios, John	Madera, 5-4, *41-6
Rodriguez, Alex	Covis East, *37-2
Watts, David	El Diamante, 4-2
Cruz, Jonah	Bakersfield
Pavone, Chris	Porterville, 10-3
Thomas, John	Clovis
Ballard, Austin	Centennial, Fall, :52
Beck, Dylan	Covis West

140
Larson, Troy	Covis East Fall, 2:52, *30-2
Rubio, Vincent	Lemoore,
Sakaguchi, Scott	Clovis, 11-0
Box, Timmy	Bakersfield
Watts, Randall	El Diamante, 4-3
Miller, Justin	East
Ellison, Dustin	Covis West, 9-5
Flores, Dwight	Tulare

145
Rassussen, Travis	Bakersfield, 7-2
Moralez, Mitch	Tulare
West, Stephen	Buchanan, Fall, 2:47
Christenson, Colton	Liberty
Ends, Dalton	Centennial, Fall, 2:27
Dupras, Jake	Covis West
Sierra, Nick	Lemoore, 5-4
Vera, Hugo	Central

152
Balch, Andrew	Buchanan, 1-0
Esparza, Josh	Clovis
Rodriguez, Jamie	Bakersfield, 7-2
Morales, Jesus	Tulare
Cook, James	Covis West, Fall, 1:18
Smith, Chris	West
Jenkins, Brock	Tulare, Western, Fall, 4:25
Roughton, Cory	Golden, West

160
Montelongo, Daniel	Madera, 3-0
Bracamonte, Paul	Central
Delarosa, Eric	Foothill, 2-0
West, Craig	Buchanan
Hernandez, Cruz	East, 3-0
Magana, Xavier	Fresno
Rogers, Kail	Liberty, Fall, 1:55
Pfitzer, Brent	Tulare

170
Smith, Eric	Buchanan, 9-3
Brant, Phil	Bullard
Allison, Dustin	Madera, 4-3
Carls, Brad	Bakersfield

YOSEMITE DIVISIONAL – Covis
East February 16-17, 2007

170 - continued
Villasenor, Sergio	Monache, 10-4
Shaver, Zack	Clovis
Sanchez, Derek	Hanford, Fall, 5:47
Enus, Johnny	Golden, West

191
Garcia, Matt	Lemoore, 3-2
Sanchez, Brett	Clovis
Travis, David	Foothill, Fall, 1:56
Ryder, Glen	Centennial
Medellin, Brandon	Madera, Default
Lowe, Tim	Sunnyside
Gingold, Jake	Buchanan, Forfeit
Leavell, Jaron	Hoover

215
Flores, Ryan	Buchanan, 1-0
Lopez, Vince	Clovis
Perez, Jose	Porterville, Fall, 1:01
Terrell, Lake	North
Gonzalez, Alex	Sunnyside, Forfeit
Trujillo, Robert	Hanford
Cummings, Eddie	East, Fall, 3:18
Shipman, Cameron	McLane

285
Maxon, Jacob	Redwood, 1-0
Zamora, Jonathan	Clovis
Garza, Austin	Buchanan, 6-5
Baize, Lloren	Lemoore
Alvarez, Lamar	Bakersfield, Default
Bernard, Tyler	Central
Cisneros, Efren	Golden, Valley
McClintock, Coby	Delano

*Records

TEAM SCORES
1	Buchanan	299.5
2	Clovis	237.5
3	Bakersfield	220.5
4	Lemoore	185.5
5	Madera	158
6	Clovis West	132
7	East	118.5
8	Centennial	114
9	Clovis East	107.5
10	Tulare Union	105
11	Bullard	90.5
12	Sunnyside	85.5
13	El Diamante	74.5
13	Porterville	74.5
15	Liberty	73
16	Redwood	72.5
17	Central	68
18	Foothill	66.5
19	Monache	59
20	Golden West	58
20	Sanger	58
22	Highland	52
23	Hanford	48
24	North	46
25	Edison	43
25	Tulare Western	43
27	Hanford West	36.5
28	Cesar Chavez	35.5
29	Ridgeview	33.5
30	Delano	31
31	Fresno	28
32	Stockdale	27
33	Golden Valley	24.5
34	McLane	24
34	West	24
36	Hoover	23
37	Reedley	17
38	Roosevelt	16
39	Mt. Whitney	15
39	South	15
41	Granite Hills	3

Most Outstanding Wrestlers

Lower Weight: John Rios   Madera
Upper Weight: Jacob Maxon   Redwood

YOSEMITE DIVISIONAL – East
February 15-16, 2008

103
Zimmer, Zach	Clovis West, Fall, 3:37
Collier, Marc	East
Yacuta, Shane	Porterville, 6-5
Diaz, Chris	Sanger
Gambrell, Mason	Clovis Fall, 1:31
Gomez, Eric	Madera
Rodriguez, Adrian	Buchanan, 2-0
Esparza, Silverio	Lemoore

112
Martinez, Chris	Clovis West, 4-2, *51-8
Gonzalez, Peter	East
McAlester, Clinton	Clovis 1-0
Jaramillo, A. J.	Lemoore
Elmer, Jordan	Redwood, 16-5
Sanchez, Cesar	Porterville
Meredith, Stephen	Buchanan, Fall, ?
Casper, Torrey	Frontier

119
Rocha, Brandon	Lemoore, 2-1
Walters, Anthony	Buchanan, *40-9
Gay, Jonathan	Clovis, 6-5
Burger, Riley	Golden West
Orozco, Sam	Monache, 3-0
Rizo, Derek	Foothill
Knoblach, Steven	Clovis West, 9-4
Gonzalez, Nick	East

125
Fitgerald, Steven	Clovis East, Fall, 5:15
Box, Timmy	Bakersfield, *36-14
Nam, Chanta	Sunnyside, 3-2
Roberts, Nathan	Buchanan
Zinkin, Josh	Clovis West, 4-2
Dieter, Alec	Clovis
Valle, Ramiro	Redwood, Fall, 5:15
Perez, Alex	Lemoore

130
Arredondo, Justin	Buchanan, 3-2
Weimer, Stephen	Clovis
Perez, Julian	Lemoore, Fall, 1:46
Rivera, Vince	Liberty, *46-13
Magno, Bryan	Ridgeview, Fall, 3:56
Williams, Chino	Tulare, Western
Voth, Nick	El Diamante, 6-5
Galaviz, John	East

135
Watts, Randall	El Diamante, 7-5, *32-3
Fisher, Nick	Clovis West
Kapler, Greg	Liberty, 5-4, *45-14
Gutierrez, Isido	Buchanan
Ballard, Austin	Centennial, Fall, 3:05
Masuta, Armajit	Madera
Phanthavong, Micky	Granite Hills, Fall, 5:12
Garcia, Rene	Ridgeview

140
Watts, David	El Diamante, 5-4
Sakaguchi, Scott	Clovis *43-5
Sierra, Nicholas	Lemoore, Fall, 2:56
Hicks, Seth	Centennial
Cruz, Jonah	Bakersfield, 5-2
Martin, Fabbian	Bullard
Ruelas, Nester	Golden West, Default
Vanhaater, Josh	Bullard

145
Balch, Andrew	Buchanan, Fall, 1:17
Rasmussen, Travis	Bakersfield
Rubio, Vincent	Lemoore, 6-4
Dupras, Jake	Clovis West
Rios, Robert	Liberty, Fall, 2:51
Aguilar, Anthony	Edison
Rios, Jamie	Madera, 4-0
Whitten, Brandon	Hanford West

152
Cook, James	Clovis West, Fall, 3:26
Ceremello, Tyler	Clovis
Hammond, Bryce	Bakersfield, Fall, 3:45, *41-12
Bullock, Brad	El Diamante
Rivera, Cisco	Central, 16-5
Matthews, Eric	Stockdale
March, Jeff	Highland, 11-6
Servin, Benny	East

160
West, Stephen	Buchanan, 10-1
Esparza, Josh	Clovis
Ramirez, Jose	Bakersfield, 5-3, *41-13
Morales, Matt	Tulare, Union
Batshon, Nadim	El Diamante, Fall, 3:57
Singh, Amandeep	Delano
Narvaez, Mark	Ridgeview, Fall, 3:57
Gonzales, Angelo	Central

171
Burriel Tommy	Clovis 8-4
Carls, Brad	Bakersfield
Bracamonte, Paul	Central, 10-9
Musquez, John	Centennial

YOSEMITE DIVISIONAL – East
February 15-16, 2008

Villasenor, Sergio — Monache, 4-2
Poteete, Nathan — Buchanan
Heath, Chris — Sunnyside, Fall, ?
Woods, Matt — Lemoore

189
Brandt, Phil — Bullard, 10-4
Gingold, Jake — Bullard, *43-15
Martinez, Steven — Lemoore, Fall, 1:47
Thomason, Joey — North
Shipman, Cameron — McLane, Default
Cox, Matt — Clovis
Ryder, Glenn — Centennial, Fall, 1:14
Perez, Carlos — Monache

215
Sanchez, Brett — Clovis 8-2
Travis, David — Foothill, *25-7
Papendorf, Kyle — Bullard, 6-0
Schoene, Brian — Bakersfield
Garcia, Jonathan — Hanford, West, Fall, 1:29
Luna, Jesus — Madera
Hernandez, Juan — Sunnyside, Fall, 3:45
Castillo, Michael — Centennial

285
Zamora, Johnathan — Clovis 3-0
Hernandez, Anthony — East, *46-7
Padilla, Anthony — Bakersfield, Fall, 1:13
Willis, Brent — North
Zamora, Jose — Sanger, 2-1
Smith, Holden — Buchanan
Baize, Loren — Lemoore, 6-2
Mancia, Byron — Sunnyside

*Season records

Most Outstanding Wrestlers

Lower Weight: Randall Watts El Diamante
Upper Weight: Andrew Balch Buchanan

TEAM SCORES

1	Clovis	304
2	Buchanan	268
3	Bakersfield	209
4	Lemoore	197.5
5	Clovis West	190
6	El Diamante	131
7	East	115.5
8	Centennial	110
9	Sunnyside	90
10	Liberty	87
10	Madera	87
12	Foothill	84
13	Golden West	66.5
14	Clovis East	65.5
15	Bullard	64.5
16	Porterville	63
16	Ridgeview	63
18	Monache	62.5
19	Central	59
20	Frontier	56.5
21	Sanger	53.5
22	Redwood	52
23	Hanford West	51
24	North	48
25	Hanford	43
26	Tulare Union	42.5
27	Highland	42
28	Edison	40.5
29	Stockdale	39
30	Hoover	38.5
31	Tulare Western	33.5
32	Fresno	31
33	Reedley	30
34	Granite Hills	28
35	Cesar Chavez	24.5
36	Delano	23
37	McLane	22
38	Golden Valley	16
38	Roosevelt	16
38	Mt. Whitney	16
41	South	15
42	West	10

YOSEMITE DIVISIONAL - Lemoore
February 20-21, 2009

103
Gaytan, Daniel	Clovis, 5-2
Knoblauch, Steven	Clovis West
Jauregui, Justin	Clovis East, 4-3
Rodriguez, Adrian	Buchanan
Gonzalez, Julio	East, 5-3, *27-12
Davis, Harley	Monache
Magnusson, Adam	Madera, 6-1
Esquivel, Kevin	Porterville

112
Rodriguez, Vince	Clovis, North, 8-2
Diaz, Chris	Sanger
Zimmer, Zack	Clovis West, 3-2
Demison, Natrelle	Bakersfield
Collier, Marc	East, Fall, 5:34
Esparza, Silerio	Lemoore
Gambrell, Madison	Clovis, Fall
Sanchez, Cesar	Porterville, *35-8

119
Meredith, Stephen	Buchanan, 5-4
Perez, Sonny	Hoover
Gonzalez, Peter	East, 10-5
Larsen, Conner	Clovis East
Martinez, Chris	Clovis West, Default
Perez, Alex	Lemoore
Orozco, Sammy	Monache, 7-2
Macias, Jose	Edison

125
Rocha, Brandon	Lemoore, 14-2
McAlister, Clinton	Clovis
Arredondo, Damien	Buchanan, 10-2
Calcagno, Chris	Clovis, North
Perez, Richard	Hoover, Default
Elmer, Jordan	Redwood
Velazquez, Gabriel	Hanford, 7-2
Xiong, Richard	Sunnyside

130
Waters, Anthony	Buchanan, 8-3
Estrada, Raul	Madera
Box, Timmy	Bakersfield, 14-10
Yacuta, Shane	Porterville
Rizo, Derik	Foothill, 19-1
Cervantes, Sonny	Clovis
Navarro, Luis	Lemoore, 12-4
Valle, Ramiro	Redwood

135
Hicks, Seth	Centennial, 4-2
Dieter, Alec	Lemoore
Phanthavong, Micky	Granite Hills, 4-2
Ramirez, Gabe	Monache
Kapler, Greg	Liberty, Default
Quezeda, Moses	Clovis East
Lujan, Brian	Clovis West, Fall
Gomez, Jonathan	Madera

140
Sierra, Nicholas	Lemoore, 13-1
Cruz, Jonah	Bakersfield
Sanchez, Javier	Ridgeview, 3-1
Negrete, Matt	Buchanan
Zinkin, Josh	Clovis West, 11-6
Gevorian, David	Bullard
Kelley, Ben	Clovis, 4-1
Ballard, Austin	Centennial

145
Sakaguchi, Scott	Clovis, 7-2
Fierro, Adam	Bakersfield
Cueto, Martin	Liberty, Default
Castaneda, Lance	Frontier
Perreaylt, Brian	Clovis East, TF, 20-5
Pedraza, Johnny	Hanford
Gomez, Fernando	Golden Valley, 12-7, *30-9
Matthews, Richard	Golden Valley

152
Kelley, Cameron	Clovis, 4-1
Rubio, Vincent	Clovis East
Hammond, Bryce	Bakersfield, 6-5
Martin, Fabbian	Buchanan
Reyes, Nikko	Clovis West, 9-2
Ramos, Mago	Hoover
Gonzales, Angelo	Central, 7-6
Bullock, Brad	El Diamante, *28-12, 98-49

160
West, Stephen	Buchanan, Fall, :26
Cook, James	Madera
Pedraza, Lewis	Madera, South, 5-4
Ramirez, Jose	Bakersfield
Endes, Dalton	Centennial, Fall, :52
Singh, Amandeep	Delano
Lujan, Jose	Redwood, 18-6, *24-12
Vega, Florencia	Clovis East

171
Flores, Dwight	Tulare, 3-1
Nevills, Zach	Clovis
Poteete, Nathan	Buchanan, 10-2
Wykoff, Matt	Mt. Whitney

YOSEMITE DIVISIONAL - Lemoore
February 20-21, 2009

Heath, Chris	Sunnyside, 13-1	11 East	81
Quiddan, Michael	Delano	12 Tulare Union	80.5
Gallardo, David	Golden West, 5-4	13 Madera	79.5
Costa, Rio	Redwood	14 Clovis North	75.5
		15 Central	69
189		16 Porterville	68
Burriel, Tommy	Clovis, 5-4	17 Sunnyside	64
Gingold, Jacob	Bullard	18 Hoover	61
Juarez, Rodolfo	Central, 3-2	19 Sanger	59
Corona-Zamarripa, Nick	Hanford West	20 Liberty	57.5
Ellis, Shane	Frontier, 11-7	21 Monache	56.5
Andersen, Michael	Tulare, *31-11	22 Redwood	55
Lareau, Garrett	Clovis West, Fall	22 Foothill	55
Sepsey, Aaron	Lemoore	24 Golden West	52
		25 Delano	50
215		26 Bullard	48.5
Schoene, Brian	Bakersfield, 5-4	27 Cesar Chavez	48
Smith, Holden	Buchanan	28 El Diamante	46.5
Yates, Rakeem	Edison, 11-6	29 Ridgeview	42.5
Garcia, Jonathan	Hanford	30 Edison	41
Gomez, Noel	Cesar, Chavez, Fall, 5:00	31 Granite Hills	37.5
Hernandez, Juan	Sunnyside	32 Stockdale	34.5
Oropeza, Diego	Frontier, 10-6	33 Golden Valley	30
Robinson, Trever	Golden West, *30-9	34 Mt. Whitney	29
		35 South	21
285		35 Tulare Western	21
Papendorf, Kyle	Buchanan, 4-1	35 McLane	21
Posadas, Angel	Foothill	38 Roosevelt	19
Baize, Loren	Lemoore, 13-1	39 Hanford	12.5
Mancia, Byron	Sunnyside	40 Reedley	11
Hernandez, Tony	East, 4-1	40 Highland	11
Contreras, Luis	Madera	42 West	5.5
Davis, Josh	Frontier, Fall		
Perez, Paul	Tulare		

*Season and career record

Most Outstanding Wrestlers

Lower Weight: Nicholas Sierra, Lemoore
Upper Weight: Stephen West, Buchanan

TEAM SCORES
1	Buchanan	275.5
2	Clovis	255.5
3	Bakersfield	190.5
4	Lemoore	154
5	Clovis West	149.5
6	Clovis East	146
7	Madera South	119.5
8	Centennial	85
9	Hanford West	84
10	Frontier	83

Stephen West (Buchanan) against Jonathan Urango (Camarillo) Photographer: John Sachs, Tech-Fall.com 2009

YOSEMITE DIVISIONAL - Buchanan
February 19-20, 2010

103
Gomez, Vincent	Frontier, 4-3
Rocha, Dillion	Lemoore
Gaytan, Jonas	Clovis, 6-0
Tamez, Chris	Clovis East
Gonzalez, Julio	East, 3-2
Rodriguez, Adrian	Buchanan
Nickell, Ian	Bakersfield, 3-0
Rodriguez, Brandon	Clovis West

112
Diaz, Chris	Sanger, 8-6
Gaytan, Daniel	Clovis
Jauregui, Justin	Clovis East, Fall, :37
Esparza, Silverio	Lemoore
Elizondo, Paul	Bullard, 13-6
Navarro, Jose	Madera
Hernandez, Daniel	Madera South, 5-2
Esquivel, Kevin	Porterville

119
Zimmer, Zach	Clovis West, 8-2
Phaysamone, Patrick	Clovis East
Perez, Alex	Lemoore, 4-3
Cruz, Micah	Bakersfield
Everk, Devin	Clovis North, Fall, 2:56
Aguilar, Chris	Stockdale
Enriquez, Matt	Tulare, 5-4
Ruiz, Michael	?

125
Rodriguez, Vince	Clovis, North, 3-2, OT
Martinez, Chris	Clovis West
Martinez, Isaiah	Lemoore, 10-2
Salas, Juan	Clovis
Larson, Conner	Clovis East, Default
Lanier, Jeff	Bakersfield
Lozano, Matt	Central, Fall, 3:07
Wade, Kyle	Madera South

130
Yacuta, Shane	Porterville, 5-3
Valles, A, J.	Sanger
Cervantes, Sonny	Clovis, Fall, :57
Arredondo, Damien	Buchanan
Calcagno, Chris	Clovis, North, Default
Demison, Natrelle	Bakersfield
Lozano, Mitch	Central, 4-3
Xiong, Shaseng	Sunnyside

135
Hill, Spencer	Buchanan, 12-9
Williams, Chino	Tulare
Quezeda, Moses	Clovis East, Fall, 3:44
Ramirez, Maxx	Bakersfield
Rodriguez, Miguel	Madera, 10-1
Steiber, Ryan	Liberty
Lucatero, Adrian	Mt., Whitney, 11-5
Muldrew, Tillman	Sunnyside

140
Box, Timmy	Bakersfield, 7-2
Bersano, Brady	Clovis
Gomez, Jonathan	Madera South, Fall, 3:06
Poindexter, Devin	Clovis North
Solis, Josue	Sanger, Fall, :33
Mariscal, Frankie	Stockdale
Ontiveros, Joseph	Central, 8-4
Villalobos, Jovan	Centennial

145
Hammond, Coleman	Bakersfield, 8-4
Rizo, Derik	Foothill
Sotomayer, Brandon	Centennial, Fall, :55
Rodriguez, Dylin	Sanger
Gevorgyan, Davit	Bullard, Default
Roberts, Nathan	Buchanan
Salas, Adrian	Clovis, Fall
Lopez, Pedro	Sunnyside

152
Sierra, Nick	Lemoore, 6-2
Negrete, Matt	Buchanan
Fierro, Adam	Bakersfield, 6-4
Estrada, Andrew	Madera South
Castaneda, Lance	Frontier, 8-1
Thompson, Blake	Clovis
Greynolds, Clayton	Liberty, Fall, 5:02
Dupras, Jared	Clovis West

160
Reyes, Nikko	Clovis West, 4-2
Pendleton, Jacob	Lemoore
Ceremello, Tyler	Clovis, Fall, 2:37
Lopez, Mike	Golden West
Ramos, Mago	Hoover, Default
Hammond, Brice	Bakersfield
Haidze, Jeremy	Stockdale, Fall
Martinez, Pablo	Monache

171
Cook, James	Madera, 9-2
Nevills, Zach	Clovis
Martin, Fabbian	Buchanan, Fall, :32
Flores, Roman	Stockdale
Wykoff, Matt	Mt. Whitney, 10-5

YOSEMITE DIVISIONAL - Buchanan
February 19-20, 2010

Buffington, Levi — Liberty
Nacita, Silas — Bakersfield, 7-2
Delfino, Santino — Frontier

189
Burrial, Tommy — Clovis, 5-0
Juarez, Rodolfo — Central
Ellis, Shane — Frontier, Forfeit
Barnes, Tanner — Buchanan
Ali, David — Porterville, Fall, :37
Velas Quez, Dakota — Bakersfield
Hernandez, Sergio — Madera, 5-3
Yslas, Ben — Fresno

215
Schoene, Brian — Bakersfield, 5-0
Gomez, Noe — Cesar Chavez
Ferguson, Taylor — Clovis, Fall, 5:24
Brantley, Nick — Edison
Sanchez, Andrew — Golden West, 4-2, *30-13
Zamaramo, John — Sunnyside
Hulse, Kevin — Porterville, Fall, 4:14
Garcia, Juan — Reedley

285
Contreras, Luis — Madera, 2-1
Davis, Josh — Frontier
Mancia, Bryan — Sunnyside, 3-1, OT
Yates, Rakeem — Edison
Wood, Steven — Lemoore, Fall, 1:46
Howard, Max — Clovis
Perez, Paul — Tulare, 3-1
Nelson, Tanner — North

*Season Record

Outstanding Wrestlers
Lower Weight: Zach Zimmer — Clovis West
Upper Weight: James Cook — Madera

TEAM SCORES
1 Clovis 281
2 Bakersfield 238
3 Lemoore 184.5
4 Buchanan 172.5
5 Frontier 157.5
6 Madera 153
7 Clovis East 142
8 Sanger 129.5
9 Madera South 120
10 Clovis West 117
11 Porterville 97
12 Central 92
13 Clovis North 91
14 Stockdale 76
15 Sunnyside 71
16 Centennial 66.5
17 Liberty 64.5
18 Bullard 62
19 Tulare Union 59
20 Foothill 57.5
21 Edison 52.5
22 Golden West 47
23 Hanford West 43
23 Monache 43
25 Mt. Whitney 41.5
26 ?
27 Cesar Chavez 37
28 ?
29 North 36
30 ?
31 ?
32 South 28
33 East 27
33 Ridgeview 27
35 ?
36 ?
37 Delano 23
38 ?
39 ?
40 Golden Valley 19
41 ?
42 ?
43 West 8
44 Highland 3

Coleman Hammond – Bakersfield High School

YOSEMITE DIVISION - East
February 18-19, 2011

103
Pengilly, Mason	Porterville, 2-1
Tamez, Chris	Clovis East
Rodriguez, Brandon	Clovis West, 6-0
Camposano, Adrian	Central
Williams, Sean	Lemoore, 7-3
Ia, Andy	Clovis
Marin, Manny	Buchanan, 6-0
Onsurez, Arik	Bakersfield

112
Nickell, Ian	Bakersfield, 7-6
Gomez, Vincent	Frontier
Navarro, Jose	Madera, 11-6
Marquez, Nick	Foothill
Gaytan, Jonas	Clovis, 11-5
Knoblauch, Mikey	Clovis West
Hood, Seth	Buchanan, 4-0
Ontiveros, Matt	Central

119
Knoblauch, Stevan	Clovis West, 7-6
Gasca, Javier	Central
Esparza, Silverio	Lemoore, 3-2
Jauregui, Justin	Clovis East
Sandoval, Martin	Porterville, Default
Gaytan, Daniel	Clovis
Cancino, Gene	Hoover, 7-2
Gonzalez, Nick	East

125
Rodriguez, Vince	Clovis North, Major 14-6
Cruz, Micah	Bakersfield
Larson, Conner	Clovis East, 6-4
Gay, Matt	Clovis
Lopez, Josh	Frontier, Default
Rocha, Dillion	Lemoore
Garcia, Chris	Clovis West, Default
Enriquez, Matt	Tulare

130
Demison, Natrelle	Bakersfield, 8-7
Calcagno, Chris	Clovis North
Salas, Juan	Clovis, 8-3
Physamone, Patrick	Clovis East
Zimmer, Tyler	Clovis West, Default
Cardenas, Racelis	Buchanan
Navarro, Jimmy	Madera, 7-2
Brown, Devin	Mission Oak

135
Yacuta, Shane	Porterville, 7-2
Box, Timmy	Bakersfield
Everk, Devin	Clovis North, Default
Ladd, Jason	Clovis
Hernandez, Josue	Madera South, Fall, 4:47
Valenzuela, C. J.	Madera
Lucatero, Arian	Mt. Whitney, 3-2,
Perez, Sonny	Hoover

140
Martinez, Isaiah	Lemoore, TF, 17-2
Bersano, Brady	Clovis
Rodriguez, Miguel	Madera, Fall, 3:21
Ramirez, Maxx	Bakersfield
Perrault, Kyle	Clovis East, 10-7
Duran, Joe	Porterville
Fambrough, Jawan	Independence, 4-3
Ayala, Martin	Granite Hills

145
Arrendondo, Damien	Buchanan, 3-1
Hammond, Coleman	Bakersfield
Sotomayor, Brandon	Centennial, Fall, 5:32
Thompson, Colby	Clovis
Gomez, Jonathan	Madera South, 5-3, OT
Poindexter, Devin	Clovis North
Lopez, Daniel	Kennedy, Major, 10-1
Corona, Oscar	Foothill

152
Fierro, Adam	Bakersfield, 2-1
Thompson, Blake	Clovis
Yllan, Charles	Madera South, 4-2
Zecchini, Jason	Mt. Whitney
Martinez, Jaime	Lemoore, 8-5
Ruiz, Miguel	Madera
Karam, Josh	Clovis North, 4-1
Callender, Nick	Clovis East

160
Hammond, Bryce	Bakersfield, TF, 20-5
Salas, Adrian	Clovis
Luna, Cesar	West, Fall, 2:36 #
Rodriguez, Dylin	Sanger
Worth, Andrew	Stockdale, 6-4, OT
Schoenborn, Aaron	Centennial
Ashjian, Cas	Bullard, Fall, 1:41
Williams, Chris	Clovis North

171
Reyes, Nikko	Clovis West, 5-2
Nevills, Zach	Clovis
Pendleton, Jacob	Lemoore, Major, 15-6
Nacita, Silas	Bakersfield
Vega, Florence	Clovis East, Major, 14-0
Spears, Jacob	Ridgeview

YOSEMITE DIVISION - East
February 18-19, 2011

Valladores, Juan	Madera South, 3-0	13	Sanger	76
Mata, Raul	Granite, Hills, *27-7	14	Central	72.5
		15	Centennial	70.5
189		16	Liberty	56
Gordan, Dakota	Clovis, Fall, 1:08	17	West	53.5
Sizemore, Chris	Liberty	18	Mt. Whitney	49
Delfierro, Gannon	Clovis East, 3-1, OT	19	Ridgeview	43
Murphy, Jack	Frontier	20	Redwood	40.5
Lopez, Nate	Lemoore, Default	21	Monache	39
Pope, Kyle	Bakersfield	21	Mission Oak	39
Rubalcado, Jesse	Foothill, Fall, 3:02	23	El Diamante	38
Mechikoff, Alex	Clovis North	24	Edison	37
		25	Stockdale	36
215		26	Independence	35
Ali, David	Porterville, 3-1	27	Granite Hills	34.5
Amaya, Rudy	Foothill	28	Reedley	31.5
Ferguson, Taylor	Clovis, TF, 18-1	29	Fresno	31
Salinas, Arnold	Fresno	29	South	31
Mendoza, Eric	Madera, Default	31	Tulare Union	28.5
Salazar, Jorge	Sanger	32	Golden Valley	25
Morales, Cortes	Clovis West, Fall, 3:26	32	Hoover	25
Sanders, Reno	Tulare Western	34	Bullard	23
		35	Delano	22
285		35	North	22
Nevills, Nick	Clovis, 3-2, OT	37	East Bakersfield	19
Wood, Steven	Lemoore	38	Roosevelt	16
Hurtado, Frankie	Liberty, 3-1	38	R F Kennedy	16
Crawford, Carson	Centennial	40	Tulare Western	15
Hunter, Jumoke	Clovis West, 5-3	41	Highland	14
Olgin, Jordan	Foothill	42	Hanford West	12
Juarez, Narciso	Sanger, Fall, 3:26	43	Mira Monte	8.5
Popek, John	Frontier	44	Golden West	6
		45	Sunnyside	4
		45	Hanford	4

Lost his first match, then pinned 7 straight
* Season, Record

Most Outstanding Wrestlers
Lower Weight: Shane Yacuta   Porterville
Upper Weight: Bryce Hammond   Bakersfield

TEAM SCORES

1	Clovis	310.5
2	Bakersfield	271.5
3	Lemoore	185
4	Clovis West	180.5
5	Clovis East	173.5
6	Porterville	149.5
7	Clovis North	147
8	Madera	138.5
9	Foothill	111
10	Frontier	108.5
11	Buchanan	94.5
12	Madera South	91

Colman Hammond - Bakersfield High School

YOSEMITE DIVISIONAL - Lemoore
February 17-18, 2012

106
Martinez, Miguel	Madera, 13-6
Camposano, Adrian	Central
Cisneros, Joey	Redwood, 7-5
Gaytan, Julian	Clovis
Gamble, Matt	Monache, Fall, 5:00
Velasquez, Marco	Foothill
Jimenez, Javier	Porterville, 17-4
Herrera, Carlos	Bakersfield

113
Gaytan, Jonas	Clovis, 5-0
Pengilly, Mason	Porterville
Hood, Seth	Monache, 1-0
Delacruz, Jason	Buchanan
Williams, Sean	Lemoore, 3-0
Tamez, Chris	Clovis East
Ruiz, Daniel	Madera, 4-3
Onsurez, Arik	Bakersfield

120
Gaytan, Daniel	Clovis, 11-3
Rodriguez, Brandon	Clovis West
Ontiveros, Matt	Central, 4-2
Marin, Oscar	Bakersfield
Contreras, Abel	Porterville, Default
Headrix, Delano	Mission Oak
Navarro, Jose	Madera, Fall, 4:36
Jimenez, Alejandro	Buchanan

126
Knoblauch, Michael	Clovis West, 10-9
Hernandez, Vicente	Clovis
Hansen, Kyler	Buchanan, 4-2
Saavedra, William	Foothill
Ozuna, Izaiah	Frontier, 14-4
Martin, Bryce	Bakersfield
Deorian, Nick	Buchanan, Fall, 3:46, *35-9
Johnstone, Reily	Mission Oak

132
Gay, Matt	Clovis, 11-5
Sandoval, Martin	Porterville
Cruz, Micah	Bakersfield, Default
Phaysamone, Patrick	Clovis East
Zimmer, Tyler	Clovis West, 16-2
Rodriguez, Christian	Reedley
Francis, Conner	Buchanan, 7-0
Holmes, Matthew	Sanger

138
Demison, Natrelle	Bakersfield, 9-1
Cardenas, Racelis	Buchanan
Ladd, Jason	Clovis, 4-3
Hernandez, Josue	Madera South
Garcia, Chris	Clovis West, Default
Rocha, Dillon	Lemoore
Lopez, Daniel	R F Kennedy, 22-9
Sanchez, Rosario	Sanger

145
Ramirez, Maxx	Bakersfield, 12-7
Osunde, Osamuyimen	Lemoore
Hartsfield, Tyler	Liberty, 6-2
Toro, James	West
Perez, Jorge	Edison, 9-1
Corona, Oscar	Foothill
Kincaid, Dominic	Clovis, 12-6
Fiddler, Chase	Centennial

152
Martinez, Isaiah	Lemoore, 12-5
Perreault, Kyle	Clovis East
Hammond, Coleman	Bakersfield, Default
Thompson, Colby	Clovis
Medley, Jason	Mission Oak, 2-1
Ruiz, Miguel	Madera
Trejo, Miguel	West, Fall, 3:22
Elisarraraz, Jorge	Sanger

160
Salas, Adrian	Clovis, 5-0
Fierro, A. J.	Bakersfield
Sulkowsky, Sebastian	Hoover, 3-2
Yilan, Charles	Madera South
Shepherd, Kyle	Frontier, Default
Martinez, Jaime	Lemoore
Zechin, Jason	Mt. Whitney, Decision?
Jepsen, David	Central

170
Nevills, Zach	Clovis, 6-3
Nacita, Silas	Bakersfield
Ashijian, Caz	Bullard, 10-0
Valladores, Juan	Madera South
Holmes, Ryan	Stockdale, 8-6
Bailey, Josh	Frontier
Robinson, Gregory	Edison, Major, 11-2
Robles, Angel	Lemoore

182
Reyes, Nikko	Clovis West, 2-1
Davies, Ryan	Clovis
Brandt, Richie	Bullard, Fall, 4:53
Pedraza, Jacob	Hanford, West
Daise, DeAndre	Lemoore, Default

YOSEMITE DIVISIONAL - Lemoore
February 17-18, 2012

Pope, Kyle	Bakersfield	13	Bullard	76
Gutierrez, Gerardo	Madera, 4-1,	15	Clovis East	74.5
Ribiero, Brooks	Mission Oak	16	Centennial	60
		17	Mission Oak	58.5

195

Gordan, Dakota	Clovis, Fall, 4:53
Murphy, Jack	Frontier
Lopez, Nate	Lemoore, 2-0
Pedraza, Lenny	Madera
Pyzer, Jordan	Clovis North, 8-3
Placido, Luis	Madera South
Willis, Cameron	Liberty, Fall, 3:43
Rocha, Raul	Fresno

18	Clovis North	56
19	Monache	49.5
20	Mt. Whitney	49
21	El Diamante	48
22	Liberty	46
23	West Bakersfield	45.5
24	Hoover	45
25	Redwood	43.5
26	Stockdale	40
27	Hanford West	38
28	Reedley	37
28	Fresno	37
28	Golden West	37
31	Ridgeview	33
32	North Bakersfield	28
33	Highland	25
34	South	24
35	Independence	23
36	Tulare Western	18.5
37	Golden Valley	18
38	R F Kennedy	16.5
39	Granite Hills	15
40	East Bakersfield	14
41	Mira Monte	10
42	Roosevelt	8

220

Morales, Cortes	Clovis West, 5-2
Salinas, Arnold	Fresno
Mendoza, Eric	Fall, 5:20
Carrillo, Otillo	Edison
Weiss, Matt	Clovis, Fall, 2:58
Olgin, Jordan	Foothill
Sanchez, Andrew	Golden West, 4-3
Santos-Valles, Joseph	Hoover

285

Nevills, Nick	Clovis, 6-4
Amaya, Rudy	Foothill
Popek, John	Frontier, 4-2
Crawford, Carson	Centennial
Juarez, Narciso	Sanger, Fall, 1:50
Roa, Johnathan	Lemoore, 4-1
Mahmood, Mustaff	Clovis West

*Season, Record

Most Outstanding Wrestlers

Lower Weight: Michael Knoblauch Clovis West
Upper Weight: Zach Nevills   Clovis

TEAM SCORES

1	Clovis	362
2	Bakersfield	237.5
3	Clovis West	177.5
4	Lemoore	176.5
5	Madera	153.5
6	Buchanan	136.5
7	Frontier	114
8	Madera South	111.5
9	Porterville	110.5
10	Foothill	112
11	Edison	83.5
12	Central	81.5
13	Sanger	76

Jordan Olgin- Foothill High School (02/11/2011)
Photographer: Casey Christie

YOSEMITE DIVISIONAL – Madera, South
February 15-16, 2013

106
Camposano, Adrian	Central, 10-6
Gambel, Matt	Monache
Lloren, Durbin	Buchanan 2-1
Gaytan, Julian	Clovis
Cisneros, Joey	Redwood, 5-3
Jimenez, Javier	Porterville
Campbell, David	Lemoore, Fall, 2:22
Herrera, Carlos	Bakersfield, 10-4
Perez, Fern	Foothill

113
Williams, Sean	Lemoore, 11-3
Jauregui, Joseph	Clovis East
Olivas, Khristian	Clovis, 6-1
Gaxiola, Greg	Buchanan
Velasquez, Marco	Foothill, 7-3
Orosco, Alex	Edison
Rosas, A. J.	Reedley, 10-2
Torres, Isaiah	Redwood
Nickell, Sean	Bakersfield

120
Pengilly, Mason	Porterville, 3-1
Gaytan, Jonas	Clovis
Ruiz, Daniel	Madera, 4-2
Delacruz, Jason	Buchanan
Marquez, Nick	Foothill, 6-0
Onsurez, Arik	Bakersfield
Armijo, Etienne	Centennial, Default
Wright, Shaquwan	Fresno
Hood, Seth	Monache

126
Knoblauch, Michael	Clovis West, 8-7
Gomez, Vincent	Frontier
Sibayan, Josh	Monache, 4-2
Esquibel, Dean	Buchanan
Barnes, Lane	Clovis, 13-9
Bracamonte, Adam	East
Jimenez, Elijah	Clovis North, 7-6
Munoz, Antony	Madera
Jackson, Jacqueall	Edison

132
Hansen, Kyler	Buchanan, 8-3
Contreras, Abel	Porterville
Ozuna, Izaiah	Frontier, Fall, 1:28
Holmes, Matt	Lemoore
Velarde, Xesus	Clovis, Default
Gutierrez, Antonio	Bakersfield
Lane, Chris	Clovis West, Fall, 2:22
Trieberg, Alex	Centennial
Valenzuela, James	Madera

138
Sandoval, Martin	Porterville, 11-6
Garcia, Chris	Clovis West
Rodriguez, Christian	Reedley, 10-1
Romero, Abner	Buchanan
Lopez, Dominic	Lemoore, 12-10
Sanchez, Rosario	Sanger
Ontiveros, Matt	Central, 14-3
Trace, Caeleb	Clovis
Santore, Johnny	Liberty

145
Zimmer, Tyler	Clovis West, 2-1, 2OT
Ladd, Jason	Clovis
Fierro, A, J.	Bakersfield, 7-2
Perez, Jorge	Edison
Francis, Conner	Buchanan, 6-5OT
Arroyo, Isidro	Reedley
Gomez, Aaron	Frontier, 8-4
Garcia, Isaac	Madera
Bonilla, Victor	Hanford

152
Perreault, Kyle	Clovis East, Fall, :39
Hammond, Coleman	Bakersfield
Pagela, Gregory	Porterville, Fall, 5:49
Thompson, Teddy	Buchanan
Kincaid, Dominic	Clovis, 3-0
Ruiz, Miguel	Madera
Robles, Angel	Lemoore, Default
Moran, Chris	Sanger
Corona, Oscar	Foothill

160
Martinez, Isaiah	Lemoore, TF22-7
Hodges, Hunter	Bakersfield
Robinson, Yusuf	Buchanan, 7-3
Brand, Brody	Clovis
Sheperd, Kyle	Frontier, Fall, 4:49
Padilla, Jose	Sanger
Jepson, David	Central, Fall, 5:07
Marple, Blake	Redwood
Mass, Jacob	Liberty

170
Martin, Bryce	Bakersfield, Fall, 2:49
Flores, Austin	Clovis North
Gamboa, Alex	Madera, 1-0
Callender, Nick	Clovis East
Stuckey, Kalvin	Bullard, Fall, 3:38
Holmes, Ryan	Stockdale
Reyes, Javier	Buchanan, Default
Martinez, Jaime	Lemoore
Solorio, Jess	Hanford

YOSEMITE DIVISIONAL – Madera, South
February 15-16, 2013

182
Salas, Adrian	Clovis, Default
Pope, Kyle	Bakersfield
Grout, Jackson	Buchanan, Default
Brandt, Richie	Bullard
Harroun, Dillon	Tehachapi, 7-6
Montejo, Carlos	Frontier
Taylor, Dejon	Clovis East
Avila, Michael	East
Webb, Landyn	Independence

195
Weiss, Matt	Clovis, 8-4
Bailey, Josh	Frontier
Kidd, Nick	Bakersfield, 6-2
Lopez, Jacob	Ridgeview
Young, Woo, An	Buchanan, Default
Karam, Josh	Clovis North
Heinsohn, Jacob	Liberty, Default
Galvan, Jaime	Mt. Whitney
Ku, Alex	Clovis West

220
Morales, Cortes	Clovis West, Fall, 3:18
Alcantar, Auggie	Frontier
Coronado, Hexton	Clovis, 10-2
Ponce, Marcus	Central
Valles, Joseph	Hoover, 6-2
Garza, Adrian	Lemoore
Mendoza, Peter	Madera South, 6-0
Mask, Kyle	Madera
An, Hyun, Woo	Buchanan

285
Nevills, Nick	Clovis, Fall, 1:52
Roa, Jonathan	Lemoore
Dill, Kai	Buchanan, 4-1OT
Garcia, Cristian	Reedley
Rosas, Gabriel	Ridgeview, Fall, 1:11
Marez, Jesus	Sanger
Garrett, Shaq	Bakersfield, 4-2OT
Guerrero, Mark	North
Harris, Dartanyan	South

Most Outstanding Wrestlers

Lower Weight: Michael Knoblauch Clovis West
Upper Weight: Kyle Perreault   Clovis East

TEAM SCORES
1	Clovis	297
2	Buchanan	269
3	Bakersfield	215
4	Lemoore	194
5	Clovis West	176
6	Frontier	166
7	Porterville	161
8	Clovis East	116.5
9	Madera	100
10	Central	92.5
11	Monache	89.5
12	Sanger	81
13	Reedley	76
14	Bullard	69
15	Clovis North	66
16	Edison	63
17	Madera South	54.5
18	Redwood	54
19	Hoover	51
19	Ridgeview	51
21	Stockdale	48
22	Foothill	46
23	South	43
24	Golden Valley	42
25	Liberty	41.5
26	East	40
27	North	36
28	Tehachapi	34.5
29	El Diamante	34
30	Centennial	33.5
31	Mission Oak	33
32	Hanford	31
33	Fresno	30
34	Mt. Whitney	25
35	Roosevelt	21
36	Sunnyside	13
37	Highland	12
37	Golden West	12
39	Delano	11.5
40	Independence	11
41	Mira Monte	10
41	Hanford West	10
43	West	7
44	McLane	6
44	Tulare Union	6
44	Tulare Western	6

YOSEMITE DIVISIONAL - East
February 21-22, 2014

106
Mejia, Justin	Clovis, Fall, 5:51
Cisneros, Joey	Redwood
Demison, Navonte	Bakersfield, Fall, 5:24
Marin, Chris	Clovis West
Campbell, David	Mission, Oak, 4-2
Alaniz, Javier	Clovis East
Arve, Ross	Buchanan, 7-6
Nelms, Andrew	Porterville
Demerath, Artur	Monache, TF15-0
Bracamonte, Matthew	East

113
Camposano, Adrian	Central, 6-3
Lloren, Durbin	Buchanan
Gamble, Matt	Monache, 5-4
Gilliland, Tristan	Clovis
Figueroa, JJ.	Bakersfield, 6-4
Rosas, A. J.	Reedley
Perez, Fern	Foothill, 4-2
Morita, Bryce	Clovis West
Deloza, Chris	Clovis North, 13-7
Pena, Sammy	Redwood

120
Gaytan, Julian	Clovis, 12-11
Delgado, Jacob	El Diamante
Herrera, Carlos	Bakersfield, Fall, 2:30
Jimenez, Alejandro	Buchanan
Quintos, Victor	Central, 14-6
Flores, Gilbert	Sanger
Weldon, Brock,	Frontier, 7-0
Torres, Isaiah	Redwood
Velasquez, Marco	Foothill, Fall, 4:42
Perez, Isaac	Porterville

126
Pengilly, Mason	Porterville, 11-4
Knoblauch, Michael	Clovis West
Ruiz, Daniel	Madera, 10-3
Olivas, Khristian	Clovis
Gaxiola, Greg	Buchanan, 10-6
Nickell, Sean	Bakersfield
Martin, Joef	Stockdale, 10-3
Hill, Jaylen	Lemoore
Rodriguez, Michael	Hoover, 15-13
Tejada, Alex	Tulare Union

132
Ontiveros, Matthew	Central, 4-2
Hokit, Isaiah	Clovis
Enriquez, Jaden	Mission Oak, 10-0
Hansen, Kyler	Buchanan
Harris, Darrin	Redwood, 14-1
Onsurez, Arik	Bakersfield
Miguel, Bobby	Clovis West, 11-9
Allen, Fletcher	Tehachapi
Garcia, Jonathan	Frontier, Fall, 3:10
Baker, Mark	North

138
Lane, Chris	Clovis West, Fall, 5:57
Contreras, Abel	Porterville
Esquibel, Dean	Buchanan, 4-3
Barnes, Lane	Clovis
Soto, Justin	Sanger, 7-1
Cerda, Brian	Sunnyside
Annis, Josh	Bakersfield, Default
Jauregul, Joseph	Clovis East
Santoro-Tovar, Johnny	Liberty, Fall, 1:04
Treiberg, Alex	Centennial

145
Garcia, Chris	Clovis West, Fall, 1:11
Francis, Conner	Buchanan
Hill, Jared,	Clovis, 12-5
Sanchez, Rosario	Sanger
Gutierrez, Antonio	Bakersfield, Default,
Demaree, Aston	El Diamante
Lopez, Conrado	Hoover, Default
Guerrero, Ronnie	Ridgeview
McGuire, Brenden	Clovis North, 2-0
Lemus, Ruben	East

152
Zimmer, Tyler	Clovis West, 3-2
Kincaid, Dominic	Clovis
Romero, Abner	Buchanan, Fall, 4:45
Alvarado, Danny	Mission Oak
Ruiz, Gabe	Monache, Default
Pagela, Greg	Porterville, *32-11
Lee, Andrew	Centennial, Fall, 1:03
Quintana, James	Clovis East
Chocoteco, Juan	Foothill, Fall, :59
Ibarra, Anthony	Sanger

160
Hokit, Josh	Clovis, Fall, 1:11
Callender, Nick	Clovis East
Leypon, Bryan	Monache, Fall, :54
White, Levi	Centennial
Mass, Jake	Liberty, 3-2
Loera, Sam	Bakersfield
Fuentes, Julio	Golden Valley, 13-1
Duran, Thomas	Tehachapi
Booth, Reese	Hanford, Fall, 5:19
Belshay, Cade	Buchanan

YOSEMITE DIVISIONAL - East
February 21-22, 2014

170
Martin, Bryce — Bakersfield, 8-6
Flores, Austin — Clovis North
Brand, Brody — Clovis, 8-2
Moran, Chris — Sanger
Padilla, Enriquez — El Diamante, 9-7
Ames, Josh — Porterville
Chavez, Nathan — Madera South, 13-9
Macias, Marcus — Central
Marple, Blake — Redwood, 9-5
Mass, Jeremy — Liberty

182
Gamboa, Alex — Madera, 4-3
Nevills, A. J. — Clovis
Woo, An, Young — Buchanan, 4-3
Montejo, Carlos — Frontier
Alvarado, Robert — Mission Oak, 6-0
Moreno, Erick — Sunnyside
Rosales, Elias — Bakersfield, 5-3
Perez, Jose — Roosevelt
Taylor, Dejon — Clovis East, Fall, 1:24
Ramirez, Fabian — Central

195
Weiss, Alex — Madera, 4-3
Lopez, Jacob — Ridgeview
Bailey, Josh — Frontier, 2-2
Bohanon, Lawrence — Sunnyside
Parker, Justin — Clovis East, 4-2
Dill, Kai — Buchanan
Valladares, Jacob — Madera South, 3-1
Ku, Alex — Clovis West
Lucas, Jacob — North, 17-16
Lowe, Brett — Lemoore

220
Morales, Cortes — Clovis West, 5-2
Prentice, Adam — Clovis
Sanchez, Cornelio — Sanger, Fall, 2:47
Yarbrough, Travis — Bakersfield
Levatino, Zak — Buchanan, 4-2
Mask, Kyle — Madera
Gonzalez, Joseph — Foothill, Fall, 2:48
Madrigal, Eduardo — Porterville
Magee, Alton — Sunnyside, 9-3
Halajian, John — Clovis North

285
Nevills, Nick — Clovis, Fall, 1:52
Villanueva, Miguel — Madera South
Vance, Kevin — Edison, Fall, :33
Madrigal, Edgar — Porterville
Moreno, Alen — Sunnyside, 5-4

Powell, Roy — Madera
Guerrero, Mark — North, Fall, 3:24
Delgado, Cesar — Golden Valley
Epiritu, Ivan — Reedley, Fall, 1:34
Bueno, Chris — East

* Season, record

Justin Mejia – Clovis High School

YOSEMITE DIVISIONAL - East
February 21-22, 2014

Most Outstanding Wrestlers

Lower Weight: Mason Pengilly Porterville
Upper Weight: Nick Nevills Clovis

TEAM SCORES

1	Clovis	370.5
2	Buchanan	226.5
3	Clovis West	212.5
4	Bakersfield	198.5
5	Porterville	154
6	Sanger	138
7	Central	129
8	Madera	114.5
9	Mission Oak	112
10	Madera South	95
11	Frontier	92.5
12	Clovis East	88.5
13	Monache	86
14	Redwood	80
15	Sunnyside	77
16	El Diamante	64
17	Clovis North	62.5
18	Foothill	58.5
19	North	57
20	Liberty	53
21	Ridgeview	50
22	Centennial	49
23	Lemoore	48
24	South	42
25	Edison	35
25	Golden Valley	35
27	Hanford	33
27	Hoover	33
29	Reedley	31
30	Mt. Whitney	29.5
31	East	26
32	Stockdale	24.5
33	Fresno	24
33	Golden Valley	24
33	Tehachapi	24
36	Tulare Union	18.5
37	West	17
38	Delano	15
38	Roosevelt	15
40	Bullard	12
41	Highland	11
42	Mira Monte	7
43	McLane	3
43	Tulare Western	3
45	Hanford West	0

MASON PENGILLY PORTERVILLE

Isaiah Hokit – Clovis High School

YOSEMITE DIVISIONAL - Lemoore
February 20-21, 2015

108
Leake, Ethan	Buchanan, 8-4
Olejnik, Izzak	Bakersfield
Morita, Bryce	Clovis West, 4-1
Pacheco, Anthony	Sanger
Cornelison, Wyatt	Clovis, Fall, 1:30
Zertuche, Julian	Madera South
Sanchez, Mateo	Central, 3-2
Sarabia, Pedro	Frontier
Moreno, Mario	Madera, 6-0
Bernal, Estevan	Tulare Union

115
Mejia, Justin	Clovis, 3-1
Campbell, David	Mission Oak
Alaniz, Javier	Clovis, 5-3
Gaxiola, Chris	Buchanan
Nelms, Andrew	Porterville, Major, 9-1
Chavez, Anthony	Central
Zavala, Hector	Lemoore, 7-1
Arenas, Anthony	Bakersfield
Reyes, Ronnie	Hanford, Fall, 2:48
Cruz, Jose	Ridgeview

122
Lloren, Durben	Buchanan, 3-1
Demison, Navonte	Bakersfield
Deloza, Chris	Clovis North, Default
Delgado, Jacob	El Diamante
Gonzalez, Ruben	Sanger, 9-5
Delacruz, Lorenzo	Redwood
Gilliland, Tristan	Clovis, 7-5
Walls, Isaiah	Clovis West
Acala, Justin, Chris	Frontier, Fall, 1:43
Lopez, Chris	Golden West

128
Figeroa, J. J.	Bakersfield, 3-1
Ozuna, Elijah	Frontier
Perez, Fern	Foothill, 9-7
Romero, Joel	Buchanan
Martinez, Dylan	Clovis, 6-3
Rodriguez, Michael	Hoover
Perez, Isaac	Porterville, Fall, 5:53
Villarreal, Brett	Redwood
Flores, Gilbert	Sanger, Fall, 3:03
Butler, William	West

134
Enriquez, Jaden	Mission Oak, 2-1OT
Mora, Aaron	Clovis West
Martino, Brandon	Clovis, 6-5
Gaxiola, Greg	Buchanan
Herrera, Carlos	Bakersfield, 12-5
Torres, Isaiah	Redwood
Armijo, Etienne	Centennial, 16-8
Guzman, Greg	Lemoore
Cerda, Brian	Sunnyside, 6-2
Zeeshan, Raul	Clovis North

140
Olivas, Khristan	Clovis, MD 17-4
Esquilbel, Dean	Buchanan
Garcia, Johnathan	Frontier, 15-9
Perez, Bailey	Reedley
Miguel, Bobby	Clovis West, 13-10
Gutierrez, Bailey	Hoover
Rodriguez, Mark	Bakersfield, 6-1
Watts, Aaron	Redwood
Saucedo, Abraham	Delano, 8-1
Zargoza, Ryan	Madera South

147
Hill, Jared	Clovis, 5-3OT
Francis, Conner	Buchanan
Lopez, Conrado	Hoover, 10-7
Sanchez, Rosario	Sanger
Annis, Josh	Bakersfield, Fall, 4:38
Morphis, Calloway	Frontier
Hooten, Tyson	Monache, 10-4
Quintana, James	Clovis East
Carranza, Alexis	Porterville, 5-3
McMillon, Joshua	Madera

154
Romero, Abner	Buchanan, 3-1
Hokit, Isaiah	Clovis
Jauregui, Joseph	Clovis East, Major 8-0
Gonzales, Ricky	Bakersfield
Zendejas, Adrian	Porterville, Fall, 1:13
Duran, Thomas	Tehachapi
Mattson, Jacob	North, 1-0
Miracle, Dylan	Madera South
Stanley, Jordan	Central, 10-8OT
Mendendez, Nico	Highland

162
Kincaid, Dominic	Clovis, 7-2
Lorea, Sam	Bakersfield
Montalvo, Anthony	Buchanan, Fall, 1:20
Medley, Anthony	Mission Oak
Chocoteco, Juan	Foothill, Major, 10-2
Jones, Phelan	South
Solis, Angel	Lemoore, 5-0
Ocotlan, Josue	Sunnyside
Garcia, Augustine	Madera South, 5-4
Romero, Marin	Madera

YOSEMITE DIVISIONAL - Lemoore
February 20-21, 2015

172
Hokit, Josh — Clovis, 3-2
Belshay, Cade — Buchanan
Gutierrez, Antonio — Bakersfield, 5-2
Hunter, Johnathan — Golden Valley
Godinez, Adrian — Foothill, 15-9
Macias, Marcus — Central
Maiden, Nic — Stockdale, 3-2
Padilla, Enriquez — El Diamante
Binger, Andrew — North, 6-5
Mass, Jeremy — Liberty

184
Nevills, A. J. — Clovis, Fall, :41
Moreno, Erik — Sunnyside
Fuentes, Julio — Golden Valley, Fall, 3:54
Trever, Ervin — Buchanan
Osunde, Osaze — Lemoore, 7-6
Rodriguez, Noah — Bakersfield
Chavez, Nathan — Madera South, 3-2
Morris, Grant — Mt. Whitney
Washington, Marcus — Clovis East, 5-3
Ramirez, Fabian — Central

197
Flores, Austin — Clovis North, 5-3
Prentice, Adam — Clovis
Gamboa, Alec — Madera, 10-3
Woo, An, Young — Buchanan
Rosales, Elias — Bakersfield, 6-3
Stutte, Matt — Fresno
Saavedra, Eric — Highland, 4-0
Rodriguez, Rene — Sunnyside
Torres, Montana — South, Fall, 4:57
Negrete, Christian — Tulare Union

222
Nevills, Seth — Clovis, 10-4
Lopez, Jacob — Ridgeview
Brandt, Bevan — Bullard, 6-2
Dill, Kai — Buchanan
Halajiah, John — Clovis North, 7-3
Mariscal, Angel — Delano
Bocanegra, Demarco — Highland, Forfeit
Parks, Hunter — Hanford, Disqualified
Parker, Justin — Clovis East, 3-2
Maniss, Drew — Porterville

287
Levatino, Zakary — Buchanan, 5-2OT
Coronado, Hexton — Clovis
Snyder, Jarrod — Frontier, Fall, 3:00
Moreno, Alan — Sunnyside
Varela, Gilbert — Independence, Fall, 3:56
Barcenas, Armando — Hanford
Holloway, Nathaniel — Clovis North, Default
Quintanilla, Nimrod — Golden, Valley
Villanueva, Miguel — Madera South, Fall, 1:07
Delgado, Cesar — Golden West

Most Outstanding Wrestlers

Lower Weight: Khristian Olivas Clovis
Upper Weight: Zakary Levatino Buchanan

Seth Nevills - Clovis High School

YOSEMITE DIVISIONAL - Lemoore
February 20-21, 2015

TEAM SCORES

1	Clovis	366.5
2	Buchanan	334
3	Bakersfield	241.5
4	Clovis North	113
5	Frontier	103
6	Clovis West	99
7	Mission Oak	95
8	Foothill	93
9	Porterville	92.5
10	Sanger	90.5
11	Madera	90
12	Golden Valley	89.5
13	Madera South	87.5
14	Sunnyside	84
15	Central	76
16	Clovis East	69
17	Lemoore	65
18	Hoover	63.5
19	Redwood	58.5
20	El Diamante	54
21	Ridgeview	53.5
22	South	53
23	Mt Whitney	49
24	Highland	48
25	Monache	46.5
26	Bullard	40.5
26	North	40.5
28	Delano	39
29	Golden West	35
29	Hanford	35
31	Liberty	30.5
32	Reedley	26
33	Independence	25
34	Tehachapi	24.5
35	Centennial	23.5
36	Tulare Union	22.5
37	Stockdale	20
38	West	19
39	East	18
40	Fresno	16
41	Edison	14.5
42	Roosevelt	12
43	McLane	7
44	Hanford West	6
44	Tulare Western	6
46	Mira Monte	3

YOSEMITE DIVISIONAL - Clovis
February 19-20, 2016

108
Olguin, Matthew	Buchanan, 4-0
Rivera, Eric	Clovis North
Betancourt, Brandon	Clovis, 4-2
Olejnik, Izzak	Bakersfield
Reyes, Cole	Frontier, 10-4
Sanchez, Matt	Central
Terrence, Thomas	Clovis East, 12-2
Moreno, Mario	Madera
Jimenez, Ruben	Foothill, 9-4
Viramonte, Jared	Tulare Union

115
Alaniz, Javier	Clovis West, Fall, 5:43
Leake, Ethan	Buchanan
Cornelison, Wyatt	Clovis, Medical Forfeit
Pacheco, Anthony	Sanger
Beckett, Rocky	Clovis North, 5-3
Morphis, Ryan	Frontier
Tristan, Jayson	Clovis East, Fall, 4:52
Callison, Jared	Monache
Bustos, Paul	Madera, 2-0
Castillo, Ramiro	Central

122
Mejia, Justin	Clovis, 14-4
Abas, Jaden	Frontier
Chavez, Anthony	Central, 5-2
Diaz, Matt, Clovis	North
Gonzalez, Ruben	Sanger, 3-0
Gaxiola, Chris	Buchanan
Bracamonte, Matt	Foothill, Fall, 1:08
Estrada, Keithan	East Bakersfield
Bernal, Estevan	Tulare Union, 8-2
Heasley, Ukiah	Mission Oak

128
Joint, Gary	Lemoore Fall, 5:00
Deloza, Chris	Clovis North
Villarreal, Brett	Buchanan, 3-1
Walls, Isaiah	Clovis West
Corona, Peter	Independence Medical Forfeit
Campbell, David	Mission Oak
Rhoads, Brandon	Clovis, 10-6
Deltoro, Abraham	Madera
Patoc, Jordan	Liberty, 5-4
Gonzalez, Adrian	Bakersfield

134
Lloren, Durban	Buchanan, Fall, 1:44
Watts, Aaron	Redwood
Geiger, Jordan	Clovis, 14-2
Peturcelli, Niko	Clovis North
Contreras, Moses	Madera, 9-2
Ball, Tavian	Central
Perez, Issac	Porterville, Fall, 1:58
Espinoza, Issac	Madera, South
Neal, Elijah	McLane, Medical, Forfeit
De La Cruz, Christian	Delano

140
Demison, Navonte	Bakersfield, 3-1
Romero, Joel	Buchanan
Miguel, Bobby	Clovis West, Fall, 3:38
Rojas, Santana	Liberty
Martinez, Dylan	Clovis, Medical Forfeit
Enriquez, Jaden	Mission Oak
Corona, Estaban	Independence, Fall, 2:49
Alvarado, Nathan	Clovis North, 9-4, SV, OT
Beltran, Julian	Bullard

147
Gaxiola, Greg	Buchanan, 9-2
Torres, Isaiah	Redwood
Ladd, Jake	Clovis, 8-5
Bradley, Beau	Monache
Cravens, Dillion	Bakersfield, Fall, 1:55
Garcia, Augustine	Madera South
Espana, Issak	Clovis West, 9-7
Huskey, Skyler	El Diamante
Surez, Ralphy	Foothill, 11-6
Urias, Albert	Ridgeview

154
Martino, Brandon	Clovis, 3-1
Lane, Chris	Clovis West
Quintana, James	Clovis East, Fall, 3:18
Garcia, Jonathan	Frontier
Gonzalez, Ricky	Bakersfield, 6-2
Levatino, Jake	Buchanan
Cardinell, Mark	Monache, 9-4
Zendejas, Adrian	Porterville
McMillon, Josh	Madera, Fall, 3:17
Vasquez, Isaac	Sunnyside

162
Ramero, Abner	Buchanan, Major, 14-3
Loera, Sam	Bakersfield
Hunter, Jonathan	Golden Valley, Fall, 2:44
Vargas, Victor	Clovis
Miracle, Dylan	Madera, 5-4
Corona, Isaiah	Hanford

YOSEMITE DIVISIONAL - Clovis
February 19-20, 2016

Stanley, Jordan — Central, 8-4
Sandaval, Joey — Porterville
Manzo, Armando — Liberty, 5-0
Sherwood, Riley — Clovis North

172
Belshay, Cade — Buchanan, Major, 10-0
Reyes, Ryan — Clovis West
Wyneken, Ruger — Clovis, 6-5
Maiden, Nic — Stockdale
Macias, Marcus — Central, Medical Forfeit
Moreno, Eric — Sunnyside
Chapa, Chris — Madera, Medical Forfeit
Gutierrez, Antonio — Bakersfield
Deboer, Willem — Frontier, 15-0, Tech, Fall, 5:29
Gonsalves, Jacob — Lemoore

184
Hokit, Josh — Clovis, Major, 12-4
Montalvo, Anthony — Buchanan
Solis, Angel — Lemoore, 6-4
Rodriguez, Noah — Bakersfield
Mass, Jeremy — Liberty, Fall, 2:57
Halajian, Mark — Clovis North
Kelley, Jeffrey — Redwood, Fall, 5:00
Chavez, Nathan — Madera South
Sandhu, Jasman — Bullard, Major, 12-4
Castillo, Juan — South

197
Nevills, A.J. — Clovis, 5-1
Ervin, Trevor — Bullard
Godinez, Adrian — Foothill, Major, 10-1
Rosales, Elias — Bakersfield
Ramirez, Fabian — Central, 6-4
Halajian, John — Clovis North
Lopez, Andy — Liberty, Fall, 4:51
Slatic, Tommy — Bullard
Bautista, Amador — Redwood, Major, 12-2
Torres, Andrew — Frontier

222
Levatino, Zakary — Buchanan, 5-2
Collier, Tyler — Clovis
Brant, Beven — Bullard, 8-3
Holloway, Nathaniel — Clovis North
Mariscal, Angel — Delano, Fall, 2:32
Torres, Montana — South
Parks, Hunter — Hanford, Fall, 3:11
Villanueva, Miguel — Madera South
Abbott, Brian — Stockdale, 4-3
Barrientos, A.J. — Bakersfield

287
Nevills, Seth — Clovis, Fall, 3:23
Snyder, Jarrod — Frontier
Varela, Gilbert — Independence, 5-2
Barcenas, Armando — Hanford
Garcia, Ricky — Reedley, Fall, 3:29
Jaramillo, Ricardo — Golden Valley
Organista, Victor — South, Fall, 5:13
Gardner, Gunner — Clovis North
Valenzuela, Robert — Madera South, Fall, 2:49
Ortiz, Isaiah — Buchanan

Most Outstanding Wrestlers

Lower Weight: Gary Joint — Lemoore
Upper Weight: Seth Nevills — Clovis

TEAM SCORES

1	Buchanan	357.5
2	Clovis	342
3	Clovis North	192.5
4	Bakersfield	180.5
5	Frontier	154
6	Clovis West	141.5
7	Madera	113
8	Central	112.5
9	Redwood	105
10	Madera South	91
11	Liberty	87.5
12	Lemoore	84.5
13	Foothill	82
14	Bullard	79.5
15	Independence	78
16	Clovis East	73
17	Golden Valley	67.5
18	Hanford	66
19	Porterville	57
19	South	57
21	El Diamante	54
22	Sunnyside	51
23	Sanger	49.5
24	Delano	47
24	Mt. Whitney	47
26	Monache	40.5
27	Mission Oak	39.5
28	Reedley	37
29	Centennial	35
29	Stockdale	35
31	East	27
31	Hoover	27

YOSEMITE DIVISIONAL - Clovis
February 19-20, 2016

31 Ridgeview	27
34 North	26
34 Highland	26
36 Tulare Union	24
37 McLane	16.5
38 Edison	16
38 Hanford West	16
40 Tulare Western	15
41 West	12
42 Fresno	11
43 Tehachapi	8
44 Golden West	4
44 Roosevelt	4
46 Mira Monte	3

YOSEMITE DIVISIONAL - East
February 17-18, 2017

106
Petrucelli, Giano	Clovis, 5-4
Reyes, Cole	Frontier
Castillo, Ramero	Central, 6-1
Poor, Josh	Buchanan
Benevidez, Brian	Porterville, 7-2
Bermudez, Manuel	Mission Oak
Reyes, Gabriel	Hanford, 10-6
Jimenez, Ruben	Foothill, *24-14
Terrence, Thomas	Clovis East, 8-6
Maldanado, Laz	Clovis West
Rojas, Jayven	Golden Valley

113
Olguin, Mathew	Buchanan, 3-1
Murphy, Devin	Clovis North
Paulson, Brandon	Clovis, 11-2
Sanchez, Mateo	Central
Pacheco, Anthony	Sanger, 5-4,
Moreno, Mario	Madera
Navarro, Elijah	Bakersfield, Major, 16-2, *21-6
Salazar, Bobby	Golden Valley
Benevidez, Marco	Porterville, 10-4
Nava, Angel	Delano
Moreno, Sebastian	Madera South

120
Leake, Ethan	Buchanan, Major 10-0
Cornelison, Wyatt	Clovis
Rivera, Eric	Clovis North, Major, 12-4
Morphis, Ryan	Frontier, *38-16
Hutcherson, Marcus	West, 6-4, *41-8
Bloemhof, Andrew	Bakersfield
Ortega, Mikey	Bullard, 3-1
Heasley, Ukiah	Mission Oak
Callison, Jared	Monache, Major, 11-1
Bustos, Paul	Madera
Ramirez, Pedro	Clovis

126
Mejia, Justin	Clovis, 10-4
Deen, Tyler	Buchanan
Sihavong, Dawson	Bullard, 6-2
Beckett, Rocky	Clovis North
Chavez, Anthony	Central, 6-2
Olenik, Izzak	Bakersfield, *27-13
Fletcher, Garrett	Frontier, Major, 9-0, *34-16
Lopez, Jesse	Golden West
Cannavino, Angelo	Hanford, 8-4
Rios, Isaiah	Monache
Rodriguez, Johnathon	Clovis

132
Deloza, Chris	Clovis, 9-7
Joint, Gary	Lemoore
Ozuna, Elijah	Frontier, 9-3
Peverill, Wyatt	Buchanan,
Reyes, Ronnie	Hanford, 7-1
Espana, Isack	Clovis
Gonzalez, Adrian	Bakersfield, Major, 8-0, *27-16
Soto, Sal	Reedley
Del, Torro, Abraham	Madera, Fall, 3:09
Rhodes, Brandon	Clovis
Hernandez, Florencio	Madera South

138
Villarreal, Brett	Buchanan, 6-4, OT
Enriquez, Jaden	Mission Oak
Figueroa, J, J	Bakersfield, 4-3
Contreras, Moses	Madera
Hernandez, Marco	Frontier, Default, *23-16
Romero, Joe	Lemoore
Walls, Isaiah	Clovis, Default
Kuntz, Emmett	Highland
Neal, Eligah	McLane, 8-7
Petrucelli, Niko	Clovis North
Garcia, Juan	Madera South

145
Demison, Navonte	Bakersfield TF, 17-1
Bradley, Beau	Monache
Zamilpa, Tristan	Buchanan, 5-3
Guzman, Greg	Lemoore
Chiaramonte, Mikelli	Clovis, Fall, 1:59
Tracy, Trent	Frontier, *33-16
Cardoso, Jose	Hanford, 11-10
Beltran, Julian	Bullard
Alvarado, Nathan	Madera, 3-2
Aranda, Ray	Clovis West
Cuttone, Vito	Clovis North

152
Garcia, Jonathan	Frontier, 3-0
Cravens, Dillion	Bakersfield, *36-10
Gianakopulos, Tyler	Clovis, 4-2
Gaxiola, Chris	Buchanan
McMillian, Joshua	Madera, 10-3
Garcia, Augustine	Madera South
Urias, Albert	Ridgeview, 3-2
De, La, Rosa, R, J	Foothill
Badilla, Daniel	Reedley, 9-7
Chairez, Jacob	West
Rodriguez, Felipe	Clovis West

YOSEMITE DIVISIONAL - East
February 17-18, 2017

160
Martino, Brandon	Clovis, 3-1
Ramero, Joel	Buchanan
Gonzalez, Ricky	Bakersfield, 5-1, OT
Zendejas, Adrian	Porterville
Gonzalez, Jorge	Madera, Default
Cardwell, Mark	Monache
Aguirre, Max	Frontier, Major, 9-1, *24-16
Wirowek, Chance	Liberty
Weir, Matt	Centennial, 5-2
Adame, Ricardo	Madera South
Quintana, James	Clovis East

170
Vargas, Victor	Clovis, 11-4
Mass, Jeremy	Liberty, *39-7
Miracle, Dylan	Madera South, 2-1
Levantino, Jake	Buchanan
Corona, Isaiah	Hanford, 3-2, OT
Cantoriano, Chris	Clovis West
Sandoval, Joey	Porterville, Default
Ponce, Eric	Golden Valley, *20-12
Panduro, John	Lemoore, 3-2
Ortega, Anthony	Centennial
Potts, Devonte	Edison

182
Montalvo, Anthony	Buchanan, 5-0
Loera, Sam	Bakersfield
DeBoer, Willem	Frontier, 3-2
Good, Jacob	Clovis
Solis, Angel	Lemoore, Default
Maiden, Nic	Stockdale, *34-16
Lindsey, Trent	Clovis North, 11-6
Azusa, Andrew	Sanger
Contras, Jonathon	Madera South, 9-5
Morales, Meteo	Clovis West
Phillips, Brent	Hoover

195
Reyes, Ryan	Clovis West, 4-3
Ervin, Trevor	Buchanan
Wyneken, Ruger	Clovis, Major, 9-1
Halajian, Mark	Clovis North
Chavez, Nathan	Madera South, Default
Godinez, Adrian	Foothill, *34-8
Aparicio, Chris	Central, Fall, 1:39
Gonzalves, Jacob	Lemoore
Watson, Kwabena	Edison, Major, 9-1
Saltic, Tommy	Bullard
Slayton, Codi	Madera

220
Belshay, Cade	Buchanan, Fall, 3:34
Halajian, John	Clovis North
Parks, Hunter	Hanford, 3-1
Jaramillo, Joey	Clovis
Sandhu, Jasman	Bullard, 3-1
Lopez, Rigoberto	Tulare Western
Garcia, Ricardo	Highland, Fall, 3:14, *32-13
Valle, Antonio	Centennial
Graham, Dakota	North, 4-2, *32-13
Vasquez, Jake	Bakersfield
Reyes, Pedro	Reedley

285
Nevills, Seth	Clovis, Fall, 1:38
Barcenos, Amando	Hanford
Holloway, Nathaniel	Clovis North, 3-2
Wright, Noah	Lemoore
Ortiz, Isaih	Buchanan, Fall, 2:20
Saltic, Patrick	Bullard
Wendt, Brien	Tulare Union, 3-2
Chavez, Xzavier	Delano
Deleon, Cesar	Clovis West
Ramirez, Walter	Stockdale, *38-16
Scales-Edwards, Isaiah	Hoover

* Season, Record

Most Outstanding Wrestlers

Lower Weight: Chris De Loza — Clovis North
Upper Weight: Seth Nevills — Clovis

TEAM SCORES 2017

1	Buchanan	342.5
2	Clovis	309.5
3	Clovis North	209.5
4	Frontier	191
5	Bakersfield	179
6	Hanford	135.5
7	Madera	122
8	Clovis West	120.5
8	Lemoore	120.5
10	Madera South	101.5
11	Central	93.5
12	Bullard	84
13	Porterville	83
14	Monache	70
15	Mission Oak	61

YOSEMITE DIVISIONAL - East
February 17-18, 2017

16	Centennial	59.5
17	Golden Valley	59
18	Ridgeview	50
19	Liberty	48.5
20	Hoover	44
20	South	44
22	Foothill	42
22	Stockdale	42
24	North	41
25	Golden West	40
25	Sanger	40
27	Highland	39.5
28	Independence	36
29	Delano	34.5
30	Edison	33
31	El Diamante	31
31	Reedley	31
33	Clovis East	28
34	Sunnyside	27
35	East	26
35	Tulare Western	26
37	West	22.5
38	Tulare	21
39	Redwood	17.5
40	Mt. Whitney	11
41	Mira Monte	10
42	Hanford West	9
43	McLane	8.5
44	Roosevelt	4
45	Fresno	0
45	Tehachapi	0

L-R Rick McKinney and Justin Mejia - Clovis

YOSEMITE DIVISIONAL - Lemoore
February 16-17, 2018

108
Negrete, Carlos	Clovis North, 5-1
Castillo, Ramiro	Central
Leake, Hunter	Buchanan, 5-0
Maldanado, Laz	Clovis West
Bermudez, Nicholas	Mission Oak, 5-3
Mouritsen, Justen	Clovis
Martinez, Armondo	Golden, West, Fall, 3:15
Acala, Josh	Frontier
Eng, Jovonni	Clovis East, 5-3
Carrillo, Vincent	Independence, 7-5
Diaz, Nick	Mt. Whitney

115
Renteria, Maximo	Buchanan, 10-3
Petrucelli, Giano	Clovis
Moreno, Mario	Madera, Fall, 3:26
Ozuna, Noah	Frontier
Joint, Wayne	Lemoore
Nava, Angel	Delano
Chavez, Adrian	Central, Fall, 5:33
Bencomo, Taylor	Clovis North
Lopez, Kalob	North, 10-4
King, Jordan	Clovis West, Fall, 1:12
Soto, Sergio	Mission Oak

122
Murphy, Devin	Clovis North, 3-1
Reyes, Cole	Frontier
Paulson, Brandon	Clovis, 12-2
Poore, Josh	Buchanan
Lucio, Cade	Bakersfield, 7-2
Miranda, Jude	Hanford
Murphy, James	Central, 8-5
Gayton, Jesse	Lemoore
Rojas, Jayven	Golden Valley, Fall, 2:59
Sanchez, Gerado	Ridgeview
Romero, Pete	South

128
Franco, Ryan	Clovis North, 6-3
Leake, Ethan	Buchanan
Callison, Jared	Monache, Fall, 1:04
Granada, Emiliano	Clovis
Valdovinos, Raul	Clovis West, 9-6
Rosales, Angel	Bakersfield
Landin, Jose	Frontier, Fall, 5:30
Maldonado, Johnny	Liberty
Alejo, Mauro	Madera, Fall, 2:30
Rueda, Everardo	Golden Valley
Heasley, Ukiah	Mission Oak

134
Grier, Lajon	Clovis North, 10-5
Bloemhof, Andrew	Bakersfield
Chavez, Anthony	Central, 8-6
Deen, Tyler	Buchanan
Fletcher, Garrett	Frontier, 7-0
Leon, Dominic	Golden Valley
Martino, Nick	Clovis, Fall, 1:43
Rodriguez, Alex	Redwood
Flores, Jose	Monache, 5-3, OT
Caldwell, Tyler	El Diamante
Cooper, Jordan	Garces

140
Olguin, Matthew	Buchanan, 7-3
Dawson, Sihavong	Bullard
Marin, Valentin	Bakersfield, 11-10
Beckett, Rocky	Clovis North
Delacruz, Lorenzo	Redwood, Default
Romero, Joe	Lemoore
Morphis, Ryan	Frontier, 14-5
Hernandez, Florencio	Madera, South
Caballero, Andrew	Porterville, 15-10
Christopherson, J, J	Clovis East, 17-9
Zuniga, George	Central

147
Gaxiola, Chris	Buchanan, 3-1
Olejnik, Izzak	Bakersfield
Neal, Elijah	McLane, 3-2
Watts, Zach	Clovis North
Sekhon, Abheybir	Central, 9-5
Reyes, Ronnie	Hanford
Frantzich, Austin	Clovis, Major, 10-2
Aranda, Steven	Clovis West
Garcia, Juan	Madera, 12-1
Salcedo, Gabe	Mission Oak
Landin, Christian	Frontier

154
Bradley, Beau	Monache, 11-2
Zamilpa, Tristan	Buchanan
Anderson, Max	Clovis, 8-4
Gonzalez, Adrian	Bakersfield
Zavala, Nicholas	Mission Oak, 5-4
Adame, Ricardo	Madera, South
Cuttone, Vito	Clovis North, Fall, 1:44
Mayall, Julias	North
Carter, Andrew	Frontier, 5-0
Brazet, Lance	Bullard
Gaeath, Julian	Central

YOSEMITE DIVISIONAL - Lemoore
February 16-17, 2018

162
Romero, Joe	Buchanan, 16-1
Kloster, Will	Lemoore
Aguirre, Max	Frontier, 7-3
Priest, Jared	Bakersfield
Rodriguez, Felipe	Clovis West, 2-1, OT
Garcia, Augstine	Madera, South
Urias, Albert	Ridgeview, Major, 13-4
Sandoval, Joey	Porterville
Castro, Rigoberto	Redwood, 3-1
Ortega, Roman	Monache
Hokit, Scott	Clovis

172
Caldwell, Mark	Monache, 6-3
Tracy, Trent	Frontier
Miracle, Dylan	Madera, South, Fall, 2:41
Martin, Jadon	Buchanan
Gianakopulos, Tyler	Clovis, 5-2
Annis, Jordan	Bakersfield
Cantoriano, Chris	Clovis West, Fall, 3:06
Aguirre, Michael	Highland
Pantoja, Bryan	Garces, Fall, 1:21
Panduro, John	Lemoore
Ramirez, Jesse	Liberty

184
Montalvo, Anthony	Buchanan, 17-4
Vardanyan, David	Bullard
Lindsey, Trent	Clovis North, Default
Avila, Tyler	Porterville
Maiden, Nick	Stockdale, Default
Contreras, Jonathan	Madera, South
Sayles, Freddy	Clovis, Fall, 1:58
Lopez, Anthony	Bakersfield
Bordon, John	Ridgeview, 14-4
Pafford, Jack	Frontier
Alcala, Daniel	Redwood

197
Good, Jacob	Clovis, 11-2
Poore, Zach	Buchanan
Watson, Kwabena	Edison, 8-6
Bautista, Amador	Redwood
Aparicio, Chris	Central, Default
Reyes, Ryan	Clovis West
Cardenas, Javier	El Diamante, 10-8
Gonzalez, Jonathon	Liberty
Shepherd, Ty	Frontier, 5-1
Garcia, Jorge	Monache, 5-1
Dorado, Jacob	Bakersfield

222
Ervin, Trevor	Buchanan, Fall, 3:49, *41-6, 152-32
Darter, Justin	Bakersfield
Washington, Marcus	Central, 3-1
Martin, Isaiah	Garces
Valle, Antonio	Centennial, 6-2
Gonsalves, Jacob	Lemoore
Morales, Mateo	Clovis West, 6-2
Miranda, Rangel	Madera
Sanchez, Sabastian	El Diamante, Default
Slatic, Tommy	Bullard
Medina, Fernando	Golden Valley

287
Nevills, Seth	Clovis, Fall, 1:12
Abernathy, Kaleb	Centennial
Slatic, Patrick	Bullard, 8-0
Bryant, Grant	Frontier
Schmidtke, Jonah	Clovis East, 12-10, OT
Duchett, Naishaw	Buchanan, *35-16
Hill, Josiah	Bakersfield, 4-0
Brewer, Mateo	Lemoore
Scales-Edwards, Isaiah	Hoover, 3-1
Bonilla, Milton	South
Lee, Regan	Golden, West

* Season and Career Records

Most Outstanding Wrestlers

Lower Weight: Ryan Franco   Clovis North
Upper Weight: Mark Caldwell   Monache

TEAM SCORES
1	Buchanan	357
2	Clovis North	241.5
3	Clovis	235
4	Bakersfield	200.5
5	Frontier	193
6	Central	170
7	Monache	125.5
8	Clovis West	115
9	Bullard	111
10	Lemoore	103
11	Madera South	93.5
12	Redwood	85.5
13	Madera	79.5
14	Mission Oak	67.5
15	Centennial	65.5

YOSEMITE DIVISIONAL - Lemoore
February 16-17, 2018

15	Golden Valley	65.5
17	Porterville	58
18	Ridgeview	57
19	Clovis East	56
20	Highland	55
21	Edison	43
22	Hanford	40
22	Mt. Whitney	40
24	Foothill	36.5
25	El Diamante	36
26	Garces	34.5
27	Liberty	34
27	South	34
29	Golden West	31
29	North	31
31	Hoover	30
32	Sunnyside	29
33	Stockdale	28
34	McLane	26
35	Sanger	25.5
36	Tulare Western	22
37	Independence	17
38	Delano	14
39	Tulare Union	12
40	Fresno	11
41	Hanford West	10
41	Reedley	10
43	Mira Monte	9.5
44	Tehachapi	7
45	?	5.5
46	East	5
47	Roosevelt	4

Garrett Fletcher – Frontier High School

Izzak Olenik – Bakersfield High School

Garret Fletcher – Frontier High School

SIERRA-SEQUOIA DIVISION

2007-2018

SIERRA-SEQUOIA DIVISIONAL CHAMPIONSHIP TEAMS

Date	Champion	Coach	Location
2-19-1966	Arvin	John Buntin	Sequoia Divisional
			Corcoran Southern Divisional
1967 & 68			
2-21-1969	Tulare Western	Jerry Vinson	Small School Divisional: Selma
2-21-1970	Selma	Dick Ravalin	Sequoia Divisional: Sanger
2-20-1971	Washington Union	Bill Griffin	Sierra–Tollhouse
2-26-1972	Washington Union	Bill Griffin	College of Sequoia-Visalia
2-17-1973	Kingsburg	Sam Crandell	Arvin
2-16-1974	Washington Union	Russ Simpson	Sierra-Tollhouse
2-22-1975	Chowchilla	Eric Hansen	College of Sequoia-Visalia
2-21-1976	Washington Union	Russ Simpson	Wasco
2-19-1977	Kingsburg	Sam Crandell	Sierra-Tollhouse
2-18-1978	Washington Union	Howard Zink	Sierra-Tollhouse
2-17-1979	Shafter	Darrell Fletcher	Shafter
2-23-1980	Washington Union	Howard Zink	Sierra-Tollhouse
2-21-1981	Washington Union	Howard Zink	Central
2-20-1982	Kingsburg	Sam Crandell	Wasco
2-19-1983	Kingsburg	Sam Crandell	Firebaugh
2-18-1984	Selma	Nick Quintana	Central
2-16-1985	Washington Union	Howard Zink	Wasco
2-22-1986	Selma	Nick Quintana	Dos Palos
2-21-1987	Selma	Nick Quintana	Selma
2-20-1988	Selma	Nick Quintana	Central
2-18-1989	Selma	Nick Quintana	Central
2-17-1990*	Selma/Tranquility	Nick Quintana/Joe Gomez	Shafter

*The CIF ruled that Tranquility used two ineligible wrestlers, making Selma the champions

Date	Champion	Coach	Location
2-16-1991	Selma	Nick Quintana	Corcoran
2-22-1992	Selma	Nick Quintana	Dos Palos
2-20-1993	Dos Palos	Frank Lemos	Shafter
2-19-1994	Firebaugh	Bill Magnusson	Washington Union-Easton
2-18-1995	Exeter	John Conley	Dos Palos
2-17-1996	Firebaugh	Bill Magnusson	Shafter
2-22-1997	Kingsburg	Ramiro Pereschica	Dos Palos
2-21-1998	Dos Palos	Frank Lemos	Firebaugh
2-20-1999	Dos Palos	Frank Lemos	Arvin
2-19-2000	Dos Palos	Frank Lemos	Dos Palos
2-17-2001	Dos Palos	Frank Lemos	Shafter
2-22-2003	Shafter	Gary Pederson	Dos Palos
2-20,21-2004	Washington Union	Howard Zink	Farmersville
2-18,19-2005	Firebaugh	Bill Magnusson	Shafter
2-17,18-2006	Dos Palos	Frank Lemos	Firebaugh
2-16,17-2007	Selma	Naser Husein	Tehachapi
2-15,16-2008	Selma	Naser Husein	Farmerville
2-20,21-2009	Selma	Sam Lopez	Mendota
2-19,20-2010	Washington Union	Ryan Stockman	Shafter
2-18,19-2011	Selma	Sam Lopez	Dinuba
2-17,18-2012	Selma	Sam Lopez	Washington Union
2-15,16-2013	Selma	Sam Lopez	Shafter
2-21,22-2014	Dinuba	Michael Wright	Dinuba
2-20,21-2015	Selma	Sam Lopez	Liberty Madera
2-19,20-2016	Selma	Sam Lopez	Shafter
2-17,18-2017	Selma	Sam Lopez	Sierra Pacific-Hanford
2-15,16-2018	Selma	Sam Lopez	Sierra Pacific-Hanford

SIERRA-SEQUOIA DIVISIONAL
MOST OUTSTANDING WRESTLERS

Lower Weight		Upper Weight	
1996 Charlie Uribe	Washington Union	Clemente Moreno	Dinuba
1997 George Moreno	Firebaugh	Dan Jackson	Kingsburg
1998 Keil Crane	Dos Palos	Narcy Martinez	Wasco
1999 Jason Moreno	Firebaugh	Narcy Martinez	Wasco
2000 Jorge Evangelis	Parlier	Mike Van Worth	Dos Palos
2001 Jorge Evangelis	Parlier	Riley Young	Sierra
2002 Matt Maldonado	Shafter	Elvis Villegas	Mendota
2003 Matt Gonzales	Exeter	Jason Carrasco	Shafter
2004 Pedro Olea	Farmersville	Orlando Landios	Wasco
2005 Dan Weatherly	Exeter	Marvin Statler	Shafter
2006 Frank Castillo	Arvin	Lucas Espericueta	Shafter
2007 Gilbert Comacho	Washington Union	Joseph Ames	Shafter
2008 Robert Pino	Exeter	Josh Boger	Coalinga
2009 Nick Pena	Selma	Theodore Furnish	Kerman
2010 Adrian Pandura	Corcoran	Justin Lozano	Selma
2011 Alex Cisneros	Selma	Eric Marquez	McFarland
2012 Alex Cisneros	Selma	Sean Medley	Wasco
2013 Javier Gasca	Kingsburg	Sean Medley	Wasco
2014 Chris Cisneros	Selma	Michael Wright	Dinuba
2015 Isaiah Perez	Dinuba	Jose Alvarez	Selma
2016 Jacob Wright	Dinuba	Ramiro Macias	R F Kennedy
2017 Jacob Wright	Dinuba	Brett Schuler	Bakersfield Christian
2018 Richard Figueroa	Selma	Fabian Maldonado	Avenal

** Most Outstanding Wrestler Awards paid by the Coyote Club Membership

Jacob Wright - Dinuba High School

SIERRA – SEQUOIA DIVISIONAL - Tehachapi
February 16-17, 2007

103
Camacho, Gilbert — Washington Union, Fall, 2:58
Valles, A. J. — Selma
Martinez, Chris — Firebaugh, 12-9
Diaz, Edgar — Arvin
Gagnon, Jason — Exeter, Fall, 3:02
Bacasegue, Marcos — Mendota

112
Quintana, Diego — Selma, Fall, 1:48, *28-3
Gonzalez, Juan — Kerman, *25-1
Steinbach, Jared — Tehachapi, Fall, 2:57
Doi, Eugene — Kingsburg
Rico, David — Washington Union, 12-7
Casper, Torry — Frontier

119
Mendoza, Jose — Selma, Fall, 2:26, *36-7
Tomaya, Luis — Arvin
Gutierrez, Emmanuel — Firebaugh, 8-4
Martinez, Sergio — Tehachapi
Arroyo, Jay, — Dos Palos, 20-2
Huerta, Rusvel — Chowchilla

125
Patino, Robert — Exeter, 9-7OT
Sanchez, Efren — Arvin
Reyes, Josh — McFarland, 11-3
Rojas, Kevin — Kerman
Felipe, Joseph — Coalinga, 10-9
Allardyce, Rafe — Sierra

130
Castillo, Frankie — Arvin, 6-3
Areloa, Berto — Washington Union
Estrada, Raul — Madera South, 4-2
Alvarado, Nick — Fowler
Vanni, Garret — Liberty, Madera, 14-1
Langford, Michael — Dos Palos

135
Hail, Jason — Tehachapi, 7-1
Hamerslagh, Will — Exeter
Solario, Phillip — Wasco, Default
Torres, Jorge — Caruthers
Gomez, Kevin — Madera South, 9-6
Alvarado, Eli — Fowler

140
Tovar, Archie — Selma, 5-2, *38-7
Varella, Abel — Arvin
Doss, Nolan — Liberty, Madera, Default
Ferrer, Ruben — Caruthers

Hicks, Chris — Kerman, 4-1
Jauregui, Luis — Madera South

145
Cisneros, Joe — Selma, Fall, 3:53
Rojo, Adolfo — Arvin
Padraza, Lewis — Madera South, 9-7
Pena, Manuel — Firebaugh,
Belew, Anthony — Caruthers, Default
Prieto, Raul — Parlier

152
Eskew, Bryan — Kingsburg, 9-1, *25-7
Satelo, Eric — Yosemite
Mariscal, David — Farmerville, Fall, 2:32
Jaime, Jeff — Caruthers
Mulligan, Mackenzie — Shafter, Default
Molina, Guillermo — Arvin

160
Ames, Joseph — Shafter, Fall, 2:29
Wilson, Josh — Exeter
Wehust, Jerry — Tehachapi, Fall, 2:49
Delfino, Santino — Frontier
Guerrero, Raul — Washington Union, Default
Dunn, Chad — Yosemite

171
Walker, Justin — Sierra, 9-5
Medina, Rene — Shafter
Hack, Tyler — Tehachapi, Fall, 1:39,
Terrones, David — Washington Union
Cuen, Gillero — Firebaugh, Fall, 3:22
Cummins, Saxon — Yosemite

189
Ruiz, Abel — Selma, 7-6, *38-8
Abarquez, Marcus — Tehachapi
Avila, Joey, — Exeter Fall 2:48
Cervantez, Johnny — Firebaugh
Chase, Nathan — Yosemite, 7-3
Doyle, Curtis — Bakersfield Christian

215
Jimenez, Leobardo — Dos Palos, 5-4
Vanderpool, Shane — Liberty, Madera
McBride, Evan — Tehachapi, 4-3
Renteria, Michael — Washington Union
Perez, Mike — Selma, Default
Madrid, Matt — Corcoran

SIERRA – SEQUOIA DIVISIONAL - Tehachapi
February 16-17, 2007

285

Romero, Enrique	Corcoran, Fall, 5:29	
Celedon, Jacob	Selma	
Hood, Cameron	Tehachapi, Fall, 3:46	
Rodriguez, Edger	Wasco	
Rodriguez, Galardo	Arvin, Default	
Tapia, David	Parlier	

Most Outstanding Wrestlers

Lower Weight: Gilbert Camacho — Wash Union
Upper Weight: Joseph Ames — Shafter

TEAM SCORES

1	Selma	217.5
2	Tehachapi	179
3	Arvin	155.5
4	Exeter	119.5
5	Firebaugh	114
6	Washington Union	106.5
7	Caruthers	74.5
8	Madera South	72.5
9	Kerman	69
10	Liberty Madera	67.5
11	Dos Palos	64
12	Shafter	62.5
13	Kingsburg	59
14	Sierra	58
15	Yosemite	53
16	Wasco	52
17	Corcoran	47
18	Frontier	38
19	Fowler	33
20	Parlier	31
21	Farmersville	26
22	McFarland	24
23	Coalinga	21
24	Mendota	20
25	Bakersfield Christian	15
26	Chowchilla	8
27	Dinuba	7
28	Woodlake & Tranquility	0

*Record

SIERRA – SEQUOIA DIVISIONAL - Farmersville
February 15-16, 2008

103
Camacho, Gilbert	Washington Union, 7-1
Diaz, Edgar	Arvin
Magnusson, Adam	Firebaugh, 7-3
Metiver, Dalton	Clovis North
Munoz, Jorge	Dos Palos, 9-7
Gonzalez, Chris	Kerman

112
Valles, A. J.	Selma, 11-0
Steinbach, Jared	Tehachapi
Gonzalez, Juan	Kerman, 11-3
Rico, David	Washington Union
Poindexter, Devin	Clovis North, 3-2
Wade, Kyle	Madera South

119
Quintana, Diego	Selma, 5-0
Martinez, Sergio	Tehachapi
Calcagno, Chris	Madera South, Fall, 1:41
Castillo, Eddie	Madera South
Gutierrez, Emmanuel	Firebaugh, 17-2
Hallmark, Michael	Wasco

125
Patino, Robert	Exeter, 6-4
Pena, Nick	Selma
Perez, Michael	Firebaugh, 8-5
Ramirez, Ronnie	Corcoran
Pimentel, Guillermo	Dos Palos, Forfeit
Perez, Santiago	Woodlake

130
Mendoza, Jose	Selma, 13-5
Rojas, Kevin	Kerman
Langford, Michael	Dos Palos, 5-4
Filipe, Joseph	Coalinga
Gomez, Johnathan	Madera South, 6-2
Garza, Jason	Corcoran

135
Arreola, Alberto	Washington Union, 8-1
Escalera, Nick	Selma
Hail, Jason	Tehachapi, 10-7
Estrada, Raul	Madera South
Alvarado, Eli	Fowler, 11-8
Romero, Beau	Wasco

140
Lozano, Justin	Selma, 10-1
Contreras, Jaime	Firebaugh
Estrada, Andrew	Madera South, 9-0
Gizzo, Nick	Liberty Madera
Alvarado, Jose	Exeter, Fall, 1:57
St., John, James	Tehachapi

145
Tovar, Archie	Selma, 18-2
Harroun, Eric	Tehachapi
Doss, Nolan	Liberty Madera, 9-6
Pena, Manuel	Firebaugh
Hammerslagh, Will	Exeter, 6-4
Peterson, Jonathan	Kingsburg

152
Mariscal, David	Farmerville, 9-4
Tirado, Anthony	Kingsburg
Gomez, Hector	Dos Palos, 7-0
Gonzalez, Jose	Mendota
Sanchez, Luke	Kerman, Fall
Gutierrez, Ulysses	Firebaugh

160
Medina, Joseph	Shafter, 8-3
Hack, Tyler	Tehachapi
Pedraza, Luis	Madera South, Fall, 4:11
Marin, Luis	Mendota
Grandal, Tyler	Kingsburg, 7-1
Guerrero, Anthony	Dos Palos

171
Ames, Joseph	Shafter, Fall, 4:48
Sotelo, Erik	Yosemite
Eskew, Bryan	Kingsburg, Fall, 1:12
Terronez, David	Washington Union
Resendez, Rene	Partier, Fall
Wehust, Jerry	Tehachapi

189
Ruiz, Abel	Selma, 12-3
Abarquez, Marcus	Tehachapi
Jackson, Wade	Kingsburg, Fall, 3:27
Hernandez, Joel	Mendota
Vallederas, Alex	Orange Cove, Fall, 3:11
Acosta, Arturo	Washington Union

215
Boger, Josh	Coalinga, Fall, 1:35
Renteria, Michael	Washington Union
Perez, Mike	Selma, 7-4
Vanderpool, Shane	Liberty Madera
Furnish, Teddy	Kerman, 9-5
Moses, Michael	Kingsburg

SIERRA – SEQUOIA DIVISIONAL - Farmersville
February 15-16, 2008

285
Romero, Enrique	Corcoran, Fall, 5:59
Celodon, Jacob	Selma
Rodriguez, Edgar	Wasco, 8-5
Tapia, David	Parlier
Hood, Cameron	Tehachapi, 3-1
Medina, Marcus	Caruthers

Most Outstanding Wrestlers

Lower Weight: Robert Patino — Exeter
Upper Weight: Josh Boger — Coalinga

TEAM SCORES

1	Selma	257
2	Tehachapi	171
3	Washington Union	132.5
4	Madera South	117
5	Firebaugh	103
6	Kerman	98.5
7	Kingsburg	90
8	Dos Palos	85
9	Exeter	78.5
10	Corcoran	68
10	Liberty Madera	68
12	Shafter	62.5
13	Mendota	59
14	Wasco	54
15	Clovis North	53
16	Coalinga	49
17	Parlier	42
18	Farmersville	34
19	Yosemite	28
20	Caruthers	23
21	Arvin	21.5
22	Orange Cove	19
23	Bakersfield Christian	14
24	Fowler	13
25	Woodlake	8
25	McFarland	8
27	Dinuba	7.5
28	Sierra	4
29	Chowchilla	3
30	Tranquility	?

SIERRA – SEQUOIA DIVISIONAL - Mendota
February 20-21, 2009

103
Cisneros, Alex	Selma, 3-2
Rico, David	Washington Union
Flores, Lupe	Exeter, Fall, 2:45
Gonzales, Chris	Kerman
Navarrete, Gabriel	Dinuba, 11-4
Deverrick, Cameron	Coalinga

112
Quintana, Diego	Selma, 6-4
Gonzalez, Juan	Kerman
Santos, Juan	Farmerville, 8-7
Gutierrez, Lalo	Firebaugh
Anguiano, Roger	Exeter, 8-3
Gaubhman, Austin	Liberty Madera

119
Valles, A. J.	Selma, 4-1
Rodriguez, Dylin	Washington Union
Leladais, Joel	Dos Palos, Fall, 3:00
Gagnon, Jason	Exeter
Rodas, Mario	Shafter, Default
Garza, Nick	Parlier

125
Pena, Nick	Selma, 6-4
Patino, Robert	Exeter
Steinbach, Jared	Tehachapi, 10-4
Spencer, Tyler	Liberty Madera
Gomez, Adrian	Corcoran, 8-0
Quiroz, Angel	Dos Palos

130
Mendoza, Jose	Selma, 10-2
Rojas, Kevin	Kerman
Jimenez, Robert	Kingsburg, 4-2
Solorio, Justin	Wasco
Perez, Mike	Firebaugh, Default
Avalos, Jose	Parlier

135
Zarate, Nathan	Selma, 9-3
Filipe, Joe	Coalinga
Maciel, Louie	Kingsburg, 4-2
Ruiz, Mikael	Kerman
Barrow, Juan	Shafter, 15-1
Monsibras, Jacob	Independence

140
Escalera, Nick	Selma, 8-1
Bugambilia, Francisco	Arvin
Martinez, Michael	Wasco, Fall, :05
Carrillo, Junior	Corcoran
Flores, Adrian	Kerman, Default
Agredano, Alonzo	Firebaugh

145
Gomez, Hector	Dos Palos, 7-4
Aguilar, Rico	Selma
Rodriguez, Alex	Washington Union, TF, 3:39
Gizzo, Nick	Liberty Madera
Peterson, Jonathan	Kingsburg, 3-1
Velasco, Estephan	Mendota

152
Lozano, Justin	Selma, 13-0
Tirado, Anthony	Kingsburg
Davila, Eric	Firebaugh, Fall, 2:37
Mireles, Rosendo	Yosemite
Schilhable, David	Independence, Default
Aleman, John	Parlier

160
Grandal, Tyler	Kingsburg, Fall, 6:00
St. John, James	Tehachapi
Gutierrez, Chico	Firebaugh, Fall, 2:54
Lincoln, Kyle	Yosemite
Guerrera, Anthony	Dos Palos, Fall, :53
Mesa, Daniel	Woodlake

171
Medina, Rene	Shafter, 6-3
Narvaez, Mark	Washington Union
Sotelo, Erik	Yosemite, 11-3
Roberts, Tanner	Kingsburg
Hail, Jason	Tehachapi, Fall, 1:23
Rodriguez, Victor	Firebaugh

189
Machado, Michael	Arvin, 2-1
Ferrea, Hugo	Caruthers
Jackson, Wade	Kingsburg, Default
Parker, John	Exeter
Hernandez, Joel	Mendota, 3-2
Wilson, Wyatt	Shafter

215
Renteria, Michael	Washington Union, TF, 6:00
Urree, Jesus	McFarland
Stilson, Ross	Sierra, Fall, 3:04
Jackson, Troy	Kingsburg
Carter, Max	Exeter, Fall, 4:48
Martinez, Jorge	Firebaugh

SIERRA – SEQUOIA DIVISIONAL - Mendota
February 20-21, 2009

285
Furnish, Theodore	Kerman, 3-2
Enos, Logan	Dos Palos
Smith, Dakota	Yosemite, Default
Tovar, Juan	Woodlake
Taliulu, Niko	Tehachapi, Fall, 1:02
Ledesma, Juan	Mendota

Most Outstanding Wrestlers

Lower Weight: Nick Pena — Selma
Upper Weight: Theodore Furnish — Kerman

TEAM SCORES

1	Selma	267
2	Kingsburg	194
3	Washington Union	168
4	Kerman	155
5	Exeter	154
6	Dos Palos	148
7	Firebaugh	148
8	Tehachapi	112
9	Shafter	100
10	Yosemite	77
11	Liberty Madera	73.5
12	Arvin	72.5
13	Mendota	67
14	Wasco	57
15	Independence	49
16	Parlier	46
17	McFarland	40
18	Corcoran	39.5
19	Woodlake	38
20	Coalinga	33
21	Dinuba	32.5
22	Caruthers	31.5
23	Sierra	31
24	Fowler	30
25	Farmersville	29
26	Orange Cove	22
27	Mira Monte	9
28	Mission Oak	8
29	Bakersfield Christian	7
30	Tranquility	4

SIERRA – SEQUOIA – DIVISIONAL - Shafter
February 19-20, 2010

103
Olea, Arnulfo	Exeter, 6-5
Rico, David	Washington Union
Navarrete, Gabrial	Dinuba, 12-1
Govea, Ivan	Kerman
Marin, Oscar	Arvin, 4-3
Johnstone, Reily	Mission Oak

112
Cisneros, Alex	Selma, TF, 15-0
Flores, Lupe	Exeter
Gonzalez, Christopher	Wash. Union, Fall, 2:36
Torres, Victor	Caruthers
Madera, Noe	Tehachapi, 9-7
Cancino, Adolfo	Dinuba

119
Panduro, Adrian	Corcoran, Fall, :40
Gagnon, Jason	Exeter
Rodas, Mario	Shafter, 6-5
Acevdo, Armando	Washington Union
Ayala, Daniel	Farmerville, 14-5
Deverick, Cameron	Coalinga

125
Barron, Juan	Shafter, 6-2
Anguiano, Roger	Exeter
Gonzalez, Jose	Mendota, Fall, 3:26
Mendoza, Michael	Washington Union
Jimenez, Tony	Dinuba, Fall, 3:32
Singh, Kuijit	R F Kennedy

130
Pena, Nick	Selma, Fall, 1:23
Blanco, Jose	Wasco
Moreno, Jaime	Wash. Union, Fall, 2:39
Torres, Joseph	Caruthers
Panuco, Juan	Orange Cove, Fall, 2:29
Hernandez, Jorge	Mendota

135
Morfin, Isish	Selma, 7-1
Renteria, Monte	Dinuba
Quiroz, D, J.	Dos Palos, 1-0
Gomez, Adrian	Corcoran,
Flores, Adrian	Kerman, 15-7
Hernandez, Richard	Washington Union

140
Zarate, Nathan	Selma, Fall, :35
Castro, Rayko	Kerman
Medley, Jason	Mission Oak, 5-4
Marquez, Mario	Washington Union
Garcia, Bruno	Dos Palos, 10-4
Heir, Cody	Kingsburg

145
Martinez, Michael	Wasco, 3-2
Alvarado, Joshua	Exeter
Aguilar, Rico	Selma, 13-3
Peterson, Jonathan	Kingsburg
Amey, Danzella	Wash Union, Fall, 1:54
Loera, Felipe	Mira Monte

152
Terrones, Josue	Washington Union, 4-0
Fulce, Jacob	Bakersfield, Christian
Aispuro, Josh	Wasco, 6-1
Hienrichs, Jacob	Kingsburg
Forfeit	
Forfeit	

160
Lozano, Justin	Selma, 24-9
Tirado, Anthony	Kingsburg
Gonzalez, Fabian	Orange Cove, 8-6
Marquez, Eric	McFarland
Reichmuth, Karl	Liberty Madera, Fall, 1:09
Mesa, Daniel	Woodlake

171
Medina, Rene	Wasco, Fall, 1:32
Lincoln, Kyle	Yosemite
Grandal, Tyler	Kingsburg, 4-3
Hernandez, Joel	Mendota
Castellow, Jonathan	Exeter, 12-3
Valdovinos, Jesus	McFarland

189
Avery, Will	Tehachapi, Fall, 4:02
Parker, John	Exeter
Hernandez, Robert	Washington Union, 13-5
Tovar, Edward	Fowler
Hernandez, Robert	Dinuba, Fall, 4:45
Olin, Jordan	Mira Monte

215
Corona, Nick	Kingsburg, 6-4, OT
Medley, Sean	Wasco,
Wilson, Wyatt	Shafter, 8-6
Garcia, Fred	Dos Palos,
Acosta, Juan	Washington Union, 7-5
Carter, Max	Exeter

SIERRA – SEQUOIA – DIVISIONAL - Shafter
February 19-20, 2010

285
Smith, Dakota — Yosemite, Fall, 3:23
Tovar, Juan — Woodlake
Taliulu, Niko — Tehachapi, 8-3
Portillo, George — Shafter
Alonzo, Mario — Dinuba, Forfeit
Enos, Logan — Dos Palos

Most Outstanding Wrestlers

Lower Weight: Adrian Panduro Corcoran
Upper Weight: Justin Lozano   Selma

* Firebaugh was late for weigh-ins could not compete

TEAM SCORES

1	Washington Union	196
2	Exeter	180
3	Selma	177.5
4	Wasco	134
5	Kingsburg	117
6	Dinuba	109
7	Shafter	92
8	Dos Palos	84.5
9	Tehachapi	79
10	Yosemite	64
10	Mendota	64
12	Corcoran	62.5
13	Kerman	55
14	Liberty Madera	44
15	Orange Cove	42.5
16	McFarland	41.5
17	Woodlake	36
18	Mission Oak	35
18	Caruthers	35
20	Arvin	30
21	Bakersfield Christian	25.5
22	Mira Monte	23
23	Farmersville	19.5
24	Fowler	19
25	Independence	18
26	Coalinga	10
26	Sierra	10
28	R F Kennedy	9
29	Chowchilla	7
30	Parlier	0
30	Firebaugh	0

Justin Lozano - Selma High School and University of Buffalo

Justin Lozano
Photo: John Sachs – Tech-Fall.com

SIERRA – SEQUOIA DIVISIONAL - Dinuba
February 18-19, 2011

105
Pena, Johnny — Selma, 4-2
Thomas, Brandon — Corcoran
Navarette, Isaac — Dinuba, 7-6
Errecart, Anthony — Kerman
Mendez, Michael — Washington Union, 4-2
Flores, Jonny — Exeter

114
Flores, Lupe — Selma, 10-6
Olea, Arnulfo — Exeter
Gonzales, Chris — Wash. Union, Fall, 5:08
Lopez, Anthony — McFarland
Reyna, P. J. — Yosemite, Fall, 4:45
Ramirez, Joe — Shafter

121
Panduro, Adrian — Corcoran, Fall, 2:31
Gutierrez, Eduardo — Firebaugh
Anguiano, Roger — Exeter, 7-2
Arroyo, Jose — Coalinga
Govea, Ivan — Kerman, 10-7
Ayala, Daniel — Farmersville

127
Cisneros, Alex — Selma, TF, 18-1
Mendoza, Michael — Washington Union
Arambula, Jobani — Firebaugh, Major, 13-5
Thomas, Hank — Dos Palos
Gutierrez, Basilio — Kerman, Fall, 4:59
Jaime, Christian — Coalinga

132
Pena, Nick — Selma, Fall, 3:27
Torres, Joseph — Caruthers
Rodas, Mario — Shafter, Major, 10-1
Akers, Brandon — Exeter
Ramirez, Norberto — Arvin, Fall, 2:46
Suarez, Issac — Dos Palos

137
Quirez, D. J. — Dos Palos, Fall, 3:37
Jimenez, Tony — Dinuba
Escalera, Ryan — Selma, 7-5
Hernandez, Richard — Washington Union
Marquez, Adrien — Corcoran, Fall, :42
Paez, Simon — Orange Cove

142
Aguilar, Rico — Selma, Major, ?-8
Gomez, Adrian — Corcoran
Aispuro, Josh — Wasco, 3-1
Renteria, Monte — Dinuba
Castro, Rayko — Kerman, Fall, 4:58
Navaro, Oscar — Mendota

147
Morfin, Isiah — Selma, Major, 12-4
Gonzalez, Gabriel — Washington Union
Solorio, Justin — Wasco, 7-3
Rangel, Issac — Firebaugh
Thompson, Matthew — Yosemite, Fall, 3:54
Valdez, Jesus — Dos Palos

154
Terrones, Josue — Wash. Union, Fall, 1:59
Martinez, Michael — Wasco
Alvarado, Caleb — Exeter, 9-3
Howell, Kevin — Yosemite
Valasco, Estafan — Mendota, 6-3
Rodriguez, Rudy — McFarland

162
Marquez, Eric — McFarland, 4-3
Tirado, Anthony — Kingsburg
Davila, Eric — Firebaugh, Fall, 2:53
Gardner, Trent — Tehachapi
Morin, Christian — Selma, 4-3
Mess, Nathaniel — Woodlake

173
Lozano, Justin — Selma, Fall, 3:59
Heinrich, Jacob — Kingsburg
Tenorio, Mike — Firebaugh, 6-5
Salazar, Carlos — Kerman
Harroun, Dillon — Tehachapi, Fall, 2:27
Hernandez, Oshmar — Washington Union

191
Lincoln, Kyle — Yosemite, 7-3
Castellow, Jonathan — Exeter
Hernandez, Jose — Washington Union, Fall, 1:50
Cunningham, Conner — Sierra
Obrien, Patrick — Kingsburg, 6-3
Cervantez, Brian — Firebaugh

217
Medley, Sean — Wasco, Fall, 5:24
Alvarez, Ismael — Orange Cove
Cortez, Justice — Selma, 7-2
Hendrickson, Grant — Yosemite
Figueroa, Chris — Mendota, Fall, 1:44
Vandergiff, Paul — Liberty Madera

SIERRA – SEQUOIA DIVISIONAL - Dinuba
February 18-19, 2011

287
Tovar, Juan	Woodlake, 5-1
Taliulu, Niko	Tehachapi
Trevino, Mark	Corcoran, 1-0
Enos, Logan	Dos Palos
Dhaliwal, Gurlabe	Fowler, Fall, 1:22
Kyle, Brian	Exeter

Most Outstanding Wrestlers

Lower Weight: Alex Cisneros Selma
Upper Weight: Eric Marquez McFarland

TEAM SCORES

1	Selma	254
2	Washington Union	173.5
3	Wasco	120
4	Exeter	119.5
5	Firebaugh	114.5
6	Corcoran	113
7	Yosemite	108
8	Dos Palos	93
9	Kerman	89.5
10	Dinuba	71.5
11	Kingsburg	67
11	Mendota	67
13	McFarland	62
14	Tehachapi	59
15	Shafter	49
16	Woodlake	47
17	Sierra	36
18	Coalinga	35.5
19	Caruthers	31
19	Orange Cove	31
21	Fowler	25
22	Liberty Madera	20
23	Arvin	19
24	Farmersville	14
25	Bakersfield Christian	3
25	Parlier	3

Alex Cisneros, Selma High School (2011)
Photographer: John Sachs, Tech-Fall.com

SIERRA – SEQUOIA DIVISIONAL – Washington Union
February 17-18, 2012

108
Hokit, Isaiah	Wasco, 7-1
Mora, Aaron	Firebaugh
Pena, Johnny	Selma, 8-1
Errecart, Anthony	Kerman
Ramirez, Noel	Kingsburg, Fall, 3:51
Gonzalez, Braulio	Washington Union

115
Olea, Arnulfo	Exeter, Fall, 3:30
Arroyo, Jose	Coalinga
Thomas, Brenden	Corcoran, 18-2
Flores, Gilbert	Selma
Kelley, Clint	Yosemite, 3-0
Salgado, Antonio	Wasco

122
Flores, Lupe	Selma, 14-8
Panduro, Adrian	Corcoran
Ferrer, Jose	Washington Union, 11-5
Tirado, Jonas	Kingsburg
Molina, Armand	Firebaugh, 19-5
Waybright, Michael	Yosemite

128
Perez, Jose	Caruthers, 9-1
Velasquez, Daniel	Firebaugh
Delgado, Steven	Selma, 11-5
Macias, Isaac	Wasco
Reyna, P. J.	Yosemite, Default
Lelandais, Nick	Dos Palos

134
Cisneros, Alex	Selma, 3-1
Gasca, Javier	Kingsburg
Valdez, Jesus	Dos Palos, 8-6
Gutierrez, Basilio	Kerman
Marquez, Adrien	Corcoran, 6-4
Serna, Trini	Firebaugh

140
Gomez, Adrain	Corcoran, 4-3
Gova, Ivan	Kerman
Pimentel, Nathan	Dos Palos, 8-2
Tirado, Jacob	Kingsburg
Pena, Tre	Selma, Default
Figueroa, Francisco	Mendota

147
Martinez, Michael	Wasco, 5-1
Morfin, Isish	Selma
Panuco, Juan	Orange Cove, 6-4
Suarez, Izzac	Dos Palos
Dhanda, Arshdeep	Dinuba, 3-0
Ferrer, Miguel	Caruthers

154
Escalera, Ryan	Selma, 3-2
Temple, Mason	Liberty Madera
Alvarado, Caleb	Exeter, 2-1
Rangel, Isaac	Firebaugh
Segura, Edgar	Mendota, 16-3
Guzman, Joe	Corcoran

162
Terrones, Josue	Washington Union, 3-0
Wright, Michael	Dinuba
Robledo, Jose	Wasco, 5-3
Morin, Christian	Selma
Acosta, Joseph	Kerman, 7-0
Medel, Juan	Farmerville

172
Del, Fierro, Dolan	Sierra, Fall, 1:16
Jimenez, Juan	Dos Palos
Morin, Keanu	Selma, 11-9
Hernandez, Oshmar	Washington Union
Valdivia, Rene	Kerman, Fall, 5:24
Caballero, Aaron	Firebaugh

184
Tenorio, Mike	Firebaugh, 9-5
Gonzalez, Gabriel	Washington Union
Padilla, David	Dinuba, 5-0
Meza, Nathaniel	Woodlake
Carranza, Enrique	Corcoran, 15-3
Diaz, Nick	Selma

197
Lincoln, Kyle	Yosemite, Fall, 3:51
Lopez, Christian	Selma
Gamez, Anthony	Mendota, 5-3
Torres, Eric	Shafter
Acevedo, Eric	Wasco, Fall, :29
Negrete, Nicholas	Woodlake

222
Medley, Sean	Wasco, 3-1
Varela, Luis	Dos Palos
Figueroa, Chris	Mendota, 6-4
Vandergriff, Paul	Liberty Madera
Rocha, Gerardo	Exeter, Fall, 2:45
Harrison, Javin	Washington Union

SIERRA – SEQUOIA DIVISIONAL – Washington Union
February 17-18, 2012

287
Trevino, Mark	Corcoran, Fall, 1:33
Kyle, Brian	Exeter
Dhaliwal, Gurlabe	Fowler, Fall, 3:42
Johnson, Garret	Wasco
Alvarez, Jose	Selma, Fall, 1:42
Garza, Eric	Kerman

Most Outstanding Wrestlers

Lower Weight: Alex Cisneros — Selma
Upper Weight: Sean Medley — Wasco

TEAM SCORES

1	Selma	248.5
2	Wasco	186.5
3	Washington Union	145.5
4	Corcoran	135
5	Firebaugh	133.5
6	Dos Palos	128.5
7	Exeter	115
8	Kerman	108
9	Yosemite	74
10	Mendota	73
11	Kingsburg	72
12	Dinuba	55
13	Caruthers	50
14	Liberty Madera	44
14	Woodlake	44
16	Orange Cove	40
17	Sierra	39.5
18	Shafter	38
19	Coalinga	27.5
20	Fowler	25
21	Sierra Pacific	14
21	Tehachapi	14
23	Farmersville	9
23	McFarland	9
25	Parlier	8
25	Strathmore	8
25	Bakersfield Christian	8
28	Arvin	0

Brady Garner - North High School

SIERRA – SEQUIOA DIVISIONAL - Shafter
February 15-16, 2013

106
Cisneros, Alex — Selma, Major, 14-5
Errecart, Anthony — Kerman
Ortega, Anthony — Dos Palos, Fall
Licea, Jose — Caruthers
Gonzalez, Brauilo — Washington Union, 9-1
Madriz, Marcelino — Firebaugh

113
Hokit, Isaiah — Wasco, Fall, 4:50
Jiminez, Roberto — Washington Union
Arciga, Eduardo — Caruthers, Major, 13-3
Ramirez, Noel — Kingsburg
Ramirez, Tomas — Dinuba, 16-5
Suarez, Ozzire — Dos Palos

120
Olea, Arnulfo — Exeter, 5-2
Brenden, Thomas — Corcoran
Tirado, Jonas — Kingsburg, 13-3
Ferrer, Alejandro — Washington Union
Maximo, Jose — Mendota, Fall
Delbosque, Davide — Orange Cove

126
Hokit, Josh — Wasco, 5-2
Molina, Armand — Firebaugh
Garcia, Ruben — Selma, Fall
Mendoza, Ismiel — Caruthers
Ledesma, Gabriel — Exeter, Default
Alvarez, Andy — Granite Hills

132
Gasca, Javier — Kingsburg, Fall, 2:29
Panduro, Adrian — Corcoran
Mora, Aaron — Firebaugh, Major, 13-5
Valdes, Jesus — Dos Palos
Diaz, Jacob — Wasco, 10-8
Jackson, Tevin — Caruthers

138
Pena, Ralph — Selma, Major, 14-3
Pimentel, Nathan — Dos Palos
Reyna, Paul — Yosemite, 11-4
Smith, Devin — Kingsburg
Serna, Trini — Firebaugh, 5-2
Ruiz, Christian — Mendota

145
Nutt, Boyce — Selma, 4-3
Suarez, Izzac — Dos Palos
Jones, Kyle — Exeter, 2-0
Guitierrez, Basilio — Kerman
Marquez, Adrian — Corcoran, TF, 18-3
Arreola, Ruben — Granite Hills

152
Escalera, Ryan — Selma, 4-2
Govea, Ivan — Firebaugh
Ferrer, Miguel — Caruthers, 4-1
Dhanda, Arshedeep — Dinuba
Fernandez, Humberto — Kerman, 9-5
Tirado, Jacob — Kingsburg

160
Terrones, Josue — Washington Union, 6-2
Temple, Mason — Liberty Madera
Wright, Michael — Dinuba, 2-1
Morin, Keanu — Selma
Maldonado, Gerado — Avenal, Fall
Cole, Ben — Shafter

170
Rangel, Isaac — Firebaugh, 5-0
Hernandez, Oshmar — Washington Union
Segura, Edgar — Mendota, 3-2
Hernandez, Adrian — Kennedy
Acosta, Joseph — Kerman, Forfeit
Medel, Juan — Farmersville

182
Robledo, Jose — Wasco, 1-0
Jimenez, Juan — Dos Palos
Mesa, Nathan — Woodlake, 5-2
Vivanco, Nathaniel — Firebaugh
Trevino, Frankie — Kerman, 1-0
Perez, Michocan — Dinuba

195
Gonzalez, Gabriel — Wash. Union, Fall, 5:30
Padilla, David — Dinuba
Carranza, Enrique — Corcoran, 8-6
Torres, Eric — Shafter
Jones, Clayton — Sierra, 9-2
Caballero, Aaron — Firebaugh

220
Medley, Sean — Wasco, Fall, 3:15
Figueroa, Chris — Mendota
Vandergriff, Paul — Liberty Madera, Fall
Loomis, Eric — Sierra Pacific
Toon, Kaleb — Corcoran, Fall
Bosiquez, Raul — Cesar Chavez

SIERRA – SEQUIOA DIVISIONAL - Shafter
February 15-16, 2013

285
Alvarez, Joey   Selma, 4-2OT
Johnson, Garret   Wasco
Barrios, Robert   Sierra Pacific, 4-2
Anaya, Anthony   Corcoran
Pineda, Christian   Wash. Union, Disqualified
Gonzales, Adrian   Firebaugh

*Season, Records

Most Outstanding Wrestlers

Lower Weight: Javier Gasca   Kingsburg
Upper Weight: Sean Medley   Wasco

TEAM SCORES

1	Selma	221
2	Wasco	215
3	Washington Union	192.5
4	Dos Palos	181
5	Firebaugh	180
6	Corcoran	141.5
7	Mendota	128
8	Caruthers	126.5
9	Dinuba	122
10	Kingsburg	120.5
11	Kerman	115.5
12	Shafter	89
13	Exeter	77.5
14	Liberty Madera	70
15	R F Kennedy	61.5
16	Sierra Pacific	56
17	Coalinga	48
18	Granite Hills	44
19	Sierra	56
19	Yosemite	56
21	McFarland	32
22	Parlier	29
23	Fowler	23
24	Orange Cove	22.5
25	Woodlake	18
25	Farmersville	18
27	Avenal	17
28	Strathmore	13
29	Arvin	10
30	Tranquility	9
31	Cesar Chavez *	7
32	Lindsey	0
32	Bakersfield Christian	0

* Team has a non-scoring wrestler

Mason Pengilly - Porterville High School

SIERRA – SEQUIOA DIVISIONAL - Dinuba
February 21-22, 2014

106
Ortiz, Tommy — Kennedy, 7-0
Perez, Isaiah — Dinuba
Castro, Carl — Mendota, 5-4
Ramirez, Noel — Kingsburg
Miramonies, Gus — Caruthers, Fall, 2:33
Armenta, Jesus — Dos Palos

113
Garcia, Robert — Selma, TF, 17-2
Errecart, Anthony — Kerman,
Pimentel, Armando — Dos Palos, Fall, 1:49
Aguilar, Anthony — Kingsburg
Birrueta, Mario — Wasco, Fall, 5:32
Mendoza, Luis — Kern Valley

120
Cisneros, Chris — Selma, Fall, 1:50
Wright, Jacob — Dinuba
Marrufo, Adrian — Dos Palos, TF, 15-0
Paez, Jose — Orange Cove,
Hawk, Chase — Kern Valley, Fall, 3:15
Arredondo, Jason — Coalinga

126
Alvarez, Andy — Granite Hills, 3-1
Del, Bosque, David — Dinuba,
Vasquez, Freddy — Caruthers, 7-5
Ledesma, Gabriel — Exeter,
Bedrosian, Zack — Coalinga, Fall, 4:23
Gonzalez, Andrew — Dos Palos

134
Garcia, Ruben — Selma, 12-7
Molina, Armando — Firebaugh,
Alvarez, Michael — Granite Hills, Major, 11-2
Del, Bosque, Alex — Dinuba
Suarez, Ozvaldo — Dos Palos, Default
Tovar, David — Fowler

138
Mora, Aaron — Firebaugh, 8-1
Mata, Joseph — Kingsburg,
Boland, Dowson — Exeter, 4-0
Bedrosian, Jake — Coalinga
Cisneros, Jordan — Dinuba, Major, 23-13
Lopez, Alex — McFarland

147
Macias, Michael — Wasco, 5-1
Pimental, Nathan — Dos Palos
Serna, Trini — Firebaugh, Fall, 1:44
Jones, Tanner — Exeter

Samano, Saul — Granite Hills, 2-0
Gaytan, Xavier — Kerman

154
Lopez, Casper — Wasco, 3-2
Gutierrez, Basio — Kerman
Suarez, Izzac — Dos Palos, 9-5
Jones, Kyle — Exeter
Simon, Saul — Selma, Fall, 1:15
Guzman, Ryan — Firebaugh

160
Wright, Michael — Dinuba, Fall, 1:34
Fernandez, Hunberto — Kerman
Coker, Tyler — Exeter, 9-2
Galindo, John — Dos Palos
Quintanar, Jesus — Mendota, 8-6OT
Ruiz, Santanana — Fowler

172
Serura, Edgar — Mendota, 7-4
Dhanda, Arshdeep — Dinuba
Potter, Dillain — Caruthers, Fall, :34
Samaniego, Zoloman — Kingsburg
Acosta, Joseph — Kerman, 6-3
Maldonado, Gerardo — Avenal

184
Rangel, Isaac — Firebaugh, 3-1
Robledo, Jose — Wasco
Rosas, Kobe — Coalinga, Fall, 1:22
Muxlow, Ty — Kingsburg
Hernandez, Michael — Parlier, Fall, 1:28
Stencska, Anthony — Sierra Pacific

195
Ybarra-Brant, Richard — Liberty Madera, 16-3
Cunningham, Christian — Sierra
Vivanco, Nathaniel — Firebaugh, 15-9
Harrison, Javin — Washington Union,
Barron, Vic — Dos Palos, Fall, 4:06
Serna, Tony — Dinuba

220
Gonzalez, Gabriel — Wash. Union Fall, 3:49
Ybarra-Brant, Bevan — Liberty Madera
Padilla, David — Dinuba, Major, 9-0
Caballero, Aaron — Firebaugh
Figueroa, Chris — Mendota, 1-0
Loomis, Eric — Sierra Pacific

SIERRA – SEQUIOA DIVISIONAL - Dinuba
February 21-22, 2014

285
Alvarez, Jose   Selma, 3-1
Barrios, Robert   Sierra Pacific
Davis, Dawson   Dinuba, Default
Jones, Casey   Sierra Pacific
Anaya, Anthony   Caruthers, 6-2
Garza, Eric   Kerman

Most Outstanding Wrestlers

Lower Weight: Chris Cisneros Selma
Upper Weight: Michael Wright Dinuba

TEAM SCORES

1	Dinuba	250.5
2	Firebaugh	193.5
3	Dos Palos*	167.5
4	Selma	155
5	Kerman*	147
6	Wasco	143
7	Exeter*	111
8	Kingsburg	105.5
9	Washington Union	100.5
10	Granit Hills	93
11	Coalinga*	91.5
12	Mendota	91
13	Caruthers	78.5
14	Liberty Madera*	66
15	Sierra Pacific*	57
16	Flower*	51.5
17	R F Kennedy	49.5
18	Corcoran*	47
18	Sierra	47
20	McFarland	34
21	Woodlake	33
22	Kern Valley	32.5
23	Shafter*	27.5
24	Chowchilla	27
25	Parlier*	24
26	Farmersville	23
27	Orange Cove	19
28	Cesar Chavez	13
29	Avenal	12.5
30	Arvin*	11
31	Bakersfield Christian	9
32	Tranquility	6
33	Rosamond	4
33	Yosemite	3

* Team has non-scoring wrestler

Dinuba High School, 2014 Sequioa Division Champs

Coach Wright and Michael Wright,
Dinuba High School

SIERRA – SEQUOIA DIVISIONAL – Liberty Madera
February 20-21, 2015

106
Perez, Isaiah — Dinuba, 6-2
Areyano, Robert — Selma
Madnz, Marcelino — Firebaugh, 4-0
Miramontes, Gus — Caruthers
Ortega, Anthony — Dos Palos, Fall, :37
Cervantez, Johnny — Coalinga

115
Ortiz, Tommy — R F Kennedy, 4-2
Castro, Carl — Mendota
Ramos, Luis — Selma, Major, 10-0
Stimpel, Ethan — Exeter
Terrigues, Joseph — Cesar Chavez, 3-0
Rangel, Chris — Dinuba

122
Garcia, Robert — Selma, 8-3
Marrufo, Adrian — Dos Palos
Hernandez, Marco — R F Kennedy, 5-0
Bedrosian, Zachary — Coalinga
Briseno, Daniel — Washington Union, 6-3
Vasquez, Alfredo — Caruthers

128
Pymentel, Armondo — Dos Palos, Fall, 3:42
Memdoza, Tony — Selma
Rangel, Julius — Dinuba, Fall, 3:29
Ramos, Ethan — Shafter
Xiong, Toules — Wash. Union, Fall, :55
Sierra, Juan — Arvin

134
Molina, Armand — Firebaugh, 7-5
Romero, Joe — Corcoran
Diaz, Oscar — Selma, 9-8
Grimsley, Kevin — Exeter
Gonzalez, Andrew — Dos Palos, 3-2
Villa, Chris — Shafter

140
Garcia, Ruben — Selma, 8-1
Mata, Joseph — Kingsburg
Tamayo, Alvaro — Arvin, 11-8
Garcia, Andrew — Exeter
Arzola, Moises — Farmersville, 8-6
Walker, Andrew — Dos Palos

147
Ramos, Jonathan — Selma, 5-3
Del, Bosque, Alex — Dinuba
Berrosian, Jacob — Corcoran, 9-6

Macias, Michael — Wasco
Coker, Tyler — Exeter, 2-1
Benadum, Chance — Dos Palos

154
Pimentel, Nathan — Dos Palos
Boland, Dawson — Exeter
Arreola, Ruben — Granite Hills
Zamilpa, Tristan — Selma
DeBoer, Willem — Frontier
Mata, Anthony — Fowler

162
Robler, Skyler — Parlier, 5-0
Jones, Kyle — Exeter
Mendoza, Juan — Mendota, 3-1
Montelejano, Edgar — Dinuba
Sevilla, Ivan — Coalinga, 7-3
Smith, Brandon — Chowchilla

172
Wright, Michael — Dinuba, Fall, 1:27
Ruiz, Santana — Fowler
Martin, Isaiah — Garces, Default
Gomez, Nino — Exeter
Fransen, Alex — Selma, Fall, 2-1
Hernandez, William — ?

184
Jiminez, Juan — Dos Palos, Major, 11-0
Bracamontes, Jesse — Granite Hills
Muxlow, Ty — Kingsburg, Fall, 2:42
Ramirez, Jose — Wasco
Jiminez, Isaiah — Selma, Fall, 3:03
Alba, Diego — Washington Union

197
Rosas, Kobe — Coalinga, 9-5
Stenschke, Anthony — Sierra Pacific
Darden, Marcus — Wasco, 5-0
Butterfield, Quin — Sierra Pacific
Metz, Daniel — Granite Hills, Fall, :42
Maravilla, Ricardo — Mendota

222
Padilla, David — Dinuba, TB, 2-1
Barrios, Robert — Sierra Pacific
Macias, Ramiro — R F Kennedy, Fall, 2:43
Marshall, Tallion — Fowler
Alvarez, Rogi — Selma, 12-5
Martinez, Rodney — Wasco

SIERRA – SEQUOIA DIVISIONAL – Liberty Madera
February 20-21, 2015

287
Alvarez, Jose	Selma, Fall, 4:54
Jones, Casey	Sierra
Davis, Dawson	Fall, 3:30
Vorhees, Andrew	Kingsburg
Echeveste, Nick	Firebaugh, Fall, 2:45
Martinez, Rodney	Wasco

Most Outstanding Wrestlers

Lower Weight: Isaiah Perez — Dinuba
Upper Weight: Jose Alvarez — Selma

TEAM SCORES

1	Selma	286
2	Dinuba	227
3	Dos Palos	193
4	Exeter	153.5
5	Coalinga	115
6	Firebaugh	103
7	Granite Hills	102
8	R F Kennedy	98
9	Wasco	89
10	Kingsburg	84
11	Fowler	80
12	Mendota	68.5
13	Sierra Pacific	68
14	Shafter	66.5
15	Washington Union	64
16	Chowchilla	61
17	Cesar Chavez	56.5
18	Caruthers	55
19	Arvin	52
20	Sierra	50
21	Garces	49.5
22	Corcoran	48
23	Parlier	43.5
24	Kerman	33
25	Bakersfield Christian	31
26	Orange Cove	30
27	Farmersville	29
28	Yosemite	26
29	Woodlake	20
30	Liberty Madera	17
31	Kern Valley	15
32	Tranquility	12
33	Avenel	9
34	Strathmore	6
35	McFarland	0
35	Rosamond	0
35	Bishop	0

Isaiah Perez, Coach Wright and Jacob Wright
Dinuba High School

Coach Wright and son, Jacob Wright

SIERRA – SEQUOIA DIVISIONAL - Shafter
February 19-20, 2016

108
Cisneros, Josh	Selma, Fall, 1:15
Dhandia, Gurjot	Dinuba
Olea, Eric	Exeter, Major
Hernandez, Jonah	Corcoran
Licea, Jacob	Wash. Union, Decision
Chavez, Martin	Orange Cove

115
Areyano, Robert	Selma, 6-0
Briseno, Daniel	Washington Union
Arbeola, Marcus	Dinuba, Decision
Birrueta, Mario	Wasco
Morales, Jacob	Wash. Union, Decision
Price, Joseph	Corcoran

122
Garcia, Robert	Selma, 3-2
Perez, Isaiah	Dinuba
Rogers, Brock	Corcoran, Fall
Stimpel, Ethan	Exeter
Terriquez, Joseph	Cesar Chavez, Fall
Arrelland, Anselmo	Wasco

128
Panduro, Aaron	Corcoran, 5-2
Marufo, Adrian	Dos Palos,
Cisneros, Chris	Selma, Decision
Bedrosian, Zackary	Coalinga
Rangel, Chris	Dinuba, Decision
Villa, Chris	Wasco

134
Mendoza, Tony	Selma, 6-4, OT
Romero, Joe	Corcoran
Pimentel, Armando	Dos Palos, Decision
Hernandez, Mario	R F Kennedy
Alvarez, Mark	Dinuba, Decision
Ramos, Ethan	Shafter

140
Wright, Jacob	Dinuba, 4-3, OT
Diaz, Oscar	Selma
Deondre, Eason	Wash. Union, Decision
Garcia, Seth	Strathmore
Gamboa, Manuel	Cesar Chavez, Decision, *24-9
Suarez, Ozvaldo	Dos Palos

147
Garcia, Ruben	Selma, TF, 17-1
Tomayo, Alvardo	Arvin
Benadum, Chance	Dos Palos, Decision
Escalera, Brandon	Granite Hills
Long, Daniel	Dinuba, Decision
Bedrosian, Caleb	Coalinga

154
Ramos, Jonathan	Selma, Forfeit
Del, Bosque, Alex	Dinuba
Jones, Tanner	Exeter, Fall
Walker, Andrew	Dos Palos
Gayton, Xavier	Kerman, Decision
Zamudio, Rafael	Shafter

162
Boland, Dawson	Exeter, Fall, 1:45
Luchau, Jace	Selma
Sevilla, Ivan	Coalinga, Decision
Medina, Jasper	Firebaugh
Panija, Bryan	Caruthers, Forfeit
Bemardo, Busillos	Chowchilla

172
Rodriguez, Christian	Selma, Fall, 1:30
Maldonado, Fabian	Avenal
Ruiz, Santana	Fowler, Decision
Gonzalez, Richard	Tranquilly
Serrano, Antonio	Firebaugh, Decision
Carrillo, Enrique	Farmerville

184
Good, Jacob	Exeter, decision
Castelo, Rodolfo	R F Kennedy
Martin, Isaiah	Garces, Fall
English, Josh	Selma
Rodriguez, Aric	Firebaugh, Fall
Angulo, L.	Caruthers

197
Muxlow, Ty	Kingsburg, Fall, 1:57
Rosas, Kobe	Coalinga
Chcias, Eric	Firebaugh, Forfeit
Lightner, Jacob	Kern Valley
Jimenez, Isaiah	Selma, Fall
Martinez, P.	Yosemite

222
Macias, Ramiro	R F Kennedy, 5-3
Echeveste, Nicholas	Firebaugh
Madrid, Manuel	Corcoran, Decision
Sanchez, Enrique	Shafter
Garcia, Matt	Exeter, Decision
Acuna, John	Cesar Chavez

SIERRA – SEQUOIA DIVISIONAL - Shafter
February 19-20, 2016

287
Alvarez, Rogi	Selma, 3-2	
Hernandez, Edgar	Corcoran	
Ortiz, Hercules	Caruthers	
Schuler, Brett	Bak Christian, Fall	
Perez, Anthony	Exeter	
Guerra, Jesus	R F Kennedy	

Scores, and fall, times, weren't, given for, third, and fifth, place.

* Record

Most Outstanding Wrestlers

Lower Weight: Jacob Wright   Dinuba
Upper Weight: Ramiro Macias   R F Kennedy

TEAM SCORES

1	Selma	380
2	Dinuba	237
3	Exeter	200
4	Corcoran	178
5	R F Kennedy	144
6	Dos Palos	143
7	Firebaugh	136
8	Shafter	100
8	Kerman	100
10	Coalinga	99
11	Chowchilla	98
12	Washington Union	93.5
13	Caruthers	81
14	Kingsburg	79
15	Cesar Chavez	74
16	Garces	72
16	Wasco	72
18	Farmersville	65
19	Arvin	60
20	Granite Hills	58
21	Mendota	55.5
22	Kern Valley	54
23	Orange Cove	41
23	Tranquility	41
25	Avenal	40
25	Liberty Madera	40
27	Sierra Pacific	32
28	Sierra	31.5
29	Bakersfield Christian	29
29	Fowler	29
31	Yosemite	28
32	McFarland	25
33	Strathmore	18
34	Woodlake	12
35	Bishop	7
36	Rosamond	3

*44 Schools entered

Jacob Wright, Dinuba High School

Jacob Wright and Julian Flores

SIERRA – SEQUOIA DIVIONAL – Sierra Pacific
February 17-18, 2017

106
Lujan, Tristen	Selma, 1106
Arreola, Lorenzo	Dinuba
Morales, Joe	Exeter, Fall, 1:48
Gomez, Sabastian	Washington Union
Hernandez, Jonah	Corcoran, 4-0
Bedrosian, Wyatt	Coalinga
Hayie, Jauron	Firebaugh, 10-4
Cantoriano, Able	Caruthers

113
Olea, Eric	Exeter, 6-3
Dhanda, Gurjot	Dinuba
Landin, Jose	Wasco, 3-0, *24-11
Chavez, Martin	Orange Cove
Franco, Isaiah	Firebaugh, 7-6
Lica, Jacob	Washington Union
Price, Chris	Corcoran, TF, 15-0
Bedrosian, Kyle	Coalinga

120
Sosa, John	Selma, 6-1, OT
Perez, Tony	Shafter
Fonseca, Daniel	Dinuba, Fall, 1:16
Arriaza, Wilfredo	Arvin
Price, Joseph	Corcoran, Forfeit
Birrueta, Mario	Wasco
Ortiz, Adam	R F Kennedy, 8-6
Juarez, Miguel	Coalinga

126
Garcia, Robert	Selma, 3-1, OT
Perez, Isaiah	Dinuba
Rodgers, Brock	Corcoran, 11-4
Tamayo, Carlos	Mendota
Bernal, Valentine	Kerman, Injury, Forfeit
Mendoza, Luis	Kern Valley
Gomez, Luis	Coalinga, 14-2
Delarosa, Adan	Caruthers

132
Ramos, Luis	Selma, Fall, :30
Arellano, Anselmo	Wasco
Valencia, Nathan	Dos Palso, Fall, 3:23
Alvarez, Mark	Dinuba
Perez, Jose	Firebaugh, 6-4
Muratalla, Cristin	Mendota
Caevantes, Johnny	Coalinga, 11-6, OT
Vang, Aaron	Washington Union

138
Mendoza, Tony	Selma, Fall, 3:24
Panduro, Aaron	Corcoran
Cortez, Noah	Dinuba, Injury, Default
Ayon, Lupe	Exeter
Gamboa, Manuel	Cesar Chavez, Fall, 2:55
Figueroa, Byan	Mendota
Estrella, Nathan	McFarland, 15-8
Melendez, David	Firebaugh

145
Wright, Jacob	Dinuba, Fall, 3:24
Ramos, Jonathan	Selma
Molina, Esteban	Firebaugh, Injury, Default
Bedrosian, Caleb	Coalinga
Kloster, William	Sierra Pacific, Fall, 2:34
Ramirez, Victor	Chowchilla
Moreno, Antonio	Garces, 18-9
Reyes, Ivan	R F Kennedy

152
Luchau, Jace	Selma, 5-2
Long, Daniel	Dinuba
Pimentel, Armando	Dos Palso, 2-1
Galindo, Miguel	Washington Union
Vale, Jonathon	Sierra Pacific, injury, Default
Stark, Braxton	Sierra
Alexis, Gil	Granite, Hills, Falls, 2:44
Rocha, Brandon	Kingsburg

160
Diaz, Oscar	Selma, Fall, 3:27
Rivas, Arturo	Firebaugh
Benadum, Chance	Dos Palso, 2-1
Collazo, Noah	Parlier
Rangel, Julius	Dinuba, Fall, 1:11
Escalera, Brandon	Granite, Hills
Pantoja, Brian	Garces, 12-7
Carpenter, Alfred	Kingsburg

170
Rodriguez, Christian	Selma, Fall, 3:00
Maldonado, Fabian	Avenal
Cisneros, Jordan	Dinuba, Fall, 3:00
Jackson, Bo	Kingsburg
Limon, Matt	Kerman, Fall, 1:45
Barajas, Luis	Mendota
Morales, Alfredo	Washington Union, Fall, 3:11
Zamudio, Rafael	Shafter

182
Martin, Isaiah	Garces, 3-0, *34-11
Gonzalez, Richard	Tranquility
Hernandez, Richard	Kerman, Fall, 2:40
Roth, Kaleb	Liberty

SIERRA – SEQUOIA DIVIONAL – Sierra Pacific
February 17-18, 2017

Banuelos, Antonio	Shafter, Fall, 5:58	8 Dos Palos	95.5
Miramontes, Justin	Dinuba	9 Kingsburg	89
Mittlestead, Eric	Exeter, Fall, :30	10 Shafter	82.5
Navarro, Erick	Firebaugh	11 R F Kennedy	80
		12 Mendota	78
195		13 Washington Union	77
Jimenez, Isaiah	Selma, 6-0	14 Garces	76
Velez, Christopher	R F Kennedy	15 Wasco	58
Butterfield, Quinn	Sierra, Fall, 1:11	16 Chowchilla	57
Aispuro, Gerardo	McFarland	17 Kern Valley	53.5
Mendoza, Alfonso	Kerman, Fall, :30	18 Parlier	52
Duarte, Jesus	Orange Cove	19 Bakersfield Christian	49
Medina, Joshua	Firebaugh, Fall, 1:11	19 Liberty Madera	49
Ayala, Edwin	Shafter	21 Caruthers	43
		21 Orange Cove	43
220		23 Sierra Pacific	41
Muxlow, Ty	Kingsburg, 4-2, OT	24 Cesar Chavez	40
Echeveste, Nicholas	Firebaugh	25 Granite Hills	36
Sera, Tony	Dinuba, Injury, Default	26 Tranquility	34
Rosas, Kobe	Coalinga	27 Arvin	30
Walker, Tre	Dos Palso, Injury, Default	27 McFarland	30
Lightner, Jacob	Kern Valley	27 Woodlake	30
Ayon, Anthony	Exeter, Injury, Default	30 Sierra	29
Madrid, Manuel	Corcoran	31 Avenal	27
		32 Yosemite	12
285		33 Lindsey	10
Schuler, Brett,	Bakersfield Christian, Fall, 3:21*26-1	34 Rosamond	8
		35 Desert	7
Johnston, Matthew	Chowchilla	36 Farmersville	6
Moran, Xavier	Kingsburg, 8-1	37 Strathmore	4
Eliosa, Thomas	Dinuba	38 Bishop Union	0
Ortiz, Hercules	Caruthers, 9-5		
Leyva-Medina	Jasper, Firebaugh		
Covarrubia, Angel	Kerman, 2-0		
Boland, Cord	Exeter		

* Season, records

Most Outstanding Wrestlers

Lower Weight: Jacob Wright   Dinuba
Upper Weight: Brett Schuler,
              Bakersfield Christian

TEAM SCORES

1 Selma	321.5
2 Dinuba	298.5
3 Firebaugh	176
4 Coalinga	128
4 Corcoran	128
6 Kerman	123.5
7 Exeter	117

Robert Garcia, Selma High School (07/18/2018)
Photographer: Jeremiah Martinez, Selma Enterprise

SIERRA – SEQUOIA DIVISIONAL – Sierra Pacific
February 15-16, 2018

106
Figueroa, Richard	Selma, TF, 17-2	
Bedrosion, Wyatt	Coalinga	
Hernandez, Jonah	Corcoran, Fall	
Macias, Jimmy	Cesar Chavez	
Castro, Javier	Dinuba, Major, Decision, 12-2	
Garza, Michael	Parlier	
Delarosa, Ricardo	Firebaugh, Fall	
Langoria, Josh	Kingsburg	

113
- Lujan, Tristan — Selma, Major, Decision, 13-4
- Arreola, Lorenzo — Dinuba
- Vasquez, Keith — Shafter, Fall
- Gomez, Sabastian — Washington Union
- Chavez, Martin — Orange Cove, Fall
- Alejo, Andrew — Kerman
- Bartolome, Daniel — Cesar Chavez, Fall
- Velasquez, Roman — Caruthers

120
- Rivera, Eric — Selma, 7-2
- Viveros, Jonathan — Kingsburg
- Olea, Erik — Exeter, 4-3
- Bernal, Valentin — Kerman
- Haynie, Jauron — Firebaugh
- Jimenez, Joseph — Dos Palos, Fall
- Garza, Christian — Shafter, 6-5
- Avila, Ryan — Liberty Madera

126
- Sepulveda, Tyler — Selma, 3-1
- Juarez, Miguel — Coalinga
- Perez, Anthony — Shafter, Major, Decision, 12-2
- Licea, Jacob — Washington Union
- Jackson, Jeff — Kingsburg, 5-2
- Bartolme, Anthony — Cesar Chavez
- Dotson, Jarred — Liberty Madera, Fall
- Wright, Brandon — Woodlake

132
- Areyano, Robert — Selma, 3-0
- Rogers, Brock — Corcoran
- Valencia, Armando — Dos Palos, 6-1
- Vang, Aaron — Washington Union
- Arreola, Marcus — Dinuba, 4-2
- DeLa, Rosa, Adan — Caruthers
- Gonzales, Eli — Shafter, Fall
- Ruiz, Vincent — Rosamond

138
- Ramos, Luis — Selma, Fall
- Ayon, Lupe — Exeter
- Perez, Jose — Firebaugh, 5-1
- Prudek, Jake — Caruthers
- Mauratallia, Christian — Mendota, 9-4
- Fulce, James — Bakersfield Christian
- Gomez, Jose — Coalinga, Fall
- Guynn, Nicolas — Yosemite

145
- Mendoza, Tony — Selma, 5-1
- Cortez, Moah — Dinuba
- Valencia, Nathan — Dos Palos, Forfeit
- Garcia, Seth — Strathmore
- Bedrosion, Caleb — Coalinga, 11-4
- Skaugstad, David — Rosamond
- Carranza, Mike — Shafter, Fall
- Pavich, Jacob — Exeter

152
- Luchau, Jace — Selma, Fall, :58
- Molina, Estaban — Firebaugh
- Miller, Conrad — Kern Valley, Fall
- Vue, Jay — Washington Union
- Santoyo, Eduardo — R F Kennedy, Fall
- Pompa, Andrew — Shafter
- Wilson, Rashad — Sierra Pacific, Forfeit

160
- Diaz, Oscar — Selma, 4-2
- Long, Daniel — Dinuba
- Rivas, Arturo — Firebaugh, Fall
- Valle, Jonathan — Sierra Pacific
- Rocha, Brandon — Kingsburg
- Barajas, David — Mendota
- Micalleff, Justin — Yosemite, 10-3
- Ferrer, Elijah — Washington Union

170
- Rodriguez, Christian — Selma, 6-0
- Limon, Mat — Kerman
- Carpenter, Alfred — Kingsburg, 3-0
- Miramontes, Justin — Dinuba
- Zamugio, Rafael — Shafter, Fall
- Gamez, Marcos — Firebaugh
- Hussin, Basheer — Orange Cove
- Garcia, Arturo — Corcoran

182
- Maldonado, Fabian — Avenal, 8-3
- Rangel, Julius — Dinuba
- Banuelos, Anthonie — Shafter, Fall *27-9

SIERRA – SEQUOIA DIVISIONAL – Sierra Pacific
February 15-16, 2018

Manzo, Luciano — Chowchilla
Garcia, Rudy — Selma, 8-4
Hurtado, Francisco — Coalinga
Chavez, Mauricio — Tranquilly, Fall
Roth, Kaleb — Liberty Madera

195
Jimenez, Isaiah — Selma, Fall
Mendoza, Alfonso — Kerman
Mittlestead, Eric — Exeter, Fall
Rodriguez, Matthew — Washington Union
Stockton, Dylan — Kingsburg, Fall
Renteria, Brandon — Woodlake
Tapia, Diego — Kern Valley, Fall
Alaniz, Jason — Dos Palos

220
Aispuro, Gerardo — McFarland, 5-3
Madrid, Manuel — Corcoran
Campos, Eric — R F Kennedy, Fall
Guzman, Anthony — Woodlake
Lugo, Angel — Liberty Madera, 6-5
Solorio, Jose — Kerman
Nutt, Jordan — Washington Union, Fall
Steele, David — Bakersfield Christian

285
Boland, Cord — Exeter, Default
Lightner, Jacob — Kern Valley
Cavamubia, Angel — 3-2
Moran, Xavier — Selma
Rojas, Francisco — Liberty Madera, 4-0
Almanza, Jose — Firebaugh
Cuellar, William — Dos Palos, Fall
Amaya, Jesus — McFarland

* Fall, times, not given

Most Outstanding Wrestlers

Lower Weight: Richard Figueroa   Selma
Upper Weight: Fabian Maldonado   Avenal

TEAM SCORES

1	Selma	363
2	Dinuba	162.5
3	Shafter	157
4	Exeter	147
5	Firebaugh	146
6	Kingsburg	130.5
7	Kerman	121.5
8	Washington Union	120
9	Coalinga	112.5
10	Corcoran	106.5
11	Liberty Madera	90
11	Dos Palos	90
13	Kern Valley	84
14	Caruthers	77
15	Cesar Chavez	76.5
16	R F Kennedy	73
17	McFarland	62
18	Woodlake	51
19	Orange Cove	48.5
20	Mendota	39.5
21	Wasco	39
21	Yosemite	39
23	Bakersfield Christian	38
24	Chowchilla	33
25	Sierra Pacific	32.5
26	Granite Hills	30
26	Rosamond	30
28	Fowler	26
29	Avenal	24
30	Sierra	22
31	Lindsey	20
32	Parlier	19
33	Strathmore	18
34	Tranquility	15
35	Arvin	13
36	Desert	11.5
37	Bishop Union	4
38	Farmersville	0

Joey Cruz - Clovis North High School and
Richard Figueroa – Selma High School

CENTRAL SECTION CHAMPIONSHIPS
TEAM CHAMPIONS & OUTSTANDING WRESTLERS

1952-2000

CIF CENTRAL SECTION CHAMPIONSHIPS
TEAM CHAMPIONS

Date	Champion	Coach	Location
1-26-1952	Roosevelt	Vico Bondietti	Oakdale
1-31-1953	Roosevelt	Vico Bondietti	Fresno High
2-06-1954	Roosevelt	Vico Bondietti	Tulare Union
2-12-1955	Roosevelt	Vico Bondietti	Roosevelt/Fresno
2-11-1956	Madera	Vern Brooks	Fresno High
1957	No CIF Finals	N/A	N/A
2-15-1958	Fresno	Dick Frances	Roosevelt/Fresno
2-21-1959	Madera	Vern Brooks	Tulare Union
2-20-1960	Madera	Vern Brooks	Bakersfield High
2-18-1961	Madera	Vern Brooks	McLane/Fresno
2-17-1962	East Bakersfield	Leon Tedder	Mt. Whitney/Visalia
2-16-1963	East Bakersfield	Leon Tedder	Bakersfield College
2-22-1964	Madera	Vern Brooks	McLane/Fresno
2-27-1965	South Bakersfield	Joe Seay	Tulare Western
2-26-1966	South Bakersfield	Joe Seay	South Bakersfield
2-25-1967	South Bakersfield	Joe Seay	McLane/Fresno
2-24-1968	Bakersfield High	Olan Polite	Reedley College
3-01-1969	Madera	Al Kiddy	Bakersfield College
2-28-1970	Madera	Al Kiddy	McLane/Fresno
2-27-1971	South Bakersfield	Joe Seay	Monache/Porterville
3-04-1972	Bakersfield High	Olan Polite	McLane/Fresno
3-04-1973	Clovis	Dennis Deliddo	Highland/Bakersfield
2-23-1975	Clovis	Dennis Deliddo	Mt. Whitney/Visalia
2-28-1976	Clovis	Dennis Deliddo	Fresno City College
2-26-1977	Highland	Joe Barton	West Bakersfield
2-25-1978	Monache	Drew Williams	Hanford
2-24-1979	South Bakersfield	Eugene Walker	Clovis
3-01-1980	Highland	Jim Seay	Bakersfield College
2-28-1981	Clovis	Dennis Deliddo	Monache/Porterville
2-27-1982	Clovis West	Lennis Cowell	Clovis West
2-26-1983	Clovis West	Lennis Cowell	Bakersfield High
2-25-1984	Clovis West	Lennis Cowell	Hanford
2-23-1985	Clovis	Rodney Balch	Clovis West
3-01-1986	Clovis	Rodney Balch	Bakersfield High
2-28-1987	South Bakersfield	Eugene Walker	Monache/Porterville
2-27-1988	Clovis	Rodney Balch	Bullard/Fresno
2-25-1989	Selma	Nick Quintana	Arvin
1-24-1990	Madera	Corky Napier	Hanford
2-23-1991	Clovis	Rodney Balch	Clovis
2-29-1992	Clovis	Rodney Balch	Bakersfield College
2-27-1993	Clovis	Rodney Balch	Mt. Whitney/Visalia
2-26-1994	Clovis	Rodney Balch	Clovis
2-25-1995	Bakersfield	David East	Arvin
2-24-1996	Buchanan	Chris Hansen	Monache/Porterville
3-01-1997	Buchanan	Chris Hansen	Clovis
2-28-1998	Buchanan	Chris Hansen	Shafter
2-27-1999	Clovis	Steve Tirapelle	Mt. Whitney/Visalia
2-26-2000	Clovis	Steve Tirapelle	Buchanan

CIF CENTRAL SECTION CHAMPIONSHIPS
MOST OUTSTANDING WRESTLERS

Year		School	Wrestler
1952		Roosevelt	George Kezarian
1953		Hughson	Don Taylor
1954		Tulare Union	Don Westerling
1955		Roosevelt	Marvin Powell
1956		Roosevelt	Bob Carr
1959		East Bakersfield	Larry Carpenter
1966		South Bakersfield	Richard Simmons
1992	Lower Weight	Bakersfield	Colby Wright
1992	Upper Weight	Hanford	Lalo Moz
1993	Lower Weight	Wasco	Aaron Rodriguez
1993	Upper Weight	Monache	Ryan Silva
1994	Lower Weight	Madera	Moises Perez
1994	Upper Weight	Hanford	Demes Cabral
1995	Lower Weight	Sanger	Albert Garza
1995	Upper Weight	Kingsburg	Don Jackson
1996	Lower Weight	Corcoran	Alex Ortiz
1996	Upper Weight	Kingsburg	Sonny Pereschica
1997	Lower Weight	Sanger	Jamie Garza
1997	Upper Weight	Buchanan	Tyler Lunn
1998	Lower Weight	Clovis West	Ralph Lopez
1998	Upper Weight	Buchanan	Tyler Lunn
1999	Lower Weight	Firebaugh	Jason Moreno
1999	Upper Weight	Centennial	Josh Naus
2000	Lower Weight	Centennial	Daniel Chapman
2000	Upper Weight	Lemoore	Chris Pendleton

Starting in 1992 the Coyote Club sponsored the Lower/Upper Weights Most Outstanding Wrestlers Awards

Floyd "Doc" Buchanan is credited with installing a competitive athletic spirit throughout the Clovis Unified school District. A high school and elite wrestling tournament are named for him.

CENTRAL SECTION DIVISIONAL CHAMPIONSHIPS
DIVISION I - II - III - IV - V

2019-2020

CENTRAL SECTION DIVISION I CHAMPIONSHIPS – Clovis North
February 8-9, 2019

108
Figueroa, Richard	Selma, Fall, 4:34
Gioffre, Jack	Buchanan
Arsitio, Noah	Clovis North, Fall, :27
Matthew, Terrence	Clovis
Alcala, Josh	Frontier, 12-9
McDonald, Dylan	Lemoore
Becerra, Johnny	Bakersfield, Fall, 1:02
Estrada, John	Central
Torres, Alex	Bullard, 8-3
Torres, Steven	Mission Oak

115
Lujan, Tristan	Selma, SV, 3-1
Negrete, Carlos	Buchanan
Zinkin, Hayden	Clovis North, 3-1
Mouritsen, Justin	Clovis
Madrigal, Giovani	Madera, 5-2
Onsurez, Ashton	Bakersfield
Corona, Shane	Foothill, Fall, 4:00
Castro, Javier	Dinuba
Romero, Xander	Lemoore, 5-2
Alcantar, Derek	Frontier
Herrera, Jonathan	Bullard

122
Renteria, Maximo	Buchanan, 3-2
Cruz, Joey	Clovis North
Rivera, Jacob	Selma, 11-7
Paulson, Brandon	Clovis
Gayton, Jesse	Lemoore, 3-2
Murphy, James	Central
Appleton, Jay, T	Frontier, Medical Forfeit
Arreola, Lorenzo	Dinuba
Vasquez, Romero	Clovis East, 8-7
Casimiro, Angel	Foothill
Takeuchi, Elijah	Clovis West, Forfeit
Solorio, Christian	Madera

128
Murphy, Devin	Clovis North, 5-3
Reyes, Cole	Frontier
Joint, Wayne	Lemoore, 2-0
Valdovinos, Raul	Clovis West
Leake, Hunter	Buchanan, 9-2
Rhoads, Austin	Clovis
Solorio, Jonathan	Central, Medical Forfeit
Chavez, Adrian	Central
Khachtryan, Daniel	Bullard, Fall, 1:54
Estrada, Blake	Selma
East, McKay	Bakersfield, Fall, :36
Moreno, Vincent	Madera South

134
Franco, Ryan	Clovis North, 14-7
Petrucelli, Giano	Clovis
Gioffre, Logan	Buchanan, 4-3, TB-2
Lucio, Cade	Bakersfield
Fletcher, Garrett	Frontier, Fall, 1:01
Amaya, Luis	Foothill
Jaramillo, Manny	Selma, 8-5
Wilson, Zach	Mission Oak
Bejarano, Alejandro	Clovis East, Fall, 3:15
Garcia, Adrian	Dinuba
Paredes, Rudy	Madera, Fall, 3:08
Benevidez, Javier	Porterville

140
Deen, Tyler	Buchanan, 5-3, SV
Bloemhof, Andrew	Bakersfield
Morphis, Ryan	Frontier, Major 13-2
Zuniga, George	Central
Watts, Zach	Clovis North, 5-3, SV
Sepulveda, Tyler	Selma
Logan, Barajas	Avina, Clovis, 16-0, TF
Corchado, Abraham	Clovis West
Chimkey, Daniel	Clovis East, Major 13-4
Evans, Ean	Mission Oak
Esquivel, Christian	Dinuba, 6-1
Yrigollen, Ryan	Madera South

147
Sihavong, Dawson	Bullard, Major 11-3
Martin, Joseph	Buchanan
Cuttone, Vito	Clovis North, 4-3
Landin, Jose	Frontier
Martin, Nick	Clovis, Major 9-0
Sekhon, Abheybir	Central
Spears, Jacob	Bakersfield, 10-4
Christopherson, J. J.	Clovis East
Cantoriano, Andrew	Clovis West, 3-1
Ruiz, Oscar	Madera
Calderon, Andrew	Mission Oak, Major 13-3
Ortiz, Giovanni	Madera South

154
Luchau, Jace	Selma, 7-3
Anderson, Max	Clovis
Gonzalez, Adrian	Bakersfield, 3-2, TB-2
Raiz, Rey	Buchanan
Almaguer, Evan	Clovis North, Medical Forfeit
Brazet, Lance	Bullard
Gaeth, Julien	Central, Fall, 1:07
Nava, Hector	Porterville
Yanez, Alex	Lemoore, Medical Forfeit
Ceccato, Jared	Frontier

CENTRAL SECTION DIVISION I CHAMPIONSHIPS – Clovis North
February 8-9, 2019

Wren, Victor — Madera South, Forfeit

162
- Olguin, Matthew — Buchanan, Major 14-6
- Aguirre, Max — Frontier
- Zavala, Nicholas — Mission Oak, 9-7
- Chiaramonte, Mikelli — Clovis
- Sanchez, Jaden — Bakersfield, Medical Forfeit
- Kloster, Will — Lemoore
- Sherwood, Reid — Clovis North, Fall, 3:56
- Grantham, Tayte — Madera South
- Brar, Yadwinder — Clovis East, Fall, 2:15
- Hernandez, Isaiah — Selma
- Martinez, Jaylen — Central, Fall, :43
- Perez, Bryan — Clovis West

172
- Long, Daniel — Dinuba, 7-4
- Contino, Rocco — Buchanan
- Rodriguez, Christian — Selma, 3-2
- Priest, Jarad — Bakersfield
- Frantzich, Austin — Clovis, 11-7
- Landin, Christian — Frontier
- Smith, DeAndre — Clovis East, Fall, :40
- Brand, Rowdy — Clovis North
- Reyes, Angel — Madera South, Fall, 4:56
- Quintanilla, Robert — Bullard
- Davis, Koy — Lemoore

184
- Tracy, Trent — Frontier, Major 9-1
- Gianakopulos, Tyler — Clovis
- Annis, Jordan — Bakersfield, 8-4
- Rodriguez, Felipe — Clovis West
- Peralta, Jalen — Buchanan, Fall, 2:27
- Garcia, Rudy — Selma
- Sharp, Paul — Clovis North, 13-10
- Mannion, Andrew — Clovis East
- Ayala, David — Porterville, Medical Forfeit
- Im, Romany — Central
- Carrillo, Alex — Madera, Fall, 4:48
- Martinez, Jonathan — Mission Oak

197
- Martin, Jadon — Buchanan, Fall, 1:45
- Shepherd, Ty — Frontier
- Sayles, Fredrick — Clovis, 7-4
- Mendivel, Michael — Bakersfield
- Vaca, Alex — Madera, Fall, 2:00
- Valdez, Andrew — Central
- Underwood, Cody — Clovis North, Fall, 1:01
- Gonzales, Isaac — Mission Oak
- Ruiz, Christian — Clovis West, Fall, 2:26

Arechiga, Matthew — Bullard
Duran/Lopez, Hector — Lemoore, 10-6
Reyes, Jorge — Foothill

222
- Good, Jacob — Clovis, Major 17-5
- Morales, Mateo — Clovis West
- Darter, Justen — Bakersfield, 7-0
- Cardwell, Branden — Buchanan
- Pafford, Jack — Frontier, 9-2
- Sandiago, Hulise — Madera
- Calderon, Mateo — Clovis East, Fall, 2:21
- Martinez, Javier — Dinuba
- Mojarras, Christian — Clovis North, Fall, 1:26
- Lopez, Diego — Mission Oak
- Florez, Flavio — Lemoore

287
- Hill, Josiah — Bakersfield, 4-1
- Slatic, Tommy — Bullard
- Schmidtke, Jonah — Clovis East, Fall, :26
- Cook, John — Madera
- Campbell, Kade — Clovis, Fall, 3:16
- Herrera, Christian — Mission Oak
- Rix, Zane — Buchanan, Medical Forfeit
- Renovato, Mike — Selma
- Vasquez, Anthony — Clovis West, Fall, 3:30
- Harmon, Clarence — Porterville
- Torres, Roman — Clovis North, 2-1
- Valdez, Arturo — Lemoore

Most Outstanding Wrestlers
Lower Weight: Tristan Lujan — Selma
Upper Weight: Trent Tracy — Frontier
Championship Coach: Troy Tirapelle — Buchanan

TEAM SCORES

1	Buchanan	324
2	Clovis	276.5
3	Clovis North	235.5
4	Frontier	221
5	Bakersfield	219.5
6	Selma	175.5
7	Central	110.5
8	Bullard	103
9	Madera	99.5
10	Clovis East	97
11	Lemoore	96.5
12	Clovis West	93
13	Mission Oak	72
14	Dinuba	61
15	Madera South	38
16	Foothill	37
17	Porterville	19

CENTRAL SECTION DIVISION I CHAMPIONSHIPS - Lemoore
February 14-15, 2020

108
- Lopez, Raymond — Buchanan, 10-1
- Terrence, Matthew — Clovis
- Mendez, Dominic — Righetti, 11-1
- Gonzalez, Nate — Selma
- McDonald, Dylan — Lemoore, 8-4
- Galicia, Nathan — Madera
- Becerra, Johnny — Bakersfield, 8-4
- Richardson, Anthony — Clovis West
- Lorraine, Tristian — Frontier, SV, 9-7
- Kobashi, Colton — Clovis North
- Carrasco, Jasias — Dinuba, TF, 15-0, 4:44
- Montoya, Eduardo — Central

115
- Figueroa, Richard — Selma, 3-1
- Cruz, Joey — Clovis North
- Lemus, Dario — Clovis, 5-1
- Gioffre, Jack — Buchanan
- Acala, Josh — Frontier Fall, 5:17, *21-11
- Quintana, Coen — Dinuba
- Diaz, Andrew — Bakersfield, 9-4
- Tataglia, Josh — Kingsburg
- Mecedo, Sebastian — Lemoore, 7-3
- Tamayo, Armando — Central
- Zacarias, Sajin — Clovis West, Fall, 1:39
- Estrada, Cameron — Clovis East

122
- Negrete, Carlos — Buchanan, Fall, ?:30
- Lujan, Tristan — Selma
- Rosas, George — Clovis, 2-0
- Maldonado, Laz — Clovis West
- Zinkin, Hayden — Clovis North, 5-3
- Ozuna, Noah — Bakersfield
- Escebdo, Tyson — Righetti, Default
- Gaytan, Jesse — Lemoore
- Castro, Javier — Dinuba, 2-0
- Longoria, Josh — Kingsburg
- Wiles, Chase — Frontier, 6-5, *17-15
- Sanchez, Gabriel — Bullard

128
- Renteria, Maximo — Buchanan, 13-3
- Watts, Ryan — Clovis North
- Joint, Wayne — Lemoore, SV, 6-4
- Leia, Kimo — Selma
- Mouritsen, Justin — Clovis, 5-2
- Chavez, Adrian — Central
- Ibarra, Aaron — Righetti, 5-1
- Spears, Jacob — Bakersfield
- Appleton, Johnny — Frontier, Fall, 1:27, *23-8

- Brar, Toji — Clovis East
- Takeuchi, Elijah — Clovis West, 11-1
- Hernandez, Alex — Kingsburg

134
- Leake, Hunter — Buchanan, 4-3
- Franco, Ryan — Clovis North
- Landin, Jose — Frontier, Forfeit, *20-7
- Murphy, Devin — Selma
- Swan, Sloan — Clovis, Fall, 3:16
- Bautista, Jason — Righetti
- East, McKay — Bakersfield, 3-1
- Ruacho, Matthew — Central
- Leyva, Daniel — Clovis West, Major, 12-0
- Ordaz, Apolonio — Madera
- Moreno, Atzel — Dinuba, Forfeit
- Gonsalves, Lucas — Lemoore

140
- Lake, Kyle — Buchanan, Fall, 3:59
- Viveros, Jonathan — Kingsburg
- Lucio, Cade — Bakersfield, Major, 12-4
- Watts, Zach — Clovis North
- Sekon, Abheybir — Central, Forfeit
- Rodriguez, Matt — Righetti
- Rhoads, Austin — Clovis, Fall, 3:49
- Combs, Luke — Frontier, *16-7
- Arias, Mathew — Selma, 7-0
- Chaidez, Amadeo — Clovis East
- Valencia, Isaac — Mission Oak, Default
- Alvarado, Tony — Clovis West

147
- Gioffre, Logan — Buchanan, Major, 11-3
- Fletcher, Garrett — Frontier, *25-6
- Avina-Barajas — Logan, 3-0
- Montoya, Sergio — Clovis North
- Juarez, James — Bakersfield, 4-2
- Garrett, Gregory — Central
- Jimenez, Xsavier — Kingsburg, Fall, 1:18
- Zepeda, Jaden — Righetti
- Corchado, Abraham — Clovis West, Major, 14-0
- Gutierrez, Dominic — Madera
- Febela, Chris — Selma, MD, 12-3
- Fernandez, Damian — Lemoore

154
- Cortez, Noah — Dinuba, 6-3
- Raiz, Reymundo — Buchanan
- Zuniga, George — Selma, 3-2
- Almaguer, Evan — Clovis North
- Smith, DeAndre — Clovis East, 6-3
- Cantoriaano — Clovis West
- Martinez, Rickieh — Clovis, Fall, 2:35

CENTRAL SECTION DIVISION I CHAMPIONSHIPS - Lemoore
February 14-15, 2020

Weimer, Dwight — Bakersfield
Trevino, Ricardo — Central, 8-6
Combs, Ben — Frontier
Brooks, Robert — Lemoore, Fall, 2:48
Farris, Nick — Righetti

162
Contino, Rocco — Buchanan, Fall, 3:56
Kloster, Will — Lemoore
Sanchez, Jaden — Bakersfield, 5-2, TB, 2
Sepulveda, Tyler — Selma
Merkord, Wyatt — Clovis, Fall, 5:58
Lopez, Jacob — Clovis North
Hansen, Nico — Clovis East, 5-2
Stimson, Anthony — Central
Muxlow, Cal — Kingsburg, SV, 6-4
Barajas, Jeremiah — Frontier
Madrigal, Adan — Madera, Forfeit
Ruiz, Brayden — Righetti

172
Petrecelli, Giano — Clovis, 2-0
Martin, Joseph — Buchanan
Priest, Jarad — Bakersfield, 5-3
Zavala, Nichlas — Mission Oak
Landin, Christian — Frontier, 9-4, *21-5
Florentino, Ryan — Clovis North
Perez, Derian — Central, 9-2
Brar, Yadi — Clovis East
Guerrero, Luke — Righetti, Fall, 5:21
Carpenter, Alfred — Kingsburg
Juarez, Abelardo — Madera, Fall, 5:30
McCouley, Nathan — Bullard

184
Martin, Jaden — Buchanan, 5-2
Smith, Christian — Clovis
Stout, Adrian — Righetti, 12-6
Hernandez, Isaiah — Selma
Steiner, Spencer — Clovis North, 6-3
Meyer, Luke — Bakersfield
Shepard, Jake — Frontier, Fall, 1:02
Ruiz, Christian — Clovis West
Angulo, Luis — Central, 4-2
Moua, Ethan — Clovis East
Jackson, Trace — Kingsburg, 4-1
Bonderer, Gaige — Madera

197
Gianakopulos, Tyler — Clovis, 5-0
Rodriguez, Felipe — Clovis West
Sharp, Paul — Clovis North, 11-6

Trujillo, Chente — Bakersfield
Rodgers, Caden — Buchanan, Forfeit
Garcia, Rudy — Selma
Mannion, Andrew — Clovis East, Fall, 2:00
Smith, Eli — Kingsburg
McCormack, John — Righetti, Fall, 5:08
Martinez, J. J. — Dinuba
Carrillo, Alex — Madera, 6-0
Morris, Brockman — Central

222
Darter, Justin — Bakersfield, 3-2
Morales, Mateo — Clovis West
Hilford, Jordan — Clovis, 3-2
Duran, Noah — Clovis North
Shepard, Ty — Frontier, Default, *22-7
Peralta, Jalen — Buchanan
Gorone, Tyler — Central, 5-2
Santiago, Hulise — Madera
Morales, Jose, Isaiah — Lemoore, Fall, 1:11
Herrera, Alan — Selma
Vea, Julian — Righetti
Mann, Armeet — Clovis East

287
Hill, Josiah — Bakersfield, 8-3
Schmidtke, Jonah — Clovis East
Martinez, Iavier — Dinuba, 1-0
Campbell, Kade — Buchanan
Watson, Isa — Central, Fall, 3:20
Brown, Josh — Righetti
Alaniz, Joe — Clovis East, 5-4
Foraker, Cade — Clovis North
Andrews, Jake — Frontier, 4-2, *27-11
Miller, Matthew — Clovis
Roque, Julian — Selma, Fall, 3:04
Valdez, Arturo — Lemoore

* Records as of 2-14-2020

Most Outstanding Wrestlers

Lower Weight: Carlos Negrete   Buchanan
Upper Weight: Josiah Hill   Bakersfield
Championship Coach: Troy Tirapelle   Buchanan

CENTRAL SECTION DIVISION I CHAMPIONSHIPS - Lemoore
February 14-15, 2020

TEAM RESULTS

1. Buchanan — 321
2. Clovis — 237
3. Clovis North — 199.5
4. Bakersfield — 192
5. Selma — 167.5
6. Frontier — 126
7. Clovis West — 111
8. Righetti — 105
9. Central — 101
10. Lemoore — 83
11. Clovis East — 75
12. Dinuba — 69
13. Kingsburg — 58.5
14. Madera — 42
15. Mission Oak — 19
16. Bullard — 6

JOSIAH HILL
BAKERSFIELD

CENTRAL SECTION II DIVISION CHAMPIONSHIPS - Shafter
February 8-9, 2019

108
Mendez, Dominic	Righetti, MD, (31-8)
Hernandez, Jonah	Corcoran
Longoria, Josh	Kingsburg
Reyes, Jimmy	Hanford
Eastham, Logan	Exeter
Sechslingloff, Jacob	Pioneer Valley
Butts, Zach	Sanger
Nagatani, Jacob	Liberty

115
Jimenez, Xavier	Redwood, MD, (19-8)
Sechslingloff, Matt	Pioneer Valley
Tartaglia, Josh	Kingsburg, Decision
De, LaRosa, Ricardo	Firebaugh
Johnson, Will	Exeter, Fall
Marmolejo, Jacob	Paso Robles
Gonzalez, Christian	Sanger, Fall
McElroy, Carson	Liberty

120
Leia, Kimo	Kingsburg, Fall
Flores, Marco	Exeter
Kilber, Peyton	Paso Robles, Fall
Rojas, Javen	Paso Valley
Ojeda, Andy	Pioneer Valley, Default
Calderon, Alex	Redwood
Garza, Christian	Shafter, Fall
Alejo, Andrew	Kerman

122
Bedrosian, Wyatt	Coalinga, Decision
Olea, Eric	Exeter
Gonzalez, Fernando	Sanger, Decision
Ibarra, Aaron	Righetti
Reyes, Gabriel	Hanford, Decision
Hunt, Colton	Liberty
Lowery, Reily	Paso Robles, Decision
Martinez, Xavier	Golden Valley

134
Viveros, Jonathon	Kingsburg, Decision
Tanner, Porter	Paso Robles
Miranda, Jude	Hanford, Decision
Juarez, Miguel	Coalinga
Haynie-Meraz Jauron,	Firebaugh, Fall
Rodriguez, Alex	Redwood
Rueda, Everardo	Golden Valley, Fall
Limon, Jacob	Pioneer Valley

140
Perez, Angel	Firebaugh, Decision
Leon, Dominick	Golden Valley
Jackson, Jett	Kingsburg, Decision
Bautista, Jasun	Righetti
Valencia, Armando	Dos Palos, Fall
Clawson, Ryan	Liberty
Ward, Joe	Pioneer Valley, Fall
Bedrosian, Kyle	Coalinga

147
Rogers, Brock	Corcoran, Fall, (31-5)
Machado, Ernesto	Golden Valley
Jimenez, Xsavier	Kingsburg, Decision
Miller, Kyle	Paso Robles
Servin, Fernando	R F Kennedy, Default
Rodriguez, Matt	Righetti
Bustamante, Matt	Liberty, Fall
Roldan, Isaiah	Exeter

154
Banduenga, Don, Beni	Righetti, Decision, (31-10)
Garcia, Nathan	Paso Robles
Santoyo, Eduardo	R F Kennedy, Decision
Jimenez, Noah	Kingsburg
Stafford, Vincent	Sanger, Fall
Olivera, Danny	Firebaugh
Sullivan, Jarron	Firebaugh, Redwood, Default
Villasenor, Leo	Corcoran

162
Gamez, Marcos	Firebaugh, Fall
Solis, Adan	Righetti
Vera, Eric	Pioneer Valley, Decision
Muxlow, Cal	Kingsburg
Pavich, Gabriel	Exeter, Decision
Ramirez, Marcus	Dos Palos
Perez, Oscar	R F Kennedy, Default
Gonzalez, Nate	Shafter

172
Lucas, Anthony	Liberty, Decision, (25-3)
Gonzalez, Cameron	Paso Robles
Kim, Ronald	Righetti, Decision
Alonso, Juan	R F Kennedy
Zamudio, Rafael	Shafter, Fall
Carpenter, Alfred	Kingsburg
Longoria, Skyler	Coalinga, MD
Romero, Sebastian	Exeter

184
Ruiz, Oskar	Pioneer Valley, Decision, (22-15)
Flores, Gerardo	Firebaugh
Aguirre, Ricardo	R F Kennedy, MD
McCormack, John	Righetti
Perez, Alejandro	Golden Valley, MD

CENTRAL SECTION II DIVISION CHAMPIONSHIPS - Shafter
February 8-9, 2019

Hernandez, Josh — Dos Palos
Olea, Francisco — Coalinga, Fall
Gonzalez, Trace — Hanford

197
Jackson, Bo — Kingsburg, MD, (28-5)
Cruz, Carlos — Kerman
Stout, Adrian — Righetti, Decision
Ayala, Kevin — Pioneer Valley
Garcia, Sonny — Liberty, MD, (31-13)
Maldanado, Dominic — Hanford
Bega, David — Corcoran, Fall
Escareno, Eloy — Sanger

222
Mittlestead, Eric — Exeter, Fall, (25-5)
Pulis, Hayden — Hanford
Haupt, Blake — Paso Robles, Fall
Maldonado, Joe — Dos Palos
Zapeda, Alejandro — Pioneer Valley, Default
Vea, Julian — Righetti
Hernandez, Andrew — Kingsburg, Fall
Espino, Isaiah — Sanger

287
Houston, Travone — Hanford, MD, (21-7)
Cortez, Josh — Dos Palos
Brown, Josh — Righetti, Fall
DeLaPena — Pioneer Valley
Almanza, Jose — Firebaugh, Fall
Takeda, Tomas — Sanger
Tinnes, Dominic — Coalinga, Default
Bejarano, Abram — Exeter

MD - Major Decision
( ) – Season Record
No fall times or decision points given.

Righetti Head Coaches:
Justin Bronson, Andrew Domingues

Most Outstanding Wrestlers

Lower Weight: Kimo Leia — Kingsburg
Upper Weight: Eric Mittlestead — Exeter

TEAM SCORES

1	Righetti	249
2	Kingsburg	242
3	Pioneer Valley	207
4	Firebaugh	189
5	Hanford	180
6	Exeter	179
7	Paso Robles	171.5
8	Sanger	135
9	Golden Valley	124
10	Dos Palos	120.5
11	Liberty	115
12	Redwood	109
13	Corcoran	102
14	R F Kennedy	99.5
15	Coalinga	90
16	Kerman	85
17	Shafter	80

Ryan Morphis - Frontier High School 2019

CENTRAL SECTION DIVISION II CHAMPIONSHIPS – Madera South
February 14-15, 2020

108
Come, Nathan	Arroyo Grande, 5-2, *23-7
Reyes, Jimmy	Hanford
Delatorre, Elijah	Pioneer Valley, MD, 10-0
Nagatani, Jacob	Liberty
Vaughn, Shaen	Paso Robles, 9-4
Mendez, Lorenzo	Firebaugh
Casas, Andres	Foothill, Fall, 3:13
Felex, Geovanny	Porterville

115
Whittington, Wanderlei	Monache, 4-3, *26-8
Calderon, Alex	Redwood, *34-8
Gacad, Brinion	Liberty
Sheriff, Damion	Madera South, *28-7
Rivera, Gabriel	Arroyo Grande, 5-1
Gonzalez, Christian	Sanger
Eastham, Logan	Exeter, Fall, :44
DeLaRosa, Ricardo	Firebaugh, 5-1

122
Benevidez, Brian	Porterville, 2-0, *27-6
Corona, Shane	Foothill, *33-7
Gomez, Juan	Arroyo Grande
Rojas, Jayven	Golden Valley, *29-6
Moreno, Josh	Redwood, Fall, 5:12
Jaimes, Diego	Madera South
Marmelejo, Jacob	Paso Robles, Fall, 2:59
Jimenez, Joseph	Dos Palos, MD, 10-2, *34-8

128
Florez, Marco	Exeter, 6-2, *27-5
Velasquez, Jacob	Pioneer Valley
Maduena, Dylan	Paso Robles, 8-1, *29-8
Casimiro, Angel	Foothill
Galvan, Adrian	Monache
Vicente, Moreno	Madera South
Guiltron, Anthony	Redwood, Fall, 4:19
Saldana, Devin	Golden Valley, 9-3, *29-8

134
Reyes, Gabriel	Hanford, TB, 1, 4-3, *20-6
Rueda, Everardo	Golden Valley, *34-7
Kilber, Peyton	Paso Robles, 6-4, *27-8
Ojeda, Andy	Pioneer Valley
Cabeje, Landen	Monache, 7-1
Benevidiez, Javier	Porterville
Catalan, Henry	Arroyo Grande, Fall, 3:06
Hunt, Calton	Liberty

140
Flores, Jose	Monache, 8-2, *29-8
Rodriguez, Alex	Redwood, *34-6
Garcia, Jaime	Madera South, 5-4
Vargas, Nathan	Firebaugh
Ochoa, Angel	Foothill, Fall, 1:44
Saldana, Rafael	Golden Valley
Rodriguez, Ian	Paso Robles, Disqualified
Salas, Gabriel	Porterville

147
Munoz, Joseph	Madera South, Fall, 4:57
Estrada, Anthony	Monache
Amaya, Luis	Foothill, MD, 10-2
Sing, Randeep	Sanger
Davidson, Cameron	Paso Robles, Fall, 4:00
Garcia, David	Redwood
Daly, Damen	Exeter, Fall, :30
Nieblas, Tristan	Porterville

154
Stafford, Vincent	Sanger, 5-0, *32-5
Guerrero, Rudy	Golden Valley *33-6
Fragoso, Andrew	Arroyo Grande, 9-7, *26-11
Vera, Eric	Pioneer Valley, *35-11
Nuno, Juan	Hanford, Fall, 4:19, *26-11
Pavich, Jacob	Exeter
Batres, Edgar	Monache, Forfeit
Perez, Arturo	Madera South

162
Leon, Dominic	Golden Valley, 4-3, *37-3
Gamez, Marcos	Firebaugh, *34-5
Collins, Devin	Hanford, 3-1, *29-12
Cardenas, Abel	Madera South, *24-12
Nava, Hector	Porterville, 2-1
Roldan, Isaiah	Exeter, *21-10
Williams, Yance	Monache, 4-1
Salazar, Adrian	Pioneer Valley

172
Clift, Zachary	Arroyo Grande, Fall, 2:26, *22-8
Flores, Gerardo	Firebaugh, *21-8
Ramirez, Marcos	Dos Palos, Fall, 1:08
Castaneda, Giovanni	Pioneer Valley
Ortiz, Giovanni	Madera South, Injury, Default
Encisco, Xavior	R F Kennedy
Romero, Sabastian	Exeter, Fall, 2:41
Castillo, Brian	Sanger

CENTRAL SECTION DIVISION II CHAMPIONSHIPS – Madera South
February 14-15, 2020

184
Avila, Tyler	Porterville, 6-0, *27-5
Alonso, Juan	R, F, Kennedy, *18-5
Garcia, Adrian	Exeter, Fall, 3:08, *24-7
Olivera, Danny	Firebaugh
Ayala, Kevin	Pioneer Valley, Forfeit, *30-16
Reyes, Angel	Madera South, *15-5
Alcala, Brandon	Redwood, 7-0
Diaz, Cameron	Sanger

197
Garcia, Mason	Arroyo Grande, Fall, 3:44, *24-6
Garcia, Sonny	Frontier Liberty, *32-12
Orozco, Juan	Pioneer Valley, Fall, 1:19
Kemp, Leo	Paso Robles
Escareno, Eloy	Sanger, Forfeit
Garcia, Salvador	Monache
Herrera, Kevin	Firebaugh, Fall, 3:08
Navarro, Sebastian	Redwood

222
Pulis, Hayden	Hanford, Fall, 2:28, *26-5
Weimer, Hunter	Monache, *32-9
Zepeda, Alejandro	Pioneer Valley, MD, 12-4
Elisea, Isaiah	Foothill, *24-13
Raygoza, Zane	Firebaugh, Fall, 3:32
Herrejon, Emillano	R F Kennedy
Baines, Ajveer	Sanger, Fall, :19
Silva, David	Redwood

287
Huston, Travon	Hanford, 6-3, *30-4
Avila, Taven	Monache, *27-8
Wilson, Vicente	Pioneer Valley, 1-0, *37-11
Rangel, Brian	Redwood
Arellano, Rivaldo	Arroyo Grande, Fall, 1:28
Haupt, Blake	Paso Robles
Struggs, Tommy	Golden Valley, Fall, :39
Harmon, Clarence	Porterville

* Records as of February 14-15, 2020

Most Outstanding Wrestlers

Lower Weight: Gabriel Reyes Hanford
Upper Weight: Mason Garcia Arroyo Grande
Pioneer Valley Coach - Kent Olson

TEAM RESULTS

1	Pioneer Valley	183
2	Monache	181.5
3	Arroyo Grande	158.5
4	Firebaugh	149
5	Madera South	144.5
6	Golden Valley	138.5
7	Paso Robles	138
8	Hanford	135
9	Redwood	128
10	Exeter	112.5
11	Porterville	112
12	Foothill	107
13	Sanger	98
14	Liberty	60
15	R F Kennedy	50
16	Dos Palos	37.5

Kent Olson - Head Coach, Pioneer Valley High School
Photographer: Joe Baily, Santa Maria Times

CENTRAL SECTION DIVISION III CHAMPIONSHIPS
February 8-9, 2019

108
Cerda, Abraham	Hoover, Fall, (28-4)
Candray, Matthew	Washington Union
Vasquez, Tomas	Wasco, 5-2
Maradiaga, Jacob	Ridgeview
Martinez, Ivan	South, Fall
Martinez, Valentin	Santa Maria
Galindo, Cristian	Independence, 10-8
Tabrez, Devin	Arroyo Grande

115
Garcia, Roman	El Diamante, 12-2(34-10)
Lopez, Rodrigo	Wasco
Sandoval, Ivan	Caruthers, Fall
Barajas, Emilio	Santa Maria
Apodaca, Isaiah	Arroyo Grande, 8-7
Bartolome, Daniel	Cesar, Chavez
Castillo, Victor	Granite Hills, Fall
Gonzalez, Joel	Washington Union

122
Macias, Jimmy	Cesar Chavez, 7-3(21-5)
Hubert, Coleman	Arroyo Grande
Gutierrez, Elijah	Ridgeview, 4-2
Velasques, Roman	Caruthers
Gonzalez, Xavier	Atascadero, Fall
Kittredge, Jacob	Centennial
Carrillo, Vincent	Independence, Fall
Galvan, Adrian	Monache

128
Bartolome, Anthony	Cesar Chavez, 6-4(26-6)
Perez, Francisco	Monache
Straeck, Trent	Atascadero, 11-4
Figueroa, Jason	Mendota
Buyni, Bryan	Tulare Western, Fall
Saldana, Devin	Independence
Vargas, Felix	Garces, 14-12
Donath, Noah	Centennial

134
Kephart, Isaac	Arroyo Grande, 8-7(26-8)
Zalala, Joey	Sunnyside
Arguijo, Elijah	Santa Maria, 16-5, MD
DeLa, Rosa, Adan	Caruthers
Job, Amador	South, 9-5
Cooper, Cael	Atascadero
Rioffrio-VanTassel	Chowchilla, Fall
Segura, Jacob	Centennial

140
Flores, Jose	Monache, 9-2(24-9)
Flores, Angel	Caruthers
Cardona, Andrew	Sunnyside, 7-3
Catalan, Henry	Arroyo Grande
Magana, Anthony	Centennial, Fall
Gonzalez, Fredi	Washington Union
Shallberger, Zayne	Chowchilla, 10-3
Macias, Matt	Atascadero

147
Wills, Zachary	Centennial, Fall (26-9)
Frey, Levi	Arroyo Grande,
Estrada, Anthony	Monache,
Injury, Default	
Munoz, Sergio	Sunnyside
Lewis, Josh	Independence, Fall
Montanez, Bryan	Santa Maria
Hall, Sean	Atascadero, 5-3
Cervantes, Juan	Tulare Western

154
Prudek, Jake	Caruthers, Fall (36-6)
Avila, Hunter	Monache
Molina, Anthony	Hoover, Fall
Torres, Raymond	South
Guerrero, Rudy	Ridgeview, Fall
McKenzie, Wyatt	Atascadero
Vue, Jay	Washington Union, 6-5
Ramirez, Josh	Centennial

162
Fragoso, Andrew	Arroyo Grande, 10-7(21-7)
Jacuinde, Steven	Granite Hills
Olejnik, Lucas	Centennial, Fall (25-11)
Ruiz, Joncarlo	Wasco
Raucho, Christian	Washington Union, 7-2
Quang, Nicholas	Santa Maria
Stansbury, Dylan	Independence, 11-10
Chavez, Alex	Atascadero

172
Cardwell, Mark	Monache, Fall (35-4)
Spainhoward, Justin	Ridgeview
Rivera, Adrian	South, Fall
Clift, Zachary	Arroyo Grande
Christie, Shane	Granite Hills, Fall
Gamez, Nelsen	Santa Maria
Hernandez, David	Hoover, 4-2
Romero, Michael	Independence

CENTRAL SECTION DIVISION III CHAMPIONSHIPS
February 8-9, 2019

184
Manzo, Luciano	Chowchilla, 4-3 (24-4)
Bordon, John	Ridgeview
Maez, Isaac	Arroyo Grande, Fall
Newsom, Joshua	Monache
Ortega, Anthony	Centennial, 4-3
Ferrer, Elijah	Washington Union
Ruiz, Erik	Hoover, 8-7
Ensaldo, Tommy	Granite Hills

197
Garcia, Mason	Arroyo Grande, 9-4(31-8)
Cardenas, Javier	El Diamante
Castellanos, Moises	Mendota, Fall
Young, Andrew	Chowchilla
Garcia, Salvador	Monache, Fall
Weir, Nathan	Centennial
Blanco, Harvey	Hoover, 3-2
Robledo, Matthew	Wasco

222
McDermott, Caleb	Hoover, 9-3(29-9)
Enriquez, Nathan	Independence
Weimer, Hunter	Monache, Fall
Nutt, Jordan	Washington Union
Gonzalez, Edward	South, Fall
Schwartz, David	Centennial
Rodriguez, Jose	Sunnyside, Fall
Cervantes, Johan	Granite Hills

287
Castro, Emmauel	Garces, 9-3(20-3)
Avila, Taven	Monache
Velasquez, Vincent	Granite Hills, Fall
Arellano, Rivaldo	Arroyo Grande
Lopez, David	Sunnyside, Forfeit
Blanco, Issac	Hoover
Ornelas, Alexander	Tulare Western, Fall
Valera, Jonathan	Wasco

No fall times were given
( ) – Records
Arroyo Grande Head Coach: Kent Hubert

Most Outstanding Wrestlers

Lower Weight: Zachary Wills   Centennial
Upper Weight: Mark Cardwell Monache

TEAM SCORES

1	Arroyo Grande	220.5
2	Monache	220
3	Centennial	144
4	Hoover	119
5	Caruthers	118
6	South	104
7	Ridgeview	101
8	Sunnyside	91.5
9	Santa Maria	90
10	Wasco	82
11	Washing Union	80.5
12	Granite Hills	78
13	Atascadero	77.5
14	Independence	76
15	El Diamante	69
16	Cesar Chavez	65
16	Chowchilla	65
18	Tulare Western	46
19	Garces	43
19	Mendota	43

DIVISION III SECTION CHAMPIONS
North High School

CENTRAL SECTION DIVISION III CHAMPIONSHIPS - North
February 14-15, 2020

106
Rivera, Abellino	South, Major, 12-3
Bartolome, Daniel	Cesar Chavez
Harton, Howard	Kerman, Fall, 3:54, *23-9
Hernandez, Noah	Corcoran, *27-10
Candray, Matthew	Washington Union, 8-3
Galindo, Christian	Independence
Taguada, Lorenzo	Caruthers, Fall, 4:27, *23-5
Clark, Cody	Wasco

115
Cerda, Abraham	Hoover, TF, 17-3, *32-5
Ornelaz, Daniel	North, *24-8
Onsurez, Ashton	Centennial, Fall, 4:37, *23-5
Riley, John	Morro Bay
Vasquez, Tomas	Wasco, Fall, 3:28
Jiminez, Manuel Miguel	Santa Maria
Medina, Josh	Ridgeview, Fall, 3:31, *23-10
Gonzales, Joel	Washington Union, *23-13

122
Lopez, Kalob	North, 8-2, *23-6
Macias, Jimmy	Cesar Chavez
Garza, Christian	Shafter, Fall, 1:49
Ochoa, Jesus	Ridgeview, *24-7
Campos, Bobby	Kerman, Forfeit
Contreras, Isaiah	Centennial
Garcia, Samuel	El Diamante, 6-0
Morales, Oswaldo	Santa Maria

128
Bedrosian, Wyatt	Coalinga, Fall, 4:27, *28-4
Bartolome, Anthony	Cesar Chavez
Gutierrez, Elijah	Ridgeview, Fall, 1:40, *34-6
Ornelaz, Athony	North, *26-8
Silva, Brandon	Hoover, Fall, 2:58
Brown, Zerek	Atascadero, *28-15
Delgado, Emmanuel	Santa Maria, 5-3
Macias, Ruben	Wasco

134
Ruvacalba, Anthony	South, 3-2, *23-7
Farias, Jose	Kerman, *29-14
Guzman, Elijah	Cesar Chavez, 12-6
Yelland, Martin	North, *22-12
Price, Christopher	Corcoran, Major, 13-2
Segura, Jacob	Centennial
Garcia, Juventino	Santa Maria, 3-2
Phommaseng, Kevin	Washington Union

140
Aginiga, Jose	Coalinga, Fall, :38, *13-4
Benitez, Samuel	Santa Maria
Lewis, Joshua	Independence, 6-3, *25-15
Armbruster, Dalton	Corcoran, *21-10
Royal, Bailey	South, 11-6
Cooper, Cale	Atascadero, *26-13
Perez, Noah	Caruthers, Fall, :57, *24-10
Gonzales, Mario	North

147
Ocampo, Javier	North, Fall, 3:12
Oregel, Brian	Kerman, *24-14
Arafi, Amiradeen	Sunnyside, 4-2, *28-11
Carizal-Ramirez, Erik	Santa Maria
Navarrete, Jesus	Wasco, Forfeit
Vang, Jonathan	Hoover
Aguilar, Manuel	Granite Hills, Forfeit
Martinez, Carlos	Shafter

154
Cardona, Andrew	Sunnyside, 9-4, *33-6
Wilson, Wesley	Morro Bay
Stansbury, Dylan	Ridgeview, Fall, :49, *33-7
Renteria, Jose	North, *24-11
Navarro, Jose	Wasco, Major, 11-0
Garcia, Richard	South
Hall, Sean	Atascadero, Fall, 4:57
Garcia, Valente	Granite Hills

162
Prudek, Jake	Caruthers, Fall, 1:42, *30-5
Ruacho, Christian	Washington Union
Chavez, Alex	Atascadero, Fall, 3:02, *32-9
McBride, Drew	North
Olejnik, Lucas	Centennial, Fall, 2:51, *16-10
Grijalva, Victor	Chowchilla
Helm, Jeremy	South, Fall, 1:47, *23-9
Galvan, Martin	Independence

172
Christie, Shane	Granite Hills, Fall, 5:31, *31-7
Spainhoward, Justin	Ridgeview, *30-6

CENTRAL SECTION DIVISION III CHAMPIONSHIPS - North
February 14-15, 2020

Longoria, Skyler — Coalinga, 1-0, *23-9
Sullivan, Keenan — Centennial
Maldonado, Samuel — Sunnyside, Fall, 1:53
Murillo, Leonardo — Kerman
Gleason, Isaiah — Atascadero, Major, 17-1
Carty, Peter — Chowchilla

184
Valla, Alex — Centennial, Fall, 1:54, *22-9
Gonzalez, Daniel — Cesar Chavez
Quang, Nicholas — Santa Maria, Major, 12-3
Zertuche, Vincent — Atascadero
Marquez, Alejandro — North, Fall, 3:10
Reid, Ben — Morro Bay
Hernandez, David — Hoover, Fall, 3:52
Bege, David — Corcoran

197
Ferrer, Elijah — Washington Union, Fall, 4:50, *25-3
Cruz, Carlos — Kerman
Chuca, Zion — North, Fall, 1:52, *22-6
Vecere, Justin — Centennial
House, James — Shafter, Fall, 5:20
Arredondo, Ullices — Cesar Chavez
Millan, Pascual — Wasco, Fall, 1:07
Ebright, Marcus — Morro Bay

222
Lopez, Daniel — Sunnyside, Fall? *36-6
Garcia, Justin — Centennial, *25-14
Costa, Brett — El Diamante, Fall, 1:00
Barajas, Freddy — South
Brander, Carson — Atascadero, 8-6
Romero, Michael — Independence
Whitby, Larry — North, Fall, :53
Ornelas, Moses — Hoover

287
Tinnes, Dominic — Coalinga, Default, *28-7
Hayden, Brenden — Atascadero
Ibrahim, Nathan — El Diamante, 5-0
Burch, Wyatt — North, *20-6
West, Jacob — Centennial, Fall, 5:56, *20-4
Alvarez, Anthony — Corcoran
Hernandez, Andrew — Cesar Chavez, Fall, 5:57
Vargas, Angel — Hoover

* Records as of 2-14-15, 2020
North Coach: Brady Garner

Most Outstanding Wrestlers

Lower Weight: Wyatt Bedrosia — Coalinga
Upper Weight: Jake Prudex — Caruthers

TEAM SCORES

1	North	281
2	Centennial	222.5
3	Kerman	196
4	Atascadero	178
5	Cesar Chavez	174
6	Coalinga	174
7	Hoover	171.5
8	Santa Maria	162.5
9	South	157.5
10	Ridgeview	142
11	Wasco	141
12	Sunnyside	140
13	Shafter	133
14	Washington Union	118
15	Morro Bay	112.5
16	Caruthers	113
17	Corcoran	113
18	Independence	88
19	El Diamente	85
20	Granite Hills	73
21	Chowchilla	56

Wyatt Bedrosian - Coalinga High school

CENTRAL SECTION DIVISION IV CHAMPIONSHIPS
February 8-9, 2019

108
Alcantar, Francisco	Nipomo, 10-2, MD
Sital, Stevie	North
Cisneros, Justin	Morro Bay, Fall, 1:28
Diaz, Shawn	Farmerville
Felcho, Nathon	Tulare Union, Fall, 3:25
Ugues, Jonathon	Arvin

115
Gallardo, Jonathan	Nipomo, 13-3, MD
Cisneros, Eufermio	Morro Bay
Orelaz, Daniel	North, 10-8
Diebert, Cole	Liberty Madera
Garcia, Marco	Parlier, 10-7
Alcantar, Dax	Fowler

122
Dennis, Trey	Morro Bay, 9-3
Ornelaz, Anthony	North
Arroyo, Phillip	Reedley, Fall, 3:52
Alvarado, Giovanni	Fowler
Lira, Eliseo	Highland, 11-10
Espinosa, Matthew	Strathmore

128
Beecham, Marshall	Morro Bay, 13-2, MD
Erracalde, Morgan	Highland
Able, Frankie	Tulare Union, 12-6
Fugazzi, Dante	North
Santoro, Zack	Liberty Madera, Fall, 3:14
Smithson, Josiah	Sierra

134
Ramos, Michael	Highland, Fall, 3:59
Broone, Logan	Stockdale
Offill, Ryland	Morro Bay, 11-2, MD
Riquelme, Luis	Nipomo
Dotson, Jarred	Liberty Madera, Fall, 3:56
Gonzalez, Mario	North

140
Marin, Valentin	Arvin, 10-2
Hiatt, Conner	Liberty Madera
Vejar, Victor	Highland, Fall, 3:26
Ocampo, Javier	North
Franks, Ian	Morro Bay, Fall, 1:35
Graves, Elijah	Tehachapi

147
Lopez, David	Stockdale, Fall, 3:04
Corona, Anthony	North
Perez, Fernando	Sierra Pacific, 12-4, MD
Webber, Jonathan	Fowler
Soto, Aiden	Tulare Union, Fall, 3:48
Garcia, Martin	Parlier

154
Vale, Jonathan	Sierra Pacific, Fall, 4:50
Sandoval, Allen	Delano
Valdez, Roy	Highland, Fall, 3:55
Renteria, Jose	North
Burgess, Gio	Liberty Madera, Fall, 3:01
Giambo, Sebastian	Stockdale

162
Mayall, Julias	North, 6-0
Rodriguez, Isiaih	Fowler
Hernandez, Christian	Highland, 2-0
Wilson, Rashad	Sierra Pacific
Aceves, Andrew	Stockdale, Fall, 2:49
Lindsay, Caleb	Tehachapi

172
Viconte, Cole	Morro Bay, Fall, 1:21
Alvarado, G, Alex	Parlier
Davis, Jason	Nipomo, Fall, 2:53
Rountree, Dominic	Highland
Gagliardi, Bryce	North, 11-4
Imirian, Chris	Liberty Madera

182
Burdick, Justin	Nipomo, Fall, 1:50
Bernal, Danny	Morro Bay
Hernandez, Kaden	Tulare Union, Fall, 5:48
Cunningham, Colton	Sierra
Rauschenberg, Sam	Liberty Madera, Fall, 1:55
Rushing, Blain	North

197
Garcia, Jesse	Nipomo, Fall, 4:55
Marquez, Alejandro	North
Tapia, Diego	Kern Valley, Fall, 4:19
Portnoff, David	Liberty Madera
Martinez, Bryce	Highland, Fall, 4:56
Reyes, Aaron	Fowler

222
Nunley, Bear	Tulare Union, Fall, 4:25
Lugo, Angel	Liberty Madera
Daugherty, Tanner	Morro Bay, Fall, 1:19
Chuca, Zion	North
Garza, Joseph	Nipomo, Fall, 5:11
Pardo, Guillermo	Arvin

CENTRAL SECTION DIVISION IV CHAMPIONSHIPS
February 8-9, 2019

287
Lightner, Jacob — Kern Valley, Fall, 2:30
Rojas, Francisco, III — Liberty Madera
Saucedo, Jonathan — Highland, Fall, 2:45
Dhami, Kuljit — Fowler
Brown, Max — Tulare Union, 3:08
Hanson, Chris — Nipomo

MD - Major Decision

North Head Coach: Brady Garner

Most Outstanding Wrestlers

Lower Weight: Michael Ramos Highland
Upper Weight: Jacob Lightner   Kern Valley

TEAM SCORES

1	North	200.5
2	Morro Bay	191
3	Highland	169
4	Nipomo	167.5
5	Liberty Madera	156.5
6	Tulare Union	115
7	Fowler	74
8	Stockdale	62.5
9	Sierra Pacific	60.5
10	Kern Valley	46
11	Arvin	38
12	Parlier	30
13	Sierra	29
14	Reedley	23
15	Farmerville	22
16	Delano	21
17	Tehachapi	12
18	Strathmore	11
19	Bakersfield Christian	0
19	West	0

Jacob Lightner, Kern Valley High School (02/19/2019)
Photo courtesy of Bakersfield.com

Jacob Lightner – Kern Valley

DIVISION IV SECTION CHAMPIONS
North High School
Boys Wrestling

CENTRAL SECTION DIVISION IV CHAMPIOSHIPS – Golden West
February 14-15, 2020

108
Alcantar, Francisco	Nipomo, Fall 1:22
Daiz, Shaun	Farmerville
Picar, Darius	Garces, Fall 5:27
Guzman, Jose	Highland
Moreno, Dominic	Tulare Union, Fall 1:23
Lopez, Ayden	?

115
Ruiz, Ignacio	Golden West 7-4
Alatorre, Hector	Tulare Union
Gallardo, Jonathan	Nipomo 11-10
Ugues, Jonathan	Arvin
Montion, Azreal	Mt. Whitney, Fall 2:32
Garcia, Marcos	Parlier

122
Orozco, Alejandro	Parlier Fall 3:23
Belancourt, Victor	Mt. Whitney
Luna, Cesar, Fowler	Fall 5:06
Gonzales, Rogelio	Farmerville
Riquelme, Samuel	Nipomo, Fall 2:44
Doyle, Cooper	Stockdale

128
Gonzalez, Aeneas	Mendota, Fall 1:04
Anderson, Ethan	Reedley
Kuntz, Lee	Highland, SV 6-4
Avila, Ryan	Liberty Madera Ranchos
Bugni, Bryan	Tulare Western, 15-8
Diaz, Nick	Mt. Whitney

134
Arroyo, Phillip	Reedley, MD 10-1
Santoro, Zack	Liberty Madera Ranchos
Figueroa, Jason	Mendota, Fall 1:42
Able, Frankie	Tulare Union
Solano, Jimenez Jacob	Stockdale, Default
Alvarado, Gio	Fowler

140
Errecelde, Morgan	Highland 9-7
Nevarez, William	Golden West
Mendoza, Chris	Kern Valley, Fall 5:41
Ortiz, Efrain	Reedley
Lewis, Ty	Tulare Western, Fall 2:41
Bayace, Christian	Stockdale

147
Weber, Jonathan	Fowler 4-0
Hiatt, Conner	Liberty Madera Ranchos
Reddington, Riley	Golden West 11-7
Dutra, Travis	Mendota
Madding, Jadan	Stockdale 7-0
Crippen, Cody	Mt. Whitney

154
Montiero, Tye	Garces, TF 20-4
Soto, Aiden	Tulare Union
Aceves, Andrew	Stockdale, Fall 1:23
Dotson, Jarred	Liberty Madera Ranchos
Marquez, Daniel	Fowler 6-5
Brunsen, Cayden	Golden West

162
Perez, Fernando	Sierra Pacific, SV 6-4
Reynaga, Ruben	Mt. Whitney
Kimball, Kim	Nipomo 9-6
Salas, Anthony	Liberty Madera Ranchos
Badilla, Gabrial	Reedley, Fall period 1
Mastrucci, Milo	Garces

172
Alvardo, Gabriel	Parlier 6-4
Thomas, Drake	Highland
Castillo, Eric	Golden West, Fall 4:41
Garcia, Moses	Mt. Whitney
Branco, Allen	Tulare Western, Default
Tapia, Ricardo	Kern Valley

184
Tripp, Justin	Mt. Whitney 9-2
Burdick, Justin	Nipomo
Rojas, Diego	Lib Mad Ranchos, 11-10
Lara, Ryan	Parlier
Retes, Joey	Highland, Fall 1:15
Ayon, Irvin	Delano

197
Garza, Jesse	Nipomo 8-2
Nunley, Bear	Tulare Union
Rauschenberg, Sam	Lib Mad Ranchos, 5-4
Tapia, Diego	Kern Valley
Barron, Audrey	Stockdale, 7-4
Cunningham, Colton	Sierra

CENTRAL SECTION DIVISION IV CHAMPIONSHIPS – Golden West
February 14-15, 2020

222
Beldo, DeAndre	Garces, Fall 1:43
Schuler, Brian	Bakersfield Christian
Portnoff, David	Liberty Madera, 4-2
Pike, Cody	Sierra
Gonzales, Benny	Highland, Default
Castro, Isak	Arvin

287
Brown, Max	Tulare Union, Fall 5:13
Portillo, Kurt	Tulare Western
Garcia, Marco	Stockdale 5-3
Valdez, Alex	Mt. Whitney
Saucedo, Jonathan	Highland, Fall 1:23
Ortiz, Armando	Fowler

Most Outstanding Wrestlers

Lower Weight: Francisco Alcantar — Nipomo
Upper Weight: Tye Montiero — Garces
Liberty Madera Ranchos Coach: Jay Pumarejo

Team Results

1	Liberty Madera Ranchos	184
2	Highland	162
3	Mt. Whitney	160
4	Tulare Union	152.5
5	Nipomo	141
6	Garces	114.5
7	Golden West	113
8	Stockdale	107
9	Tulare Western	105.5
10	Fowler	100
11	Parlier	99
12	Reedley	85
13	Kern Valley	71
14	Mendota	70
15	Farmerville	52
16	Sierra	46
17	Delano	41
18	Sierra Pacific	38
19	Arvin	36
20	Bakersfield Christian	22

CENTRAL SECTION DIVISION V CHAMPIONSHIPS
February 8-9, 2019

108
Martinez, Armando	Golden Valley Fall 1:30 *29-10
Nicolas, Isaiah	Woodlake
Pittarelli, Nicolas	San Luis Obispo, 4-1
Padilla, Gonzalo	Orange Cove

115
Chavez, Martin	Orange Cove, Fall 3:45 *31-6
Moraido, Elijah	Woodlake
Verduzco, Solomon	Fresno, Fall :15
Barbosa, Anthony	McLane

122
Tristen, Andy	Orange Cove, 12-10 *24-10
Diaz, Nick	Mt. Whitney
Rivera, Eric	Fresno, 5-2
Ruiz, Ignacio	Golden West

128
Mayhugh, Mark	Bishop, 4-1 *29-9
Cook, Justin	Desert
Lopez, Angelo	Golden West, Fall 3:13
Sanchez, Arturo	Mt. Whitney

134
Prado, Xavier	Edison, 11-4
Mendoza, Jonathon	McLane
Almanza, Isaiah	Mt. Whitney, Fall 3:58
Baker, Aaron	Desert

138
Lopez, Jesse	Golden West, 6-1 TF *28-12
Gonzalez, Richard	St Joseph
Xavier, Reyes	Mira Monte, 9-0 MD
Combs, Diego	Yosemite

147
Perez, Eduardo	Mira Monte, Fall 2:57
Reynaga, Ruben	Mt. Whitney
Meza, Darius	Hanford, West Fall 1:09
Polley, Noah	St. Joseph

154
Guynn, Nicolas	Yosemite, Fall 1:38 *34-4
Staley, Justin	Hanford West
Jauique, Deniceo	Fresno, Fall 5:59
Reddington, Riley	Golden West

162
Eaton, Ricardo	East, 7-0 *14-1
DeMartini, Khashayar	San Luis Obispo
Marquez, George	Mira Monte, 14-8
Harrison, Dillon	Mt. Whitney

172
Micallef, Justin	Yosemite, Fall 3:10, *27-6
Urbina, Bladimir	Fresno
Patino, Jonathan	East, Fall, 3:24
Evans, Ty	San Luis Obispo

184
Arafi, Jihad	Edison, Fall, 2:19
Jumayer, Oguzhan	Yosemite
Medrano, Jacob	St. Joseph, Fall, 4:21
Renteria, Brandon	Woodlake

197
Tripp, Justin	Mt. Whitney, 12-5 *24-9
Viahakis, Yiannis	Mira Monte
Gonzalez, Marcelino	St. Joseph, 8-6
Guzman, Anthony	Woodlake

222
Watson, Kwabena	Edison, Fall, 3:05 *23-4
Aispuro, Gerado	McFarland
Juarez, Luis	McLane, Fall :34
Lucatero, Mark	Mt. Whitney

287
Rezac, Kevin	Fresno, Fall, 3:05 *19-4
Lee, Regan	Golden West
Watson, Isa	Edison, Fall :34
Hernandez, Jacob	St. Joseph

* Record
MD - Major Decision
TF – Technical Fall

Most Outstanding Wrestlers

Lower Weight: Mark Mayhugh Bishop
Upper Weight: Kwabena Watson Edison

CENTRAL SECTION DIVISION V CHAMPIONSHIPS
February 8-9, 2019

Team Scores

1	Golden West	171.5
2	Mt. Whitney	166.5
3	Edison	137.5
4	Fresno	121.5
5	Mira Monte	116
6	Yosemite	101
7	St. Joseph	86
7	Woodlake	86
9	McLane	78.5
10	Orange Cove	73
11	San Luis Obispo	72
12	East	61
13	Desert	49.5
14	Hanford West	48
15	McFarland	45
16	Bishop	34
17	Roosevelt	26
18	Tranquility	22
19	Lindsay	17
20	Rosamond	16

Golden West Head Coach: Richard Sanchez

CENTRAL SECTION DIVISION V CHAMPIONSHIPS – Golden West
February 14-15, 2020

108
Maldonado, Petro — Roosevelt, Fall 1:08
Hernandez, Brian — Avenal
Martinez, Aidan — St. Joseph, 6-1
Maples, Aidan — San Luis Obispo

115
Kazmiski, Peter — Yosemite, 3-1
Anaya, Adian — Hanford West
Nicolas, Isaiah — Woodlake, MD 15-4
Martinez, Jose — East

122
Rivera, Eric — Firebaugh, MD 9-1
Morales, Matthew — Lindsay
Crofton, Curtis — West, 6-4
Urabetia, Giovanni — Hanford West

128
Tristen, Andy — Orange Cove, Fall :54
Vaekhan, Tom — McLane
Olsen, Taven — San Luis Obispo, Fall 4:55
Rodriguez, Shane — Woodlake

134
Lee, Cedrick — McLane, TF 19-4
Ramirez-Aguilar, Titus — Hanford West
Garcia, Alan — McFarland, Fall 1:03
Willoughby, Clint — Yosemite

140
Mendoza, Jon — McLane, Fall 5:52
Prado, Xavier — Edison
Kee, Devonya — Hanford West, Fall 1:34
Hernandez, Israel — East

147
Gonzalez, Richard — St. Joseph, Fall 2:37
Meza, Darius — Hanford West
Jonathan — Mira Monte, Fall 4:53
Brasuell, Enrique — West

154
Nicholas, Guynn — Yosemite, 8-7
Maksoudian, David — San Luis Obispo
Packard, Matthew — Edison, 8-7
Jordan, Clayton — Rosamond

162
Reyes, Xavier — Mira Monte, 7-0 *34-6
Graves, Elijah — Tehachapi
Fraysier Gavin — San Luis Obispo, Fall :31
Pina, Mario — Roosevelt

172
Eaton, Ricardo — East, Fall 1:18
Padilla, Daniel — McFarland
Corcio, Angel — Mira Monte, 7-3
Godding, Wyatt — Orange Cove

184
Pitino, Jonathan — East, 4-1
Johnson, Amir Caiden — Edison
Marquez, Jorge — Mira Monte, 5-2
Baeza, Rob — McLane

197
Evans, Ty — San Luis Obispo, Fall 2:34
Hipolito, Santiago — Edison
Vargas, Cesar — St. Joseph, 1-0
Tercero, Victor — McLane

222
Juarez, Luis — McLane, 13-8
Medrano, Jacob — St. Joseph, Fall 1:27
Ohanian, Hogiv — Edison, Fall 4:56
Davis, Christofer — Roosevelt

287
Balladarez, Adam — Edison, Fall 1:05
Sanchez, Andrew — West
Ahumada, Jose — McLane, Fall 1:49
Meraz, Roque — St. Joseph

*Record

CENTRAL SECTION DIVISION V CHAMPIONSHIPS – Golden West
February 14-15, 2020

Most Outstanding Wrestlers

Upper Weight: Nicolas Guynn — Yosemite
Lower Weight: Pedro Maldonado — Roosevelt
McLane Coach: Brian Perreault

Team Results

1. McLane — 215.5
2. San Luis Obispo — 202
3. Edison — 182.5
4. St. Joseph's — 137
5. Hanford West — 130.5
6. East Bakersfield — 115
7. Yosemite — 108
8. Orange Cove — 95.5
9. Mira Monte — 94
10. Fresno — 77.5
11. Roosevelt — 77
12. West Bakersfield — 75
13. Woodlake — 64.5
14. Bishop Union — 53
15. McFarland — 48.5
16. Rosamond — 46
17. Tehachapi — 45
18. Lindsay — 42
19. Avenal — 26
20. Desert — 10

CENTRAL SECTION MASTERS

2000-2020

CENTRAL SECTION MASTERS CHAMPIONSHIP TEAMS

Date	Champion	Coach	Location
2-24-2001	Bakersfield	David East	East Bakersfield
2-23-2002	Bakersfield	David East	Clovis
3-01-2003	Clovis	Steve Tirapelle	East Bakersfield
2-28-2004	Bakersfield	Andy Varner	Lemoore
2-26-2005	Bakersfield	Andy Varner	Buchanan
2-25-2006	Buchanan	Dustin Riley	East Bakersfield
2-24-2007	Buchanan	Dustin Riley	Lemoore
2-23-2008	Clovis	Steve Tirapelle	Clovis East
2-28-2009	Clovis	Ben Holscher	East Bakersfield
2-27-2010	Clovis	Steve Tirapelle	Lemoore
2-26-2011	Clovis	Steve Tirapelle	Buchanan
2-25-2012	Clovis	Steve Tirapelle	East Bakersfield
2-23-2013	Clovis	Co-Coaches Steve Tirapelle/Ben Holscher	Mt. Whitney
3-01-2014	Clovis	Co-Coaches Steve Tirapelle/Ben Holscher	Madera South
2-28-2015	Buchanan	Troy Tirapelle	East Bakersfield
2-26,27-2016	Clovis	Steve Tirapelle	Lemoore
2-24,25-2017	Buchanan	Troy Tirapelle	Clovis
2-23,24-2018	Buchanan	Troy Tirapelle	North
2-14,15-2019	Buchanan	Troy Tirapelle	Lemoore
2-21-22-2020	Buchanan	Troy Tirapelle	Hoover

Coach Varner and Josiah Hill
Bakersfield High School

CENTRAL SECTION MASTERS
MOST OUTSTANDING WRESTLERS

Year	Name	School
2001	Gerrard Contreras	Buchanan
	Miguel Gutierrez	Foothill
2002	Darrell Vasquez	Bakersfield
	Drew East	Bakersfield
2003	Troy Tirapelle	Clovis
	William Griffin	Madera
2004	Nathan Morgan	Bakersfield
	Chip Meredith	Central
2005	Paul Ruiz	Firebaugh
	Jake Varner	Bakersfield
2006	David Chaidez	Foothill
	Ryan Flores	Buchan
2007	Nick Fisher	Clovis West
	Daniel Montelongo	Madera
2008	Chris Martinez	Clovis West
	Josh Boger	Coalinga
2009	Chris Martinez	Clovis West
	Rykeem Yates	Edison
2010	Timmy Box	Bakersfield
	Justin Lozano	Selma
2011	Isaiah Martinez	Lemoore
	Bryce Hammond	Bakersfield
2012	Alex Cisneros	Selma
	Nikko Reyes	Clovis West
2013	Martin Sandoval	Porterville
	Isaiah Martinez	Lemoore
2014	Michael Knoblauch	Clovis West
	Gabriel Gonzalez	Washington Union
2015	Ruben Garcia	Selma
	Seth Nevills	Clovis
2016	Gary Joint	Lemoore
	Abner Romero	Buchanan
2017	Justin Mejia	Clovis
	Brandon Martino	Clovis
2018	Richard Figueroa	Selma
	Seth Nevills	Clovis
2019	Wayne Joint	Lemoore
	Trent Tracy	Frontier
2020	Richard Figueroa	Selma
	Tyler Avila	Porterville

Most Outstanding Wrestler Awards paid by the Coyote Club Membership

CENTRAL SECTION MASTERS - Lemoore
February 24, 2007

103
Camacho, Gilbert	Washington Union, 5-0
Done, Chris	Buchanan
Valles, AJ	Selma, 2-0
Martinez, Chris	Firebaugh
Diaz, Edgar	Arvin, 8-7 *34-11
Collier, Marc	East, *44-7
Zimmer, Zach	Clovis West, 3-2
Diaz, Chris	Sanger

112
Quintana, Diego	Selma, 3-2 *34-4
Gonzalez, Peter	East, *32-10
Demison, Nektoe	Bakersfield, 12-1 *40-6
Jaramillo, AJ	Lemoore
Fitzgerald, Steven	Clovis East, Fall 5:17 *50-7
Roberts, Nathan	Buchanan
Everwine, Chase	Clovis West, 8-4
Gonzales, Juan	Kerman

119
Lomas, Frank	Bakersfield, 4-1 *42-8 170-35
Weimer, Steve	Clovis, *50-8
Mendoza, Jose	Selma, 1-0 *39-6
Rocha, Brandon	Lemoore
Tarkington, Richard	Ridgeview, 15-4 *39-12
Tomayo, Luis	Arvin, *27-10
Waters, Anthony	Buchanan, 12-4
Gutierrez, Emmanuel	Firebaugh

125
Fisher, Nick	Clovis West, 8-4
Arredondo, Justin	Buchanan
Ramos, Chris	Bullard
Reyes, Josh	McFarland, *40-8
Sanchez, Efrain	Arvin, Default *30-9
Patino, Robert	Exeter
Perez, Julian	Lemoore, 7-5
Chatman, Charles	Edison

130
Roman-Marin, Sean	Lemoore, 5-3 *40-8
Castillo, Frankie	Arvin, *36-6
Kelly, Cameron	Clovis, 9-5
Gutierrez, Isidio	Buchanan
Hicks, Seth	Centennial, 8-7 *38-14
Arreola, Albert	Wasco
Gonzalez, Freddy	East, 12-4 *39-15
Estrada, Raul	Madera South

135
Rios, Johnny	Madera, 1-0 *41-7 125-50
Rodriguez, Alex	Clovis West, *38-5
Watts, David	El Diamante, 1-0
Pavone, Chris	Porterville, 11-2
Cruz, Jonah	Bakersfield, 11-2
Thomas, John	Clovis
Hail, Jason	Tehachapi, 15-5 *37-13
Hamerslagh, Will	Exeter

140
Sakaguchi, Scott	Clovis, 3-1
Rubio, Vincent	Lemoore
Watts, Randall	El Diamante, 3-1
Tovar, Archie	Selma
Box, Timmy	Bakersfield, 1-0 *13-7
Ellison, Dustin	Clovis West
Miller, Justin	East, Fall 4:54 *39-12
Hicks, Chris	Kerman

145
Cisneros, Joe	Selma, 6-2 *50-5
Rasmussen, Travis	Bakersfield, *44-5
West, Stephen	Buchanan, Default, *44-12
Moralez, Mitch	Tulare
Christensen, Colton	Liberty, Default
Dupras, Jake	Clovis West
Endes, Dalton	Centennial, 10-3 *23-9
Rojo, Aldolfo	Arvin

152
Balch, Andrew	Buchanan, 1-0 *48-4 12 Falls
Cook, James	Clovis West
Rodriguez, Jamie	Bakersfield, 7-4 *33-14
Esparza, Josh	Clovis
Morales, Matt	Tulare, 8-1
Sotelo, Eric	Yosemite
Eskew, Bryan	Kingsburg, 5-2
Mariscal, David	Farmerville

160
Montelongo, Daniel	Madera, 6-5 *44-10
Dela Rosa, Eric	Foothill, *46-6
West, Craig	Buchanan, Default, *40-14
Hernandez, Cruz	East, *22-10
Bracamonte, Paul	Central, 10-4
Magana, Xavier	Fresno
Ames, Joseph	Shafter, 8-2
Wilson, Josh	Exeter

CENTRAL SECTION MASTERS - Lemoore
February 24, 2007

171
Smith, Eric	Buchanan, 10-1 *46-12
Allison, Dustin	Madera
Carls, Brad	Bakersfield, Fall 5:03 *31-15
Shaver, Zach	Clovis
Hack, Tyler	Tehachapi, 6-3 *34-14
Walker, Justin	Sierra
Villasenor, Sergio	Monache, 10-4
Terrones, David	Wasco

189
Sanchez, Brett	Clovis, 7-5 *34-8
Garcia, Mat	Lemoore, *42-12
Travis, David	Foothill, 6-5 *36-11 95-16
Medelin, Brandon	Madera
Avila, Joey	Exeter, 6-5
Abarquez, Marcus	Tehachapi, *30-11
Ruiz, Able	Selma, Fall, 5:11
Cervantez, Johnny	Firebaugh

215
Flores, Ryan	Buchanan, 3-0 *56-1 39 Falls
Lopez, Vince	Clovis, *39-7
Perez, Jose	Porterville, Fall 1:31
Jiminez, Leobardo	Dos Palos
Terrell, Lake	North, 2-1 37-9
McBride, Evan	Tehachapi, *36-18
Gonzalez, Alex	Sunnyside, 3-2
Vanderpool, Shane	Liberty Madera

275
Zamora, Jonathan	Clovis, 6-3 *38-9
Maxson, Jacob	Redwood
Garza, Austin	Buchanan, 11-3
Alvarez, Lamar	Bakersfield, *30-17
Baize, Loren	Lemoore, Fall 1:10
Bernard, Tyler	Central
Celedon, Jacob	Selma, Fall 2:25
Romero, Enrique	Corcoran

Most Outstanding Wrestler
Lower Weight: Nick Fisher
Upper Weight: Daniel Montelongo

* Season and career records

TEAM SCORES

1	Buchanan	189
2	Clovis	148
3	Bakersfield	125.5
4	Lemoore	106.5
5	Selma	101.5
6	Madera	76
7	Clovis West	65
8	East	52
9	Arvin	47
10	Washington Union	35.5
11	Porterville	35
12	Foothill	32
13	Clovis East	31
14	Exeter	24
15	Tulare Union	23
16	Tehachapi	22
17	Kerman	19
17	Redwood	19
19	Dos Palos	16
19	Firebaugh	16
21	Central	14
22	Bullard	12
22	El Diamante	12
22	Liberty	12
22	McFarland	12
26	Highland	10
27	Fresno	9
27	North	9
29	Sierra	7
30	Monache	5
31	Edison	3
31	Liberty Madera	3
31	West	3
35	Farmersville	2
35	Sanger	2
37	Kingsburg	1
37	Shafter	1

CENTRAL SECTION MASTERS – Clovis East
February 23, 2008

103
Camacho, Gilbert — Washington Union, 10-2
Zimmer, Zach — Clovis West
Collier, Marc — East, 7-5, *41-3
Diaz, Edgar — Arvin, *41-6
Magnusson, Adam — Firebaugh, 6-5
Gambrell, Madison — Clovis
Metiver, Dalton — Clovis North, 3-1
Gomez, Eric — Madera

112
Martinez, Chris — Clovis West, *48-6
Valles, AJ — Selma, *42-6
Jaramillo, AJ — Lemoore, 8-2
Gonzalez, Peter — East, *33-4
McAlester, Clinton — Clovis, Fall 3:08 *35-11
Sanchez, Cesar — Porterville
Jordon, Elmer — Redwood, Fall 1:47 *40-10
Steinbach, Jared — Tehachapi

119
Rocha, Brandon — Lemoore, 10-4
Quintana, Diego — Selma, *40-7
Waters, Anthony — Buchanan, 5-0
Orozco, Sam — Monache
Burger, Riley — Golden West, 9-4 *37-12
Martinez, Sergio — Tehachapi, *37-12
Rizo, Derek — Foothill, 10--4 *41-10
Calcagno, Chris — Clovis North

125
Fitzgerald, Steven — Clovis East, 12-2
Patino, Robert — Exeter, *38-10
Pena, Nick — Selma, 4-2
Dieter, Alec — Clovis
Box, Timmy — Bakersfield, 8-2 *36-12
Zinkin, Josh — Clovis West
Roberts, Nathan — Buchanan, 7-2
Nam, Chantra — Sunnyside

130
Arredondo, Justin — Buchanan, 3-1
Weimer, Steven — Clovis
Mendoza, Jose — Selma, 9-6
Perez, Julian — Lemoore
Rojas, Kevin — Kerman, 5-4
Rivera, Vince — Liberty, *43-11
Magno, Bryan — Ridgeview, 14-4 *37-7
Williams, Chino — Tulare Western, *22-15

135
Fisher, Nick — Clovis West, 6-4 OT
Watts, Randall — El Diamante
Arreola, Alberto — Washington Union, 13-8 *52-5 156-35
Gutierrez, Isidro — Buchanan
Masuta, Armajit — Madera, 5-2
Kapler, Greg — Liberty, *43-12
Escalera, Nick — Selma, 9-5
Estrada, Raul — Madera South

140
Sakaguchi, Scott — Clovis, 5-4 *45-9
Watts, David — El Diamante
Lozano, Justin — Selma, 4-2
Cruz, Jonah — Bakersfield, *39-8
Martin, Fabian — Buchanan, Default
Hicks, Seth — Centennial, *38-10
Sierra, Nicholas — Lemoore, 15-1
Contreras, Jaime — Firebaugh

145
Rasmussen, Travis — Bakersfield, 8-3 *40-4
Dupras, Jake — Clovis West
Balch, Andrew — Buchanan, 14-10
Tovar, Archie — Selma
Rubio, Vincent — Lemoore, 11-4
Doss, Nolan — Liberty Madera, *44-12
Rios, Robert — Liberty, 9-0 *44-12
Pena, Manuel — Firebaugh

152
Cook, James — Clovis West, TF16-1 *36-4
Mariscal, David — Farmerville, *34-5
Ceremello, Tyler — Clovis, 12-4
Matthews, Eric — Stockdale, *33-13
Bullock, Brad — El Diamante, Default
Hammond, Bryce — Bakersfield, *40-10
Tirado, Anthony — Kingsburg, 9-7
Gonzalez, Jose — Mendota

160
West, Stephen — Buchanan, 1-0
Esparza, Josh — Clovis
Luis, Madera — South, 3-1
Morales, Matt — Tulare, *31-12
Ramirez, Jose — Bakersfield, Fall 2:25 *40-11
Medina, Rene — Shafter, *23-5
Batshon, Nadim — El Diamante, 9-8
Marin, Luis — Mendota

171
Burriel, Tommy — Clovis, 5-4
Carls, Brad — Bakersfield, *32-5

CENTRAL SECTION MASTERS – Clovis East
February 23, 2008

Bracamonte, Paul — Central, Fall :38
Eskew, Brian — Kingsburg
Ames, Joseph — Shafter, *40-2
Musquez, John — Central, *40-5
Villasenor, Sergio — Monache, Fall 3:24 *30-10
Terronez, David — Washington Union

189
Brant, Phil — Bullard, 9-4
Ruiz, Abel — Selma, *39-8
Gingold, Jake — Bullard, Fall 5:55
Martinez, Steven — Lemoore
Abarquez, Marcus — Tehachapi, *27-7
Thompson, Joey — North, *42-7
Jackson, Wade — Kingsburg, 9-6
Shipman, Cameron — McFarland

215
Boger, Josh — Coalinga, 9-4
Sanchez, Brett — Clovis, *34-5
Renteria, Michael — Washington Union
Travis, David — Foothill, *25-7
Perez, Mike — Selma, 2-1
Papendorf, Kyle — Buchanan
Schoene, Brian — Bakersfield, 8-4 *37-17
Vanderpool, Shane — Liberty Madera

285
Zamora, Jonathan — Clovis, Fall 1:53 *39-1
Romero, Enrique — Corcoran
Hernandez, Antonio — East, Fall 1:10 *44-5
Willis, Brent — North, *39-6
Zamora, Jose — Sanger, 3-1
Smith, Holden — Buchanan
Padilla, Anthony — Bakersfield, Fall 2:51 *12-4
Celodon, Jacob — Selma

*Records and career records

Most Outstanding Wrestlers

Lower Weight: Chris Martinez — Clovis West
Upper Weight: Josh Boger — Coalinga

TEAM SCORES

1	Clovis	181
2	Buchanan	135
3	Selma	130
4	Clovis West	121
5	Bakersfield	96
6	Lemoore	78.5
7	Washington Union	58
8	El Diamante	56
9	East	52
10	Coalinga	26
11	Bullard	25
11	Clovis East	25
13	North	21
13	Tehachapi	21
15	Corcoran	20
15	Kingsburg	20
17	Farmersville	19.5
18	Foothill	19
18	Liberty	19
20	Exeter	18
20	Shafter	18
22	Central	16
22	Monache	16
24	Centennial	14
24	Firebaugh	14
24	Madera South	14
27	Arvin	12
27	Stockdale	12
27	Tulare Union	12
30	Golden West	11
30	Liberty Madera	11
32	Kerman	10.5
33	Sanger	9
34	Madera	8
35	Clovis North	7
35	Porterville	7
37	Redwood	6.5
38	Ridgeview	5
39	Mendota	4
40	McLane	2
40	Sunnyside	2
40	Tulare Western	2
43	Yosemite	0

CENTRAL SECTION MASTERS - East
February 28, 2009

103
Cisneros, Alex	Selma, 4-3 2nd OT
Gaytan, Daniel	Clovis
Knoblauch, Steven	Clovis West, 6-4 *30-6
Rico, David	Washington Union
Rodriguez, Adrian	Buchanan, 3-0
Jauregul, Justin	Clovis East
Flores, Lupe	Exeter, 7-5 *36-9
Davis, Harley	Monache

112
Zimmer, Zach	Clovis West, 2-1 2nd OT
Rodriguez, Vince	Clovis North
Diaz, Chris	Sanger, Fall 1:25
Demison, Natrelle	Bakersfield, *35-11
Quintana, Diego	Selma, 10-1
Esparza, Silverio	Lemoore
Collier, Marc	East Bakersfield, 11-3 *35-9
Santos, Juan	Farmerville

119
Martinez, Chris	Clovis West, Fall 3:53
Meredith, Stephen	Bullard
Valles, AJ	Selma, Default
Perez, Sonny	Hoover
Larsen, Connor	Clovis East, 4-0
Perez, Alex	Lemoore
Gonzalez, Peter	East, 6-0 *35-3
Gagnon, Jason	Exeter, *23-14

125
Rocha, Brandon	Lemoore, 18-5
McAlester, Clinton	Clovis
Pena, Nick	Selma, 4-0
Arredondo, Damien	Buchanan
Calcagno, Chris	Clovis East, 5-3
Patino, Robert	Exeter, *34-8 139-46
Velasquez, Gabriel	Hanford, Fall 5:36
Steinbach, Jared	Tehachapi, *33-12

130
Estrada, Raul	Madera South, 5-3 *46-6
Yacuta, Shane	Porterville, 18-6
Box, Timmy	Bakersfield, 14-12 *24-2
Mendoza, Jose	Selma
Rojas, Kevin	Kerman, Fall 1:57
Waters, Anthony	Buchanan
Rizo, Derik	Foothill, 11-6 *44-10
Cervantes, Sonny	Clovis

135
Hicks, Seth	Centennial, 6-3 *43-0
Kapler, Greg	Liberty, *44-6
Zarate, Nathan	Selma, 7-6
Dieter, Alex,	Clovis
Ramirez, Gabe	Monache, 7-5
Quesada, Moses	Clovis East
Phanthavong, Micky	Granite Hills, Fall 1:30 *42-8 94-24
Ruiz, Mikeal	Kerman

140
Sierra, Nicholas	Lemoore, 6-4
Cruz, Jonah	Bakersfield, *39-4
Escalera, Nick	Selma, 3-2
Sanchez, Javier	Ridgeview, *35-3
Negrete, Matt	Buchanan, Fall 2:28
Martinez, Michael	Wasco, *34-7
Gevorian, David	Bullard, Fall 4:45
Bugambilia, Francisco	Arvin

145
Sakagucki, Scott	Clovis, Fall 3:05
Fierro, Adam	Bakersfield, *34-9
Rodriguez, Alex	Washington Union, Fall 1:30 *45-4
Cueto, Martin	Liberty, *43-11
Perrault, Brian	Clovis East, Default
Castenada, Lance	Frontier
Gizzo, Nick	Liberty Madera, 1-0
Gomez, Hector	Dos Palos

152
Hammond, Bryce	Bakersfield, 5-3 2nd OT *32-3
Kelley, Cameren	Clovis
Reyes, Nikko	Clovis West, 3-1
Fabbian, Martin	Buchanan
Lozano, Justin	Selma, Fall 1:10
Ramos, Mago	Hoover
Rubio, Vincent	Clovis East, 9-4
Tirado, Anthony	Kingsburg

160
West, Stephan	Buchanan, 10-4
Cook, James	Madera
Ramirez, Jose	Bakersfield, 10-4 *35-10
Pedraza, Lewis	Madera South
Sing, Amandeep	Delano, 15-6 *37-10
Grandal, Tyler	Kingsburg

CENTRAL SECTION MASTERS - East
February 28, 2009

St. John, James — Tehachapi, 11-6 *32-13
Endes, Dalton — Centennial

171
Medina, Rene — Shafter, 5-2 *36-12
Narvaez, Mark — Washington Union
Nevills, Zach — Clovis, 1-0
Sotelo, Eric — Yosemite
Heath, Chris — Sunnyside, 3-5
Wykoff, Michael — Mt. Whitney
Flores, Dwight — Tulare, Fall :28
Roberts, Tanner — Kingsburg

189
Burriel, Tommy — Clovis, 8-1
Juarez, Rodolfo — Central
Gingold, Jake — Buchanan, 11-0
Corona-Zamarripa, Alex — Hanford West
Ellis, Shane — Frontier, 6-4 *28-14
Jackson, Wade — Kingsburg
Machado, Michael — Arvin, Fall 5:59
Ferrer, Hugo — Caruthers

215
Yates, Rykeem — Edison, 11-3
Schoene, Brian — Bakersfield, *41-3
Renteria, Michael — Washington, 5-2
Gomez, Noel — Ceasar Chavez, *37-9
Hernandez, Juan — Sunnyside, Fall 3:35
Garcia, Jonathan — Hanford West
Smith, Holden — Buchanan, Fall 3:28
Urrea, Jesus — McFarland

275
Baize, Loren — Lemoore, 1-0 *46-6 38 Falls
Papendorf, Kyle — Buchanan
Posadas, Angel — Foothill, 1-0 *35-6
Mancia, Byron — Sunnyside
Contreras, Luis — Madera, Default
Hernandez, Antonia — East, *34-8
Furnish, Teddy — Kerman, Fall :44
Enos, Logan — Dos Palos

Most Outstanding Wrestlers

Lower Weight: Chris Martinez   Clovis West
Upper Weight: Rykeem Yates   Edison

*Records and career records

TEAM SCORES

1	Clovis	138
2	Buchanan	137.5
3	Bakersfield	128
4	Selma	118
5	Lemoore	92.5
6	Clovis West	78
7	Washington Union	61.5
8	Clovis East	46
9	Sunnyside	36
9	Madera South	36
11	Madera	33
12	Liberty	32
13	Clovis North	29
14	Shafter	26
14	Central	26
16	Centennial	25
17	Hanford West	23
18	Central	21
19	Hoover	20.5
20	Sanger	20
21	East	19
21	Foothill	19
21	Kerman	19
21	Kingsburg	19
25	Porterville	18
26	Frontier	17.5
27	Exeter	17
28	Ridgeview	13
28	Delano	13
30	Cesar Chavez	12
30	Yosemite	12
32	Monache	11
33	Granite Hills	8
33	Tehachapi	8
35	Bullard	7
35	Mt. Whitney	7
35	Wasco	7
38	Arvin	6.5
39	Dos Palos	5
39	Hanford	5
41	Tulare Union	3
41	Liberty Madera	3
43	McFarland	2
43	Farmersville	2
43	Caruthers	2

CENTRAL SECTION MASTERS - Lemoore
February 27, 2010

103
Gomez, Vincent	Frontier, Fall 3:32
Olea, Arnulfo	Exeter
Rocha, Dillion	Lemoore, 3-1
Rico, David	Washington Union
Nickell, Ian	Bakersfield, Default
Gaytan, Jonas	Clovis
Tamez, Chris	Clovis East, Default
Rodrigues, Adrian	Buchanan

112
Cisneros, Alex	Selma, 5-2
Diaz, Chris	Sanger
Gaytan, Daniel	Clovis, Default
Jauregui, Justin	Clovis East
Navarro, Jose	Madera, Default
Esparza, Silverio	Lemoore
Elizondo, Pau	Bullard, 18-13
Flores, Lupe	Exeter, *38-8

119
Zimmer, Zach	Clovis West, Fall 3:23
Everk, Devin	Clovis
Cruz, Micah	Bakersfield, 5-4 *37-12
Aguilar, Chris	Stockdale
Phaysamone, Patrick	Clovis East, Default
Perez, Alex	Lemoore
Gagnon, Jason	Exeter, TF 16-1 *20-8
Panduro, Adrian	Corcoran

125
Martinez, Chris	Clovis West, 6-4 OT
Rodriguez, Vince	Clovis North
Martinez, Isaiah	Lemoore, 10-7
Salas, Juan	Clovis
Larson, Conner	Clovis East, Default
Lanier, Jeff	Bakersfield, *36-11
Barron, Juan	Shafter, 6-5
Mendoza, Michael	Washington Union

130
Pena, Nick	Selma, 2-1 2 OT
Arredondo, Damien	Buchanan
Valles, AJ	Sanger, 3-1 OT
Cervantes, Sonny	Clovis
Yacuta, Shane	Porterville, 6-2
Calcagno, Chris	Clovis North
Demision, Natrelle	Bakersfield, Major 15-3
Torres, Joseph	Caruthers

135
Quezeda, Moses	Clovis East, 4-3
Hill, Spencer	Buchanan, *39-12
Ramirez, Maxx	Bakersfield, TF 21-4
Steiber, Ryan	Liberty
Gomez, Adrian	Corcoran, 8-6
Williams, Chino	Tulare Western
Quiroz, DJ	Dos Palos, 14-6
Renteria, Monte	Dinuba

140
Box, Timmy	Bakersfield, 14-8
Zarate, Nathan	Selma
Poindexter, Devin	Clovis North, 8-4 *41-12
Bersano, Brady	Clovis
Gomez, Johnathan	Madera, Fall
Castro, Rayko	Kerman
Solis, Josue	Sanger, Fall 1:36
Medley, Jason	Mission Oak, *36-10

145
Hammond, Colman	Bakersfield, 6-5
Rizo, Derik	Foothill, *52-4
Sotomayor, Brandon	Centennial, Fall 1:20
Martinez, Michael	Wasco
Alvardo, Joshua	Exeter, 4-3 *44-13
Rodriguez, Dylin	Sanger
Aguilar, Rico	Selma, 11-4
Gevargyan, Davit	Bullard

152
Sierra, Nick	Lemoore, 3-1
Fierro, Adam	Bakersfield, *23-6
Negrett, Matt	Buchanan, 3-0
Thompson, Blake	Clovis
Castaneda, Lance	Frontier, 4-3
Estrada, Andrew	Madera South
Aispuro, Josh	Wasco, Fall 1:37
Hienrichs, Jacob	Kingsburg

160
Lozano, Justin	Selma, 8-1
Reyes, Nikko	Clovis West
Ceremello, Tyler	Clovis, Default
Pendleton, Jacob	Lemoore
Ramos, Mago	Hoover, 9-6
Lopez, Mike	Golden West, *37-15
Hammond, Bryce	Bakersfield, TF 15-0
Tirado, Anthony	Kingsburg

171
Cooks, James	Madera, Default
Nevills, Zach	Clovis
Fabbian, Martin	Buchanan, Major 13-1
Flores, Roman	Stockdale
Nacita, Silas	Bakersfield, 8-1

CENTRAL SECTION MASTERS - Lemoore
February 27, 2010

Wykoff, Matt — Mt. Whitney
Medina, Rena — Wasco, 9-4 *36-9
Lincoln, Kyle — Yosemite

189
Burriel, Tommy — Clovis, Major 9-1
Juarez, Rodolfo — Central
Hernandez, Robert — Washington Union, 15-2
Barnes, Tanner — Buchanan
Ellis, Shane — Frontier, Default *37-12
Ali, David — Porterville, *21-13
Avery, Will — Tehachapi, 11-9
Parker, John — Exeter

215
Schoene, Brian — Bakersfield, 4-2
Gomez, Noe — Cesar Chavez
Ferguson, Taylor — Clovis, 3-1
Wilson, Wyatt — Shafter
Brantley, Nick — Edison, Default
Corona, Nick — Kingsburg, *34-5
Medley, Sean — Wasco, Fall :30
Zamarano, John — Sunnyside

275
Conteras, Luis — Madera, 6-2
Davis, Josh — Frontier, *36-9
Mancia, Bryan — Sunnyside, 7-3 *43-9
Tovar, Juan — Woodlake
Woods, Steven — Lemoore, 4-2
Smith, Dakota — Yosemite
Howard, Max — Clovis, 3-2
Perez, Paul — Tulare, *24-9

*Record

Most Outstanding Wrestlers

Lower Weight: Timmy Box — Bakersfield
Upper Weight: Justin Lozano — Selma

TEAM SCORES

1 Clovis	168	
2 Bakersfield	154	
3 Lemoore	88	
4 Buchanan	85.5	
5 Selma	84	
6 Clovis East	74.5	
7 Madera	71	
8 Clovis West	61.5	
9 Frontier	61	
10 Sanger	42	
11 Clovis North	36	
12 Centennial	35	
13 Exeter	33.5	
14 Washington Union	32	
15 Foothill	31	
16 Stockdale	22.2	
17 Wasco	19	
17 Cesar Chavez	19	
19 Sunnyside	18	
20 Shafter	17	
21 Porterville	16	
22 Kingsburg	12	
23 Liberty	11	
24 Edison	9	
24 Yosemite	9	
26 Corcoran	8	
26 Hoover	8	
26 Kerman	8	
29 Madera South	7	
30 Bullard	6	
31 Golden West	5	
31 Mt. Whitney	5	
31 Tulare Western	5	
34 Dos Palos	4	
35 Tulare Union	3	
36 Caruthers	2	
36 Tehachapi	2	
38 Dinuba	1	
38 Mission Oak	1	
40 Bakersfield Christian	0	
40 Central	0	
40 East	0	
40 Fowler	0	
40 McFarland	0	
40 Mendota & Orange Cove	0	

CENTRAL SECTION MASTERS - Buchanan
February 26, 2011

103
- Pengilly, Mason — Porterville, 5-1
- Marin, Manny — Buchanan
- Rodriguez, Brandon — Clovis West, 4-2
- Tamez, Chris — Clovis East
- Camposano, Adrain — Central, Fall 1:11
- La, Andy — Clovis
- Williams, Sean — Lemoore, Major 13-2
- Pena, Nick — Selma
- Navarette, Isaac — Dinuba, DQ
- Thomas, Brandon — Corcoran

112
- Gomez, Vincent — Frontier, Major 13-2 *40-5
- Gaytan, Jonas — Clovis
- Nichell, Ian — Bakersfield, 4-3 *31-7
- Navarro, Jose — Madera
- Flores, Lupe — Selma, Fall 3:44
- Knoblauch, Mikey — Clovis West
- Olea, Arnulfo — Exeter, 3-2
- Marquez, Nick — Foothill, *38-9
- Hood, Seth — Monache, 8-2
- Lopez, Anthony — McFarland

119
- Gaytan, Daniel — Clovis, 7-5
- Knoblauch, Stevan — Clovis West
- Gasca, Javier — Central, 3-0 *41-8
- Jauregui, Justin — Clovis East
- Esparza, Silverio — Lemoore, Major 17-9
- Panduro, Adrian — Corcoran
- Sandoval, Martin — Porterville, Major 10-0 *39-4
- Cancino, Gene — Hoover
- Anguiano, Roger — Exeter, 3-2
- Arroyo, Jose — Coalinga

125
- Cisneros, Alex — Selma, 2-1 3rdOT
- Rodriguez, Vincent — Clovis North
- Larson, Conner — Clovis East, 3-1
- Gay, Matt — Clovis
- Cruz, Micah — Bakersfield, Default *32-7
- Rocha, Dillon — Lemoore
- Lopez, Josh — Frontier, 4-3 *40-8
- Garcia, Chris — Clovis West
- Aramula, Jobani — Firebaugh, 3-2
- Mendoza, Michael — Washington Union

130
- Demison, Natrelle — Bakersfield, 3-2 *36-2
- Pena, Nick — Selma
- Calcagno, Chris — Clovis North, Fall 1:40
- Salas, Juan — Clovis
- Phaysamone, Patrick — Clovis East, 6-2
- Cardenas, Racelis — Buchanan
- Zimmer, Tyler — Clovis West, 2-0
- Torres, Joseph — Caruthers
- Navarro, Jimmy — Madera, Major 13-0
- Akers, Brandon — Exeter

135
- Yacuta, Shane — Porterville, Major 12-4
- Box, Timmy — Bakersfield, *33-3
- Everk, Devin — Clovis North, Fall 5:23
- Lucatero, Adrian — Mt. Whitney
- Valenzuela, C J — Madera, Default
- Jimenez, Tony — Dinuba
- Ladd, Jason — Clovis, 5-0
- Ouiroz, D J — Dos Palos
- Hernandez, Josie — Madera South, 5-1
- Escalera, Ryan — Selma

140
- Martinez, Isaiah — Lemoore, Fall 1:38
- Rodriguez, Miguel — Madera
- Bersano, Brady — Clovis, 2-1
- Aguilar, Rico — Selma
- Ramirez, Maxx — Bakersfield, 16-12a *31-10
- Perrault, Kyle — Clovis East
- Gomez, Adrian — Corcoran
- Duran, Joe — Porterville, 3-2 2nd OT *19-10
- Rentenia, Monte — Dinuba, 12-5
- Fambrough, Jawayn — Independence

145
- Arrendondo, Damien — Buchanan, 3-1 *32-5
- Hammond, Coleman — Bakersfield, *29-3
- Poindexter, Devin — Clovis North, 2-0 *38-15
- Morin, Isiah — Selma
- Sotomayor, Brandon — Centennial, 10-6 *41-10
- Gomez, Jonathan — Madera South
- Thompson, Colby — Clovis, Default
- Lopez, Daniel — R F Kennedy
- Gonzales, Gabriel — Washington Union, 5-1
- Rangel, Isaac — Firebaugh

152
- Ferro, Adam — Bakersfield, 4-0 41-2
- Thompson, Blake — Clovis
- Terrones, Josue — Washington Union, Major 9-1
- Karam, Josh — Clovis North
- Martinez, Michael — Wasco, Fall *31-7
- Zecchini, Jason — Mt. Whitney, 36-13

CENTRAL SECTION MASTERS - Buchanan
February 26, 2011

Alvardo, Caleb — Exeter, 5-4
Yilan, Charles — Madera South
Martinez, Jaime — Lemoore, 8-4
Ruiz, Miguel — Madera

160
Hammond, Bryce — Bakersfield, TF15-0 *29-0
Salas, Adrian — Clovis
Rodriguez, Dylin — Sanger, 10-1(a)
Tirado, Anthony — Kingsburg
Gardner, Trent — Tehachapi, 7-3*33-10
Marquez, Eric — McFarland, *24-9
Davila, Eric — Firebaugh, Fall 1:10
Worth, Andrew — Stockdale, *34-13
Ashjian, Cas — Bullard, 11-6
Luna, Cesar — West

171
Reyes, Nikko — Clovis West, 9-2
Lozano, Justin — Selma
Pendleton, Jacob — Lemoore, 4-2 OT
Nevills, Zach — Clovis
Nacita, Silas — Bakersfield, TF 15-0 *29-9
Tenorio, Mike — Firebaugh
Heinrich, Jacob — Kingsburg, Fall 3:56
Vega, Florencio — Clovis East
Salazar, Carlos — Kerman, 4-3
Valladares, Juan — Madera South

189
Gordan, Dakota — Clovis, Fall 5:17
Lincoln, Kyle — Yosemite, *42-7
Castellow, Jonathan — Exeter, Fall 1:39 *36-9
Hernandez, Jose — Washington Union, *36-14
Murphy, Jack — Frontier, Fall 4:44 *36-12
Cunningham, Conner — Sierra
Lopez, Nate — Lemoore
Pope, Kyle — Bakersfield, *31-8
Delfierro, Gannoon — Clovis East, 2-1
Sizemore, Chris — Liberty

215
Furguson, Taylor — Clovis, Fall 2:29
Ali, David — Porterville, *28-6
Amaya, Rudy — Foothill, 3-1 OT *38-9
Medley, Sean — Wasco, *32-5
Salinas, Arnold — Fresno, Fall 2:37 (a)
Mendoza, Eric — Madera
Cortez, Justin — Selma, 4-3 OT
Alvarez, Ismael — Orange Cove
Morales, Cortes — Clovis West, 3-1
Henderson, Grant — Yosemite

285
Nevills, Nick — Clovis, Fall 3:15
Hurtado, Frankie — Liberty, *46-6
Wood, Steven — Lemoore, 6-1
Tovar, Juan — Woodlake, *36-6
Talliulu, Niko — Tehachapi, Fall 4:41 *32-7
Olgin, Jordan — Foothill, *33-12
Logan, Enos — Dos Palos, 5-2
Juarez, Narciso — Sanger
Jumoke, Hunter — Clovis West, Fall 3:33
Crawford, Carson — Centennial

Top 8 to state championships
*Record
a = Quarters result

Most Outstanding Wrestlers

Lower Weight: Isaiah Martinez   Lemoore
Upper Weight: Bryce Hammond   Bakersfield

TEAM SCORES

Rank	Team	Score	Rank	Team	Score
1	Clovis	241.5	26	Sierra	11
2	Bakersfield	169	28	Centennial	9
3	Lemoore	97	28	Corcoran	9
4	Selma	96	30	Dinuba	7
5	Clovis West	81.5	30	McFarland	7
6	Porterville	79	32	Dos Palos	6
7	Clovis North	78.5	33	Hover	4
8	Clovis East	62	33	Orange Cove	4
9	Madera	59	33	R F Kennedy	4
10	Buchanan	51	36	Caruthers	2
11	Frontier	44	36	Independence	2
12	Wash Union	29	38	Bullard	0
13	Exeter	28	38	Coalinga	0
14	Central	26	38	Granite Hills	0
15	Wasco	25	38	Kerman	0
16	Foothill	24.5	38	Ridgeview	0
17	Mt. Whitney	22	38	Shafter	0
18	Kingsburg	21	38	West	0
18	Sanger	21	45	Monache	-1
20	Yosemite	20			
21	Liberty	19			
21	Tehachapi	19			
23	Woodlake	16			
24	Firebaugh	12			
24	Madera South	12			
26	Fresno	11			

CENTRAL SECTION MASTERS - East
February 25, 2012

106
Martinez, Miguel	Madera, Fall 4:47 *46-5
Hokit, Isaiah	Wasco * 41-5
Camposano, Adrian	Central, Major 12-4 *47-10
Cisneros, Joey	Redwood
Gaytan, Julian	Clovis, 6-2
Gamble, Matt	Monache
Jimenez, Javier	Porterville, 5-4
Velasquez, Marco	Foothill, *37-12
Pena, Johnny	Selma, Fall 1:39
Errecart, Anthony	Kerman

113
Gaytan, Jonas	Clovis, 8-4 *55-2
Olea, Arnulfo	Exeter
Pengilly, Mason	Porterville, 4-0 *39-4
DeLaCruz, Jason	Buchanan
Hood, Seth	Monache, 3-2
Williams, Sean	Lemoore
Arroyo, Jose	Coalinga, 2-0
Tamez, Chris	Clovis East
Ruiz, Daniel	Madera, 4-2
Thomas, Brandon	Corcoran

120
Gaytan, Daniel	Clovis, 3-1 52-5
Rodriguez, Brandon	Clovis West, *33-8
Ontiveros, Matthew	Central, Decision +1
Panduro, Adrian	Corcoran
Flores, Lupe	Selma, Fall 4:54
Navarro, Jose	Madera
Marin, Oscar	Bakersfield, 4-1 *36-14
Ferrer, Jose	Washington Union
Contreras, Abel	Porterville, Fall 4:15
Hendrix, Delano	Mission Oak

126
Hernandez, Vicente	Clovis, Fall 5:20 44-5
Knoblauch, Michael	Clovis West, *34-11
Hansen, Kyler	Buchanan, Decision +1
Deorian, Nick	Central
Martin, Bryce	Bakersfield, Default *27-15
Ozuna, Izaiah	Frontier, *37-14
Saavedra, Willyam	Foothill, Default *42-10
Perez, Jose	Caruthers
Delgado, Steven	Selma, 7-5 ***
Valasquez, Daniel	Firebaugh

132
Cisneros, Alex	Selma, 5-0 *47-1
Gasca, Javier	Kingsburg, *37-3
Gay, Matt	Clovis, 1-0
Cruz, Micah	Bakersfield, 41-10
Phaysamone, Patrick	Clovis East, 5-2
Zimmer, Tyler	Clovis West
Rodriguez, Christin	Reedley, Default
Sandoval, Martin	Porterville, *33-9
Frances, Conner	Buchanan, 6-0
Valdez, Jesus	Dos Palos

138
Demison, Natrelle	Bakersfield, Major 9-1 *47-4
Ladd, Jason	Clovis, *35-8
Cardenas, Racelis	Buchanan, 10-8
Hernandez, Josue	Madera South
Gomez, Adrian	Corcoran, Decision +2
Garcia, Chris	Clovis West
Govea, Ivan	Kerman, Default
Rocha, Dillion	Lemoore
Pimentel, Nathan	Dos Palos, Default
Lopez, Daniel	R F Kennedy

145
Ramirez, Maxx	Bakersfield, 14-12 *45-9
Hartsfield, Tyler	Liberty, *35-8
Martinez, Michael	Wasco Decision +2 *34-8
Morfin, Isiah	Selma, *40-10
Osamuyimen, Osunde	Lemoore, Default
Toro, James	West
Corona, Oscar	Foothill, 3-1 *36-14
Perez, Jorge	Edison
Kincaid, Dominic	Clovis, 2-1 OT
Panuco, Juan	Orange Cove

152
Martinez, Isiah	Lemoore, Fall :43 *45-1
Hammond, Coleman	Bakersfield *39-4
Perreault, Kyle	Clovis East, 7-3
Thompson, Colby	Clovis
Escalera, Ryan	Selma, Decision +2
Medley, Jason	Mission Oak, *40-10
Ruiz, Miguel	Madera, Default
Trejo, Miguel	West, *25-8
Alvardo, Caleb	Exeter, 1-0 ***
Temple, Mason	Liberty Madera

160
Salas, Adrian	Clovis, Fall 4:52
Terrones, Josue	Wash. Union, *38-5
Ferro, A J	Bakersfield, Fall 2:30 *45-13
Wright, Michael	Dinuba, 30-12
Martinez, Jaime	Lemoore, Default
Suikowsky, Sebastian	Hoover
Yilan, Charles	Madera South, 5-4

CENTRAL SECTION MASTERS - East
February 25, 2012

Shepherd, Kyle — Frontier, *30-17
Zecchini, Jason — Mt. Whitney, 12-0
Robledo, Jose — Wasco

170
Nacita, Silas — Bakersfield, 3-1 OT *27-4
Nevills, Zach — Clovis, *52-3
Ashjian, Cas — Bullard, 7-5 *42-12
Valladares, Juan — Madera South
Robinson, Gregory — Edison, Fall 1:43
Del Fierro, Dolan — Sierra
Hernandez, Oshmar — Wash. Union, TF 21-6
Morin, Keanu — Selma
Bailey, Josh — Frontier, Fall 3:01
Jimenez, Juan — Dos Palos

182
Reyes, Nikko — Clovis West, Fall :54 *51-1
Pope, Kyle — Bakersfield, *37-5
Davies, Ryan — Clovis, Fall 4:36
Tenorio, Mike — Firebaugh
Brandt, Richie — Bullard, 7-6
Pedraza, Jacob — Hanford West
Gonzalez, Gabrial — Wash. Union, Default
Daise, Deandre — Lemoore
Meza, Nathaniel — Woodlake, 3-2 *29-5
Gutierrez, Gerardo — Madera

195
Gordan, Dakota — Clovis, Major 16-3 *40-2
Lincoln, Kyle — Yosemite, *36-3 27, Falls
Murphy, Jack — Frontier, Default *35-7
Lopez, Nathaniel — Lemoore
Pedraza, Lenny — Madera, Decision +1
Lopez, Christian — Selma
Pyzer, Jordan — Clovis, North, Major 14-3
Placido, Luis — Madera South
Wills, Cameron — Liberty, Fall 1:09
Gamez, Anthony — Mendota

220
Mendoza, Eric — Madera, 3-2 *32-6
Weiss, Matt — Clovis, 27-11
Medley, Sean — Wasco, Decision +2 *37-9
Sanchez, Andrew — Golden West *39-9
Morales, Cortes — Clovis West, Fall 4:30
Olgin, Jordan — Foothill, *18-9
Salinas, Arnold — Fresno, 7-1
Carillio, Otillo — Edison
Varela, Luis — Dos Palos, 8-3 ***
Vandergriff, Paul — Liberty Madera

285
Nevills, Nick — Clovis, 5-1 *43-1
Amaya, Rudy — Foothill, *40-4
Popek, John — Frontier, 7-3 *36-9
Trevino, Mark — Corcoran
Crawford, Carson — Centennial, 3-2 3rdOT
Juarez, Narciso — Sanger
Hiatt, Brophy — Golden West, 2-1 OT *33-17
Roa, Johnathan — Lemoore
Johnson, Garret — Wasco, Fall 3:02
Kyle, Brian — Exeter

* Record

*** 3 - 9th place finishers take Oakland spot at state

Placing criteria for sixth match

+1 Victory head to head Masters
+2 Higher divisional placing

Most Outstanding Wrestlers

Lower Weight: Alex Cisneros — Selma
Upper Weight: Nikko Reyes — Clovis West

CENTRAL SECTION MASTERS - East
February 25, 2012

TEAM SCORES

1	Clovis	281
2	Bakersfield	163
3	Clovis West	93.5
4	Lemoore	86
5	Madera	77
6	Selma	71
7	Wasco	60
8	Central	51
9	Frontier	50
10	Buchanan	43
11	Washington Union	39.5
12	Foothill	39
13	Corcoran	38
14	Madera South	33
15	Porterville	31.5
16	Clovis East	30.5
17	Bullard	26
18	Liberty	25
19	Exeter	22
20	Kingsburg	19
21	Edison	18
21	Monache	18
21	Yosemite	18
24	Golden West	17
25	Redwood	14
26	Dinuba	12
27	Centennial	11
27	West	11
29	Firebaugh	10
29	Kerman	10
31	Sanger	9
32	Hanford West	7
32	Hoover	7
32	Mission Oak	7
32	Sierra	7
36	Clovis North	6
36	Dos Palos	6
36	Fresno	6
39	Reedley	5
40	Mt. Whitney	4
41	Coalinga	3
41	Woodlake	3
43	R F Kennedy	2
43	Stockdale	2
45	Caruthers	1
45	Liberty Madera	1
45	Mendota	1
45	Orange Cove	1
49	Fowler	0
49	Shafter	0

CENTRAL SECTION MASTERS – Mt. Whitney
February 23, 2013

106
Camposano, Adrian	Central, Major 13-2
Lloren, Durbin	Buchanan
Cisneros, Joey	Redwood, 5-4
Gamble, Matt	Monache
Gaytan, Julian	Clovis, Fall 2:46
Herrera, Carlos	Bakersfield, *39-17
Jimenez, Jovier	Porterville, Major 13-3
Campbell, David	Lemoore
Cisneros, Chris	Selma, Fall 3:49
Licea, Jose	Caruthers

113
Williams, Sean	Lemoore, Major 11-3
Hokit, Isaiah	Wasco
Olivas, Khristian	Clovis 3-0
Gaxiola, Greg	Buchanan
Rosas, A J	Reedley, Major 10-1
Velasquez, Marco	Foothill, *44-11
Orosco, Alex	Edison, TF 19-4
Torres, Isaiah	Redwood
Jauergui, Joseph	Clovis East, Fall 1:34
Ramirez, Noel	Kingsburg

120
Pengilly, Mason	Porterville, 4-0
Olea, Arnulfo	Exeter
Gaytan, Jonas	Clovis, 6-4
Ruiz, Daniel	Madera
Delacruz, Jason	Buchanan
Thomas, Brenden	Corcoran, prior Fall 1:19
Marquez, Nick	Foothill, 7-0 *47-10
Onsurez, Arik	Bakersfield, *29-17
Tirado, Jonas	Kingsburg, 6-2
Hood, Seth	Monache

126
Gomez, Vincent	Frontier, 4-3
Knoblauch, Michael	Clovis West
Sibayan, Josh	Monache, 10-7
Hokit, Josh	Wasco, *35-10
Molina, Armand	Firebaugh, 11-5
Garcia, Ruben	Selma
Esquibel, Dean	Buchanan, 5-3
Barnes, Lane	Clovis
Jimenez, Elijah	Clovis North, 4-2 OT
Bracamonte, Adam	East, *33-9

132
Gasca, Javier	Kingsburg, Default
Hansen, Kyler	Buchanan
Contreras, Abel	Porterville, Fall 3:43
Ozuna, Izaiah	Frontier, *40-12
Panduro, Adrian	Corcoran, prior result
Velarde, Xesus	Clovis, *21-9
Gutierrez, Antonio	Bakersfield, 9-2 *32-14
Lane, Chris	Clovis East
Mora, Aaron	Firebaugh, Fall 3:54
Valenzuela, James	Madera

138
Sandoval, Martin	Porterville, Fall 3:51
Garcia, Chris	Clovis West
Ontiveros, Matt	Central, Fall 1:47
Pena, Ralph	Selma
Romero, Abner	Bakersfield, 6-3
Pimentel, Nathan	Dos Polos
Rodriguez, Christian	Reedley, 8-4
Sanchez, Rosario	Sanger
Lopez, Dominic	Lemoore, 11-8
Reyna, Paul	Yosemite

145
Ladd, Jason	Clovis, 3-1
Zimmer, Tyler	Clovis West
Fierro, A J	Bakersfield, 6-3
Perez, Jorge	Edison
Frances, Conner	Buchanan, Default
Garcia, Isaac	Madera
Arroya, Isidro	Reedley, 4-2
Suarez, Izzac	Dos Palos
Jones, Kyle,	Exeter, Fall 1:04
Gomez, Aaron	Frontier

152
Perreault, Kyle	Clovis East, 3-2
Hammond, Coleman	Bakersfield
Govea, Ivan	Firebaugh, Fall 2:29
Pegela, Gregory	Porterville
Kincaid, Dominic	Clovis, 9-6
Thomas, Teddy	Buchanan
Escalera, Ryan	Selma, Default
Ruiz, Miguel	Madera
Ferrer, Miguel	Caruthers, 11-6
Moran, Chris	Sanger

160
Martinez, Isaiah	Lemoore, TF 18-3
Hodges, Hunter	Bakersfield
Brand, Brody	Clovis, Default
Wright, Michael	Dinuba
Morin, Keam	Selma, Default
Terrones, Josue	Washington Union
Shepherd, Kyle	Frontier, 8-2 *39-12
Jepsen, David	Central
Robinson, Yusuf	Buchanan, 3-1
Temple, Mason	Liberty Madera

CENTRAL SECTION MASTERS – Mt. Whitney
February 23, 2013

170
- Martin, Bryce — Bakersfield, 5-4 2nd OT
- Flores, Austin — Clovis North
- Gamboa, Alex — Madera, Fall 3:24
- Callender, Nick — Clovis East
- Reyes, Javier — Buchanan, prior result
- Hernandez, Adrian — Kennedy, 3-2 *27-9
- Martinez, Jaime — Lemoore, Default
- Holmes, Ryan — Stockdale, *39-18
- Segura, Edgar — Mendota, 3-1
- Rangel, Isaac — Firebaugh

182
- Salas, Adrian — Clovis, Default
- Pope, Kyle — Bakersfield, *34-7
- Grout, Jackson — Buchanan, 6-3
- Robledo, Jose — Wasco, *36-9
- Harroun, Dillon — Tehachapi, Default*35-6
- Brandt, Richie — Bullard
- Jimenez, Juan — Dos Palos, 9-3
- Montejo, Carlos — Frontier, *32-17
- Mesa, Nathan — Woodlake, 3-1
- Vivanco, Nathanial — Firebaugh

195
- Gonzalez, Gabriel — Washington Union, 3-2
- Weiss, Matt — Clovis
- Bailey, Josh — Frontier, Default *45-7
- Kidd, Nick — Bakersfield, *29-15
- Lopez, Jacob — Ridgeview, Default *28-10
- Karam, Josh — Clovis North
- Woo An, Young — Buchanan, Default
- Padilla, David — Dinuba
- Carranza, Enrique — Corcoran, 5-3
- Galvan, Jaime — Mt. Whitney

220
- Medley, Sean — Wasco, 9-4*46-2
- Morales, Cortes — Clovis West
- Coronado, Hexton — Clovis, 2-1
- Ponce, Marcus — Central
- Alcantar, Augie — Frontier, 8-3 *45-12
- Figueroa, Chris — Mendota
- Mendoza, Peter — Madera South, Fall 2:57
- Vandergriff, Paul — Liberty Madera
- Valles, Joseph — Hoover, 5-3
- Garza, Adrian — Lemoore

285
- Nevills, Nick — Clovis, Fall 2:49
- Roa, Jonathan — Lemoore
- Barrios, Robert — Sierra Pacific, Fall time?
- Alvarez, Joey — Selma
- Dill, Kai — Buchanan, Default
- Johnson, Garret — Wasco, *33-12
- Garcia, Christian — Reedley, 4-3
- Anaya, Anthony — Corcoran
- Rosas, Gabriel — Ridgeview, 5-3 2nd OT*28-12
- Garret, Shaq — Bakersfield

10 to state championships
* Season Record

Most Outstanding Wrestlers

Lower Weight: Martin Sandoval Porterville
Upper Weight: Isaiah Martinez   Lemoore

Isaiah Martinez – Lemoore High School and University of Illinois

CENTRAL SECTION MASTERS – Mt. Whitney
February 23, 2013

TEAM SCORES

1	Clovis	201
2	Buchanan	149
3	Bakersfield	132.5
4	Porterville	94
5	Lemoore	91
6	Clovis West	90.5
7	Frontier	78
8	Wasco	74
9	Central	60.5
10	Selma	56
11	Clovis East	44
12	Madera	40
13	Firebaugh	37
14	Clovis North	32
15	Kingsburg	30.5
16	Washington Union	26
17	Monache	28
18	Corcoran	24
19	Exeter	22
20	Reedley	21.5
21	Edison	20
22	Redwood	18
22	Sierra Pacific	18
24	Dos Palos	16.5
25	Ridgeview	14
25	Dinuba	14
27	Tehachapi	13
28	Foothill	12
28	Mendota	12
30	Bullard	11
31	R F Kennedy	9
31	Madera South	9
31	Liberty Madera	9
34	Sanger	6
35	Caruthers	4
35	Centennial	4
35	Stockdale	4
38	Yosemite	3
39	Shafter	2
40	East	1
40	Hoover	1
40	Mt. Whitney	1
40	Woodlake	1
44	North	0
40	Liberty	0
40	Fresno	0
40	Kerman	0

Michael Knoblauch-Clovis West High School and Vincent Gomez – Frontier High School

CENTRAL SECTION MASTERS – Madera South
March 1, 2014

108
- Mejia, Justin — Clovis, 10-4
- Cisneros, Joey — Redwood
- Demison, Novonte — Bakersfield, 15-2
- Marin, Chris — Clovis West
- Campbell, David — Mission Oak, 2-0
- Arve, Ross — Buchanan
- Alaniz, Javier — Clovis East, 4-1
- Nelms, Andrew — Porterville
- Castro, Carl — Mendota, 9-3
- Perez, Tommy — Kennedy

115
- Figueroa, J J — Bakersfield, 3-1 *39-8
- Gamble, Matt — Monache
- Lloren, Durbin — Buchanan, 12-4
- Camposano, Adrian — Central
- Garcia, Robert — Selma, 5-0
- Rosas, A J — Reedley
- Gilliland, Tristan — Clovis, 4-3
- Perez, Fern — Foothill, *47-8
- Morita, Bryce — Clovis West, 3-2
- Pimental, Armondo — Dos Palos

122
- Gaytan, Julian — Clovis, 6-5 *40-10 20 Falls
- Herrera, Carlos — Bakersfield
- Wright, Jacob — Dinuba, Fall 4:51 *42-9
- Jimenez, Alejandro — Buchanan
- Quintos, Victor — Central, Default
- Cisneros, Chris — Selma
- Marrufo, Adrian — Dos Palos, 12-6
- Delgado, Gilbert — El Diamante
- Flores, Gilbert — Sanger, 11-5
- Welton, Brock — Frontier, *38-12

128
- Knoblauch, Michael — Clovis West, 4-3
- Pingilly, Mason — Porterville
- Ruiz, Daniel — Madera, 9-6
- Olivas, Khristian — Clovis
- Gaxiola, Greg — Buchanan, Default
- Alvarez, Andy — Granite Hills
- Nickell, Sean — Bakersfield, Fall 1:11 *38-15
- DelBosque, David — Dinuba
- Ledesma, Gabriel — Exeter, Fall 1:22
- Martin, Josef — Stockdale, *19-14

134
- Ontiveros, Matthew — Central, 5-0 *140-15 72 Falls
- Enriquez, Jaden — Mission Oak
- Hansen, Kyler — Buchanan, 11-3
- Garcia, Ruben — Selma
- Hokit, Isaiah — Clovis, 8-1
- Molina, Armand — Firebaugh
- Harris, Darrion — Redwood, Fall 3:21
- Onsurez, Arik — Bakersfield, *28-17
- Miguel, Bobby — Clovis West, Default
- Alvarez, Michael — Granite Hills

140
- Lane, Chris — Clovis West, 5-1 37-19 19 Falls
- Esquibel, Dean — Buchanan
- Contreras, Abel — Porterville, 5-2 *46-9
- Barnes, Lane — Clovis
- Annis, Josh — Bakersfield, 10-2 *36-15
- Cerda, Brian — Sunnyside
- Mata, Joseph — Kingsburg, Default
- Jauregui, Joseph — Clovis East
- Mora, Aaron — Firebaugh, 3-2
- Bedrosian, Jake — Coalinga

147
- Garcia, Chris — Clovis West, 10-1 42-5 22 Falls
- Frances, Conner — Buchanan
- Hill, Jared — Clovis, Fall :33
- Gutierrez, Antonio — Bakersfield, *23-14
- Serna, Trini — Firebaugh, Default
- Pimental, Nathan — Dos Palos
- Sanchez, Rosario — Sanger, Fall 4:36
- Macias, Michael — Wasco, *41-9
- Demaree, Ashton — El Diamante, Fall 1:59 *37-9
- Jones, Tanner — Exeter

154
- Kincaid, Dominic — Clovis, 2-1 *44-8 21 Falls
- Zimmer, Tyler — Clovis West
- Romero, Abner — Buchanan, Default
- Alvarado, Danny — Mission Oak
- Lee, Andrew — Centennial, 4-2 *31-12
- Suarez, Izzac — Dos Palos
- Quintana, James — Clovis East, Fall 3:01
- Gutierrez, Basiio — Kerman
- Jones, Kyle — Exeter, 7-3
- Ruiz, Greg — Monache

160
- Hokit, Josh — Clovis, Fall 4:48
- Wright, Michael — Dinuba, *39-7
- Callender, Nick — Clovis East, 3-2
- Mass, Jake — Liberty, *34-9
- Loera, Sam — Bakersfield, 5-2 42-12

CENTRAL SECTION MASTERS – Madera South
March 1, 2014

Leypon, Bryan — Monache
Fuentes, Julio — Golden Valley, Default *40-12
Fernandez, Hunberto — Kerman
Coker, Tyler — Exeter, 13-4
Galindo, John — Dos Palos

172
Martin, Bryce — Bakersfield, 7-3
Flores, Austin — Clovis North
Brand, Brody — Clovis, 13-4
Moran, Chris — Sanger
Segura, Edgar — Mendota, Default
Dhanda, Arshdeep — Dinuba, *41-16
Potter, Dillain — Caruthers, Fall :35
Padilla, Enrique — El Diamante
Ames, Josh — Porterville, Default
Macias, Marcus — Central

184
Gamboa, Alec — Madera, 10-9
Nevills, A J — Clovis
Rangel, Isaac — Firebaugh, 12-7
Woo an, Young — Buchanan
Alvarado, Robert — Mission Oak, Default *43-11
Montejo, Carlos — Frontier, *37-10
Moreno, Erick — Sunnyside, Fall 3:50
Robledo, Jose — Wasco, *43-10
Rosas, Kobe — Coalinga, Fall 2:22
Rosales, Elias — Bakersfield

197
Weiss, Matt — Clovis, Fall 5:32
Bailey, Josh — Frontier, *36-9
Dill, Kai — Buchanan, 7-6
Ybarra-Brandt, Richard — Liberty Madera
Lopez, Jacob — Ridgeview, *27-5
Bohanon, Lawrence — Sunnyside
Parker, Justin — Clovis East, Default
Cunningham, Christian — Sierra
KU, Alex — Clovis West, 6-1
Valladares, Jacob — Madera South

220
Gonzales, Gabriel — Washington Union, 2-1OT
Morales, Cortes — Clovis West
Prentice, Adam — Clovis, Default
Yarbrough, Travis — Bakersfield, *27-10
Sanchez, Cornelio — Sanger, 5-3OT
Levatino, Zak — Buchanan
Ybarra-Brandt, Bevan — Liberty Madera, Fall 4:35 *35-4

Padilla, David — Dinuba, *14-8
Mask, Kyle — Madera, 2-1OT
Gonzalez, Joseph — Foothill

287
Nevills, Nick — Clovis, Fall 3:42
Alvarez, Jose — Selma
Barrios, Robert — Sierra Pacific, Default
Jones, Casey — Sierra
Powell, Roy — Madera, Fall 3:09
Vance, Kevin — Edison
Villanueva, Miguel — Madera South, Default
Guerrero, Mark — North, *33-11
Davis, Dawson — Dinuba, Fall 5:07 39-21
Moreno, Alan — Sunnyside

* Season and career records

Most Outstanding Wrestlers

Lower Weight: Michael Knoblauch Clovis West
Upper Weight: Gabriel Gonzales Wash. Union

TEAM SCORES

1	Clovis	284.5
2	Buchanan	157
3	Bakersfield	144
4	Clovis West	140
5	Madera	56
6	Mission Oak	52
7	Dinuba	51
8	Selma	50
9	Central	48
10	Porterville	40
11	Firebaugh	35.5
12	Clovis East	30.5
13	Frontier	30
13	Sanger	30
15	Washington Union	27
16	Monache	25
17	Redwood	24
18	Clovis North	19
18	Sierra Pacific	19
18	Sunnyside	19
21	Dos Palos	18
21	Liberty Madera	18
23	Sierra	16
24	Liberty	14
25	Mendota	13
25	Ridgeview	13
27	Centennial	12

CENTRAL SECTION MASTERS – Madera South
March 1, 2014

27	Foothill	12
29	Kingsburg	11
30	Edison	9
31	Kerman	8
32	Caruthers	7
32	Exeter	7
32	Golden Valley	7
32	Madera South	7
36	El Diamante	6
36	Granite Hills	6
36	Reedley	6
39	North	4
39	Wasco	4
41	Coalinga	0
41	Golden West	0
41	Hoover	0
41	Orange Cove	0
41	R F Kennedy	0
41	Roosevelt	0
41	Stockdale	0
41	Tehachapi	0
41	Lemoore	0

Sean Nickell – Bakersfield High School

Michael Wright – Dinuba High School

CENTRAL SECTION MASTERS - East
February 28, 2015

106
Perez, Isaiah	Dinuba, Fall 6:25
Leake, Ethan	Buchanan
Morita, Bryce	Clovis West, 6-0
Olejnik, Izzak	Bakersfield, *34-12
Cornelison, Wyatt	Clovis, 8-1
Madriz, Marcelino	Firebaugh
Areyano, Robert	Selma, 2-0
Pacheco, Anthony	Sanger
Sanchez, Meteo	Central, 6-2
Zertuche, Julian	Madera South

113
Mejia, Justin	Clovis, 11-2
Alaniz, Javier	Clovis West
Ortiz, Tommy	R F Kennedy, *43-7
Campbell, David	Mission Oak
Nelms, Andrew	Porterville
Gaxiola, Chris	Buchanan
Zavala, Hector	Lemoore, 2-1
Chavez, Anthony	Central
Arenas, Anthony	Bakersfield, 10-8 *23-12
Stimpel, Ethan	Exeter

120
Lloren, Durbin	Buchanan, 5-0
Deloza, Chris	Clovis North
Demison, Navonte	Bakersfield, Default
Gilliland, Tristan	Clovis
Marrufo, Adrian	Dos Palos, Major 19-4
Delgado, Jacob	El Diamante
Garcia, Robert	Selma, 7-5
Delacruz, Lorenzo	Redwood
Gonzales, Ruben	Sanger, 3-1
Hernandez, Marco	R F Kennedy, *30-10

126
Figeroa, J J	Bakersfield, 4-0
Perez, Fern	Foothill, *48-8
Ozuna, Elijah	Frontier, 2-1 *33-10
Romero, Joel	Buchanan
Mendoza, Tony	Selma, 5-4
Rodriguez, Michael	Hoover
Martinez, Dylan	Clovis, Major 18-9
Villarreal, Brett	Redwood
Perez, Isaac	Porterville, Fall 3:39
Ramos, Ethan	Shafter, *29-11

132
Gaxiola, Greg	Buchanan 3-0
Martino, Brandon	Clovis
Enriquez, Jaden	Mission Oak, 6-4
Herrera, Carlos	Bakersfield
Molina, Armand	Firebaugh, 3-2
Mora, Aaron	Clovis West
Diaz, Oscar	Selma, 4-2
Armijo, Etienne	Centennial
Romero, Joe	Corcoran, 4-0
Grimsley, Kevin	Exeter

138
Garcia, Ruben	Selma, Default
Olivas, Khristian	Clovis
Esquibel, Dean	Buchanan, 3-1
Perez, Bailey	Reedley
Garcia, Jonathan	Frontier, 11-8 *34-13
Miguel, Bobby	Clovis West
Rodriguez, Mark	Bakersfield, 4-2 *26-14
Tamayo, Alvaro	Arvin
Mata, Joseph	Kingsburg, 6-5
Gutierrez, Bailey	Hoover

145
Hill, Jared	Clovis, Default
Frances, Conner	Buchanan
Annis, Josh	Bakersfield, 9-2 *34-12
Sanchez, Rosario	Sanger
Lopez, Conrado	Hoover, Fall 4:49
Hooten, Tyson	Monache
Morphis, Calloway	Frontier, Default *34-14
Ramos, Jonathon	Selma, 5-1
Quintana, James	Clovis East, 7-4
Bedrosian, Jacob	Coalinga

152
Jauregul, Joseph	Clovis East, 6-4
Romero, Abner	Buchanan
Hokit, Isaiah	Clovis, 8-2
Gonzales, Ricky	Bakersfield, *28-12
Zamilpa, Tristan	Selma, 5-1
Zendejas, Adrian	Porterville
Dawson, Boland	Exeter, Major 9-0 *38-14
Arreola, Ruben	Granite Hills
Duran, Thomas	Tehachapi, Fall 1:57 *37-16
Miracle, Dylan	Madera South

160
Kincaid, Dominic	Clovis, Fall 1:19
Loera, Sam	Bakersfield
Montalvo, Anthony	Buchanan, Fall 3:06
Robles, Skyler	Parlier
Medley, Anthony	Mission Oak, Fall :18
Jones, Phelan	South, *46-9
Jones, Kyle	Exeter, Default
Montejano, Edgar	Dinuba
Chocoteco, Juan	Foothill, 4-3 *35-9
Solis, Angel	Lemoore

CENTRAL SECTION MASTERS - East
February 28, 2015

170
Hokit, Josh	Clovis, 6-3
Wright, Michael	Dinuba, *36-5
Gutierrez, Antonio	Bakersfield, 6-5 *31-8
Belshay, Cade	Buchanan
Macias, Marcus	Central, Fall 4:24
Hunter, Jonathan	Golden Valley, *26-12
Godinez, Adrian	Foothill, Fall :43 *40-9
Gomez, Nino	Exeter
Maiden, Nic	Stockdale, 14-9
Ruiz, Santana	Fowler

182
Nevills, A J	Clovis, 8-4
Fuentes, Julio	Golden Valley
Ervin, Trever	Buchanan, 3-2
Moreno, Erick	Sunnyside
Muxlow, Ty	Kingsburg, Defalt
Jimenez, Juan	Dos Palos
Osunde, Osaze	Lemoore, Major 11-3
Bracamonte, Jesse	Granite Hills
Chavez, Nathan	Madera South, 2-1
Rodriguez, Noah	Bakersfield, *27-13

195
Flores, Austin	Clovis North, 3-2
Prentice, Adam	Clovis
Gamboa, Alec	Madera, Major 15-4
Woo An, Young	Buchanan
Stenschke, Anthony	Sierra Pacific, 7-6
Rosas, Kobe	Coaling
Metz, Daniel	Granite Hills, Fall 1:06
Stutte, Matt	Fresno
Rosales, Elias	Bakersfield, 5-2 *29-13
Saavedra, Eric	Highland, 39-12

220
Nevills, Seth	Clovis, Fall 2:56
Brandt, Bevan	Bullard
Padilla, David	Dinuba, 1-0
Lopez, Jaccob	Ridgeview, *32-4
Dill, Kai,	Buchanan, Fall 4:30
Barrios, Robert	Sierra Pacific
Halajian, John	Clovis North, 3-1
Mariscal, Angel	Delano, *28-14
Parker, Justin	Clovis East, Major 12-3
Macias, Romiro	Kennedy, *38-13

285
Coronado, Hexton	Clovis, Fall 3:49
Jones, Casey	Sierra
Alvarez, Jose	Selma, Fall 2:10
Snyder, Jarrod	Frontier
Davis, Dawuud	Dinuba, 5-1*29-13

Moreno, Alan	Sunnyside
Holloway, Nathaniel	Clovis North, Forfeit
Quintanilla, Nimrod	Golden Valley, *28-11
Vorhees, Andrew	Kingsburg, Fall :12
Levatino, Zakary	Buchanan

*Season Record

Most Outstanding Wrestlers

Lower Weight: Ruben Garcia   Selma
Upper Weight: Seth Nevills   Clovis

A J Nevills – Clovis High School and Fresno State University

CENTRAL SECTION MASTERS - East
February 28, 2015

TEAM SCORES

Rank	Team	Score
1	Clovis	310.5
2	Buchanan	226
3	Bakersfield	148
4	Dinuba	71.5
4	Selma	71.5
6	Clovis North	56
7	Clovis West	51
8	Frontier	46
9	Mission Oak	41
10	Golden Valley	34
10	Foothill	34
12	Clovis East	29
13	Porterville	25
14	Sierra Pacific	23
14	Lemoore	23
16	Sunnyside	21
17	Dos Palos	19.5
18	Exeter	19
18	Bullard	19
18	Hoover	19
21	Central	18
21	Sierra	18
23	Firebaugh	17
23	Granite Hills	17
23	Kingsburg	17
23	Madera	17
27	R F Kennedy	16
28	Ridgeview	14
28	Sanger	14
30	Reedley	11
31	Coalinga	10
31	Parlier	10
33	Monache	9
33	South	9
35	Highland	7
35	Madera South	7
37	Redwood	6
38	El Diamante	5
38	Tehachapi	5
40	Arvin	4
40	Centennial	4
40	North	4
43	Stockdale	1
43	Corcoran	1
43	Fowler	1
43	Shafter	1
47	Bakersfield Christian	0
47	Caruthers	0
47	Cesar Chavez	0
47	Farmersville	0
47	Garces	0
47	Independence	0
47	Mendota	0
47	Mt. Whitney	0
47	Wasco	0
47	Washington Union	0
57	Hanford	-1

Izzak Olejnik – Bakersfield High School

CENTRAL SECTION MASTERS - Lemoore
February 26-27, 2016

108
Olguin, Matthew	Buchanan, 10-1
Betancourt, Brandon	Clovis
Rivera, Eric	Clovis North, 11-4
Reyes, Cole	Frontier
Cisneros, Josh	Selma, Fall 1:06
Moreno, Mario	Madera
Terrence, Thomas	Clovis East, Default
Olenik, Izzak	Bakersfield
Sanchez, Matt	Central, 9-5
Olea, Eric	Exeter

115
Leake, Ethan	Buchanan, 12-6
Alantz, Javier	Clovis West
Cornellison, Wyatt	Clovis, TF 16-0
Areyana, Robert	Selma
Pacheco, Anthony	Sanger, 14-1
Morphis, Ryan	Frontier
Beckett, Rocky	Clovis North, 6-3
Briseno, Daniel	Independence
Birrueta, Mario	Wasco, Fall 1:11
Callison, Jared	Monache

122
Mejia, Justin	Clovis 16-4
Abas, Jaden	Frontier
Perez, Isaiah	Dinuba, 7-2
Gaxioia, Chris	Buchanan
Garcia, Robert	Selma, Fall :48
Chavez, Anthony	Central
Diaz, Matt	Clovis North, Fall 5:07
Bracamonte, Matt	Foothill
Rodgers, Brock	Corcoran, 3-1 OT
Gonzales, Ruben	Sanger

128
Joint, Gary	Lemoore, 5-2
Villarreal, Brett	Buchanan
Campbell, David	Mission Oak, Fall :52
Marufu, Adrian	Dos Palos
Deloza, Chris	Clovis North, Fall :45
Deltoro, Abraham	Madera
Corona, Pete	Independence, 10-1
Bedrosian, Zackary	Coalinga
Rhoads, Brandon	Clovis, 7-1
Walls, Isaiah	Clovis West

134
Lloren, Durbin	Buchanan, 9-4
Mendoza, Tony	Selma
Geiger, Jordan	Clovis, Criteria
Perez, Isaac	Porterville
Hernandez, Marco	Kennedy, 6-2
Peturell, Niko	Clovis North
Pimentel, Armando	Dos Palos, Fall 1:44
Espinoza, Issac	Madera South
Watts, Aaron	Redwood, Fall :46
Contreras, Moses	Madera

140
Demison, Navonte	Bakersfield, 3-1 OT
Wright, Jacob	Dinuba
Martinez, Dylan	Clovis, 3-1
Miguel, Bobby	Clovis West
Ramero, Joel	Buchanan, Fall 1:04
Corona, Esteban	Independent
Diaz, Oscar	Selma, 5-0
Gamboa, Manuel	Cesar Chavez
Deandre, Eason	Wash. Union, Default
Garcia, Seth	Strathmore

147
Garcia, Ruben	Selma, 6-5
Gaxiola, Greg	Buchanan
Bradley, Beau	Monache, Fall 4:21
Cravens, Dillon	Bakersfield
Torres, Isaiah	Redwood, Criteria
Ladd, Jake	Clovis
Espana, Issak	Clovis West, 8-5
Benadum, Chance	Dos Palos
Garcia, Augustine	Madera South, 11-2
Huskey, Skyler	El Diamante

154
Martino, Brandon	Clovis, 11-0
Lane, Chris	Clovis West
Garcia, Jonathan	Frontier, 6-2
Gonzalez, Ricky	Bakersfield
Quintana, James	Clovis East, Criteria
Cardwell, Mark	Monache
Ramos, Jonathan	Selma, Default
Jones, Tanner	Exeter
Levatino, Jake	Buchanan, Fall 1:35
Delbosque, Alex	Dinuba

162
Romero, Abner	Bullard, Fall 4:36
Loera, Sam	Bakersfield
Hunter, Jonathan	Golden Valley, 6-4
Varas, Victor	Clovis
Miracle, Dylan	Madera, Default
Boland, Dawson	Exeter
Corona, Isaiah	Hanford, Default
Stanley, Jordan	Central
Sandoval, Joey	Porterville, 3-1
Sevilla, Ivan	Coalinga

CENTRAL SECTION MASTERS - Lemoore
February 26-27, 2016

172
Belshey, Cade — Buchanan, 4-2
Reyes, Ryan — Clovis West
Wyneken, Ruger — Clovis, Default
Macias, Marcus — Central
Gutierrez, Antonio — Bakersfield, Default
Moreno, Eric — Sunnyside
Maiden, Nic — Stockdale, Default
Chapa, Chris — Madera
Rodriguez, Christian — Selma, 8-1
Ruiz, Santana — Fowler

184
Hokit, Josh — Clovis, 13-5
Montalvo, Anthony — Buchanan
Solis, Angel — Lemoore, 6-0
Rodriguez, Noah — Bakersfield
Mass, Jeremy — Liberty, Default
Good, Jacob — Exeter
Halajian, Mark — Clovis North, Fall 5:55
English, Josh — Selma
Chavez, Nathan — Madera South, 4-3
Martin, Isaiah — Garces

197
Nevills, A J — Clovis, 9-2
Godinez, Adrian — Foothill
Rosales, Elias — Bakersfield, 9-3
Rosas, Kobe — Coalinga
Halajian, John — Clovis North, Default
Ramirez, Fabian — Central
Erwin, Fabian — Buchanan
Muxlow, Ty — Kingsburg
Cicas, Eric — Firebaugh, Default
Lightner, Jacob — Kern Valley

220
Brant, Bevan — Bullard, 7-3
Levatino, Zakary — Buchanan
Macias, Ramiro — R F Kennedy, Criteria
Collier, Tyler — Clovis
Holloway, Nathaniel — Clovis North, Fall 3:32
Torres, Montana — South
Parks, Hunter — Hanford, Default
Mariscal, Angel — Delano
Villanueva, Miguel — Madera South, Fall 2:26
Madrid, Manuel — Corcoran

287
Nevills, Seth — Clovis, 3-1
Snyder, Jarrod — Frontier
Varela, Gilbert — Independence, 8-4
Barcenas, Armando — Hanford
Alvarez, Rogi, Selma — Default

Jaramillo, Ricardo — Golden Valley
Perez, Anthony — Exeter, Default
Garcia, Ricky — Reedley
Schuler, Brett — Bakersfield Christian Fall 1:40
Cruz, Hercules — Caruthers

Most Outstanding Wrestlers

Lower Weight: Gary Joint — Lemoore
Upper Weight: Abner Romero — Buchanan

TEAM RECORDS

1	Clovis	270
2	Buchanan	245
3	Bakersfield	114
4	Selma	101.5
5	Frontier	79
6	Clovis West	78.5
7	Clovis North	75.5
8	Central	42
9	Lemoore	40
10	Dinuba	36
11	Independence	29
11	Monache	29
13	Exeter/Foothill	27
13	Golden Valley	27
13	Hanford	27
17	Bullard	22
18	Dos Palos	21.5
19	R F Kennedy	21
20	Mission Oak	20
21	Clovis East	18
21	Madera	18
22	Coalinga	17
23	Porterville	14
24	Redwood	12

CENTRAL SECTION MASTERS - Clovis
February 24-25, 2017

106
Petrucelli, Giano	Clovis, 7-5
Reyes, Cole	Frontier
Lujan, Tristin	Selma, 10-0
Poore, Josh	Buchanan
Arreola, Lorenzo	Dinuba, Forfeit
Benevidez, Brian	Porterville
Terrence, Thomas	Clovis East, Forfeit
Reyes, Gabriel	Hanford
Morales, Joe	Exeter
Jimenez, Ruben	Foothill, *24-14

113
Olguin, Matthew	Buchanan, 3-0
Murthy, Devin	Clovis North
Paulson, Brandon	Clovis, Major 12-4
Sanchez, Mateo	Central, Forfeit
Dhanda, Gurjot	Dinuba, Forfeit
Pacheco, Anthony	Sanger
Moreno, Mario	Madera, Forfeit
Olea, Eric	Exeter
Navarro, Elijah	Bakersfield, 10-6
Landin, Jose	Wasco, *24-12

120
Leake, Ethan	Buchanan, Major 12-2
Cornelison, Wyatt	Clovis
Morphis, Ryan	Frontier, SV7-5 OT *38-16
Rivera, Eric	Clovis North
Bloemhof, Andrew	Bakersfield, Forfeit *28-15
Oetega, Mikey	Bullard
Hutcherson, Marcus	West, 4-2
Bustos, Paul	Madera
Callison, Jared	Monache, Fall 1:44
Perez, Tony	Shafter, *40-11

126
Mejia, Justin	Clovis, 3-1
Garcia, Robert	Selma
Olenik, Izzak	Bakersfield, 6-3 *27-13
Deen, Tyler	Buchanan
Sihavong, Dawson	Bullard, Forfeit
Perez, Isaiah	Dinuba
Chavez, Anthony	Central, Major 11-3
Beckett, Rocky	Clovis North
Rodgers, Brock	Corcoran, 10-6
Fletcher, Garrett	Frontier, *34-16

132
Deloza, Chris	Clovis North, Major 10-2
Joint, Gary	Lemoore
Ozuna, Elijah	Frontier, 3-1
Reyes, Ronnie	Hanford
Peverill, Wyatt	Buchanan, Fall 5:43
Ramos, Luis	Selma
Gonzalez, Adrian	Bakersfield, SV 8-4OT *27-16
Espana, Isack	Clovis West
Del Toro, Abraham	Madera, Fall 3:41
Arellano, Anselmo	Wasco, *24-11

138
Villerreal, Brett	Buchanan, 3-2 OT
Enriquez, Jaden	Mission Oak
Figueroa, J J	Bakersfield, 7-5
Mendoza, Tony	Selma
Contreras, Moses	Madera, Forfeit
Ayon, Lupe	Exeter
Hernandez, Marco	Frontier, Forfeit *23-16
Romero, Joe	Lemoore
Petrucelli, Niko	Clovis North, Fall 2:29
Cortez, Noah	Dinuba

145
Demison, Navonte	Bakersfield, Forfeit
Wright, Jacob	Dinuba
Zamilpa, Tristan	Buchanan, 4-3
Ramos, Jonathan	Selma
Bradley, Beau	Monache, 4-2
Tracy, Trent	Frontier, *33-16
Chiaramonte, Mikelli	Clovis, 6-5
Guzman, Greg	Lemoore
Cardoso, Jose	Hanford, 7-6
Beltran, Julian	Bullard

152
Garcia, Jonathan	Frontier, SV 8-6 OT
Luchau, Jace	Selma
Gianakopuloa, Tyler	Clovis, 5-2
McMillion, Josh	Madera
Cravens, Dillion	Bakersfield, 4-0 *36-10
Gaxiola, Chris	Buchanan
Garcia, Augustine	Madera South, Fall 5:30
Long, Daniel	Dinuba, *31-15
Badilla, Daniel	Reedley, Fall :47
De La Rosa, R J	Foothill, *26-15

160
Martino, Brandon	Clovis, 5-4
Romero, Joel	Buchanan
Gonzalez, Ricky	Bakersfield, 3-2
Diaz, Oscar	Selma
Zendejas, Adrian	Porterville, Forfeit
Rivas, Arturo	Firebaugh
Aguirre, Max	Frontier, *24-16
Cardwell, Mark	Monache

CENTRAL SECTION MASTERS - Clovis
February 24-25, 2017

Benadum, Chance — Dos Palos
Gonzalez, Jorge — Madera

170
Vargas, Victor — Clovis, 3-2
Rodriguez, Christian — Selma
Mass, Jeremy — Liberty, 7-4 *39-7
Levatino, Jake — Buchanan
Miracle, Dylan — Madera South, 11-5
Sandoval, Joey — Porterville
Corona, Isaiah — Hanford, Fall 2:38
Cantoriano, Chris — Clovis West
Jackson, Bo — Kingsburg, 4-3
Maldonado, Fabian — Avenal

182
Montalvo, Anthony — Buchanan, 8-0
Loera, Sam — Bakersfield
Solis, Angel — Lemoore, 6-3
Good, Jacob — Clovis
DeBoer, Willem — Frontier, Forfeit
Martin, Isaiah — Garces, *34-11
Maiden, Nic — Stockdale, Forfeit *33-16
Gonzalez, Richard — Tranquility
Lindsey, Trent — Clovis North, Forfeit
Azua, Andrew — Sanger

195
Reyes, Ryan — Clovis West, 5-2
Wyneken, Ruger — Clovis
Ervin, Trevor — Buchanan, Major 13-0
Jimenez, Isaiah — Selma
Chavez, Nathan — Madera South, 7-3
Halajian, Mark — Clovis North
Godinez, Adrian — Foothill, TF 17-0 4:42
Velez, Chris — R F Kennedy, *35-14
Watson, Kwabna — Edison, Fall 3:24
Gonzalves, Jacob — Lemoore

220
Belshay, Cade — Buchanan, 10-4
Halajian, John — Clovis North
Rosas, Kobe — Coalinga, Fall :37
Serna, Tony — Dinuba
Parks, Hunter — Hanford, 5-3
Echeveste, Nicholas — Firebaugh
Muxlow, Ty — Kingsburg, 6-0
Jaramillo, Joey — Clovis
Sandhu, Jasman — Bullard, 4-1
Garcia, Ricardo — Highland, *32-13

285
Nevills, Seth — Clovis, Fall 1:47
Holloway, Nathaniel — Clovis North
Barcenos, Armando — Hanford, Major 12-3
Wright, Noah — Lemoore
Ortiz, Isaiah — Buchanan, Fall 3:10
Went, Brian — Tulare Union
Schuler, Brett — Bakersfield Christian, Fall 1:35
Moran, Xavier — Kingsburg
Johnson, Matt — Chowchilla, Forfeit
Static, Patrick — Bullard

* Record

Most Outstanding Wrestlers

Lower Weight: Justin Mejia — Clovis
Upper Weight: Brandon Martino — Clovis

Robert Garcia – Selma High School

CENTRAL SECTION MASTERS - Clovis
February 24-25, 2017

TEAM SCORES

1 Buchanan	285.5	
2 Clovis	232.5	
3 Selma	158.5	
4 Bakersfield	137	
5 Clovis North	127	
6 Frontier	119.5	
7 Dinuba	84	
8 Lemoore	65.5	
9 Hanford	64.5	
10 Madera	53	
11 Clovis West	46	
12 Central	39	
13 Madera South	38	
14 Bullard	30	
14 Porterville	30	
16 Mission Oak	26	
17 Coalinga	20	
17 Firebaugh	20	
19 Monache	19	
20 Liberty	16.5	
21 Kingsburg	16	
22 Sanger	15.5	
23 Exeter	15	
24 Foothill	14.5	
25 Garces	12	
26 Bakersfield Christian	11	
27 Stockdale	9	
28 Reedley	8	
29 Dos Palos	7.5	
30 West	7	
30 Clovis East	7	
30 Tulare Union	7	
33 R F Kennedy	5	
33 Edison	5	
33 Highland	5	
33 Chowchilla	5	
37 Avenal	4	
37 Corcoran	4	
37 Wasco	4	
37 Sierra	4	
41 Centennial	3	
41 Tranquility	3	
41 Golden Valley	3	
45 Shafter	1	
45 Mendota	1	
45 Golden Valley	1	
45 Orange Cove	1	
45 Delano	1	
50 Parlier	0	
50 Granite Hills	0	
50 Arvin	0	
50 Kerman	0	
50 Kern Valley	0	
50 McFarland	0	
50 Cesar Chavez	0	
50 Washington Union	0	
50 McLane	0	
50 Sierra Pacific	0	
50 North	0	
50 Caruthers	0	

CENTRAL SECTION MASTERS - North
February 23-24, 2018

108
Figueroa, Richard	Selma, 8-0
Negrete, Carlos	Clovis North
Leake, Hunter	Buchanan, 4-0
Mouritsen, Justin	Clovis
Castillo, Ramiro	Central, 5-0
Maldanado, Laz	Clovis West
Bermudez, Nicholas	Mission Oak, 6-4
Bedrosian, Wyatt	Coalinga
Hernandez, Jonah	Corcoran, 2-0
Martinez, Armondo	Golden West

115
Renteria, Maximo	Buchanan, 4-2 OT
Lujan, Tristan	Selma
Petrucell, Giano	Clovis, 6-2
Moreno, Mario	Madera
Arreola, Lorenzo	Dinuba, Fall 1:44
Ozuna, Noah	Frontier, *24-13
Chavez, Adrian	Central, Default
Nava, Angel	Delano, *27-11
Bencomo, Taylor	Clovis North, Fall 5:41
Joint, Wayne	Lemoore

122
Murphy, Devin	Clovis North, 5-2
Reyes, Cole	Frontier
Paulsen, Brandon	Clovis, 8-1
Viveros, Jonathan	Kingsburg
Lucio, Cade	Bakersfield, Default *40-17
Miranda, Jude	Hanford
Rivera, Eric	Selma, 3-1
Poore, Josh	Buchanan, *29-19
Olea, Erik	Exeter, Fall 1:51
Gayton, Jesse	Lemoore

128
Franco, Ryan	Clovis North, 6-1
Leake, Ethan	Buchanan
Callison, Jared	Monache, Fall 3:59
Sepulveda, Tyler	Selma
Landin, Jose	Frontier, 10-5 *38-15
Valdovinos, Raul	Clovis West
Rosales, Angel	Bakersfield, 5-2 *35-16
Alejo, Mauro	Madera
Maldonado, Johnny	Liberty, Fall 5:21 *30-18
Granada, Emiliano	Clovis

134
Areyano, Robert	Selma, Fall 4:41
Deen, Tyler	Buchanan, *27-8
Bloemhof, Andrew	Bakersfield, 6-5 *39-14
Chavez, Anthony	Central
Grier, Lajon	Clovis North, Fall 4:36
Fletcher, Garrett	Frontier, *34-16
Rogers, Brock	Corcoran, Default
Leon, Dominic	Golden Valley, *29-12
Caldwell, Tyler	El Diamante, Default
Vang, Aaron	Washington Union

140
Olguin, Matthew	Buchanan, 8-4
Sihavong, Dawson	Bullard
Delacruz, Lorenzo	Redwood, Default
Beckett, Rocky	Clovis North
Morphis, Ryan	Frontier, 11-6 *39-16
Ayon, Lupe	Exeter
Romero, Joe	Lemoore, Default
Ramos, Luis	Selma
Marin, Valentin	Bakersfield, Default *30-12
Hernandez, Florencio	Madera South

147
Mendoza, Tony	Selma, Default
Gaxiola, Chris	Buchanan
Olejnik, Izzak	Bakersfield, Fall 1:14 *31-5
Neal, Elijah	McLane
Cortez, Noah	Dinuba, 8-1
Watts, Zach	Clovis North
Frantzich, Austin	Clovis, Default
Bedrosian, Caleb	Coalinga
Valencia, Nathan	Dos Palos, Fall :58
Sekhon, Abheybir	Central

154
Luchau, Jace	Selma, 7-4
Bradley, Beau	Monache
Zamilpa, Tristan	Buchanan, 3-1
Anderson, Max	Clovis
Gonzalez, Adrian	Bakersfield, 3-1 *35-16
Molina, Estaban	Firebaugh
Cuttone, Vito	Clovis North, 2-0
Adame, Ricardo	Madera South
Carter, Andrew	Frontier, 10-8 *35-16
Zavala, Nicholas	Mission Oak

162
Romero, Joel	Buchanan, Fall 1:28
Urias, Albert	Ridgeview, *34-9
Diaz, Oscar	Selma, 4-3
Aguirre, Max	Frontier, *46-14
Priest, Jared	Bakersfield, 8-7 *33-17
Long, Daniel	Dinuba, *36-14
Kloster, Will	Lemoore, Default
Rivas, Arturo	Firebaugh

CENTRAL SECTION MASTERS - North
February 23-24, 2018

Rodriguez, Felipe — Clovis West, 5-3
Garcia, Augustine — Madera South

172
Rodriguez, Christian — Selma, 9-1
Cardwell, Mark — Monache
Tracy, Trent — Frontier, Fall :40
Miracle, Dylan — Madera South
Martin, Jadon — Buchanan, 14-3 *44-16
Gianakopulos, Tyler — Clovis
Annis, Jordan — Bakersfield, 4-1 *31-16
Cantoriano, Chris — Clovis West
Limon, Mat — Kerman, Fall :58
Pantoja, Bryan — Garces, *30-16

184
Montalvo, Anthony — Buchanan, Fall :30
Vardanyan, David — Bullard
Maiden, Nic — Stockdale, Fall 1:37 *38-8
Bordon, John — Ridgeview, *32-11
Maldonado, Fabian — Avenal, 3-1
Lopez, Anthony — Bakersfield, *29-18
Rangel, Julius — Dinuba, Fall 2:30
Manzo, Luciano — Chowchilla
Avila, Tyler — Porterville, 5-2
Lindsey, Trent — Clovis North

197
Reyes, Ryan — Clovis West, 6-4
Good, Jacob — Clovis
Poore, Zach — Buchanan, 4-2*27-8 -98-48
Bautista, Amador — Redwood
Jimenez, Isaiah — Selma, Forfeit
Watson, Kwabena — Edison
Aparicio, Chris — Central, Fall :13
Cardenas, Javier — El Diamante
Mittlestead, Eric — Exeter, Fall 1:39
Gonzalez, Jonathon — Liberty, *30-18

222
Ervin, Trevor — Buchanan, 6-0
Darter, Justin — Bakersfield
Martin, Isaiah — Garces, Fall 2:17 *32-10
Gonsalves, Jacob — Lemoore
Morales, Mateo — Clovis West, 13-3
Slatic, Tommy — Bullard
Valle, Antonio — Centennia,l 3-1 *32-17
Sanchez, Sebastian — El Diamante
Aispuro, Gerardo — McFarland, 6-3 *28-10
Campos, Eric — R F Kennedy, *27-14

287
Nevills, Seth — Clovis, Fall :18
Moran, Xavier — Selma
Duchett, Naishawn — Buchanan, Fall 5:06
Hill, Josiah — Bakersfield, *28-15
Boland, Cord — Exeter, Default
Lightner, Jacob — Kern Valley, *26-8
Slatic, Patrick — Bullard, 6-3
Cavarrubia, Angel — Kerman
Abernathy, Kaleb — Centennial, Fall 3:15 *42-7
Schmidtke, Jonah — Clovis East

Most Outstanding Wrestlers

Lower Weight: Richard Figueroa — Selma
Upper Weight: Seth Nevills — Clovis

*Season Record – Career Record

Jacob Lightner – Kern Valley High School

CENTRAL SECTION MASTERS - North
February 23-24, 2018

TEAM SCORES

1 Buchanan	290.5	
2 Selma	229.5	
3 Clovis	143	
4 Bakersfield	130.5	
5 CLOVIS North	128	
6 Frontier	101	
7 Clovis West	67	
7 Monache	67	
9 Bullard	51	
9 Central	51	
11 Dinuba	43.5	
12 Lemoore	39	
13 Redwood	36	
14 Ridgeview	32	
15 Exeter	30	
16 Madera South	23	
17 Garces	21	
18 Madera	19.5	
19 Kerman	18	
20 Stockdale	16	
21 Kingsburg	14	
21 Mission Oak	14	
23 El Diamante	13	
23 Firebaugh	13	
25 Centennial	12	
25 McLane	12	
27 Avenel	11	
27 Coalinga	11	
29 Corcoran	10	
30 Edison	9	
31 Hanford	8	
32 Kern Valley	7	
32 Porterville	7	
34 Clovis East	6	
35 Delano	5	
35 North	5	
35 Shafter	5	
38 Golden West	4	
38 Liberty	4	
38 McFarland	4	
41 Chowchilla	3	
41 Golden Valley	3	
41 Highland	3	
44 Dos Palos	2	
44 R F Kennedy	2	
46 Crothers	1	
46 South	1	
46 Strathmore	1	
46 Washington Union	1	
50 Bakersfield Christian	0	
50 Cesar Chaves	0	
50 Hoover	0	
50 Independence	0	
50 Liberty Madera	0	
50 Mendota	0	
50 Orange Cove	0	
50 Parlier	0	
50 Rosamond	0	
50 Sierra Pacific	0	
50 Woodlake	0	

CENTRAL SECTION MASTERS - Lemoore
February 14-15, 2019

108
Figueroa	Selma, 12-3, MD
Gioffre, Jack	Buchanan
Mendez, Dominic	Righetti, 11-1 MD
Arsitio, Noah	Clovis North
Terrence, Matthew	Clovis, Fall 3:36
Hernandez, Jonah	Corcoran
Cerda, Abraham	Hoover, Injury Default
Alcantar, Francisco	Nipomo
Martinez, Armando	Golden West, Fall 1:24
Acala, Josh	Frontier, *26-18

115
Lujan, Tristan	Selma, 5-1
Negrete, Carlos	Buchanan
Mouritsen, Justin	Clovis, 5-3 OT
Zinkin, Hayden	Clovis North
Chavez, Martin	Orange Cove, 5-2
Garcia, Roman	El Diamante
Madrigal, Giovani	Madera, Injury Default
Castro, Javier	Dinuba
Onsurez, Ashton	Bakersfield, Injury Default *23-16
Jimenez, Xavier	Redwood

122
Renteria, Maximo	Buchanan, 18-2 TF
Rivera, Jacob	Selma
Paulson, Brandon	Clovis, 8-7 OT
Cruz, Joey	Clovis North
Gayton, Jesse	Lemoore, Injury Default
Arreola, Lorenzo	Dinuba
Murphy, James	Central, Injury Default
Leia, Kimo	Kingsburg
Flores, Marco	Exeter, 6-4
Appleton, Jay T	Frontier *20-11

128
Joint, Wayne	Lemoore, 6-2
Leake, Hunter	Buchanan, *42-14
Murphy, Devin	Clovis North, 10-7
Valdovinos, Raul	Clovis West
Rhoads, Autin	Clovis North, Injury Default
Reyes, Cole	Frontier
Olea, Erik	Exeter, Injury Default
Bedrosian, Wyatt	Coalinga
Gonzalez, Fernando	Sanger, Injury Default
Reyes, Gabriel	Hanford

134
Franco, Ryan	Clovis North, 11-4
Petrucelli, Giano	Clovis
Viveros, Jonathan	Kingsburg, 5-3
Gioffre, Logan	Buchanan
Lucio, Cade	Bakersfield, 9-3 *34-10
Fletcher, Garrett	Frontier, *40-15
Tanner, Porter	Paso Robles, 5-2
Miranda, Jude	Hanford
Rodriguez, Alex	Redwood, 8-4
Kephart, Isaac	Arroyo Grande

140
Deen, Tyler	Buchanan, 9-4 OT 38-8 *140-37
Bloemhof, Andrew	Bakersfield, *34-10
Morphis, Ryan	Frontier, Fall :14
Watts, Zach	Clovis North
Sepulveda, Tyler	Selma, 4-3
Perez, Angel	Firebaugh
Jackson, Jett	Kingsburg, 3-2
Zuniga, George	Central
Logan, Avina Barajas	Clovis, 5-1
Leon, Dominick	Golden Valley

147
Siavong, Dawson	Bullard, 7-3
Martin, Joseph	Buchanan
Cuttone, Vito	Clovis North, 1-0
Rogers, Brock	Corcoran
Sekhon, Abheybir	Central, Injury Default
Rodriguez, Matt	Righetti
Martino, Nick	Clovis, Fall 3:59
Wills, Zachary	Centennial, *23-13
Machado, Ernesto	Golden Valley, Injury Default
Landin, Jose	Frontier

154
Luchau, Jace	Selma, 8-2
Anderson, Max	Clovis
Garcia, Nathan	Paso Robles, 11-3
Avila, Hunter	Monache
Raiz, Rey	Buchanan, Injury Default
Beni, Bandueng	Righetti
Gonzalez, Adrian	Bakersfield, 10-3 *34-14
Almaguer, Evan	Clovis North
Stafford, Vincent	Sanger, 16-7 MD
Sullivan, Jarron	Redwood

162
Olguin Matthew	Buchanan, 12-1 MD
Aguirre, Max	Frontier
Zavala, Nicholas	Mission Oak, 8-5
Kloster, Will	Lemoore
Chiaramonte, Mikelli	Clovis, Fall :58

CENTRAL SECTION MASTERS - Lemoore
February 14-15, 2019

Sanchez, Jaden — Bakersfield
Sherwood, Reid — Clovis North, Fall 2:44
Brar, Yadwinder — Clovis East

Grantham, Tayte — Madera South, Fall 1:28
Hernandez, Isaiah — Selma

172
Rodriguez, Christian — Selma, 4-3
Cardwell, Mark — Monache
Contino, Rocco — Buchanan, 5-3
Priest, Jarad — Bakersfield
Frantzich, Austin — Clovis, Injury Default
Long, Daniel — Dinuba
Landin, Christian — Frontier, Fall 2:22 *33-18
Visconte, Cole — Morro Bay
Micallef, Justin — Yosemite, 3-1
Spainhoward, Justin — Ridgeview

184
Tracy, Trent — Frontier, 17-2 TF
Gianakopulos, Tyler — Clovis
Annis, Jordan — Bakersfield, 4-2
Rodriguez, Felipe — Clovis West
Manzo, Luciano — Chowchilla, 7-6
Maez, Isaac — Arroyo Grande
Garcia, Rudy — Selma, 7-2
Mannion, Andrew — Clovis East
Sharp, Paul — Clovis North, Injury Default
Bordon, John — Ridgeview

197
Martin, Jadon — Buchanan, 10-0 MD
Jackson, Bo — Kingsburg
Sayles, Fredrick — Clovis, 5-0
Shepherd, Ty — Frontier
Garcia, Mason — Arroyo Grande, 4-3
Mendivel, Michael — Bakersfield
Vaca, Alex — Madera, 4-3
Cardenas, Javier — El Diamante
Tripp, Justin — Mt. Whitney, 8-0 MD
Underwood, Cody — Clovis North

222
Good, Jacob — Clovis, 9-0 MD
Darter, Justen — Bakersfield
Morales, Mateo — Clovis West, 7-6
Watson, Kwabena — Edison
Nunley, Bear — Tulare Union, Injury Default
Cardwell, Branden — Buchanan
Mittlestead, Eric — Exeter, Fall 1:36

Aispuro, Gerardo — McFarland
Pafford, Jack — Frontier, Injury Default *30-18
Pulis, Hayden — Hanford

287
Hill, Josiah — Bakersfield, 3-2
Schmidtke, Jonah — Clovis East
Slatic, Tommy — Bullard, 7-0
Cook, John — Madera
Houston, Travone — Hanford, Injury Default
Lightner, Jacob — Kern Valley, 26-8 23, Falls *100-26 69 Falls
Rojas III, Francisco — Liberty Madera, Fall 2:38
Lee, Regan — Golden West
Campbell, Kade — Clovis, Fall 1:13
Herrera, Christian — Mission Oak

MD – Major Decision
TF – Technical Fall
* Record

Most Outstanding Wrestlers

Lower Weight: Wayne Joint — Lemoore
Upper Weight: Trent Tracy — Frontier

4X CIF Masters Champion:
Matthew Olguin, Buchanan

TEAM SCORES

1	Buchanan	307
2	Clovis	272
3	Clovis North	214.5
4	Bakersfield	192.5
5	Selma	184.5
6	Frontier	168.5
7	Clovis East	89
8	Kingsburg	82.5
9	Righetti	81.5
10	Monache	80.5
11	Clovis West	77
12	Lemoore	73
13	Arroyo Grande	62
14	Central	56
15	Madera	52
16	Bullard	50.5
17	Hanford	45
18	Paso Robles	43.5
19	Dinuba	42
20	Exeter	37
20	Morro Bay	37

CENTRAL SECTION MASTERS - Lemoore
February 14-15, 2019

22 Mission Oak	36	
23 Edison	35	
24 Corcoran	33	
25 Hoover	31.5	
26 Golden Valley	30	
27 Coalinga	28	
28 Pioneer Valley	27	
29 Nipomo	26.5	
30 Redwood	25	
31 Centennial	23	
32 Firebaugh	22.5	
33 Golden West	22	
33 Liberty Madera	22	
33 North	22	
33 Orange Cove	22	
37 Kern Valley	21	
38 Chowchilla	19	
38 El Diamante	19	
38 Sanger	19	
41 Caruthers	18	
42 Highland	17	
43 Tulare Union	16	
44 Yosemite	14	
45 South	13.5	
46 Ridgeview	13	
46 Sunnyside	13	
48 Cesar Chavez	11	
48 McFarland	11	
48 Wasco	11	
51 Dos Palos	10	
51 Porterville	10	
53 Granite Hills	9	
53 Liberty	9	
53 R F Kennedy	9	
53 Shafter	9	
57 East	8	
57 Mira Monte	8	
57 Santa Maria	8	
57 Sierra	8	
57 Tulare Western	8	
62 Stockdale	7.5	
63 Foothill	7	
63 Independence	7	
63 McLane	7	
63 Parlier	7	
63 Woodlake	7	
68 Atascadero	6	
68 Fresno	6	
68 Madera South	6	
68 Mendota	6	
68 Mt. Whitney	6	
68 Sierra Pacific	6	
74 Arvin	4	

74 Delano	4
74 Farmersville	4
74 Fowler	4
74 Reedley	4
74 Washing Union	4
80 Bishop	3
80 Garces	3
80 Hanford West	3
80 Kerman	3
80 San Luis Obispo	3
85 Desert	2
85 St. Joseph	2

Trent Tracy – Frontier High School

CENTRAL SECTION MASTERS - Hoover High
February 21-22, 2020

108
- Lopez, Richard — Buchanan, 3-0
- Mendez, Dominic — Righetti
- Terrence, Matthew — Clovis, 13-4
- Gonzalez, Nate — Selma
- Reyes, Jimmy — Hanford, Medical Forfeit
- McDonald, Dylan — Lemoore
- Galicia, Nathan — Madera, Forfeit
- Harton, Howard — Kerman
- Delatorre, Elijah — Pioneer Valley, 7-5
- Candray, Matthew — Washington Union

115
- Figueroa, Richard — Selma, 5-0 *34-0
- Cruz, Joey — Clovis North *31-3
- Gioffre, Jack — Buchanan, 4-2
- Lemus, Darin — Clovis
- Cerda, Abraham — Hoover, 7-4
- Acala, Josh — Frontier, *32-19
- Onsurez, Austin — Centennial, Fall 4:26
- Diaz, Andrew — Bakersfield, *23-19
- Calderon, Alex — Redwood, Medical Forfeit
- Whittington, Wanderlei — Monache

122
- Negrete, Carlos — Buchanan, 4-3
- Lujan, Tristan — Selma
- Rosas, George — Clovis, 3-2
- Maldonado, Laz — Clovis West
- Zinkin, Hayden — Clovis North, 2-1
- Ozuna, Noah — Bakersfield, *17-11
- Escebdo, Tyson — Righetti, Medical Forfeit
- Benevidez, Brian — Porterville
- Gayton, Jesse — Lemoore, 2-1
- Corona, Shane — Foothill, *36-12

128
- Renteria, Maximo — Buchanan, 7-1
- Joint, Wayne — Lemoore
- Leia, Kimo — Selma
- Mouritsen, Justin — Clovis
- Watts, Ryan — Clovis North, 3-2
- Chavez, Adrian — Central
- Ibarra, Aaron — Righetti, 8-1
- Folorez, Marco — Exeter
- Spears, Jacob — Bakersfield, Medical Forfeit
- Ornelaz, Anthony — North, *31-12

134
- Leake, Hunter — Buchanan, 4-3
- Franco, Ryan — Clovis North
- Swan, Sloan — Clovis, 4-3
- Murphy, Devin — Selma
- Landin, Jose — Frontier, Major 13-4 *35-10
- Bautista, Jasun — Righetti
- Rueda, Everardo — Golden Valley, Medical Forfeit *37-9
- East, Makay — Bakersfield, *23-17
- Reyes, Gabriel — Hanford, 3-1
- Kilber, Peyton — Paso Robles

140
- Lake, Kyler — Buchanan, 3-1
- Viveros, Johnathan — Kingsburg
- Lucio, Cade — Bakersfield, 4-3 *29-13
- Rodriguez, Matt — Righetti
- Watts, Zach — Clovis North, Fall :57
- Combs, Luke — Frontier, *20-13
- Roads, Austin — Clovis, Fall 4:30
- Rodriguez, Alex — Redwood
- Sekhon, Abheybir — Central, 6-2
- Flores, Jose — Monache

147
- Gioffre, Logan — Buchanan, 10-3
- Fletcher, Garrett — Frontier, *35-10
- Montoya, Sergio — Clovis North, 4-2
- Avina-Barajas, Logan — Clovis
- Garrett, Gregory — Central, 7-3
- Ocampo, Javier — North, *24-10
- Gonzalez, Richard — St. Joseph, 8-1
- Estrada, Anthony — Monache
- Juarez, James — Bakersfield, Fall 1:03
- Davidson, Cameron — Paso Robles

154
- Raiz, Reymundo — Buchanan, 4-0
- Cortez, Noah — Dinuba
- Almaguer, Evan — Clovis North, SV 8-7
- Zuniga, George — Selma
- Monteiro, Tye — Garces, Fall 5:28 *37-11
- Martinez, Rickieh — Clovis
- Stafford, Vincent — Sanger, Major 14-2
- Wilson, Wesley — Morro Bay
- Weimer, Dwight — Bakersfield, 5-1 *23-15
- Cantoriano, Andrew — Clovis West

CENTRAL SECTION MASTERS – Hoover High
February 21-22, 2020

162
- Contino, Rocco — Buchanan, Major 12-3
- Kloster, Will — Lemoore
- Prudek, Jake — Caruthers, Fall 2:46
- Sepulveda, Tyler — Selma
- Sanchez, Jaden — Bakersfield, 9-3 *27-11
- Lopez, Jacob — Clovis North
- Merkord, Wyatt — Clovis, 8-2
- Gamez, Marcos — Firebaugh
- Leon, Dominic — Golden Valley, Forfeit *42-7
- Perez, Feradon — Sierra Pacific

172
- Petrucelli, Giano — Clovis, 3-0
- Martin, Joseph — Clovis
- Priest, Jarad — Bakersfield, 5-4 *40-11
- Zavala, Nicolas — Mission Oak
- Landin, Christian — Frontier, Major 14-3 *33-11
- Perez, Derian — Central
- Florentino, Ryan — Clovis North, Medical Forfeit
- Christie, Shane — Granite Hills
- Spainhoward, Justin — Ridgeview, Major 14-4
- Brar, Yadi — Clovis East

184
- Avila, Tyler — Porterville, 10-5
- Martin, Joseph — Buchanan, **35-8
- Tripp, Justin — Mt. Whitney, 4-1
- Alonso, Juan — R F Kennedy
- Smith, Christian — Clovis, Medical Forfeit
- Stout, Adrian — Righetti
- Steiner, Spencer — Clovis North, 7-0
- Myer, Luke — Bakersfield, *19-13
- Hernandez, Isaiah — Selma, Medical Forfeit
- Valle, Alex — Central

197
- Gianakopulos, Tyler — Clovis, 5-1 **33-5
- Rodriguez, Felipe — Clovis West
- Sharp, Paul — Clovis North, Medical Forfeit
- Garcia, Rudy — Selma
- Garcia, Mason — Arroyo Grande, 9-2
- Garza, Jesse — Nipomo
- Rodgers, Caden — Buchanan, Fall 5:08
- Mannion, Andrew — Clovis East
- Trujillo, Chente — Bakersfield, Medical Forfeit
- Nunley, Bear — Tulare Union

222
- Morales, Meteo — Clovis West, Fall 1:01
- Peralta, Jalen — Buchanan
- Hilford, Jordan — Clovis, TB 3-2
- Weimer, Hunter — Monache
- Pulis, Haydon — Hanford East, Medical Forfeit
- Darter, Justin — Bakersfield, *36-5
- Shepard, Ty — Frontier, Medical Forfeit
- Medrano, Taven — Monache
- Duran, Noah — Clovis North, Fall 1:59
- Garone, Tyler — Central

287
- Hill, Josiah — Bakersfield, 5-1 *43-1
- Martinez, Javier — Dinuba, ** 27-6
- Campbell, Kade — Buchanan, Fall 5:19
- Schmidtke, Jonah — Clovis East
- Huston, Travone — Hanford, Medical Forfeit
- Alaniz, Joe — Clovis East
- Watson, Isa — Central, Medical Forfeit
- Avila, Taven — Monache
- Andrews, Jake — Frontier, Fall 4:43 *34-17
- Foraker, Cade — Clovis North

* Season records
** Record as of 2-14,15-20

Most Outstanding Wrestlers

Lower Weight: Richard Figueroa — Selma
Upper Weight: Tyler Avila — Porterville

Giano Petrucelli – Clovis High School
Joseph Martin – Buchanan High School

CENTRAL SECTION MASTERS - Hoover High
February 21-22, 2020

Team Results

Rank	Team	Score
1	Buchanan	380
2	Clovis	256.5
3	Clovis North	216.5
4	Selma	191
5	Bakersfield	175.5
6	Frontier	137
7	Righetti	113
8	Clovis West	102
9	Central	90.5
10	Lemoore	84
11	Dinuba	66
12	Monache	61.5
13	Kingsburg	60
14	Hanford	59
15	North	52
16	Arroyo Grande	51
17	Porterville	48
18	Clovis East	46
19	Centennial	37.5
20	Paso Robles	28
20	Redwood	28
22	Mt. Whitney	27
23	Exeter	26.5
24	Pioneer Valley	26
24	Hoover	26
24	Nipomo	26
27	Garces	25.5
27	Golden Valley	25.5
29	Caruthers	25
29	Madera South	25
31	St. Joseph	24
32	Madera	23.5
33	Sanger	23
34	Sunnyside	22
34	Mission Oak	22
36	Edison	21.5
37	Coalinga	21
37	Ridgeview	21
39	R F Kennedy	19
39	Firebaugh	19
41	Kerman	17
42	Liberty Madera	16
42	Golden West	16
44	Foothill	15
44	Morro Bay	15
44	McLane	15
44	Tulare Union	15
48	Liberty	14
49	East Bakersfield	13
49	Cesar Chavez	13
49	Washington Union	13
52	Parlier	12
52	Kern Valley	12
54	Tulare Western	11
54	San Luis Obispo	11
56	Shafter	10
56	Mira Monte	10
56	Yosemite	10
56	Granite Hills	10
60	Dos Palos	9.5
61	Independence	9
61	Sierra Pacific	9
63	Reedley	8
64	Atascadero	7
64	Hanford West	7
64	Santa Maria	7
64	Bkfd. Christian	7
68	West Bakersfield	4
68	Farmerville	4
68	Roosevelt	4
68	Orange Cove	4
68	Sierra	4
73	Fresno	3
73	Arvin	3
73	Chowchilla	3
76	Fowler	2
76	Highland	2
76	Wasco	2
79	Stockdale	1
80	Lindsay	0
80	Avenal	0
80	McFarland	0
80	Mendota	0
80	Woodlake	0

LUKE COMBS
BAKERSFIELD

CALIFORNIA STATE CHAMPIONSHIPS

2007-2020

CENTRAL SECTION STATE CHAMPIOSHIPS TOP 10 TEAMS

Year	School	Place	Points	Year	School	Place	Points
1973	Clovis	2	38	2001	Buchanan	7	60.5
1974	Clovis	Champion	57	2001	Lemoore	8	54
1975	Clovis	Champion	46	2001	Madera	9	48.5
1975	Madera	2	40	2002	Bakersfield	Champion	226.5
1976	Clovis	Champion	65.5	2002	Buchanan	2	101.5
1976	Hanford	5	40	2002	Clovis	3	96
1979	South	4	38	2003	Clovis	Champion	151.5
1979	Mt. Whitney	5	34.5	2003	Bakersfield	4	106
1980	Bakersfield	5	35	2003	Clovis West	6	69.5
1981	Clovis	3	59.5	2003	Hanford	9	38.5
1982	Clovis West	5	45	2004	Bakersfield	Champion	170.5
1983	Clovis West	Champion	88.5	2004	Clovis	2	93.5
1984	Clovis West	Champion	117.5	2004	Clovis West	7	63
1984	Madera	2	69	2005	Bakersfield	2	111
1985	Clovis	6	41	2005	Lemoore	8	62
1986	Clovis	4	51.5	2006	Buchanan	Champion	134
1988	Selma	5	47	2006	Bakersfield	6	73
1988	Roosevelt	6	35	2006	Clovis	8 Tie	55
1989	Clovis West	Champion	57	2007	Buchanan	3	113
1989	Clovis	3	51.5	2007	Clovis	4	97.5
1990	Clovis	Champion	78.5	2007	Bakersfield	5	78
1990	Selma	7	42	2007	Selma	7	72
1990	South	9	36	2008	Clovis	Champion	118.5
1991	Clovis	Champion	88.5	2008	Buchanan	5	102.5
1991	Selma	4	64	2008	Clovis West	7	85.5
1991	Madera	5	53.5	2008	Selma	8	79.5
1991	Roosevelt	8	43.5	2008	Lemoore	9	78
1992	Clovis	Champion	95	2009	Buchanan	2	125.5
1992	Bakersfield	10	37	2009	Selma	2	125.5
1993	Clovis	3	65	2009	Clovis	4	124
1993	Madera	6	52	2009	Bakersfield	7	69.5
1994	Madera	3	68	2009	Clovis West	7	69.5
1994	Clovis	4	63	2009	Lemoore	9	52.5
1995	Bakersfield	3	98.5	2010	Bakersfield	Champion	126
1995	Clovis West	10	42	2010	Selma	2	113.5
1996	Buchanan	5	65.5	2010	Clovis	3	97
1996	Bakersfield	9	55.5	2010	Lemoore	4	94
1997	Clovis West	4	71.5	2010	Clovis West	8	76
1997	Madera	8	49.5	2011	Clovis	Champion	186
1998	Buchanan	2	102	2011	Bakersfield	2	177
1998	Foothill	3	93	2011	Selma	3	100
1998	Clovis West	7	81	2011	Lemoore	5	76
1999	Clovis	3	69	2011	Clovis West	7	65
1999	Foothill	6	64	2011	Porterville	9	61.5
1999	Centennial	9	57.5	2012	Clovis	Champion	256.5
1999	Tulare Union	10	53	2012	Bakersfield	2	129.5
2000	Clovis	2	106.5	2012	Clovis West	8	63
2000	Lemoore	4	66.5	2012	Lemoore	9	60
2000	Buchanan	5	61.5	2013	Clovis	Champion	174
2000	Bakersfield	6	53.5	2013	Bakersfield	6	78.5
2000	Hanford	10	41.5	2013	Porterville	7	73
2001	Bakersfield	2	129	2013	Buchanan	8	70.5
2001	Clovis	5	71.5	2013	Lemoore	8	70.5

CENTRAL SECTION STATE CHAMPIOSHIPS TOP 10 TEAMS

Year	School	Place	Points
2013	Clovis West	10	69
2014	Clovis	Champion	197.5
2014	Clovis West	2	118.5
2014	Buchanan	9	79
2014	Bakersfield	10	75
2015	Clovis	Champion	276.5
2015	Buchanan	4	120
2015	Bakersfield	7	85
2016	Buchanan	Champion	274.5
2016	Clovis	2	232.5
2016	Bakersfield	7	83
2016	Selma	8	81.5
2017	Buchanan	Champion	213.5
2017	Clovis	2	189
2017	Selma	4	108
2017	Frontier	6	85
2017	Lemoore	9	79.5
2017	Bakersfield	10	79
2018	Buchanan	Champion	219
2018	Selma	4	168
2018	Clovis	5	121.5
2018	Clovis North	6	119
2018	Frontier	9	91
2019	Buchanan	Champion	235
2019	Clovis	3	171.5
2019	Selma	4	139.5
2019	Frontier	7	99.5
2019	Clovis North	9	90.5
2020	Buchanan	1	261
2020	Clovis	4	159
2020	Selma	5	131
2020	Clovis North	6	129
2020	Bakersfield	8	99.5

2018 CIF State Wrestling Championships Weight Class 170 lbs

STATE MOST OUTSTANDING WRESTLERS

CALIFORNIA STATE WRESTLER OF THE YEAR – CENTRAL SECTION
*Named by Cal-Hi Sports Magazine

Year	Wrestler	School	Weight
1958	Ausencio Rodriguez	Madera	112
1959	Ausencio Rodriguez	Madera	112
1966	Richard Simmons	South	175
1968	John Miller	North	191
1973	Mike Bull	South	191

MOST OUTSTANDING WRESTLER OF THE CALIFORNIA STATE CHAMPIONSHIPS
*The award started in 1991 – The Dave Shultz Award was started in 1998

Year	Wrestler	School	Weight
1999	Ben Martinez	Tulare Union	130
2000	Chris Pendleton	Lemoore	145
2001	Darrell Vasquez	Bakersfield	119
2002	Darrell Vasquez	Bakersfield	125
2003	Nathan Morgan	Bakersfield	130
2004	Jake Varner	Bakersfield	189
2010	Nick Sierra	Lemoore	152
2013	Isaiah Martinez	Lemoore	160
2017	Justin Mejia	Clovis	126
2018	Seth Nevills	Clovis	285

Rick McKinney – Referee
Justin Majia – Clovis High School

Isaiah Martinez
Lemoore High School

STATE 2007

Name	School	Weight	Place	Season/Career Record
Camacho, Gilbert	Washington Union	103	Champion	50-0, 38 Falls
Valles, A J	Selma	103	2	45-6, 20 Falls
Done, Chris	Buchanan	103	4	41-9, 13 Falls
Demison, Nektoe	Bakersfield	112	3	45-6/159-46
Arredondo, Justin	Buchanan	125	7	43-13
Ramos, Chris	Bullard	125	8	43-13, 28 Falls
Roman-Marin, Sean	Lemoore	130	2	52-8, 28 Falls
Kelly, Cameron	Clovis	130	8	23-6
Cruz, Jonah	Bakersfield	135	3	
Watts, David	El Diamante	135	4	47-7
Rios, Johny	Madera	135	6	45-10, 8 Falls
Sakaguchi, Scott	Clovis	140	5	44-8, 8 Falls
Watts, Randall	El Diamante	140	8	
Cisneros, Joe	Selma	145	2	50-5/105-10, 30 Falls
Rasmussen, Travis	Bakersfield	145	3	44-5/82-18
Cook, James	Clovis West	152	7	38-13, 12 Falls
Delarosa, Eric	Foothill	160	5	45-5/ 150-25
Sanchez, Brett	Clovis	189	7	
Medellin, Brandon	Madera	189	8	
Flores, Ryan	Buchanan	215	Champion	56-1, 39 Falls 198-19, 140 Falls
Lopez, Vince	Clovis	215	3	39-7
Zamora, Jonathon	Clovis	285	2	38-9

STATE 2008

Name	School	Weight	Place	Season/Career Record
Camacho, Gilbert	Washington Union	103	Champion	40-1/125-13,102 Falls
Zimmer, Zach	Clovis West	103	2	49-4
Diaz, Edgar	Arvin	103	4	
Gambrell, Mason	Clovis	103	8	39-12
Jaramillo, A J	Lemoore	112	5	47-14, 14 Falls
Gonzalez, Peter	East	112	6	37-5
McAlaster, Clinton	Clovis	112	8	35-11
Rocha, Brandon	Lemoore	119	2	54-4, 18 Falls
Fitzgerald, Steven	Clovis East	125	3	62-4
Pena, Nick	Selma	125	6	
Arredondo, Justin	Buchanan	130	Champion	52-1/ 174-28
Weimer, Stephen	Clovis	130	2	41-7
Mendoza, Jose	Selma	130	3	48-7, 30 Falls
Perez, Julian	Lemoore	130	5	50-13, 20 Falls
Rojas, Kevin	Kerman	130	8	
Fisher, Nick	Clovis West	135	3	52-4/ 148-36, 36 Falls
Watts, David	El Diamante	140	2	52-4, 28 Falls/ 158-26
Cruz, Jonah	Bakersfield	140	7	44-11
Balch, Andrew	Buchanan	145	Champion	48-4/ 157-29
Rasmussen, Travis	Bakersfield	145	2	44-4
Tovar, Archie	Selma	145	6	49-9, 30 Falls
Rubio, Vincent	Lemoore	145	8	43-16, 12 Falls
Cook, James	Clovis West	152	2	40-4
West, Stephen	Buchanan	160	3	52-4
Esparza, Josh	Clovis	160	4	45-9
Burriel, Tommy	Clovis	171	8	44-9
Brandt, Phil	Bullard	189	2	42-2
Boger, Josh	Coalinga	215	2	30-1, 27 Falls
Sanchez, Brett	Clovis	215	5	38-7
Zamora, Jonathan	Clovis	285	4	44-3

STATE 2009

Name	School	Weight	Place	Season/Career Record
Cisneros, Alex	Selma	103	Champion	48-0
Knoblauch, Steven	Clovis West	103	2	30-6
Gaytan, Daniel	Clovis	103	4	39-11
Rodriguez, Adrian	Buchanan	103	7	
Rodriguez, Vince	Clovis North	112	3	46-2
Zimmer, Zach	Clovis West	112	4	53-6
Quintana, Diego	Selma	112	6	42-8
Martinez, Chris	Clovis West	119	5	45-10
Gonzalez, Peter	East	119	8	39-8
Rocha, Brandon	Lemoore	125	2	51-5, 42 Falls/ 201-32, 53 Falls
Pena, Nick	Selma	125	3	50-8
Arredondo, Damien	Buchanan	125	4	37-4
McAlaster, Clinton	Clovis	125	6	42-10
Mendoza, Jose	Selma	130	2	49-4
Box, Timmy	Bakersfield	130	8	28-5
Hicks, Seth	Centennial	135	Champion	48-0/ 154-42
Zarate, Nathan	Selma	135	5	45-8
Dieter, Alec	Clovis	135	6	36-13
Sanchez, Javier	Ridgeview	140	2	39-4
Sierra, Nicholas	Lemoore	140	6	51-9, 30 Falls
Cruz, Jonah	Bakersfield	140	8	42-7
Sakaguchi, Scott	Clovis	145	Champion	49-1/ 163-22 75 Falls
Rodriguez, Alex	Washington Union	145	2	45-4
Fabbian, Martin	Buchanan	152	2	40-13
Hammond, Bryce	Bakersfield	152	4	38-5
West, Stephen	Buchanan	160	2	43-1/ 164-38, 81 Falls
Cook, James	Madera	160	4	28-7
Pedraza, Lewis	Madera South	160	8	45-12
Nevills, Zach	Clovis	171	5	42-16
Flores, Dwight	Tulare Union	171	6	41-6
Burriel, Tommy	Clovis	189	6	44-7
Juarez, Rodolfo	Central	189	7	49-5
Corona-Zamarripa, Nick	Hanford West	189	8	
Yates, Rykeem	Edison	215	6	30-5
Schoene, Brian	Bakersfield	215	7	45-4
Posadas, Angel	Foothill	285	2	41-7
Papendorf, Kyle	Buchanan	285	4	42-5

STATE 2010

Name	School	Weight	Place	Season/Career Record
Rocha, Dillon	Lemoore	103	5	51-9
Gomez, Vincent	Frontier	103	6	39-4
Nickell, Ian	Bakersfield	103	7	
Cisneros, Alex	Selma	112	Champion	53-1
Diaz, Chris	Sanger	112	2	43-5
Gaytan, Daniel	Clovis	112	3	37-7, 22 Falls
Zimmer, Zach	Clovis West	119	2	54-2, 11 Falls/ 156-12
Martinez, Chris	Clovis West	125	Champion	50-6/ 149-21 3 years
Rodriguez, Vince	Clovis North	125	2	48-3/ 95-4 2 years
Martinez, Isaiah	Lemoore	125	3	51-5
Larson, Conner	Clovis East	125	8	57-12
Pena, Nick	Selma	130	Champion	49-3, 23 Falls/ 172-23
Yacuta, Shane	Porterville	130	4	43-7
Demison, Natrelle	Bakersfield	130	5	46-7
Arredondo, Damien	Buchanan	130	6	37-12
Valles, A J	Sanger	130	7	42-7
Quezada, Moses	Clovis East	135	5	50-6
Zarate, Nathan	Selma	140	2	42-6, 30 Falls
Rizo, Derik	Foothill	145	3	52-4
Hammond, Colman	Bakersfield	145	4	37-5
Sierra, Nick	Lemoore	152	Champion	42-1
Hammond, Bryce	Bakersfield	160	Champion	40-0
Reyes, Nikko	Clovis West	160	3	51-6, 20 Falls
Lozano, Justin	Selma	160	5	47-6
Pendleton, Jacob	Lemoore	160	6	44-10
Cook, James	Madera	171	Champion	41-2, 27 Falls/ 143-27
Nevills, Zach	Clovis	171	2	41-11, 19 Falls
Fabbian, Martin	Buchanan	171	5	40-8
Burriel, Tommy	Clovis	189	2	42-3, 32 Falls/ 131-9 3 years
Juarez, Rodolfo	Central	189	7	46-9
Schoene, Brian	Bakersfield	215	3	47-3
Gomez, Noel	Cesar Chavez	215	6	39-7

STATE 2011

Name	School	Weight	Place	Season/Career Record
Pengilly, Mason	Porterville	103	4	40-7
Marin, Manny	Buchanan	103	5	20-14
Olea, Arnulfo	Exeter	112	4	41-7
Gaytan, Jonas	Clovis	112	5	32-11
Nickell, Ian	Bakersfield	112	7	37-9
Gaytan, Daniel	Clovis	119	Champion	48-7, 22 Falls/ 124-25
Knoblauch, Steven	Clovis West	119	2	46-6
Esparza, Silverio	Lemoore	119	8	32-11
Cisneros, Alex	Selma	125	Champion	45-1, 15 Falls
Rodriguez, Vincent	Clovis North	125	2	50-5
Cruz, Micah	Bakersfield	125	4	36-9
Pena, Nick	Selma	130	Champion	33-5/ 172-23
Demison, Netrelle	Bakersfield	130	3	43-3
Cacagno, Chris	Clovis North	130	7	45-10, 32 Falls
Yacuta, Shane	Porterville	135	2	40-2/ 186-26
Box, Timmy	Bakersfield	135	3	38-4/ 147-29, 55 Falls
Martinez, Isaiah	Lemoore	140	Champion	50-0
Ramirez, Maxx	Bakersfield	140	6	37-13
Bersano, Brady	Clovis	140	7	46-14 , 21 Falls
Rodriguez, Miguel	Madera	140	8	43-13/ 102-47
Arredondo, Damien	Buchanan	145	3	43-5/ 108-22
Poindexter, Damien	Clovis North	145	7	38-15
Ferro, Adam	Bakersfield	152	3	47-3
Thompson, Blake	Clovis	152	5	46-15 , 16 Falls
Hammond, Bryce	Bakersfield	160	Champion	34-0/ 157-14
Rodriguez, Dylin	Sanger	160	6	44-7
Salas, Adrian	Clovis	160	7	43-11, 23 Falls
Reyes, Nikko	Clovis North	171	Champion	49-1
Lozano, Justin	Selma	171	2	31-3/ 157-25
Nevills, Zach	Clovis	171	3	48-7, 26 Falls/ 131-34
Nacita, Silas	Bakersfield	171	4	33-12
Gordan, Dakota	Clovis	189	7	43-5, 31 Falls
Ferguson, Taylor	Clovis	215	6	41-9 ,33 Falls
Nevills, Nick	Clovis	285	Champion	49-3, 27 Falls
Wood, Steven	Lemoore	285	4	48-7, 27 Falls/ 90-13

STATE 2012

Name	School	Weight	Place	Season/Career Record
Hokit, Isaiah	Wasco	106	4	41-5
Gaytan, Julian	Clovis	106	6	38-18, 19 Falls
Camposano, Adrian	Central	106	7	39-7
Gaytan, Jonas	Clovis	113	2	52-2, 25 Falls 4TF
Pengilly, Mason	Porterville	113	5	39-4, 15 Falls 1TF
Olea, Arnulfo	Exeter	113	8	44-18, 27 Falls
Gaytan, Daniel	Clovis	120	Champion	53-5, 27 Falls 2TF/ 177-30
Panduro, Adrian	Corcoran	120	8	
Hernandez, Vicente	Clovis	126	8	44-11, 21 Falls
Cisneros, Alex	Selma	132	2	47-2, 9 Falls 18TF/ 177-4
Gasca, Javier	Kingsburg	132	3	50-5, 30 Falls 7TF
Cruz, Micah	Bakersfield	132	6	41-2
Denison, Natrelle	Bakersfield	138	4	47-4
Ladd, Jason	Clovis	138	5	43-14, 25 Falls
Cardenas, Racelis	Buchanan	138	6	39-10, 9 Falls
Hernandez, Josue	Madera South	138	7	45-14, 17 Falls
Garcia, Chris	Clovis West	138	8	36-14, 17 Falls
Ramirez, Max	Bakersfield	145	7	44-7
Martinez, Isaiah	Lemoore	152	Champion	49-1/ 205-7, 103 Falls 78TF
Hammond, Colman	Bakersfield	152	3	39-4
Perreault, Kyle	Clovis West	152	7	48-9, 23 Falls 1TF
Salas, Adrian	Clovis	160	4	39-6, 22 Falls 1TF
Nevills, Zach	Clovis	170	Champion	53-3, 32 Falls/ 183-37
Nacita, Silas	Bakersfield	170	2	24-7
Reyes, Nikko	Clovis West	182	Champion	48-1/ 180-13
Pope, Kyle	Bakersfield	182	2	37-5
Davies, Ryan	Clovis	182	4	42-12, 22 Falls 3TF
Gordan, Dakota	Clovis	195	2	40-3, 31 Falls
Medley, Sean	Wasco	220	4	37-9
Nevills, Nick	Clovis	285	3	48-2, 29 Falls
Amaya, Rudy	Foothill	285	7	40-4

STATE 2013

Name	School	Weight	Place	Season/Career Record
Camposano, Adrian	Central	106	Champion	36-1
Lloren, Durbin	Buchanan	106	5	45-10, 12 Falls
Williams, Sean	Lemoore	113	2	44-7, 11 Falls
Olivas, Khristan	Clovis	113	4	43-19, 18 Falls
Hokit, Isaiah	Wasco	113	6	41-7
Pengilly, Mason	Porterville	120	Champion	42-0, 16 Falls
Gaytan, Jonas	Clovis	120	3	51-7, 16 Falls/ 190-31
Ruiz, Daniel	Madera	120	6	43-12, 16 Falls
Olea, Arnulfo	Exeter	120	8	41-8, 20 Falls
Knoblauch, Michael	Clovis West	126	3	41-6, 15 Falls
Gomez, Vincent	Frontier	126	7	42-5
Gasca, Javier	Kingsburg	132	3	52-2, 41 Falls/ 161-19
Contreras, Abel	Porterville	132	7	34-8, 12 Falls/ 82-23, 31 Falls
Sandoval, Martin	Porterville	138	3	37-4, 24 Falls/ 133-34, 85 Falls
Garcia, Chris	Clovis West	138	7	43-11, 24 Falls
Ladd, Jason	Clovis	145	5	50-5, 32 Falls
Fierro, Andrew	Bakersfield	145	8	36-12
Perreault, Kyle	Clovis East	152	3	55-5, 23 Falls/ 127-47, 63 Falls
Hammond, Coleman	Bakersfield	152	4	43-6
Martinez, Isaiah	Lemoore	160	Champion	55-1/ 205-7, 63 Falls, 78TF
Hodges, Hunter	Bakersfield	160	5	38-10
Martin, Bryce	Bakersfield	170	4	44-10
Salas, Adrian	Clovis	182	Champion	42-1, 22 Falls/ 153-28
Gonzales, Gabriel	Washington Union	182	5	53-4, 37 Falls
Morales, Cortez	Clovis West	182	7	46-9, 35 Falls
Nevills, Nick	Clovis	265	Champion	53-0, 100 Falls in 3 yrs

Khristian Olivas – Clovis High School and Fresno State University

STATE 2014

Name	School	Weight	Place	Season/Career Record
Mejia, Justin	Clovis	106	Champion	48-1, 37 Falls
Demison, Navonte	Bakersfield	106	3	41-10
Campbell, David	Mission Oak	106	4	48-7, 32 Falls
Cisneros, Joey	Redwood	106	6	51-7, 14 Falls, 10TF 6 Majors
Alaniz, Javier	Clovis East	106	7	
Marin, Chris	Clovis West	106	8	
Gamble, Matt	Monache	113	Champion	36-5
Garcia, Robert	Selma	113	2	43-9, 13 Falls
Camposano, Adrian	Central	113	3	41-7/ 156-19, 40 Falls
Lloren, Durbin	Buchanan	113	5	
Gilland, Tristan	Clovis	113	7	
Herrera, Carlos	Bakersfield	120	6	40-12
Knoblauch, Michael	Clovis West	126	Champion	48-4
Pengilly, Mason	Porterville	126	2	52-2/ 183-13
Ruiz, Daniel	Madera	126	6	
Hokit, Isaiah	Clovis	132	3	
Enriquez, Jaden	Mission Oak	132	4	45-10, 22 Falls
Garcia, Ruben	Selma	132	6	
Garcia, Chris	Clovis West	145	2	42-5, 22 Falls
Francis, Conner	Buchanan	145	6	
Zimmer, Tyler	Clovis West	152	3	42-7, 19 Falls
Romero, Abner	Buchanan	152	8	
Hokit, Josh	Clovis	160	5	47-6, 28 Falls
Martin, Bryce	Bakersfield	170	2	39-2
Brand, Brody	Clovis	170	3	
Flores, Austin	Clovis North	170	4	44-8/ 110-28
Moran, Chris	Sanger	170	6	
Gamboa, Alec	Madera	182	5	47-6/ 99-26 3 years
Nevills, A J	Clovis	182	7	
Rangels, Isaac	Firebaugh	182	8	
Weiss, Matt	Clovis	195	6	46-5, 37 Falls
Gonzalez, Gabriel	Washington Union	220	2	53-4, 37 Falls/ 164-25, 110 Falls
Morales, Cortez	Clovis West	220	5	41-7, 26 Falls
Nevills, Nick	Clovis	285	Champion	50-0, 46 Falls/ 200-5, 146 Falls
Alvarez, Jose	Selma	285	5	21-5, 15 Falls/ 85-25 3 years

* Nick Nevills 105 wins in a row

STATE 2015

Name	School	Weight	Place	Season/Career Record
Perez, Isaiah	Dinuba	106	6	33-3
Morita, Bryce	Clovis West	106	8	
Mejia, Justin	Clovis	113	Champion	44-0
Lloren, Durbin	Buchanan	120	Champion	48-1, 22 Falls
Demison, Novonte	Bakersfield	120	2	35-5
Deloza, Chris	Clovis North	120	5	/128-26
Garcia, Robert	Selma	120	6	
Figueroa, J J	Bakersfield	126	4	38-6
Enriquez, Jaden	Mission Oak	132	2	43-3
Herrera, Carlos	Bakersfield	132	8	37-12
Olivas, Khristan	Clovis	138	3	
Garcia, Ruben	Selma	138	6	42-3
Hill, Jared	Clovis	145	6	
Francis, Conner	Buchanan	145	8	
Hokit, Isaiah	Clovis	152	5	
Jauregui, Joseph	Clovis East	152	6	
Romero, Abner	Buchanan	152	7	
Kincaid, Dominic	Clovis	160	3	
Loera, Sam	Bakersfield	160	7	35-6
Hokit, Josh	Clovis	170	2	
Nevills, A J	Clovis	182	2	
Fuentes, Julio	Golden Valley	182	3	41-5
Flores, Austin	Clovis North	195	Champion	43-2
Prentice, Adam	Clovis	195	2	
Woo An, Young	Buchanan	195	6	
Nevills, Seth	Clovis	220	Champion	44-0
Brandt, Bevan	Bullard	220	2	
Padilla, David	Dinuba	220	7	32-8
Coronado, Hexton	Clovis	285	Champion	44-0
Alvarez, Jose	Selma	285	2	
Snyder, Jarrod	Frontier	285	4	49-9

David Padilla, Coach Wright, Isaiah Perez
Dinuba High School

STATE 2016

Name	School	Weight	Place	Season/Career Record
Olguin, Matthew	Buchanan	106	Champion	44-4
Rivera, Eric	Clovis North	106	3	
Betancourt, Brandon	Clovis	106	4	
Olejnik, Izzak	Bakersfield	106	5	32-10
Cisneros, Josh	Selma	106	8	
Leake, Ethan	Buchanan	113	Champion	42-9
Cornelson, Wyatt	Clovis	113	8	
Mejia, Justin	Clovis	120	Champion	38-0/ 135-1
Abas, Jaden	Frontier	120	2	43-6
Garcia, Robert	Selma	130	3	
Perez, Isaiah	Dinuba	120	4	40-7
Campbell, David	Mission Oak	126	Champion	35-3/ 165-27, 76 Falls
Joint, Gary	Lemoore	126	3	56-4
Villarreal, Brett	Buchanan	126	4	
Lloren, Durbin	Buchanan	132	Champion	42-2/ 196-27, 76 Falls
Mendoza, Tony	Selma	132	8	
Demison, Novonte	Bakersfield	138	Champion	39-4
Wright, Jacob	Dinuba	138	2	
Romero, Joel	Buchanan	138	3	
Miguel, Bobby	Clovis West	138	5	
Garcia, Ruben	Selma	145	3	49-2
Gaxiola, Greg	Buchanan	145	4	
Martino, Brandon	Clovis	152	5	
Romero, Abner	Buchanan	160	2	
Loera, Sam	Bakersfield	160	7	35-10
Belshay, Cade	Buchanan	170	5	
Reyes, Ryan	Clovis West	170	7	
Hokit, Josh	Clovis	182	Champion	36-5/ 175-18
Montalvo, Anthony	Buchanan	182	2	
Nevills, A J	Clovis	195	Champion	45-4/ 169-31
Godinez, Adrian	Foothill	195	5	55-5
Levatino, Zakary	Buchanan	220	Champion	103-35, 39 Falls
Collier, Tyler	Clovis	220	3	
Nevills, Seth	Clovis	285	Champion	46-0
Snyder, Jarrod	Frontier	285	2	40-4

STATE 2017

Name	School	Weight	Place	Season/Career Record
Reyes, Cole	Frontier	106	4	47-6
Petucelli, Geno	Clovis	106	6	
Olguin, Matthew	Buchanan	113	3	
Murphy, Devin	Clovis North	113	4	
Paulson, Brandon	Clovis	113	6	
Pacheco, Anthony	Sanger	113	8	
Leake, Ethan	Buchanan	120	4	
Mejia, Justin	Clovis	126	Champion	36-0/ 169-1, 89 Falls Fr. 41-1 So. 44-0 Jr. 38-0 Sr. 36-0
Garcia, Robert	Selma	126	2	46-6/ 139-26
Perez, Isaiah	Dinuba	126	4	41-5/ 142-22
Sihavong, Dawson	Bullard	126	6	
Deen, Tyler	Buchanan	126	7	
Joint, Gary	Lemoore	132	Champion	/180-16, 63 Falls
Elijah, Elijah	Frontier	132	2	48-7
Deloza, Chris	Clovis North	132	4	/128-26
Enriquez, Jaden	Mission Oak	138	Champion	45-2/ 178-18, 92 Falls
Mendoza, Tony	Selma	138	3	54-7
Figueroa, JJ	Bakersfield	138	6	41-11
Romero, Joe	Lemoore	138	8	
Demison, Novonte	Bakersfield	145	Champion	35-0/ 187-18, 98 Falls
Wright, Jacob	Dinuba	145	4	43-3/ 145-20
Garcia, Jonathan	Frontier	152	7	36-11
Martino, Brandon	Clovis	160	Champion	41-4/ 145-27
Romero, Joel	Buchanan	160	2	
Gonzalez, Ricky	Bakersfield	160	6	42-13
Diaz, Oscar	Selma	160	7	
Rodriguez, Christian	Selma	170	5	43-7
Vargas, Victor	Clovis	170	6	
Montalvo, Anthony	Buchanan	182	Champion	51-1/ 145-27
Lara, Sam	Bakersfield	182	4	45-11
Solis, Angel	Lemoore	182	6	
DeBoer, Willem	Frontier	182	8	30-10
Reyes, Ryan	Clovis West	195	3	
Ervin, Trever	Buchanan	195	6	41-6/ 152-32
Wyneken, Ruger	Clovis	195	7	
Godinez, Adrian	Foothill	195	8	34-8
Belshay, Cade	Buchanan	220	Champion	50-1/ 169-31
Halajian, John	Clovis North	220	7	
Nevills, Seth	Clovis	285	Champion	37-0, 37 Falls 127-0
Wright, Noah	Lemoore	285	4	
Ortiz, Isaiah	Buchanan	285	7	

STATE 2018

Name	School	Weight	Place	Season/Career Record
Figueroa, Richard	Selma	103	Champion	48-2
Negrete, Carlos	Clovis North	103	2	52-8
Mouritsen, Justin	Clovis	103	4	
Leake, Hunter	Buchanan	103	7	47-11
Reteria, Maximo	Buchanan	113	Champion	47-4
Lujan, Tristan	Selma	113	4	
Petrucelli, Giano	Clovis	113	6	
Murphy, Devin	Clovis North	120	3	
Reyes, Cole	Frontier	120	5	45-8
Franco, Ryan	Clovis North	126	2	45-6
Leake, Ethan	Buchanan	126		48-9/ 182-32, 64 Falls
Grier, Lajon	Clovis North	132	5	
Areyano, Robert	Selma	132	8	
Olguin, Matthew	Buchanan	138	3	42-2
Sihavong, Dawson	Bullard	138	4	
Ramos, Luis	Selma	138	8	
Mendoza, Tony	Selma	145	2	35-5/ 143-25
Olejnik, Izzak	Bakersfield	145	4	31-5
Gaxiola, Chris	Buchanan	145	7	47-9/ 158-54
Cortez, Noah	Dinuba	145	8	
Luchau, Jace	Selma	152	4	46-10
Bradley, Beau	Monache	152	5	
Zanilpa, Tristan	Buchanan	152	6	45-12/ 115-35
Anderson, Max	Clovis	152	8	
Romero, Joel	Buchanan	160	2	44-6/ 170-40
Aguirre, Max	Frontier	160	4	48-14
Diaz, Oscar	Selma	160	5	
Long, Daniel	Dinuba	160	6	36-14
Tracy, Trent	Frontier	170	Champion	48-6
Rodriguez, Christian	Selma	170	3	47-5
Cardwell, Mark	Monache	170	4	
Miracle, Dylan	Madera South	170	5	
Gianakopulos, Tyler	Clovis	170	7	
Montalvo, Anthony	Buchanan	182	Champion	51-1/ 178-19, 114 Falls
Reyes, Ryan	Clovis West	195	3	
Good, Jacob	Clovis	195	4	
Darter, Justin	Bakersfield	220	8	37-15
Nevills, Seth	Clovis	285	Champion	42-1/ 169-1, 141 Falls
				Fr. 44-0
				So. 46-0
				Jr. 37-0
				Sr. 42-1

Tyler Gianakopulos – Clovis High School

STATE 2019

Name	School	Weight	Place	Season/Career Record
Figueroa, Richard	Selma	106	Champion	42-0
Gioffre, Jack	Buchanan	106	2	43-4
Lujan, Tristan	Selma	113	Champion	39-3
Negrete, Carlos	Buchanan	113	2	45-4
Mouritsen, Justin	Clovis	113	4	
Renteria, Maximo	Buchanan	120	Champion	43-2
Paulson, Brandon	Clovis	120	2	42-8
Cruz, Joey	Clovis North	120	3	
Rivera, Jacob	Selma	120	6	
Joint, Wayne	Lemoore	126	5	
Reyes, Cole	Frontier	126	7	34-9
Franco, Ryan	Clovis North	132	2	46-6
Petrucelli, Giano	Clovis	132	4	
Morphis, Ryan	Frontier	138	3	44-12
Deen, Tyler	Buchanan	138	5	/146-37, 44 Falls
Sihavong, Dawson	Bullard	145	3	
Martin, Joseph	Buchanan	145	4	
Luchau, Jace	Selma	152	3	47-4/ 164-35
Olguin, Matthew	Buchanan	160	Champion	46-0/ 188-7, 90 Falls
Aguirre, Max	Frontier	160	4	
Zavala, Nicholas	Mission Oak	160	5	
Kloster, Will	Lemoore	160	8	
Contino, Rocco	Buchanan	170	2	
Long, Daniel	Dinuba	170	4	46-11/ 125-45
Rodriguez, Christian	Selma	170	5	44-8/ 168-32
Cardwell, Mark	Monache	170	6	
Priest, Jarad	Bakersfield	170	7	36-13
Tracy, Trent	Frontier	182	3	30-1/ 141-39, 90 Falls
Gianakopulos, Tyler	Clovis	182	5	
Martin, Jaden	Buchanan	195	2	47-5
Good, Jacob	Clovis	220	Champion	/133-34
Watson, Kwabena	Edison	220	8	
Darter, Justin	Bakersfield	220	4	37-8
Hill, Josiah	Bakersfield	285	7	33-7

Josiah Hill – Bakersfield High School

STATE 2019

Ryan Morphis – Frontier High School

Cole Reyes – Frontier High School

Richard Figueroa – Selma High School

State 2020

Name	School	Weight	Place	Season/Career Record
Lopez, Richard	Buchanan	106	2	43-2
Mendez, Dominic	Righetti	106	4	42-9
Figueroa, Richard	Selma	113	Champion	38-0, 22 Falls
Cruz, Joey	Clovis North	113	2	36-4
Gioffre, Jack	Buchanan	113	4	35-9
Lemus, Dario	Clovis	113	5	
Lujan, Tristan	Selma	120	Champion	37-2, 24 Falls/ 159-22, 80 Falls
Maldonado, Laz	Clovis West	120	2	18-5
Rosas, George	Clovis	120	4	
Renteria, Maximo	Buchanan	126	Champion	26-2
Leia, Kimo	Selma	126	3	41-8, 21 Falls
Chavez, Adrian	Central	126	6	
Watts, Ryan	Clovis North	126	7	
Mouritsen, Justin	Clovis	126	8	
Leake, Hunter	Buchanan	132	2	41-6
Murphy, Devin	Selma	132	4	23-7, 10 Falls
Franco, Ryan	Clovis North	132	4	
Lake, Kyler	Buchanan	138	4	38-8
Watts, Zach	Clovis North	138	5	
Viveros, Jonathon	Kingsburg	138	7	33-10, 20 Falls
Rodriguez, Matt	Righetti	138	8	29-10
Gioffre, Logan	Buchanan	145	4	38-9
Raiz, Reymundo	Buchanan	152	4	42-10
Cortez, Noah	Dinuba	152	6	46-6/ 139-36
Monteiro, Tye	Garces	152	8	37-11, 27 Falls
Contino, Rocco	Buchanan	160	3	44-4
Kloster, Will	Lemoore	160	8	
Petrucelli, Giano	Clovis	170	Champion	48-1/ 160-28
Martin, Joseph	Buchanan	170	2	40-7
Priest, Jarad	Bakersfield	170	6	40-11, 10 Falls
Martin, Jadon	Buchanan	182	5	38-10
Avila, Tyler	Porterville	182	7	33-5, 20 Falls/ 97-25, 56 Falls
Gianakopulos, Tyler	Clovis	195	2	
Rodriguez, Felipe	Clovis West	195	4	
Garcia, Rudy	Selma	195	8	35-14, 23 Falls
Darter, Justin	Bakersfield	220	6	35-5, 20 Falls
Morales, Mateo	Clovis West	220	7	
Hill, Josiah	Bakersfield	285	Champion	43-1, 21 Falls/ 120-16, 60 Falls
Schmidtke, Jonah	Clovis East	285	6	
Campbell, Kade	Buchanan	285	8	35-10

State 2020

Joey Cruz – Clovis North High School
Richard Figueroa – Selma High School

Jarad Priest – Bakersfield High School

Luke Combs – Frontier High School

SECTION II
NATIONAL HIGH SCHOOL
WRESTLING CHAMPIONSHIPS

NATIONAL HIGH SCHOOL COACHES ASSOCIATION CHAMPIONSHIPS

SENIOR

Year	Wt	Name	Place	School
1991	119	Aguirre, Jimmy	Champion	Clovis
1991	130	Quintana, Gary *	Champion	Selma
1992	189	Moz, Lalo	4	Hanford
1992	103	Wright, Colby	7	Bakersfield
1993	275	Mast, Chad	3	Clovis
1993	135	Ramos, Eddie	6	Porterville
1994	140	Perez, Moises	5	Madera
1994	160	Philp, Eric	7	Madera
1995		NONE		
1996	135	Tirapelle, Adam	Champion	Buchanan
1996	112	Ruiz, Paris	6	Clovis West
1997	103	Johnson, Cleo	7	Firebaugh
1997	189	Jackson, Dan	7	Kingsburg
1997	112	Garza, Albert	7	Sanger
1998	103	Felix, Chris	3	East Bakersfield
1998	160	Sanders, Telly	4	Buchanan
1998	152	Moore, Kirk	5	Foothill
1999	140	Odom, Max	Champion	Foothill
1999	189	Naus, Joshua	2	Centennial
1999	175	Fox, Ben	2	Buchanan
1999	119	Martinez, Ben	7	Tulare Union
2000	145	Pendleton, Chris	4	Lemoore
2000	112	Onsurez, Andrew	8	East Bakersfield
2001	135	Tirapelle, Alex	Champion	Clovis
2001	145	Gutierrez, Miguel	4	Foothill
2002	125	Vasquez, Darrell	2	Bakersfield
2002	160	Sherley, Josh	3	Bakersfield
2002	103	Contreras, Gerrard	4	Buchanan
2002	152	Hafemeister, Sven	5	Lemoore
2003	119	Mendez, Chad	3	Hanford
2003	125	Flores, Gabe	3	Clovis
2004	135	Tirapelle, Troy	3	Clovis
2005	125	Anderson, Mark	3	Lemoore
2005	135	Soto, Joe	7	Porterville
2005	189	Varner, Jake	2	Bakersfield
2006	103	Chaides, David	3	Foothill
2006	130	Betancur, Josh	8	Buchanan
2006	145	Espericueta, Lucas	5	Shafter
2007	103	Done, Chris	Champion	Buchanan
2007	112	Demison, Nektoe	2	Bakersfield
2007	215	Flores, Ryan	2	Buchanan
2008	103	Camacho, Gilbert	3	Washington Union
2008	103	Diaz, Edgar	5	Arvin
2009	112	Gambrell, Madison	2	Clovis
2009	145	Sakaguchi, Scott	3	Clovis
2010		NONE		
2011	112	Nickell, Ian	4	Bakersfield
2011	119	Larson, Connor	7	Clovis East
2011	125	Rodriguez, Vince	Champion	Clovis North
2011	135	Box, Timmy	4	Bakersfield
2011	152	Fierro, Adam	3	Bakersfield
2011	160	Hammond, Bryce	Champion	Bakersfield
2012	138	Demison, Natrelle	Champion	Bakersfield
2012	138	Cruz, Micah	6	Bakersfield

NATIONAL HIGH SCHOOL COACHES ASSOCIATION CHAMPIONSHIPS

Year	Weight	Name	Place	School
2012	170	Nacita, Silas	3	Bakersfield
2013	120	Olea, Arnulfo	5	Exeter
2013	132	Gasca, Javier	Champion	Kingsburg
2013	145	Hammond, Coleman	4	Bakersfield
2013	160	Perraut, Kyle	Champion	Clovis East
2014	120	Pengilly, Mason	Champion	Porterville
2014	126	DeLacruz, Jason	6	Buchanan
2015	126	Molina, Armand	6	Firebaugh
2015	195	Flores, Austin	3	Clovis North
2015	285	Alvarez, Jose	Champion	Selma
2016	170	Romero, Abner	Champion	Buchanan
2016	285	Snyder, Jarrod	4	Frontier
2017	113	Pacheco, Anthony	5	Selma
2017	138	Enriquez, Jaden	3	Mission Oak
2017	138	Demison, Navonte	5	Bakersfield
2017	145	Figueroa, JJ	5	Bakersfield
2018	145	Olejnik, Izzak	5	Bakersfield
2018	170	Miracle, Dylan	7	Madera South
2019	138	Bloemhof, Andrew	5	Bakersfield

*Gary Quintana named Most Outstanding Wrestler

2015 CIF Wrestling Team Champions: Clovis H.S.

NATIONAL HIGH SCHOOL COACHES ASSOCIATION CHAMPIONSHIPS

JUNIOR

Year	Weight	Name	Place	School
2005		NONE		
2006	145	Webber, Tony	5	Bakersfield
2007	103	Camacho, Gilbert	2	Washington Union
2007	112	Fitzgerald, Steven	4	Clovis East
2008	145	Sagaguchi, Scott	5	Clovis
2008	160	West, Steven	5	Buchanan
2009	112	Zimmer, Zach	5	Clovis West
2009	285	Contreras, Luis	6	Madera
2010	103	Nickell, Ian	2	Bakersfield
2010	119	Rodriguez, Vince*	Champion	Clovis North
2010	135	Box, Timmy	Champion	Bakersfield
2010	160	Lozano, Justin	2	Selma
2011	130	Phaysamone, Patrick	7	Clovis East
2011	135	Demison, Natrelle	2	Bakersfield
2011	160	Nacita, Silas	3	Bakersfield
2011	171	Reyes, Nikko*	Champion	Clovis West
2012	152	Perrault, Kyle	Champion	Clovis East
2012	152	Hammond, Coleman	3	Bakersfield
2013	106	Camposano, Adrian	3	Central
2013	106	Nickell, Sean	4	Bakersfield
2013	195	Gonzales, Gabriel	3	Washington Union
2014	106	Morita, Bryce	6	Clovis West
2014	132	Hansen, Kyle	7	Buchanan
2014	138	Francis, Conner	6	Buchanan
2014	170	Flores, Austin	4	Clovis North
2014	182	An Woo, Young	8	Buchanan
2015	113	Campbell, David	Champion	Mission Oak
2016	126	Garcia, Robert	6	Selma
2017	138	Mendoza, Tony	6	Selma
2017	152	Diaz, Oscar	5	Selma
2018	120	Reyes, Cole	4	Frontier
2018	170	Rodriguez, Christian	6	Selma
2018	170	Cardwell, Mark	7	Monache
2019		NONE		

*Vince Rodriguez Named the Most Outstanding Wrestler
*Nikko Reyes won the Most Falls Award

IAN NICKELL BAKERSFIELD

Sean Nickell – Bakersfield High School

NATIONAL HIGH SCHOOL COACHES ASSOCIATION CHAMPIONSHIPS

SOPHMORE

Year	Weight	Name	Place	School
2006	135	Rassmussen, Travis	6	Bakersfield
2007	119	Rocha, Brandon	8	Lemoore
2007	275	Baize, Lloren	6	Lemoore
2008	152	Cook, James	Champion	Clovis West
2008	215	Schoene, Brian	5	Bakersfield
2009	130	Timmy, Box	7	Bakersfield
2009	135	Zarate, Nathan	6	Selma
2009	145	Fierro, Adam	4	Bakersfield
2009	152	Hammond, Bryce	Champion	Bakersfield
2009	152	Lozano, Justin	3	Selma
2010	160	Reyes, Nikko	Champion	Clovis West
2010	160	Nacita, Silas	5	Bakersfield
2011	130	Hodges, Hunter	6	Bakersfield
2011	140	Perreault, Kyle	6	Clovis East
2011	145	Hammond, Coleman	Champion	Bakersfield
2011	285	Rea, Johnathan	8	Lemoore
2012	106	Cisneros, Joey	3	Redwood
2012	138	Martin, Bryce	6	Bakersfield
2013	106	Herrera, Carlos	4	Bakersfield
2014	120	Lloren, Durbin	3	Buchanan
2014	126	Gaxiola, Greg	6	Buchanan
2014	145	Romero, Abner	2	Buchanan
2014	145	Hill, Jared	4	Clovis
2015	126	Enriquez, Jaden	2	Mission Oak
2015	160	Solis, Angel	6	Lemoore
2016	120	Leake, Ethan	5	Buchanan
2016	132	Villarreal, Brett	7	Buchanan
2016	145	Romero, Joel	8	Buchanan
2016	182	Montalvo, Anthony	Champion	Buchanan
2017	170	Rodriguez, Christian	4	Selma
2017	195	Reyes, Ryan	Champion	Clovis West
2018	113	Lujan, Tristan	Champion	Selma
2018	285	Hill, Josiah	6	Bakersfield
2019		NONE		

NATIONAL HIGH SCHOOL COACHES ASSOCIATION CHAMPIOSHIPS

FRESHMEN

Year	Weight	Name	Place	School
2007	112	Roberts, Nathan	7	Buchanan
2007	140	Flores, Roman	2	Stockdale
2007	145	Sierra, Nick	3	Lemoore
2007	189	Papendorf, Kyle	3	Buchanan
2008	103	Rodriguez, Vincent	2	Clovis North
2008	112	Knoblauch Steven	7	Clovis West
2009		NONE		
2010	145	Hammond, Coleman	Champion	Bakersfield
2011	152	Callender, Nickolas	7	Clovis East
2012		NONE		
2013	132	Gutierrez, Antonio	5	Bakersfield
2014	126	Enriquez, Jaden	Champion	Mission Oak
2014	126	Wright, Jacob	3	Dinuba
2015	132	Diaz, Oscar	5	Selma
2015	138	Ramos, Johathan	8	Selma
2015	145	Zamilpa, Tristan	5	Selma
2016	106	Paulson, Brandon	7	Clovis
2016	113	Olguin, Matt	Champion	Buchanan
2016	112	Abas, Jaden	3	Frontier
2016	152	Caldwell, Mark	3	Monache
2016	170	Reyes, Ryan	Champion	Clovis West
2016	170	Rodriguez, Christian	3	Selma
2017		NONE		
2018	113	Ozuna, Noah	7	Frontier
2018	120	Lucio, Cade	6	Bakersfield
2018	126	Viveros, Johnathan	8	Kingsburg
2018	220	Darter, Justin	3	Bakersfield
2019	113	Zinkin, Hayden	5	Clovis North

Matthew Olguin – Buchanan High School

Coach Wright – Dinuba High School

AMATUER WRESTLING NEWS ALL AMERICANS

Year	Wrestler	Weight	School	Team
1985	Trent Barns	245	Clovis West	1
1988	Mike Ortega	126	Roosevelt	Honorable Mention
1989	Terry Watts	145	Caruthers	6
1989	Lorenzo Neal	245	Lemoore	4
1990	Jassen Froelich	175	Bakersfield	Honorable Mention
1991	Jimmy Aguirre	125	Clovis	2
1991	Detran Gant	125	Roosevelt	7
1991	Gary Quintana	130	Selma	3
1992	Lalo Maz	189	Hanford	3
1992	Nick Quintana	112	Selma	8
1992	Nick Zinkin	119	Clovis	8
1993	Chad Mast	HWT	Clovis	3
1994	Moises Perez	140	Madera	Honorable Mention
1996	Adam Tirapelle	140	Buchanan	2
1997	Don Jackson	189	Kingsburg	Honorable Mention
1998	Ralph Lopez	140	Clovis West	3
1998	Kirk Moore	152	Foothill	6
1998	Telly Sanders	160	Buchanan	Honorable Mention
1999	Ben Martinez	130	Tulare Union	2
1999	Max Odom	145	Foothill	1
1999	Joshua Naus	189	Centennial	3
1999	Ben Fox	HWT	Buchanan	9
2000	Chris Pendleton	145	Lemoore	5
2000	Marcio Botelho	215	Lemoore	5
2000	Garrett Spooner	130	Clovis	Honorable Mention
2000	Mike Van Worth	189	Dos Palos	Honorable Mention
2000	Clint Walbeck	215	Clovis	Honorable Mention
2001	Alex Tirapelle	140	Clovis	1
2001	Miguel Gutierrez	145	Foothill	8
2001	Sean Sheets	152	Centennial	Honorable Mention
2002	Darrell Vasquez	125	Bakersfield	1
2002	Josh Sherley	160	Bakersfield	5
2002	Logan Ingram	112	Buchanan	9
2002	Gerrard Contreras	103	Buchanan	11
2002	Tony Franco	119	Bakersfield	9
2002	David Roberts	135	Clovis West	11
2002	Shane Seibert	140	Madera	11
2002	Drew East	152	Bakersfield	7
2003	Chad Mendez	119	Hanford	4
2003	Gabe Flores	125	Clovis	3
2004	Nathan Morgan	130	Bakersfield	1
2004	Troy Tirapelle	140	Clovis	1
2004	Alex Herrera	145	Bakersfield	9
2004	Chris Martinez	145	Clovis East	10
2005	Mark Anderson	125	Lemoore	9
2005	Jake Varner	189	Bakersfield	1
2006	Elijah Nacita	130	Bakersfield	11
2007	Nektoe Demison	112	Bakersfield	11
2007	Ryan Flores	215	Buchanan	4
2008	Gilbert Camacho	103	Washington Union	6
2009	Jose Mendoza	130	Selma	10

AMATUER WRESTLING NEWS ALL AMERICANS

Year	Wrestler	Weight	School	Team
2009	Scott Sakaguchi	145	Clovis	8
2010	James Cook	171	Madera	9
2010	Tommy Burial	189	Clovis	12
2011	Bryce Hammond	160	Bakersfield	1
2011	Steven Knoblauch	119	Clovis West	9
2011	Nick Pena	130	Selma	5
2011	Timmy Box	135	Bakersfield	11
2012	Daniel Gaytan	120	Clovis	10
2012	Alex Cisneros	132	Selma	1
2012	Nikko Reyes	182	Clovis West	4
2012	Zach Nevills	170	Clovis	11
2013	Isaiah Martinez	160	Lemoore	2
2013	Nick Nevills	285	Clovis	4
2014	AWN did not have a High School All American Team			
2015	Justin Mejia	113	Clovis	2
2015	Hexton Coronado	285	Clovis	Honorable Mention
2016	Justin Mejia	120	Clovis	2
2016	Seth Nevills	285	Clovis	3
2017	Seth Nevills	285	Clovis	2
2018	Seth Nevills	285	Clovis	3
2019	Richard Figueroa	106	Selma	1
2020	Richard Figueroa	113	Selma	1
2020	Joey Cruz	113	Clovis North	3

WRESTLING USA MAGAZINE ALL-AMERICAN TEAM

1969
Richard Alvarez — Bakersfield All American
Larry Morgan — East All American

1970
Alex Hernandez — Corcoran All American
Charlie Freeman — Madera *
Tony Serros — Bakersfield *

1971
Pete King — Madera All American
Paul Lovelace — West *
Bill Van Worth — South *
Dan McMasters — South *

1972
Sythell Thompson — Selma All American
Tony Alvarez — Bakersfield *
Rodney Mitchell — Bakersfield *

1973
Mike Bull — South All American
Ernie Flores — Madera *
Randy Baxter — Clovis *

1974
Rodney Balch — Clovis *
Fred Bohna — Clovis *

1978
Reynaldo Martinez — Roosevelt Dream Team

1984
Randy Graham — Bakersfield All American
Brian Lewis — Clovis West *

1985
Eddie Gomez — Caruthers Dream Team

1989
Terry Watts — Caruthers All American

1991
Jimmy Aguirre — Clovis Dream Team
Gary Quintana — Selma All American

1992
Lalo Moz — Hanford All American

1996
Adam Tirapelle — Buchanan Dream Team

1999
Max Odom — Foothill Academic Team
Ben Martinez — Tulare Union All American
Josh Naus — Centennial All American
Ben Fox — Buchanan *

2000
Garrett Spooner — Clovis All American
Chris Pendleton — Lemoore All American
Marcio Botehio — Lemoore All American
Clint Walbeck — Clovis *

2001
Alex Tirapelle — Clovis Dream Team
Miguel Gutierrez — Foothill All American
Sean Sheets — Centennial *

2002
Darrell Vasquez — Bakersfield Academic Team
Drew East — Bakersfield All American
Josh Sherley — Bakersfield All American
Logan Ingram — Buchanan *
Tony Franco — Bakersfield *
David Roberts — Clovis West *
Andrew Spradlin — Bakersfield*
Sven Hafemeister — Lemoore *

2003
Gabriel Flores — Clovis All American
Chad Mendes — Hanford *

2004
Nathan Morgan — Bakersfield Dream Team
Troy Tirapelle — Clovis Dream Team
Chris Martinez — Clovis West All American
Alex Herrera — Bakersfield All American
Steve Juarez — Hanford *

Adam Tirapelle — Isaiah Martinez — Ryan Flores

2005
Mark Anderson — Lemoore All American
Joe Soto — Porterville All American
Jake Varner — Bakersfield All American

2006
Elijah Nacita — Bakersfield All American
Lucas Espericueta — Shafter *

WRESTLING USA MAGAZINE ALL-AMERICAN TEAM

2007
Ryan Flores — Buchanan Academic Team
Joe Cisneros — Selma *

2008
Justin Arredondo — Buchanan All American
Gilbert Camacho — Washington Union *
David Watts — El Diamante *
Andrew Balch — Buchanan *

2009
Seth Hicks — Centennial All American
Scott Sakagushi — Clovis All American
Brandon Rocha — Lemoore*
Stephen West — Buchanan *

2010
Chris Martinez — Clovis West All American
James Cook — Madera All American
Zach Zimmer — Clovis West *
Tommy Buriell — Clovis *

2011
Bryce Hammond — Bakersfield Dream Team
Vincent Rodriguez — Clovis North All American
Nick Pena — Selma All American
Timmy Box — Bakersfield *
Damien Arredondo — Buchanan *

2012
Alex Cisneros — Selma Academic Team
Daniel Gaytan — Clovis All American
Zach Nevills — Clovis All American
Nikko Reyes — Clovis West All American
Natrelle Demison — Bakersfield *
Silas Nacita — Bakersfield *

2013
Isaiah Martinez — Lemoore Academic Team
Adrian Salas — Clovis All American
Jonas Gaytan — Clovis *
Javier Gasca — Kingsburg *
Kyle Perrault — Clovis East *

2014
Nick Nevills — Clovis Dream Team
Mason Pengilly — Porterville All American
Michael Knoblauch — Clovis West All American

2015
Hexton Coronado — Clovis *

2016
David Campbell — Mission Oak All American
Durbin Lloren — Buchanan All American
Josh Hoket — Clovis All American
Zakary Levatino — Buchanan *

2017
Justin Mejia — Clovis All American
Gary Joint — Lemoore All American
Jaden Enriquez — Mission Oak All American
Navonte Demison — Bakersfield All American

2018
Seth Nevills — Clovis Academic Team
Anthony Montalvo — Buchanan All American
Ethan Leake — Buchanan *

2019
Matthew Olguin — Clovis All American
Jacob Good — Clovis All American
Tyler Deen — Buchanan *
Trent Tracy — Frontier *

2020
Tristan Lujan — Selma All American
Giano Petrucelli — Clovis All American
Josiah Hill — Bakersfield All American
Hunter Leake — Buchanan *
Tyler Giankopulos — Clovis *

*Honorable Mention

* 1998 All American Nominations were not received from California

BRYCE HAMMOND BAKERSFIELD
Chris Pendleton

ASICS HIGH SCHOOL ALL-AMERICANS

Year	Wrestler	Weight	School	Team
1986	Trent Barnes	HWT	Clovis West	1
1989	Lorenzo Neal	HWT	Lemoore	2
1989	Terry Watts	145	Carruthers	Honorable Mention
1990	Jimmy Aguirre	119	Clovis	Honorable Mention
1991	Jimmy Aguirre	125	Clovis	2
1991	Detran Gant	125	Roosevelt	Honorable Mention
1991	Gary Quintana	130	Selma	3
1991	Lalo Moz	189	Hanford	Honorable Mention
1992	Lalo Moz	189	Hanford	2
1993	Chad Mast	HWT	Clovis	2
1995	Adam Tirapelle	130	Hiram Johnson	Honorable Mention
1996	Adam Tirapelle	140	Buchanan	3
1998	Max Odom	130	Foothill	Honorable Mention
1998	Ralph Lopez	140	Clovis West	Honorable Mention
1998	Telly Sanders	160	Buchanan	Honorable Mention
1999	Max Odom	145	Foothill	3
1999	Josh Naus	189	Centennial	3
1999	Ben Martinez	130	Tulare Union	Honorable Mention
2000	Darrell Vasquez	112	Bakersfield	3
2000	Marcio Botelho	215	Lemoore	Honorable Mention
2001	Darrell Vasquez	119	Bakersfield	3
2001	Alex Tirapelle	140	Clovis	1
2001	Miguel Gutierrez	145	Foothill	Honorable Mention
2002	Nathan Morgan	112	Bakersfield	3
2002	Darrell Vasquez	125	Bakersfield	2
2002	Josh Sherley	160	Bakersfield	Honorable Mention
2002	Sven Hafemeister	160	Lemoore	Honorable Mention
2003	Nathan Morgan	125	Bakersfield	2
2003	Gabe Flores	125	Clovis	Honorable Mention
2003	Troy Tirapelle	130	Clovis	2
2004	Nathan Morgan	130	Bakersfield	1
2004	Troy Tirapelle	140	Clovis	2
2004	Jake Varner	171	Bakersfield	Honorable Mention
2005	Mark Anderson	125	Lemoore	2
2005	Jake Varner	189	Bakersfield	2
2006	Ryan Flores	215	Buchanan	2
2007	Ryan Flores	215	Buchanan	Honorable Mention
2008	Gilbert Camacho	103	Washington Union	Honorable Mention
2009	Alex Cisneros	103	Selma	2
2009	Scott Sakaguchi	145	Clovis	Honorable Mention
2010	Alex Cisneros	112	Selma	2
2010	James Cook	171	Madera	Honorable Mention
2011	Alex Cisneros	125	Selma	Honorable Mention
2011	Vince Rodriguez	125	Clovis North	Honorable Mention
2011	Bryce Hammond	160	Bakersfield	2
2012	Alex Cisneros	132	Selma	2
2012	Isaiah Martinez	152	Lemoore	2
2012	Nikko Reyes	182	Clovis West	Honorable Mention
2013	Javier Casca	132	Kingsburg	Honorable Mention
2013	Isaiah Martinez	160	Lemoore	3
2013	Nick Nevills	285	Clovis	Honorable Mention
2014	Justin Mejia	103	Clovis	Honorable Mention
2014	Nick Nevills	285	Clovis	1

ASICS HIGH SCHOOL ALL-AMERICANS

Year	Wrestler	Weight	School	Team
2015	Justin Mejia	113	Clovis	3
2016	Matt Olguin	106	Buchanan	Honorable Mention
2016	Justin Mejia	120	Clovis	2
2017	Seth Nevills	285	Clovis	2
2018	Richard Figueroa	106	Selma	2
2018	Anthony Montalvo	182	Buchanan	Honorable Mention
2018	Seth Nevills	285	Clovis	Honorable Mention
2019	Richard Figueroa	106	Selma	1

Isaiah Martinez – Lemoore High School

Justin Mejia – Clovis High School

JUNIOR USA NATIONAL WRESTLING CHAMPIONSHIPS

Year	Wrestler	Weight	Style	Place	School
1972	Mike Bull	191.5	Greco	Champion	South
1974	Fred Bohna	191.5	Freestyle	3	Clovis
1974	Tom Gongora	143	Greco	2	Clovis
1975	Paul Bolanos	105.5	Freestyle	3	Clovis
1976	Tom Blanco	114.5	Freestyle	6	Clovis
1976	Doug Artur	HWT	Greco	2	Clovis
1976	Doug Artur	HWT	Freestyle	6	Clovis
1978	Rey Martinez	191	Freestyle	Champion	Roosevelt
1981	Darrell Nerove	98	Greco	3	Foothill
1985	Ben Lizama	286	Greco	Champion	Foothill
1987	John Tripp	165	Greco	6	Tulare Union
1987	John Tripp	178	Freestyle	6	Tulare Union
1988	Lorenzo Neal	220	Greco	3	Lemoore
1988	Lorenzo Neal	220	Freestyle	3	Lemoore
1988	Mark Smith	275	Freestyle	8	Clovis West
1989	Jimmy Aguirre	105.5	Freestyle	7	Clovis
1990	Andy Munoz	98	Freestyle	Champion	Washington Union
1990	Gary Quintana	123	Freestyle	7	Selma
1990	Jeff Heberle	132	Greco	7	North
1990	Lalo Moz	191.5	Greco	6	Hanford
1990	Josh Selven	275	Greco	4	Clovis West
1990	Josh Selven	275	Freestyle	8	Clovis West
1991	Brad Fuqua	98	Greco	7	North
1991	Nick Zinkin	114.5	Freestyle	8	Clovis
1991	Gary Quintana	132	Freestyle	5	Selma
1991	Jeff Heberle	143	Greco	7	North
1991	Scott Silver	178	Greco	8	Bullard
1991	Lalo Moz	191.5	Greco	2	Hanford
1992	Brad Fuqua	98	Greco	5	North
1992	Lalo Moz	191.5	Greco	6	Hanford
1992	Lalo Moz	220	Freestyle	7	Hanford
1992	Nick Zinkin	123	Freestyle	8	Clovis
1992	Chad Mast	275	Freestyle	2	Clovis
1993	Jeremy Karle	275	Greco	8	Highland
1995	Adam Tirapelle	143	Greco	5	Buchanan
1995	Fred Ashley	178	Greco	4	Bakersfield
1995	Brett Clark	275	Greco	2	Bakersfield
1995	Brett Clark	275	Freestyle	4	Bakersfield
1996	Adam Tirapelle	143	Freestyle	4	Buchanan
1998	Ben Martinez	123	Greco	Champion	Tulare Union
1998	Joshua Naus	191.5	Greco	7	Centennial
1999	Ben Martinez	132	Greco	3	Tulare Union
1999	Ben Martinez	132	Freestyle	4	Tulare Union
1999	Max Odom	143	Freestyle	Champion	Foothill
1999	Marcio Botelho	220	Freestyle	3	Lemoore
2000	Darrell Vasquez	114.5	Freestyle	2	Bakersfield
2000	Sven Hafemeister	165	Greco	3	Lemoore
2000	Marcio Botelho	220	Freestyle	4	Lemoore
2000	Marcio Botelho	220	Greco	5	Lemoore
2001	Darrell Vasquez	123	Freestyle	4	Bakersfield
2001	Tony Franco	123	Freestyle	6	Bakersfield
2002	Nathan Morgan	119	Freestyle	2	Bakersfield
2002	Chad Mendez	119	Freestyle	8	Hanford
2002	James Holt	125	Greco	2	Tulare Union

JUNIOR USA NATIONAL WRESTLING CHAMPIONSHIPS

Year	Wrestler	Weight	Style	Place	School
2002	James Holt	130	Freestyle	8	Tulare Union
2002	Tony Franco	125	Freestyle	8	Bakersfield
2002	Darrell Vasquez	130	Freestyle	2	Bakersfield
2003	Brett Land	112	Greco	4	Bakersfield
2003	Brett Land	112	Freestyle	4	Bakersfield
2003	Alex Herrera	140	Freestyle	7	Bakersfield
2003	Tyler Bernacchi	160	Greco	5	Clovis East
2003	Jake Varner	160	Greco	6	Bakersfield
2004	Nathan Morgan	130	Freestyle	4	Bakersfield
2004	Jake Varner	189	Freestyle	3	Bakersfield
2006	Randall Watts	125	Freestyle	6	El Diamante
2006	Elijah Nacita	135	Freestyle	7	Bakersfield
2007	Frank Lomas	119	Freestyle	4	Bakersfield
2001	Randall Watts	135	Greco	5	El Diamante
2008	Cesar Sanchez	112	Freestyle	8	Porterville
2008	Jose Mendoza	130	Freestyle	2	Selma
2008	David Watts	143	Freestyle	5	El Diamante
2008	Stephen West	171	Freestyle	5	Buchanan
2009	Manny Marin	98	Greco	7	Buchanan
2009	Manny Marin	98	Freestyle	6	Buchanan
2009	Stephen West	160	Greco	4	Buchanan
2010	Manny Marin	105	Freestyle	6	Buchanan
2011	Colman Hammond	152	Freestyle	4	Bakersfield
2012	Sean Nickell	100	Freestyle	7	Bakersfield
2012	Joe Cisneros	106	Greco	4	Redwood
2012	Mason Pengilly	120	Freestyle	6	Porterville
2012	Isaiah Martinez	160	Freestyle	Champion	Lemoore
2012	Isaiah Martinez	160	Greco	8	Lemoore
2013	Joe Cisneros	106	Freestyle	2	Redwood
2013	Joe Cisneros	106	Greco	2	Redwood
2013	Sean Nickell	106	Freestyle	4	Bakersfield
2013	Matt Gamble	113	Freestyle	4	Monache
2013	Bryce Martin	170	Freestyle	8	Bakersfield
2014	Joe Cisneros	113	Freestyle	3	Redwood
2014	Joe Cisneros	113	Greco	4	Redwood
2015	Novonte Demison	126	Freestyle	2	Bakersfield
2016	Gary Joint	132	Freestyle	8	Lemoore
2016	Jaden Enriquez	138	Greco	6	Mission Oak
2016	Ricky Gonzalez	160	Greco	7	Bakersfield
2017	Jaden Enriquez	138	Freestyle	3	Mission Oak
2017	Jaden Enriquez	145	Greco	Champion	Mission Oak
2018	Dawson Sihavong	138	Greco	2	Bullard
2018	Jace Luchau	158	Freestyle	5	Selma
2019	Jace Luchau	152	Freestyle	Champion	Selma *
2019	Cade Lucio	138	Greco	2	Bakersfield
2019	Jace Luchau	160	Greco	5	Selma

CADET USA NATIONAL CHAMPIONSHIPS

Year	Wrestler	Weight	Style	Place	School
1986	Stricker, Tad	121	Greco	4	South
1987	La Garetta, Eric	103.5	Greco	5	Selma
1989	Munoz, Andy	94.5	Freestyle	3	Washington Union
1989	Zinkin, Nick	103.5	Freestyle	3	Clovis
1989	Moz, Lalo	182.5	Freestyle	6	Hanford
1990	Fugua, Brad	94.5	Greco	8	North
1991	Green, Stan	83.5	Freestyle	2	Clovis
1992	Perez, Moses	154	Freestyle	6	Madera
1993	Tirapelle, Adam	121	Greco	2	Buchanan
1993	Tirapelle, Adam	121	Freestyle	6	Buchanan
1993	Clark, Brett	209	Greco	2	Bakersfield
1993	Smith, Jared	242	Greco	2	Clovis West
1993	Smith, Jared	242	Freestyle	2	Clovis West
1994	Johnson, Cleo	83.5	Freestyle	8	Firebaugh
1994	Guerrero, Brian	94.5	Freestyle	6	Madera
1994	Brecedo, Sergio	112	Freestyle	8	Buchanan
1994	Jackson, Dan	182.5	Freestyle	6	Kingsburg
1995	Sanders, Telly*	154	Greco	2	Buchanan
1996	Beck, Scott	94.5	Greco	5	Tulare Union
1996	Beck, Scott	94.5	Freestyle	7	Tulare Union
1996	Odom, Max	103.5	Freestyle	5	Foothill
1996	Martinez, Ben	112	Greco	2	Tulare Union
1997	Villa, Daniel	88	Freestyle	8	South
1997	Odom, Max	121	Freestyle	Champion	Foothill
1997	Martinez, Ben	121	Greco	Champion	Tulare Union
1997	Martinez, Ben	121	Freestyle	4	Tulare Union
1997	Naus, Josh	182.5	Greco	5	Centennial
1998	Holt, James	83.5	Greco	2	Tulare Union
1998	Holt, James	83.5	Freestyle	7	Tulare Union
1998	Moreno, Jason	103.5	Greco	Champion	Firebaugh
1998	Moreno, Jason	103.5	Freestyle	Champion	Firebaugh
1998	Portillo, Angel	121	Greco	4	Tulare Union
1998	Gutierrez, Miguel	132	Freestyle	8	Foothill
1998	Patino, Edward	209	Greco	8	Porterville
1999	Morgan, Nathan	88	Freestyle	Champion	Bakersfield
1999	Holt, James	94.5	Greco	4	Tulare Union
1999	Roberts, David	121	Freestyle	8	Clovis West
1999	Gutierrez, Miguel	142	Freestyle	8	Foothill
2000	Morgan, Nathan	103.5	Freestyle	5	Bakersfield
2000	Flores, Gabe	103.5	Greco	4	Clovis
2000	Franco, Tony*	121	Freestyle	2	Bakersfield
2001	Land, Brett	83.5	Greco	Champion	Bakersfield
2001	Land, Brett	83.5	Freestyle	2	Bakersfield
2001	Mendes, Chad	112	Greco	4	Hanford

CADET USA NATIONAL CHAMPIONSHIPS

Year	Wrestler	Weight	Style	Place	School
2001	Herrera, Alex	121	Freestyle	4	Bakersfield
2001	Flores, Gabe	121	Freestyle	6	Clovis
2001	Bernacchi, Tyler	154	Greco	8	Clovis East
2002	Ruiz, Paul	98	Freestyle	3	Firebaugh
2002	Herrera, Alex	130	Freestyle	Champion	Bakersfield
2002	Sierra, Lionel	140	Greco	5	Reedley
2002	Landois, Orlando	145	Greco	7	Wasco
2002	Varner, Jake	152	Freestyle	4	Bakersfield
2002	Griffin, Kyle	160	Greco	2	Clovis East
2002	Griffin, Kyle	160	Freestyle	7	Clovis East
2003	Soto, Joe	135	Freestyle	5	Porterville
2004	Watts, Randall	98	Greco	8	El Diamante
2004	Boger, Matt	171	Greco	7	Coalinga
2004	Boger, Matt	171	Freestyle	3	Coalinga
2004	Flores, Ryan	215	Freestyle	3	Coalinga
2005	Timmerman, Nathan	189	Freestyle	7	Monache
2005	Zimmer, Zach	84	Freestyle	5	Clovis West
2006	Boger, Josh	215	Greco	3	Buchanan
2006	Boger, Josh	215	Freestyle	4	Buchanan
2007	Zimmer, Zach	98	Greco	8	Clovis West
2007	Schoene, Brian	215	Freestyle	6	Bakersfield
2007	Hernandez, Antonio	285	Freestyle	8	East
2008	Gaytan, Daniel	98	Freestyle	8	Clovis
2008	Hammond, Bryce	152	Freestyle	2	Bakersfield
2009	Demision, Natrelle	119	Freestyle	7	Bakersfield
2010	Martinez, Isaiah	135	Greco	Champion	Lemoore
2010	Pengilly, Mason	98	Freestyle	5	Porterville
2010	Demision, Natrelle	130	Freestyle	5	Bakersfield
2010	Hammond, Coleman	145	Freestyle	2	Bakersfield
2010	Perrault, Kyle	145	Freestyle	6	Clovis East
2011	Nickell, Sean	84	Freestyle	3	Bakersfield
2011	Sandoval Martin	125	Freestyle	7	Porterville
2012	NONE				
2013	Deloza, Chris	106	Freestyle	8	Clovis North
2013	Enriquez, Jaden	126	Freestyle	5	Mission Oak
2013	Enriquez, Jaden	126	Greco	3	Mission Oak
2014	Olejnik, Izzak	94	Freestyle	8	Bakersfield
2014	Olejnik, Izzak	94	Greco	7	Bakersfield
2014	Enriquez, Jaden	126	Freestyle	2	Mission Oak
2014	Enriquez, Jaden	126	Greco	Champion	Mission Oak
2014	Gonzalez, Ricky	152	Greco	5	Bakersfield
2015	Olejnik, Izzak	106	Greco	6	Bakersfield
2016	Rivera, Eric	120	Freestyle	5	Clovis North
2016	Abas, Jaden	126	Freestyle	2	Frontier
2017	Figueroa, Richard	100	Freestyle	3	Selma
2017	Franco, Ryan	126	Freestyle	2	Clovis North
2017	Franco, Ryan	126	Greco	4	Clovis North
2017	Sinavong, Dawson	132	Greco	3	Bullard
2017	Luchau, Jace	145	Freestyle	3	Selma
2017	Luchau, Jace	145	Greco	6	Selma
2018	Hill, Josiah	285	Freestyle	7	Bakersfield
2018	Franco, Ryan	132	Freestyle 16U	2	Clovis North

CADET USA NATIONAL CHAMPIONSHIPS

Year	Wrestler	Weight	Style	Place	School
2019	Harris, Ray	94	Greco	Champion	Buchanan
2019	Rodriguez, Matthew	145	Greco	5	Righetti
2019	Hilford, Jordan	195	Greco	6	Clovis

*Most Falls Award
All Placers Awarded All-American Status

Jake Varner – Bakersfield High School, Iowa State and USA Olympian

FLO NATIONALS ALL-AMERICANS

Year	Wrestler	Weight	School	Place
2010	NONE			
2011	Isaiah Martinez	140	Lemoore	2nd
2011	Brandon Sotomayor	145	Centennial	7th
2012	Mason Pengilly	113	Porterville	2nd
2012	Jonas Gaytan	113	Clovis	5th
2012	Javier Gasca	126	Kingsburg	2nd
2012	Alex Cisneros	138	Selma	Champion
2012	Isaiah Martinez	152	Lemoore	Champion
2012	Zach Nevills	170	Clovis	3rd
2012	Nikko Reyes	182	Clovis West	Champion
2012	Nate Lopez	195	Lemoore	8th
2012	Nick Nevills	220	Clovis	2nd
2012	Sean Medley	220	Wasco	6th
2013	Durbin Lloren	106	Buchanan	8th
2013	Mason Pengilly	120	Porterville	4th
2013	Martin Sandoval	138	Porterville	5th
2013	Tyler Zimmer	138	Clovis West	7th
2013	Sean Medley	220	Wasco	4th
2013	Nick Nevills	285	Clovis	Champion
2014	Justin Mejia	106	Clovis	7th
2014	Khristian Olivas	126	Clovis	8th
2014	Austin Flores	170	Clovis North	6th
2015	Isaiah Hokit	145	Clovis	5th
2015	Josh Hokit	170	Clovis	4th
2015	Austin Flores	195	Clovis North	3rd
2016	Brandon Betancourt	106	Clovis	6th
2016	Justin Mejia	120	Clovis	2nd
2016	Durbin Lloren	126	Buchanan	2nd
2017	Seth Nevills	285	Clovis	Champion
2017	Jaden Enriquez	145	Mission Oak	Champion Greco Roman
2018	Devin Murphy	120	Clovis North	5th
2019	Devin Murphy	61kg	Clovis North	2nd
2019	Jace Luchau	70kg	Selma	Champion

CADET USA NATIONAL CHAMPIONSHIP

Year	Wrestler	Weight	School	Place	
2018	Richard Figueroa	106	Selma	Champion	Cadet
2018	Joey Cruz	106	Clovis North	2nd	8th grade
2019	Justin Wells	41-45kg	Clovis North	4th	Cadet
2019	Joey Cruz	51kg	Clovis North	Champion	Cadet
2019	Richard Figueroa	51kg	Selma	2nd	Cadet
2019	Ryan Franco	60kg	Clovis North	4th	Cadet

USA WRESTLING FOLKSTYLE NATIONALS - IOWA

JUNIOR

Year	Weight	Name	Place	School
2013	113	Cisneros, Joey	3	Redwood
2014	113	Cisneros, Joey	Champion	Redwood
2014	120	Nickell, Sean	2	Bakersfield
2014	120	Herrera, Carlos	7	Bakersfield
2014	170	Martin, Bryce	4	Bakersfield
2015	120	Campbell, David	3	Mission Oak
2015	126	Demison, Navonte	Champion	Bakersfield
2015	126	Deloza, Chris		Clovis North
2015	126	Lloren, Derbin	3	Buchanan
2015	132	Enriquez, Jaden	6	Mission Oak
2016	100	Posas, Carlos	4	Madera South
2016	106	Olejnik, Izzak	3	Bakersfield
2016	132	Deloza, Chris	2	Clovis North
2016	132	Joint, Gary	3	Lemoore
2016	138	Demison, Novonte	Champion	Bakersfield
2016	160	Gonzales, Ricky	3	Bakersfield
2016	160	Loera, Sam	6	Bakersfield
2016	182	Rosales, Elias	7	Bakersfield
2016	220	Holloway, Nathaniel	5	Clovis North
2017	132	Deloza, Chris		Clovis North
2017	220	Belshay, Cade	Champion	Buchanan
2017	285	Holloway, Nathaniel		Clovis North
2018	113	Leake, Hunter	3	Buchanan
2018	138	Sihavong, Dawson	3	Bullard
2018	138	Leake, Ethan	5	Buchanan
2019	113	Bermundez, Nicholas	6	Buchanan
2019	120	Renteria, Maximo	Champion	Buchanan
2019	126	Leake, Hunter	2	Buchanan
2019	132	Gioffre, Logan	8	Buchanan
2019	145	Sihavong, Dawson	2	Bullard
2019	145	Ruiz, George	5	Buchanan
2019	152	Martin, Joseph	3	Buchanan
2019	160	Luchau, Jace	3	Selma
2019	195	Martin, Jaden	8	Buchanan

CADET USA WRESTLING FOLKSTYLE CHAMPIONSHIPS - IOWA

Year	Weight	Name	Place	School
2013	100	Nelms, Andrew	4	Porterville
2013	126	Molina, Armand	Champion	Firebaugh
2013	138	Mora, Aaron	8	Firebaugh
2014	94	Olelnik, Izzak	5	Bakersfield
2014	103	Demison, Navonte	3	Bakersfield
2014	120	Figueroa, JJ	8	Bakersfield
2014	132	Enriquez, Jaden	Champion	Mission Oak
2014	160	Loera, Sam	4	Bakersfield
2014	285	Schoene, Daniel	4	Bakersfield
2015	106	Olejnik, Izzak	6	Bakersfield
2015	126	Villarreal, Brett	6	Redwood
2015	132	Figueroa, JJ	2	Bakersfield
2015	152	Zamilpa, Tristan	5	Selma
2016	120	Rivera, Eric	5	Clovis North
2016	120	Sihavong, Dawson	8	Bullard
2017	120	Martin, Joseph	4	Buchanan
2017	132	Sihavong, Dawson	Champion	Bullard
2017	152	Luchau, Jace	2	Selma
2017	195	Watson, Kwabena	6	Edison
2018	106	Gioffre, Michael	7	Buchanan
2018	113	Lake, Kyler	3	Buchanan
2018	113	Jauron, Haynie	6	Firebaugh
2018	152	Martin, Joseph	3	Buchanan
2018	195	Peralta, J D	4	Buchanan

16U

Year	Weight	Name	Place	School
2019	106	Gioffre, Jack	Champion	Buchanan
2019	106	Cabrera, Cisco	2	Buchanan
2019	106	Mendez, Dominic	3	Righetti
2019	106	Lopez, Raymond	8	Buchanan
2019	113	Rail, Reggie	3	Buchanan
2019	120	Gioffre, Michael	3	Buchanan
2019	126	Lake, Kyler	2	Buchanan
2019	152	Rodriguez, Mathew	3	Righetti
2019	182	Rogers, Caden	7	Buchanan

USWF JUNIOR NATIONALS

Year	Wrestler	Weight	Style	Place	School
1972	Guy Campbell	165	Greco Roman	2	South
1972	Mike Bull	191.5	Greco Roman	Champion	South

NATIONAL AAU CHAMPIONSHIPS HIGH SCHOOL DIVISION

Year	Wrestler	Weight	Style	Place	School
1971	Guy Campbell	154	Greco Roman	Champion	South

JUNIOR NATIONAL AAU CHAMPIONNSHIPS

Year	Wrestler	Weight	Style	Place	School
1979	Tim Vanni	98	Freestyle	Champion	Monache
1979	Tim Vanni	105	Greco Roman	Champion	Monache

FILA JUNIOR NATIONALS

Year	Wrestler	Weight	Style	Place	School
1999	Ben Martinez	127.7	Greco Roman	2	Tulare Union
1999	Ben Martinez	127.7	Freestyle	Champion	Tulare Union
1999	Ian Nelms	167.5	Greco Roman	3	Mt. Whitney
1999	Ian Nelms	167.5	Freestyle	7	Mt. Whitney
2003	David Roberts	145.5	Freestyle	8	Clovis West
2005	Jake Varner	185	Freestyle	4	Bakersfield

FILA CADET NATIONALS

Year	Wrestler	Weight	Style	Place	School
2005	Chris Lewis	220.25	Freestyle	Champion	Clovis West

JUNIOR WORLD TOURNAMENT

Year	Wrestler	Weight	Style	Place	School	Location
1967	Larry Morgan	106	Freestyle		East	Canceled
1967	Ronnie Shearer	132	Freestyle		East	Canceled
1967	John Miller	178	Greco Roman		North	Canceled
1969	Larry Morgan	123	Freestyle	Champion	East	Colorado Springs
1969	Larry Little	132	Freestyle	2	South	Colorado Springs
1971	Randy Powers	143	Greco Roman	6	South	Tokyo, Japan
1973	Mike Bull	198	Greco Roman	Injured	South	Miami Beach, Fl.
1981	Tim Vanni	105.5	Freestyle	D.N.P.	Monache	Vancouver, BC

FILA JUNIOR WORLD TOURNAMENT

Year	Wrestler	Weight	Style	Place	School	Location
1990	Lorenzo Neal	Hwt.	Freestyle		Lemoore	
1997	Adam Tirapelle	143	Freestyle	5	Buchanan	Helsinki, Finland
1998	Nathan Vasquez	154	Greco Roman	D.N.P.	Bakersfield	
1999	Ben Martinez	127.7	Freestyle	8	Tulare Union	
2005	Jake Varner	185	Freestyle	Injured	Bakersfield	Budapest, Hungary

CADET WORLD CHAMPIONSHIPS

Year	Wrestler	Weight	Style	Place	School	Location
1998	Jason Moreno	105.5	Greco Roman	D.N.P.	Firebaugh	Pretoria, South Africa

USWF JUNIOR NATIONALS

Year	Wrestler	Weight	Style	Place	School	
UWW CADET NATIONALS						
2018	Richard Figueroa	48 Kg	Freestyle	Champion	Selma	
2018	Joey Cruz	48 Kg	Freestyle	Second	Clovis North	
2019	Richard Figueroa	51 Kg	Freestyle	Champion	Selma	
2019	Joey Cruz	51 Kg	Freestyle	Third	Clovis North	
FILA WORLD CHAMPIONSHIPS 16U						
2011	Nikko Reyes		Freestyle		Clovis	West Hungary
2018	Richard Figueroa	48 Kg	Freestyle	Second	Selma	Zagreb, Croatia
2019	Richard Figueroa	51 Kg	Freestyle	D.N.P.	Selma	Sofia, Bulgaria

RICHARD FIGUEROA SELMA

STEVE AND ADAM TIRAPELLE CLOVIS

YOUNG WRESTLER HIGH SCHOOL ALL-AMERICANS

Year	Wrestler	School	Team
1975	Robert Kiddy	Madera	Fourth Team
1975	Jewrel Thomas	Hanford	Sixth Team
1978	Rey Martinez	Roosevelt	First Team

INTERMAT ALL-AMERICAN TEAM

Year	Wrestler	Weight	School	Team
2012	Jonas Gaytan	113	Clovis	16
2012	Daniel Gaytan	120	Clovis	17
2012	Alex Cisneros	132	Selma	2
2012	Natrelle Demison	132	Bakersfield	19
2012	Isaiah Martinez	152	Lemoore	2
2012	Coleman Hammond	152	Bakersfield	19
2012	Zach Nevills	170	Clovis	12
2012	Silas Nacita	170	Bakersfield	15
2012	Nikko Reyes	182	Clovis West	4
2012	Nick Nevills	285	Clovis	8
2013	Adrian Camposano	106	Central	11
2013	Mason Pengilly	120	Porterville	9
2013	Jonas Gaytan	120	Clovis	13
2013	Javier Gasca	132	Kingsburg	12
2013	Isaiah Martinez	160	Lemoore	3
2013	Adrian Salas	182	Clovis	18
2013	Sean Medley	220	Wasco	20
2013	Nick Nevills	285	Clovis	3
2014	Nick Nevills	285	Clovis	1

USA TODAY NEWSPAPER HIGH SCHOOL ALL-AMERICAN TEAM

Year	Wrestler	Weight	School	Team
2014	Nick Nevills	285	Clovis	
2015	Justin Mejia	113	Clovis	3
2016	Justin Mejia	120	Clovis	2
2017	Justin Mejia	120	Clovis	3
2017	Seth Nevills	285	Clovis	2
2010	Richard Figueroa	106	Selma	1
2019	Matthew Olguin	160	Buchanan	2
2019	Troy Tirapelle	Coach of the Year	Buchanan High School	

THE OPEN MAT ALL-AMERICAN TEAM

Year	Wrestler	Weight	School	Team	
2017	Justin Mejia	126	Clovis	3	Senior Team
2017	Anthony Montalvo	182	Buchanan	3	Junior Team
2017	Seth Nevills	285	Clovis	2	Junior Team
2017	Matthew Olguin	113	Buchanan	1	Sophomore Team
2017	Ryan Flores	195	Clovis West	1	Sophomore Team

CLINCH GEAR ALL-AMERICAN TEAM

Year	Wrestler	Weight	School	Team
2010	Alex Cisneros	112	Selma	3
2011	Bryce Hammond	160	Bakersfield	1
2011	Steve Tirapelle	Coach of the Year	Clovis High School	

CLINCH GEAR ALL REGION TEAM WEST

Year	Wrestler	Weight	School	Team
2012	Alex Cisneros	132	Selma	
2012	Isaiah Martinez	152	Lemoore	
2012	Nick Nevills	285	Clovis	
2012	Steve Tirapelle	Coach of the Year	Clovis High School	
2015	Justin Mejia	113	Clovis	1

PITTSBURG POST-GAZETTE DAPPER DAN WRESTLING CLASSIC

The most prestigious high school All-Star wrestling meet in the United States
Began in 1975 in Pittsburg, Pennsylvania – Now called the Pittsburg Classic

Year	Wrestler	School	Weight	Won/Lost
1986	Trent Barnes	Clovis West	Heavy Weight	Lost 11-5
2001	Alex Tirapelle	Clovis	140	Won 8-6 OT
2002	Darrell Vasquez	Bakersfield	125	Lost Fall 5:45
2004	Nathan Morgan	Bakersfield	130	Won 13-5
2011	Bryce Hammond	Bakersfield	160	Won 4-2 OT
2013	Isaiah Martinez	Lemoore	160	Won 20-8
2014	Nick Nevills	Clovis	285	Won 5-3
	* Adam Tirapelle	Clovis High	Coached the team	
2017	Justin Mejia	Clovis	126	Lost 18-5

FILA CADET NATIONALS

2005	Chris Lewis	Clovis West	Freestyle	200.25	Champion

UWW CADET NATIONALS

Year	Wrestler	School	Style	Weight	Place
2018	Richard Figueroa	Selma	Freestyle	48kg	Champion
2018	Joey Cruz	Clovis North	Freestyle	48kg	Second
2019	Richard Figueroa	Selma	Freestyle	51kg	Champion
2019	Joey Cruz	Clovis North	Freestyle	51kg	Third

FILA WORLD CADET WORLD CHAMPIONSHIPS

Year	Wrestler	School	Style	Location	Place
2011	Nikko Reyes	Clovis West	Freestyle	Hungary	
2018	Richard Figueroa	Selma	Freestyle	48kg Zagreb, Croatia	Second
2019	Richard Figueroa	Selma	Freestyle	51kg Sofia, Bulgaria	D.N.P.

SECTION III
COLLEGIATE WRESTLING

UNIVERSITY DIVISION I

Before there were NCAA Division II and III, there was the NCAA College Division Created in 1963 for smaller college programs. In 1975, the NCAA split the college division into Division II and III
National Collegiate Athletic Association

NCAA DIVISION I

Year	Wrestler	Weight	Place	College	High School
1969	John Woods	167	2	Cal Poly	Redwood
1969	Ben Welch	167	5	Naval Academy	Bakersfield
1971	Lee Torres	142	3	Cal Poly	Roosevelt
1972	Larry Morgan	134	5	Cal Poly	East Bakersfield
1973	Allyn Cook	158	4	Cal Poly	Tulare Union
1976	Sythell Thompson	177	4	Cal Poly	Selma
1977	Franc Affentranger	134	3	Bakersfield	Shafter
1997	Flo Rocha	167	4	Bakersfield	Bakersfield
1978	Franc Affentranger	134	3	Bakersfield	Shafter
1979	Fred Bohna	UNL	Champion	UCLA	Clovis
1983	Al Gutierrez	118	8	Cal Poly	Redwood
1984	Jesse Reyes	142	Champion	Bakersfield	Bakersfield
1988	Darrel Nerove	142	7	Military Academy	Foothill
1992	Lorenzo Neal	275	7	Lemoore	Fresno State
1993	Harold Zinkin	134	5	Fresno State	Bullard
1994	Terry Watts	150	5	Fresno State	Caruthers
1995	DeWayne Zinkin	134	5	Fresno State	Bullard
1996	Coby Wright	126	4	Bakersfield	Bakersfield
1996	Yero Washington	134	6	Fresno State	Porterville
1997	Colby Wright	126	5	Bakersfield	Bakersfield
1997	Yero Washington	134	3	Fresno State	Bakersfield
1998	Alfonso Tucker	158	4	Fresno State	Hoover
1998	Stan Green	126	4	Fresno State	Hoover
1999	Stan Green	126	5	Fresno State	Clovis
1999	Adam Tirapelle	149	3	University of Illinois	Buchanan
2000	Adam Tirapelle	149	2	University of Illinois	Buchanan
2001	Adam Tirapelle	149	Champion	University of Illinois	Buchanan
2003	Alex Tirapelle	157	2	University of Illinois	Clovis
2003	Chris Pendelton	174	3	Oklahoma State	Lemoore
2003	Marcio Botellho	197	8	Fresno State	Lemoore
2004	Darrell Vasquez	133	4	Cal Poly	Bakersfield
2004	Alex Tirapelle	157	4	University of Illinois	Clovis
2004	Chris Pendleton	174	Champion	Oklahoma State	Lemoore
2005	Chris Pendleton	174	Champion	Oklahoma State	Lemoore
2006	Chad Mendes	125	6	Cal poly	Hanford
2006	Nathan Morgan	133	6	Oklahoma State	Bakersfield
2006	Jake Varner	184	2	Iowa State	Bakersfield
2007	Darrell Vasquez	133	5	Cal Poly	Bakersfield
2007	Nathan Morgan	141	4	Oklahoma State	Bakersfield
2007	Jake Varner	184	2	Iowa State	Bakersfield
2008	Chad Mendez	141	2	Cal Poly	Hanford
2008	Nathan Morgan	141	4	Oklahoma State	Bakersfield
2008	Jake Varner	184	2	Iowa State	Bakersfield
2009	Jake Varner	197	Champion	Iowa State	Bakersfield
2010	Jake Varner	197	Champion	Iowa State	Bakersfield
2011	Ryan Flores	285	2	American University	Buchanan

UNIVERSITY DIVISION I

Year	Wrestler	Weight	Place	College	High School
2011	Ricky Alcala	285	5	University of Indiana	Arvin
2012	Scott Sakaguchi	149	7	Oregon State	Clovis
2012	Ryan Flores	285	6	American University	Buchanan
2013	Scott Sakauchi	149	5	Oregon State	Clovis
2014	Bryce Hammond	174	8	Bakersfield	Bakersfield
2015	Isaiah Martinez	157	Champion	University of Illinois	Lemoore
2016	Isaiah Martinez	157	Champion	University of Illinois	Lemoore
2017	Isaiah Martinez	165	2	University of Illinois	Lemoore
2017	Nick Nevills	285	5	Penn State	Clovis
2018	Isaiah Martinez	165	2	University of Illinois	Lemoore
2018	Nick Nevills	285	7	Penn State	Clovis
2019	Hokit Josh	197	5	Fresno State	Clovis

Jake Varner – Bakersfield High School and Iowa State

Josh Hokit – Clovis High School and Fresno State University

NCAA DIVISION II

Year	Wrestler	Weight	Place	College	High School
1964	Roy Stuckey	123	3	Fresno	Madera
1965	Steve Johansen	115	Champion	Fresno	Madera
1965	Phillip Sullivan	177	Champion	Cal Poly	Tulare Western
1966	Steve Johansen	115	2	Fresno	Madera
1968	Sam King	123	3	Cal Poly	Madera
1968	John Woods	167	2	Cal Poly	Redwood
1969	Art Chavez	123	5	San Francisco State	South
1969	Jesse Flores	130	5	Cal Poly	East
1969	John Woods	167	Champion	Cal Poly	Redwood
1970	Lee Torres	150	2	Cal Poly	Roosevelt
1970	Richard Simmons	177	2	Cal Poly	South
1971	Larry Morgan	134	2	Cal Poly	East
1971	Allyn Cooke	150	5	Cal Poly	Tulare Union
1972	Ray Hernandez	118	2	San Francisco State	Corcoran
1972	Larry Morgan	134	2	Cal Poly	East
1972	Allyn Cooke	158	3	Cal Poly	Tulare Union
1972	Doug Stone	167	3	Humboldt State	West
1973	Larry Morgan *	134	Champion	Cal Poly	East
1973	Allyn Cooke	158	2	Cal Poly	Tulare Union
1973	Doug Stone	167	3	Humboldt State	West
1974	Dick Molina	118	4	CSU Bakersfield	South
1974	Sythell Thompson	177	3	Cal Poly	Selma
1974	Bill Van Worth	UNL	2	Humboldt State	South
1975	Dick Molina	118	3	CSU Bakersfield	South
1975	Mike Bull	190	4	CSU Bakersfield	South
1976	Dick Molina	118	3	CSU Bakersfield	South
1976	Flo Rocha	167	3	CSU Bakersfield	Bakersfield
1976	Mike Bull	190	Champion	CSU Bakersfield	South
1976	Bill Van Worth	UNL	Champion	CSU Bakersfield	South
1977	Franc Affentranger *	134	Champion	CSU Bakersfield	Shafter
1977	Rod Balch	150	2	CSU Bakersfield	Clovis
1977	Flo Rocha	167	Champion	CSU Bakersfield	Bakersfield
1977	Mike Anderson	177	2	CSU Bakersfield	Foothill
1977	Mike Bull	190	2	CSU Bakersfield	South
1978	Franc Affentranger	134	2	CSU Bakersfield	Shafter
1978	Rod Balch	142	5	CSU Bakersfield	Clovis
1978	Tom Gongora	150	4	CSU Bakersfield	Clovis
1978	Mike Johnson	190	4	CSU Bakersfield	Wasco
1979	Joe Lopez	134	6	CSU Bakersfield	Shafter
1979	Tom Gongora	142	Champion	CSU Bakersfield	Clovis
1980	Jessie Reyes	134	4	CSU Bakersfield	Bakersfield
1981	Alfredo Gonzalez	118	7	Sacramento State	Highland
1981	Steve Nickell	142	2	CSU Bakersfield	East
1982	Alfredo Gonzalez	118	8	Sacramento State	Highland
1982	Steve Nickell	142	2	CSU Bakersfield	East
1983	Jessie Reyes *	142	Champion	CSU Bakersfield	Bakersfield
1984	Jessie Reyes	142	Champion	CSU Bakersfield	Bakersfield
1987	Tony Ramirez	118	7	Chico State	Arvin
1987	Mike Dallas	126	2	CSU Bakersfield	Foothill
1988	Tony Ramirez	126	5	Chico State	Arvin

NCAA DIVISION II

Year	Wrestler	Weight	Place	College	High School
1992	Ken Fontes	275	8	Portland State	Clovis
2003	Pacifico Garcia	141	7	San Francisco State	Clovis
2005	Pacifico Garcia	149	Champion	San Francisco State	Clovis
2011	Jimmy Savala	141	7	Chardon State, NE	Clovis
2016	Brady Bersand	157	2	Cal Baptist	Clovis
2018	Natrelle Demison	149	7	Adams State	Bakersfield

* Most Outstanding Wrestler

NCAA DIVISION III

Year	Wrestler	Weight	College	Place	High School
2013	Gilbert Camacho	125	Wartburg College-IA	3	Washington Union
2014	Gilbert Camacho	125	Wartburg College-IA	5	Washington Union
2016	Arnulfo Olea	125	Wartburg College-IA	5	Exeter
2017	Arnulfo Olea	125	Wartburg College-IA	6	Exeter

NATIONAL ASSOCIATION OF INTERCOLLEGIATE ATHLETICS
NAIA WRESTLING CHAMPIOSHIPS

Year	Wrestler	Weight	College	Place	High School
2002	Ivan Sanchez	125	William Penn Univ. IA	5	Arvin
2003	Isaac Pumarejo	125	Menlo College	7	Kingsburg
2003	Jose Sanchez	133	Menlo College	4	Fresno High
2004	Cleo Johnson	125	Menlo College	4	Firebaugh
2005	Mariano Sanchez	197	Menlo College	8	Reedley
2005	Jacob Hallmark	285	Menlo College	4	Clovis
2006	Pablo Sanchez	133	Menlo College	8	Hoover
2006	Jason Moreno	133	Lindenwood Univ. MO	4	Firebaugh
2007	Jason Moreno	133	Lindenwood Univ. MO	5	Firebaugh
2007	Mariano Sanchez	184	Menlo College	5	Reedley
2007	Joe Espejo	285	Dickinson State Univ. ND	6	Stockdale
2007	Chaunney Coleman	285	William Penn Univ. IA	7	McLane
2009	Christian Martinez	141	Menlo College	7	Bakersfield
2010	Angel Olea	125	Dickinson State Univ. ND	4	Exeter
2010	Christian Martinez	141	Menlo College	4	Bakersfield
2011	AJ Valles	133	Embry Riddle Univ. AZ	5	Sanger
2014	Chris Padilla	125	Missouri Baptist	4	Clovis West
2014	Oscar Marin	125	York College, Nebraska	8	Bakersfield
2014	Michael Ruiz	133	Great Falls College, MT	5	Porterville
2014	AJ Valles	133	Simpson College	8	Sanger
2015	Michael Ruiz	133	Great Falls College, MT	2	Porterville
2016	Vicente Hernandez	133	Simpson College	6	Clovis
2017	Adrian Camposano	125	Campbellsville Univ. KY	2	Central
2017	Hunter Hodges	157	Southern Oregon Univ.	4	Bakersfield
2018	Julian Gaytan	125	Midland Nebraska Univ.	2	Clovis

MIDLANDS WRESTLING CHAMPIONSHIPS

Year	Weight	Wrestler	Place
1976	150	Larry Morgan	4
1977	134	Franc Affentranger	3
1979	HWT	Fred Bohna	2
1983	142	Jessie Reyes	2
1985	118	Pablo Saenz	3
1986	158	Jessie Reyes	6
1989	126	Mike Dallas	5
1994	190	Jassen Frohlich	3
1995	126	Colby Wright	6
1996	126	Colby Wright	Champion
1998	149	Adam Tirapelle	3
1998	165	Andy Varner	4
1999	149	Adam Tirapelle	3
1999	157	Nathan Vasquez	8
2002	157	Alex Tirapelle	5
2003	157	Alex Tirapelle	Champion
2004	125	Gabe Flores	7
2004	157	Alex Tirapelle	2
2005	149	Troy Tirapelle	7
2005	157	Alex Tirapelle	Champion
2006	184	Jake Varner	3
2009	197	Jake Varner	2
2010	197	Jake Varner	Champion
2010	285	Ryan Flores	3
2012	174	Bryce Hammond	7
2013	157	Isaiah Martinez	4
2014	157	Isaiah Martinez	Champion
2014	167	Adam Fierro	5
2014	184	Nikko Reyes	6
2015	165	Isaiah Martinez	Champion
2015	165	Adam Fierro	6
2016	165	Isaiah Martinez	Champion
2018	149	Khristian Olivas	7
2018	197	Josh Hokit	7
2018	285	AJ Nevills	4
2019	165	Izzak Olejnik	8
2019	285	Josh Hokit	6

NATIONAL WRESTLING COACHES ASSOCIATION ALL STAR CLASSIC
EAST-WEST

Year	Name	School	Weight	Result
1969	Woods, John	Cal Poly	167	Lost
1973	Morgan, Larry	Cal Poly	142	Lost
1973	Cook, Allyn	Cal Poly	158	Lost
1976	Bull, Mike	CSU Bakersfield	90	Lost
1978	Affentranger, Franc	CSU Bakersfield	134	Tie
1979	Bohna, Fred	UCLA	Unl.	Tie
1984	Reyes, Jessie	CSU Bakersfield	142	Won
1997	Wright, Colby	CSU Bakersfield	26	Lost
1997	Washington, Yero	Fresno State	134	Lost
2000	Tirapelle Adam	Illinois	149	Won
2003	Pendleton, Chris	Oklahoma State	174	Lost
2004	Pendleton, Chris	Oklahoma State	174	Won
2005	Pendleton, Chris	Oklahoma State	174	Won
2006	Vasquez, Darrell	Cal Poly	133	Won
2006	Tirapelle, Alex	Illinois	157	Won
2007	Morgan, Nathan	Oklahoma State	141	Lost
2008	Morgan, Nathan	Oklahoma State	141	Lost
2008	Varner, Jake	Penn State	184	Won
2009	Varner, Jake	Penn State	197	Won
2010	Varner, Jake	Penn State	197	Won
2011	Flores, Ryan	American University	285	Won
2017	Nevills, Nick	Penn State	285	Won

Jake Varner – Bakersfield High School

SECTION IV
NATIONAL AND INTERNATIONAL WRESTLING

USA WRESTLING SENIOR NATIONAL FREESTYLE AND GRECO ROMAN CHAMPIONSHIPS

Year	Wrestler	Weight	Place	Location
1981	Tim Vanni	105.5	2	Cedar Falls. Iowa
1983	Tim Vanni	105.5	2	Madison, Wisconsin
1984	Tim Vanni	105.5	4	Norman, Oklahoma
1985	Tim Vanni	105.5	Champion	Lock Haven, Pennsylvania
1985	Jessie Reyes	149.5	6	Lock Haven, Pennsylvania
1986	Tim Vanni	105.5	2	Las Vegas, Nevada
1987	Tim Vanni	105.5	2	Las Vegas, Nevada
1988	Tim Vanni	105.5	Champion	Reno, Nevada
1988	Pablo Saenz	114.5	6	Reno, Nevada
1989	Tim Vanni	105.5	Champion	Topeka, Kansas
1990	Jessie Reyes	149.5	5	Las Vegas, Nevada
1991	Tim Vanni	105.5	Champion	Las Vegas, Nevada
1993	Tim Vanni	105.5	2	Las Vegas, Nevada
1994	Tim Vanni	105.5	Champion	Las Vegas, Nevada
1995	Tim Vanni	105.5	2	Las Vegas, Nevada
1995	Andy Munoz	105.5	6	Las Vegas, Nevada
1996	Tim Vanni	105.5	3	Las Vegas, Nevada
1997	Yero Washington	127.5	4	Las Vegas, Nevada
1998	Yero Washington	127.5	2	Las Vegas, Nevada
1999	Yero Washington	132	4	Las Vegas, Nevada
2000	Yero Washington	132	4	Las Vegas, Nevada
2002	Adam Tirapelle	145	7	Las Vegas, Nevada
2003	Yero Washington	132	4	Las Vegas, Nevada
2003	Clint Walbeck	HWT	7	Las Vegas, Nevada
2004	Yero Washington	132	5	Las Vegas, Nevada
2007	Chris Pendleton	185	4	Las Vegas, Nevada
2007	Jake Varner	185	8	Las Vegas, Nevada
2008	Jake Varner	185	7	Las Vegas, Nevada
2009	Jake Varner	211.5	Champion	Las Vegas, Nevada
2010	Chris Pendleton	185	7	Cleveland, Ohio
2010	Jake Varner	211.5	2	Cleveland, Ohio
2011	Jake Varner	211.5	Champion	Las Vegas, Nevada
2013	Chris Pendleton	211.5	2	Las Vegas, Nevada
2014	Jake Varner	211.5	Champion	Las Vegas, Nevada
2015	Jake Varner	211.5	2	Las Vegas, Nevada
2017	Nikko Reyes	97kg	4	Las Vegas, Nevada
2018	Nikko Reyes	92kg-202	5	Las Vegas, Nevada
2018	Jake Varner	125kg-285	2	Las Vegas, Nevada
2018	Isaiah Martinez	74kg-163	Champion	Las Vegas, Nevada
2019	Isaiah Martinez	74 kg	Champion	Las Vegas, Nevada
2019	Nick Nevills	125 kg	4	Fort Worth, Texas

USA WRESTLING SENIOR NATIONAL GRECO ROMAN CHAMPIONSHIPS

Year	Wrestler	Weight	Place	Location
1986	Tim Vanni	105.5	2	Las Vegas, Nevada
1987	Tim Vanni	105.5	4	Las Vegas, Nevada
1991	John Tripp*	180.5	5	Las Vegas, Nevada

* Most Falls Award

AAU NATIONAL FREESTYLE AND GRECO ROMAN CHAMPIONSHIPS

Year	Wrestler	Weight	Place	Location
Freestyle				
1968	Art Chavez	114.5	Champion	Lincoln, Nebraska
1972	Floyd Winter	198	3	
1973	Larry Morgan	149.5	2	Cleveland, Ohio
1974	Larry Morgan	149.5	2	Long Beach, California
1975	Larry Morgan	149.5	3	Bloomington, Indiana
1975	Allyn Cook	163	6	Bloomington, Indiana
1976	Larry Morgan	149.5	2	Cleveland, Ohio
1977	Larry Morgan	149.5	2	Ames, Iowa
1977	Fred Bohna	220	3	Ames, Iowa
1981	Tim Vanni	105.5	2	Tempe, Arizona
1981	Rey Martinez	180.5	4	Tempe, Arizona
1982	Tim Vanni	105.5	4	Lincoln, Nebraska
1982	Al Gutierrez	114.5	4	Lincoln, Nebraska
1982	Jessie Reyes	149.5	6	Lincoln, Nebraska
Greco Roman				
1967	Roy Heath	114.5	3	Lincoln, Nebraska
1968	Art Chavez	114.5	Champion	Lincoln, Nebraska
1971	Art Chavez	136.5	3	San Diego, California
1974	Guy Campbell**	149.5	Champion	Omaha, Nebraska
1975	Bill Van Worth	Hwt.	2	Berkley, California
1976	Larry Morgan	149.5	Champion	Cleveland, Ohio

USWF NATIONAL FREESTYLE AND GRECO ROMAN CHAMPIONSHIPS

Year	Wrestler	Weight	Place	Location
Freestyle				
1975	Larry Morgan	149.5	2	Iowa City, Iowa
1976	Larry Morgan*	149.5	Champion	Madison, Wisconsin
1977	Larry Morgan	149.5	Champion	Eugene, Oregon
1977	Mike Anderson	180.5	5	Eugene, Oregon
1977	Fred Bohna	220	Champion	Eugene, Oregon
1981	Rey Martinez	180.5	Champion	Cedar Falls, Iowa
1982	Tim Vanni	105.5	4	Cedar Falls, Iowa
1982	Rey Martinez	180.5	4	Cedar Falls, Iowa
Greco Roman				
1970	Larry Little	136.5	3	Fullerton, California
1975	Fred Bohna	198	2	Iowa City, Iowa
1976	Larry Morgan	149.5	Champion	Cleveland, Ohio

NATIONAL YMCA CHAMPIONSHIPS

Year	Wrestler	Weight	Style	Place	Location
1972	Larry Morgan	149.5	Freestyle	2	Las Vegas, Nevada
1972	Larry Morgan	149.5	Greco Roman	2	Las Vegas, Nevada

GOODWILL GAMES

Year	Wrestler	Weight	Style	Place	Location
1994	Tim Vanni	105.5	Freestyle	D.N.P.	St. Petersburg, Russia

FILA WORLD UNIVERSITY WORLD GAMES

Year	Wrestler	Weight	Style	Place	Location
2005	Chris Pendleton	185	Freestyle	10	Izmir, Turkey

**Most Outstanding Wrestler and Most Falls Awards
*Most Outstanding Wrestler Award

OYLMPIC GAMES

Year	Wrestler	Weight	Style	Place	Location
1968	Art Chavez	114.5	Greco Roman	Medical*	Mexico City, Mexico
1976	Larry Morgan	149.5	Freestyle	Alternate	Montreal, Canada
1988	Tim Vanni	105.5	Freestyle	Fourth	Soul, Korea
1992	Tim Vanni	105.5	Freestyle	Fifth	Barcelona, Spain
1996	Tim Vanni	105.5	Freestyle	Alternate	Atlanta, Georgia
2012	Jake Varner	213.5	Freestyle	Champion	London, England

*Failed the medical examination: bleeding stomach uclcers

WORLD CHAMPIONSHIPS

Year	Wrestler	Weight	Style	Place	Location
1969	Art Chavez	114.5	Greco Roman	7	Mar Del Plata, Argentina
1969	Rocky Rasley	Hwt.	Freestyle	5	Mar Del Plata, Argentina
1973	Larry Morgan	136.5	Freestyle	4	Tehran, Iran
1974	Joe Nigos	185.5	Greco Roman	D.N.P.	Katowice, Poland
1975	Bill Van Worth	Hwt.	Greco Roman	6	Minsk, Russia
1982	Tim Vanni	105.5	Freestyle	6	Edmonton, Canada
1985	Tim Vanni	105.5	Freestyle	10	Budapest, Hungary
1986	Tim Vanni	105.5	Freestyle	6	Budapest, Hungary
1987	Tim Vanni	105.5	Freestyle	5	Claremont, France
1989	Tim Vanni	105.5	Freestyle	5	Martigny, Switzerland
1991	Tim Vanni	105.5	Freestyle	D.N.P.	Varna, Bulgaria
1994	Tim Vanni	105.5	Freestyle	9	Instanbul, Turkey
2009	Jake Varner	211.5	Freestyle	9	Herring, Denmark
2011	Jake Varner	211.5	Freestyle	3	Instanbul, Turkey
2014	Jake Varner	213.5	Freestyle	D.N.P.	Tashkent, Uzbekistan

WORLD CUP

Year	Wrestler	Weight	Style	Place	Location
1979	Fred Bohna	220	Freestyle	2	?
1986	Tim Vanni	105.5	Freestyle	3	Toledo, Ohio
1988	Tim Vanni	105.5	Freestyle	3	Toledo, Ohio
1989	Tim Vanni	105.5	Freestyle	4	Toledo, Ohio
1990	Tim Vanni	105.5	Freestyle	2	Toledo, Ohio
1991	Tim Vanni	105.5	Freestyle	2	Toledo, Ohio
1994	Tim Vanni	105.5	Freestyle	3	Chattanooga, TN
1999	Yero Washington	125.5	Freestyle		?
2015	Jake Varner	97Kg	Freestyle		Los Angles, California
2016	Jake Varner	125Kg	Freestyle		Los Angles, California
2019	Isaiah Martinez	74Kg	Freestyle		Iowa City, Iowa

PAN-AMERICAN GAMES

Year	Wrestler	Weight	Style	Place	Location
1975	Bill Van Worth	Hwt.	Greco Roman	Champion	Mexico City, Mexico
1977	Fred Bohna	220	Freestyle	Champion	?
1987	Tim Vanni	105.5	Freestyle	2	Indianapolis, Indiana
1991	Tim Vanni	105.5	Freestyle	3	Havana, Cuba
1992	Tim Vanni	105.5	Freestyle	2	Vancouver, Canada
1995	Tim Vanni	105.5	Freestyle	3	Mar Del Plato, Argentina
2011	Jake Varner	211.5	Freestyle	Champion	Guadalajara, Mexico

FILA JUNIOR NATIONALS
20 AND UNDER
ESPOIR
UWW

Year	Wrestler	Weight	Style	Place	School
1988	Tamez, Anthony	114.5	Freestyle	5	Clovis
1988	Ravalin, Rick	198	Freestyle	5	Selma – Cal Poly
1990	Lagarreta, Eric		Freestyle	3	Selma
1990	Patton, Dereck	149.5	Freestyle	5	Arvin
1990	Neal, Lorenzo	286	Freestyle	Champion	Lemoore – Fresno State
1990	Neal, Lorenzo	286	Greco	Champion	Lemoore – Fresno State
1992	Aguirre, Jim	125.5	Freestyle	2	Clovis – Stanford
1992	Salven, Josh	286	Freestyle	2	Clovis West
1992	Salven, Josh	286	Greco	4	Clovis West
1993	Aguirre, Jim	136.5	Freestyle	2	Clovis - Stanford
1993	Moland, David	136.5	Freestyle	6	Golden West
1993	Mast, Chad	286	Freestyle	5	Clovis
1997	Johnson, Cleo	108	Freestyle	3	Firebaugh
1997	Banuelos, Antonio	123.5	Freestyle	8	Clovis West
1997	Banuelos, Antonio	123.5	Greco	5	Clovis West
1997	Tirapelle, Adam	143	Freestyle	Champion	Buchanan – Illinois
1997	Davis, Jonte	143	Freestyle	5	Edison – Fresno State
1997	Varner, Andy	167	Freestyle	4	Bakersfield - CSUB
1997	Nelms, Ian	167	Freestyle	7	Mt. Whitney - CSUB
1999	Martinez, Ben	127.7	Greco	2	Tulare – Fresno State
1999	Martinez, Ben	127.7	Freestyle	Champion	Tulare – Fresno State
1999	Nelms, Ian	167.5	Greco	3	Mt. Whitney – CSUB
1999	Nelms, Ian	167.5	Freestyle	7	Mt. Whitney – CSUB
2003	Roberts, David	145.5	Freestyle	8	Clovis West – Cal Poly
2005	Varner, Jake	185	Freestyle	2	Bakersfield – Iowa State
2007	Espericueta, Lucas	154.25	Freestyle	6	Shafter – Stanford
2008	Nacita, Elijah	145	Freestyle	5	Bakersfield – CSUB
2010	Rocha, Brandon	132	Freestyle	8	Lemoore – Cal Poly
2010	Sakaguchi, Scott	154.75	Freestyle	7	Clovis – Oregon State
2012	Martinez, Isaiah	154	Freestyle	Champion	Lemoore – Illinois
2012	Martinez, Isaiah	154	Greco	All American	Lemoore - Illinois
2012	Fierro, Adam	154	Freestyle	5	Bakersfield – CSUB
2012	Hammond, Bryce	174	Freestyle	7	Bakersfield – CSUB
2013	Box, Timmy	145.5	Freestyle	5	Bakersfield – CSUB
2013	Box, Timmy	145.5	Greco	5	Bakersfield – CSUB
2013	Fierro, Adam	163	Freestyle	8	Bakersfield – CSUB
2013	Fierro, Adam	163	Greco	4	Bakersfield – CSUB
2014	Martinez, Isaiah	163	Freestyle	2	Lemoore – Illinois
2014	Reyes, Nikko	185	Freestyle	4	Clovis West – Illinois
2016	Hokit, Josh	185	Freestyle	4	Clovis – Fresno State
2017	Martinez, Isaiah	163	Freestyle	1	Lemoore – Illinois
2018	Belshay, Cade	92kg	Freestyle	8	Buchanan – Arizona St.
2018	Nevills, Seth	125kg	Freestyle	4	Clovis – Penn State

FILA JUNIORS NATIONALS

Year	Wrestler	Weight	Style	Place	School
2019	Nevills, Seth	125kg	Freestyle	2	Clovis – Penn State

U-23 Worlds

Year	Wrestler	Weight	Style	Place	School
2017	Martinez, Isaiah Bydgoszcz, Poland	163	Freestyle	5	Lemoore – Illinois

UWW
Junior Pan-American Championships

Year	Wrestler	Weight	Style	Place	School
2019	Nevills, Seth Guatemala, City, Guatemala	125kg	Freestyle	1	Clovis – Penn State

TBILISI RUSSIA
Known as the toughest tournament in the world

Year	Wrestler	Weight	Style	Place
1974	Morgan, Larry	136.5	Freestyle	
1980	Bohna, Fred	220	Freestyle	
1982	Vanni, Tim	105.5	Freestyle	6
1983	Vanni, Tim	105.5	Freestyle	
1985	Reyes, Jessie	149.5	Freestyle	
1990	Vanni, Tim	105.5	Freestyle	Bronze

UNITED STATES OLYMPIC FESTIVAL

Year	Wrestler	Weight	Style	Place	Location
1983	Vanni, Tim	105.5	Freestyle	Second	Colorado Springs, CO
1985	Vanni, Tim	105.5	Freestyle	Champion	Baton Rouge, LA.
1987	Vanni, Tim	105.5	Freestyle	Champion	Raleigh Durham, NC
1989	Vanni, Tim	105.5	Freestyle	Champion	Stillwater, OK

USA UNIVERSITY NATIONALS

USA WRESTLING NATIONAL CHAMPIONSHIPS
UNIVERSITY NATIONALS
Freestyle – Greco-Roman

Year	Wrestler	Weight	Style	Place	College	High School
	Zinkin, Harold		Freestyle	2	Fresno State	Bullard
1992	Sordi, Robbi	125.5	Freestyle	6	Fresno State	Madera
1992	Quintana, Gary	136.5	Freestyle	3	Fresno State	Selma
1996	Washington, Yero	125	Freestyle	6	Fresno State	Porterville
1997	Equivel, Benny	127.5	Greco	6		Porterville
1998	Vasquez, Nathan	152	Greco	7	CSUB	Bakersfield
1999	Varner, Andy	167	Freestyle	4	CSUB	Bakersfield
1999	Nelms, Ian	167	Freestyle	7	CSUB	Mt. Whitney
2000	Nelms, Ian	167	Freestyle	8	CSUB	Mt. Whitney
2002	Pendleton, Chris	185	Freestyle	2	Oklahoma State	Lemoore
2003	Hafemeister, Sven	163	Greco	8	Columbia	Lemoore
2005	Pendleton, Chris	185	Freestyle	Champion	Oklahoma State	Lemoore
2006	Varner, Jake	185	Freestyle	3	Iowa State	Bakersfield
2007	Maffia, Broc	264.5	Greco	4	UC Davis	Tulare Western
2010	Lomas, Frank	121	Freestyle	4	CSUB	Bakersfield
2010	West, Stephen	174	Freestyle	7	Columbia	Buchanan
2016	Martinez, Isaiah	74kg	Freestyle	Champion	Illinois	Lemoore
2016	Reyes, Nikko	213	Freestyle	2	Northern Colorado	Clovis West
2017	Martinez, Isaiah	163	Freestyle	Champion	Illinois	Lemoore

Jake Varner – Bakersfield High School and Iowa State

Isaiah Martinez – Lemoore High and University of Illinois

SECTION V
KERN COUNTY COACHING STAFFS
COACH/WRESTLERS PROFILES

Arvin High School

Year	League Record	Season	Head Coach	Assistant Coaches
1958	NA	NA	Olan Polite	
1959	1-6	NA	Olan Polite	
1960	3-5	6-4	Don Lukehart	
1961	2-6	NA	Don Lukehart	
1962	0-7	NA	John Bunton	
1963	NA	NA	John Bunton	
1964	NA	NA	John Bunton	Duane Damron
1965	NA	NA	John Burton	Duane Damron
1966	8-1	NA	John Burton	Duane Damron, Jim Young
1967	NA	NA	Jim Young	Mr. Smith
1968	NA	NA	Jim Young	
1969	NA	NA	Richard Fisher	Bill Smith
1970	NA	NA	Richard Fisher	Gordon Shuppert
1971	NA	NA	Jose Gomez	Bill Satterfield
1972	6-0	NA	Phil Bradfield	Bill Shanholtzer
1973	NA	NA	Phil Bradfield	Dwight Denney
1974	NA	NA	Phil Bradfield	A J Vasquez
1975	NA	NA	A J Vasquez	Ruben Ramirez
1976	NA	NA	Ruben Ramirez	Ken Myers
1977	NA	NA	Ruben Ramirez	Frank Borjas
1978	NA	NA	Ruben Ramirez	Frank Borjas
1979	NA	NA	Ruben Ramirez	Frank Borjas
1980	NA	NA	Rubin Ramirez	
1981	4-3	10-4	Rubin Ramirez	Tom Gault, Gil Trevino
1982	4-3	NA	Ruben Ramirez	Mike Spensko, Gil Trevino
1983	5-2	NA	Ruben Ramirez	Gil Trevino, Eddie Morales
1984	7-0	NA	Rubin Ramirez	Gil Trevino, Leon Robinson
1985	6-1	NA	Rubin Ramirez	Gil Trevino, Leon Robinson, Ric Cox
1986	4-3	NA	Rubin Ramirez	George White, Leon Robinson, Gil Trevino
1987	NA	NA	Rubin Ramirez	George White, Leon Robinson, Gil Trevino, Mike Smithee
1988	7-0	NA	Rubin Ramirez	George White, Mike Smithee
1989	4-3	NA	Rubin Ramirez	George White, Jose Morales, Mike Smithee
1990	1-6	NA	Rubin Ramirez	George White, Jose Morales, Mike Smithee
1991	NA	NA	Rubin Ramirez	George White, Jose Morales, Mike Smithee
1992	NA	NA	Rubin Ramirez	George White, Jose Morales, Mike Smithee
1993	NA	NA	Rubin Ramirez	George White, Jose Morales, Steve Scarey, Mike Leonard
1994	1-6	NA	Rubin Ramirez	Jose Morales
1995	1-3	6-5	Jack Serros	Jose Marin
1996	1-3	NA	Jack Serros	Jose Marin

Arvin High School

Year	League Record	Season	Head Coach	Assistant Coaches
1997	NA	NA	Jack Serros	Jose Marin
1998	NA	NA	Jack Serros	Jose Marin
1999	NA	NA	Jack Serros	Milo Lavario
2000	NA	NA	Jack Serros	Miguel Sanchez
2001	2-3	NA	Jack Serros	Miguel Sanchez
2002	NA	NA	Jack Serros	Miguel Sanchez
2003	NA	NA	David Manriquez	Chris Carlos, Jenard Arellano, Anthony Adame
2004	0-4	2-5	Chris Carlos	Miguel Sanchez, Jose Marin
2005	4-1	10-5	Miguel Sanchez	James Seiser, Chris Alfonso, Ivan Sanchez, Isaias Manriquez
2006	4-1	9-4	Miguel Sanchez	Chris Alfonso, Ivan Sanchez, Isaias Manriquez
2007	4-1	6-2	Miguel Sanchez	Isaias Manriquez, Chris Alfonso, Ivan Sanchez, Aaron Garza
2008	3-2	3-2	Miguel Sanchez	Chris Alfonso, Ivan Sanchez, Aaron Garza
2009	3-2	3-2	Raymond Menchaca	Francisco Tomayo, Jose Marin
2010	1-4	1-4	Raymond Menchaca	Jose Tamayo, Jose Marin, Eddie Machado
2011	0-5	0-5	Raymond Menchaca	Edgar Moreno, Eddie Machado, Mike Machado
2012	2-3	2-3	Raymond Menchaca	Eddie Machado, Juan Gutierrez,
2013	1-5	1-5	Abel Varela	Mike Karr, Raymond Menchaca
2014	2-4	2-6	Raymond Menchaca	Jose Tamayo, Richard Beltran, Isai Mirales
2015	3-3	3-3	Raymond Menchaca	Jose Tamayo, Isai Mirales
2016	2-4	3-4	Raymond Menchaca	Jose Tamayo, Francisco Tamayo
2017	1-5	1-6	Raymond Menchaca	Jose Tamayo, Joshlyn Horton-Girls
2018	1-5	1-5	Raymond Menchaca	Jose Tamayo, Alicia Llanes-Girls
2019	4-1	5-2	Joes Marin	J J Ugues
2020	1-4	1-4	Miguel Sanchez	J J Ugues, Alicia Llanes-Girls

Bakersfield Christian High School

Year	League Record	Season	Head Coach	Assistant Coaches
2007	0-5	0-5	Daniel Chapman	Gary Chapman
2008	2-4	3-4	Daniel Chapman	Gary Chapman, Matt Machado, Nathan Hodges
2009	3-2	5-2	Gary Chapman	Daniel Chapman, Jeff Davis, Matt Machado
2010	0-5	0-5	Paul Garcia	Daniel Alejandro
2011	1-4	1-4	Paul Garcia	Daniel Alejandro, Blake Henderson
2012	0-5	0-5	Paul Garcia	
2013	0-6	0-6	Paul Garcia (no varsity team)	Richard Tarkington, Richard Christensen
2014	0-6	0-6	Paul Garcia	Ryan Meloche, Carlos Hernandez, Jose Espinoza
2015	0-6	0-6	Mario Gomez	Gerry Abas, Jake Fulce
2016	0-5	0-5	Mario Gomez	Jake Fulce, Esai Gomez
2017	3-3	3-3	Mario Gomez	Esai Gomez, John Epperly
2018	1-6	1-6	Mario Gomez	Esai Gomez
2019	NA	NA	Randy Raymond	
2020	0-0	0-0	Scott Joseph	James Fulce, Ethan Myers

Bakersfield High School

Year	League Record	Season	Head Coach	Assistant Coaches
1957	NA	5-1	Paul Briggs	
1958	NA	6-0	Paul Briggs	
1959	8-1-1	NA	Olan Polite	Paul Briggs
1960	4-4	NA	Olan polite	
1961	6-2	9-5	Olan Polite	
1962	5-2	12-2	Olan Polite	
1963	6-4	10-5	Olan Polite	Don Cornett
1964	7-3	11-4	Olan Polite	Don Cornett, Pat Mitchell
1965	8-1-1	12-1-1	Olan Polite	Don Cornett, Nick Graham
1966	5-3	10-3	Olan Polite	Nick Graham
1967	4-4	4-4	Olan Polite	Mike Meek
1968	8-2	11-2	Olan Polite	Mike Meek
1969	8-2	13-2	Olan Polite	Joe McDonald
1970	10-0	12-0	Olan Polite	Willard Roberson
1971	8-2	9-2	Olan Polite	Willie Sandoval
1972	11-1	12-1	Olan Polite	Willie Sandoval
1973	11-1	NA	Olan Polite	Willie Sandoval
1974	4-2	NA	Olan Polite	Willie Sandoval
1975	7-5	9-5	Olan Polite	Steve Varner, Charles Plummer
1976	4-2	9-6	Olan Polite	Steve Varner, Charles Plummer
1977	6-0	8-2	Steve Varner	Charles Plummer
1978	5-1	NA	Steve Varner	Rick Varner
1979	5-1	NA	Steve Varner	Rick Varner
1980	7-0	NA	Steve Varner	Tom Williams
1981	6-1	NA	Steve Varner	Joe Smart
1982	7-0	NA	Steve Varner	Joe Smart
1983	3-4	NA	Jim Seay	Tony Ovalle
1984	4-3	NA	Steve Varner	Tony Ovalle
1985	4-3	NA	Steve Varner	Tony Ovalle
1986	2-5	NA	Steve Varner	David East
1987	NA	NA	Steve Varner	David East
1988	6-1	NA	David East	Bob Thisle, Richard Simmons
1989	7-0	NA	David East	Mike Taylor, Richard Simmon
1990	7-0	NA	David East	Paul Olejnik, Craig Oliver, Richard Simmons
1991	6-0	NA	David East	Paul Olejnik, Craig Oliver, Richard Simmons
1992	5-1	NA	David East	Paul Olejnik, Craig Oliver, Richard Simmons
1993	7-0	NA	David East	Craig Noble, Jack Serros, Mel East
1994	7-0	NA	David East	Jack Serros, Craig Noble, Joe Lopeteguy
1995	4-0	14-1	David East	Craig Noble, Joe Lopeteguy, Larry Vasquez Sr.

Bakersfield High School

Year	League Record	Season	Head Coach	Assistant Coaches
1996	4-0	14-0	David East	Craig Noble, Joe Lopeteguy, Mike Battistoni, Larry Vasquez Sr
1997	4-0	13-1	David East	Kenny Wright, Mike Battistoni, Mel East
1998	4-0	5-2	David East	Kenny Wright, Richard Simmons, Mel East, Dan Corpstein
1999	4-0	NA	David East	Kenny Wright, Mel East, Mike Battistoni, Larry Vasquez, Joe Lopeteguy, Richard Simmons
2000	4-0	14-0	David East	Ben Sherley, Larry Vasquez Jr., Mike Battistoni, Larry Vasquez Sr.
2001	4-0	12-0	David East	Ben Sherley, Larry Morgan, Larry Vasquez Jr., Andy Varner, Nathan Vasquez, Larry Vasquez Sr., Steve Varner
2002	4-0	5-0	David East	Andy Varner, Nathan Vasquez, Larry Morgan, Mel East, Sean Crosswhite, Larry Vasquez Jr., Steve Varner
2003	5-1	5-1	Andy Varner	Fidel Herrera, Ray Hammond, Kenny Wright, Steve Varner, Larry Morgan, Kirk Moore
2004	5-0	5-0	Andy Varner	Mel East, Kenny Wright, Larry Morgan, Steve Varner, Ray Hammond, Danny Castaneda, Fidel Herrera
2005	4-0	4-0	Andy Varner	Larry Morgan, Mel East, Ray Hammond, Kenny Wright, Danny Castaneda, Steve Varner, Fidel Herrera, Craig Schoene
2006	3-1	7-2	Andy Varner	Kenny Wright, Craig Schoene, Larry Morgan, Ray Hammond, Steve Varner, Fidel Herrera
2007	5-0	6-0	Andy Varner	Steve Varner, Craig Schoene, Mel East, Brett Clark, Fidel Herrera, Darryl Pope, Don Delfin, Ray Hammond
2008	5-0	6-1	Andy Varner	Steve Varner, Craig Schoene, Mel East, Drew East, Ray Hammond, Fidel Herrera, Darryl Pope, Jordan Danz
2009	5-0	11-0	Andy Varner	Steve Varner, Ray Hammond, Craig Schoene, Eric Parker, Darryl Pope, Fidel Herrera, Darrell Vasquez, Grant Neuman, Anthony Tobin

Bakersfield High School

Year	League Record	Season	Head Coach	Assistant Coaches
2010	5-0	9-2	Andy Varner	Steve Varner, Craig Schoene, Eric Parker, Ray Hammond, Darrell Vasquez, Darryl Pope, Grant Neuman, Fidel Herrera
2011	5-0	6-0	Andy Varner	Steve Varner, Mel East, Fidel Herrera, Darryl Pope, Todd Bassett, Eric Parker, Grant Neuman
2012	5-0	6-0	Andy Varner	Matt Olejnik, Fidel Herrera, Darryl Pope, Steve Varner, Ray Hammond, Grant Neuman, Todd Bassett
2013	5-0	6-0	Andy Varner	Matt Olejnik, Steve Varner, Darryl Pope, Ray Hammond, Anthony Box, Frank Lomas, Todd Bassett, Craig Schoene
2014	5-0	10-1	Andy Varner, Anthony Box	Frank Lomas, Justin Golding, Jeff Annis, Steve Varner
2015	5-0	9-0	Andy Varner, Anthony Box	Steve Varner, Jeff Annis, Frank Lomas, Justin Golding
2016	4-0	9-0	Andy Varner, Frank Lomas	Anthony Box, Jeff Annis, Steve Varner, Matt Olejnik, Joey Lopetguy
2017	5-0	8-1	Andy Varner, Frank Lomas	Adam Cole, Jeff Annis, Matt Olejnik, Adam Ferro, Todd Bassett, Jose Marin, Anthony Box
2018	5-0	6-0	Andy Varner, Frank Lomas	Jeff Annis, Rick Priest, Genard Valdez, Matt Olejnik, Todd Bassett
2019	4-1	5-2	Andy Varner, Frank Lomas	Jeff Annis, Genard Valdez, Adam Cole, Ray Hammond
2020	1-0	7-3	Andy Varner	Frank Lomas, Matt Olejnik, DJ Weimer, Ray Hammond

Centennial High School

Year	League Record	Season	Head Coach	Assistant Coaches
1994	NA	NA	Paul Olejnik	Claude Bradford
1995	NA	NA	Paul Olejnik	Claude Bradford, John Burns, Manuel Machado
1996	5-0	11-5	Paul Olejnik	Claude Bradford, John Burns, John Branch, Manuel Machado
1997	3-1	NA	Paul Olejnik	Claude Bradford, John Burns, John Branch
1998	4-0	5-4	Paul Olejnik	Gary Chapman, Derek Scott, John Burns
1999	4-0	7-4	Paul Olejnik	Derek Scott, Gary Chapman, John Burns, Jason Froehlich
2000	4-0	8-2	Paul Olejnik	Derek Scott, Gary Chapman, John Burns, Jason Froehlich
2001	NA	NA	Paul Olejnik	Derek Scott, Gary Chapman, John Burns, Jason Froehlich
2002	4-0	6-6	Paul Olejnik	Tom Olejnik, John Archuletta, Gary Chapman
2003	3-0-1	4-0-1	Mike Hicks	Glen Smith
2004	3-1	4-2	Mike Hicks	Greg Horton, Lawrence, Jason Mason, Brian Strain
2005	4-1	20-1	Mike Hicks	John Burns, Bob Thisle, Jason Mesa
2006	4-1	11-1	Mike Hicks	John Burns, Bob Thisle, Grant Newman, Juan Villalobos, Andy Sheffield, Jason Mesa
2007	5-0	6-0	Mike Hicks	Bob Thisle, Andy Sheffield, Jason Mesa, Jeff Heberle
2008	5-1	12-1	Mike Hicks	Bob Thisle, Andy Sheffield, Jeff Heberle, Tom Cierley
2009	5-1	10-2	Mike Hicks	Bob Thisle, Andy Sheffield, Jeremy Doyle, John Musquez
2010	4-2	6-2	Mike Hicks	Andy Sheffield, Carson McAtee, Jason Armijo, Pedro Quinterro, Jeremy Doyle
2011	3-2	3-2	Mike Hicks	Ernie Ciaccio, Pedro Quinterro, Jeremy Doyle, David Morgan
2012	3-2	7-3	Mike Hicks	Sean Crosswhite, David Morgan, Billy Ballard
2013	3-2	3-2	Sean Crosswhite	Ken Gabin
2014	2-3	6-6	Sean Crosswhite	Ken Gabin, Stewart Rojas, Nathan Poteet
2015	2-2	2-2	Ken Gabin Shawn Crosswhite	Jose Mendoza, Brian Lujan Nick Sotelo
2016	2-2	5-8	Ken Gabin	Brian Lujan, Nick Sotelo, Jose Mendoza
2017	3-2	5-4	Ken Gabin	Brian Lujan, Nick Sotelo, Paul Olejnik, Mike Olejnik, Dante Borradori, Matt Deason
2018	3-2	3-2	Ken Gabin	Brian Lujan, Paul Olejnik, Nick Stelo, Matt Deason
2019	3-2	4-2	Ken Gabin	Nick Sotello, Paul Olejnik, Matt Deason
2020	1-0	7-3	Ken Gabin	Billy Pitcher, Paul Olejnik, Michael Martinez

Cesar Chavez High School

Year	League Record	Season	Head Coach	Assistant Coaches
2003	NA	NA	Jesse Ortega	
2004	NA	NA	Jesse Ortega	
2005	NA	NA	Eugene Walker	Jesse Ortega
2006	NA	NA	Eugene Walker	Ian Tablit
2007	3-3	4-4	Ian Tablit	Mike Cardenas
2008	3-3	17-6	Ian Tablit	Mike Cardenas
2009	2-4	3-4	Brett Clark	Ian Tablit, Andrew Powell, Brenda Reed
2010	1-5	2-5	Brett Clark	Ian Tablet, Andrew Powell, Leonard Castillo, Brenda Reed
2011	0-8	0-8	Manuel Vasquez	Andrew Powell, Ian Tablit
2012	2-6	2-6	Manuel Vasquez	Noel Gomez, Andrew Powell
2013	3-3	3-3	Ernesto Gonzales	Ivan Lara, John Alcala
2014	4-2	4-2	Ernesto Gonzales	Ivan Lara, John Alcala
2015	4-2	13-8	Ernesto Gonzales	Ivan Lara
2016	5-1	7-1	Jesse Ortega	Jason Becerra, Vincent Escobedo, Johnny Rodriguez, Omar Cisneros
2017	3-3	4-3	Jesse Ortega	Jason Becerra, Vincent Escobedo
2018	4-2	4-3	Jesse Ortega	Ernie Macias, Jimmy Macias, Johnny Rodriguez, Vincent Escobedo
2019	3-3	3-4	Jesse Ortega	Ernie Macias, Jimmy Macias
2020	4-1	5-1	Roman Salcedo	Jesse Ortega, Ernie Macias, Jimmy Macias

Delano High School

Year	League Record	Season	Head Coach	Assistant Coaches
1958	1-9	NA	Ralph Allen	
1959	0-7	NA	Ralph Allen	
1960	2-5	NA	Ralph Allen	
1961	NA	NA	Ralph Allen	
1962	NA	NA	Ralph Allen	
1963	NA	NA	Ralph Allen	Jack Mason
1964	NA	NA	Ralph Allen	Phillip Tincher
1965	NA	NA	Ralph Allen	Ted Hemmock
1966	NA	2-11-1	Ralph Allen	Harold Reimer
1967	NA	NA	James Macres	Harold Reimer
1968	NA	NA	James Macres	Gene Beck
1969	NA	NA	Terry Moreland	Gene Beck, Bob Limi
1970	NA	8-2	Terry Moreland	Gene Beck
1971	NA	17-0	Terry Moreland	Gene Beck
1972	NA	14-0	Terry Moreland	Gene Beck
1973	NA	15-0	Terry Moreland	Mike Sawyer
1974	NA	13-0	Terry Moreland	Lon Gwyn
1975	NA	2-9	Lon Gwyn	John Alcala
1976	NA	4-9	Jon Talbott	John Alcala
1977	NA	9-3	Jon Talbott	Juan Garza
1978	NA	NA	Jon Talbott	Juan Garza
1979	NA	NA	Jon Talbott	Juan Garza, Greg Reimer
1980	NA	6-6	Robert Arballo	Juan Garza
1981	NA	9-4	Robert Arballo	Don Noriel
1982	NA	7-5-1	Robert Arballo	Joe Vega
1983	NA	2-11	Robert Arbollo	Joe Vega
1984	NA	5-6	Robert Arbollo	Tim Hartnett
1985	NA	6-9-1	Ray Trask	Ernie Gonzales
1986	NA	NA	Ed Sibby	Ernie Gonzales, John Alcala
1987	NA	NA	Ed Sibby	Ernie Gonzales
1988	NA	NA	John Alcala	Keith Delehoy
1989	NA	NA	John Alcala	Ernie Gonzales, Keith Delehoy
1990	NA	6-6	John Alcala	Ernie Gonzales, Keith Delehoy
1991	NA	NA	John Alcala	Jesse Ortega, John Brown
1992	NA	2-5	Keith Delehoy	Jesse Ortega
1993	NA	5-15-1	Keith Delehoy	Jesse Ortega
1994	NA	4-13	Keith Delehoy	Jesse Ortega
1995	0-4	NA	Keith Delehoy	Jesse Ortega, Johnny Rodriguez
1996	1-3	1-3	Jesse Ortega	
1997	NA	NA	Keith Delehoy	Jesse Ortega, Felicano Romero
1998	NA	7-9-1	Jesse Ortega	Liario Prieto, Ernie Macias, David Castillo, Feliciano Romero
1999	NA	NA	Jesse Ortega	Liario Prieto, Ernie Macias
2000	NA	11-10-1	Jesse Ortega	Liario Prieto, Ernie Macias
2001	NA	7-15-1	Jesse Ortega	Liario Prieto, Ernie Macias

Delano High School

Year	League Record	Season	Head Coach	Assistant Coaches
2002	NA	8-4-2	Jesse Ortega	Liario Prieto Ernie Masias
2003	NA	4-4	Eric Rodriguez	Tim Bonita
2004	NA	NA	Eric Rodriguez	Ernie Macias
2005	NA	NA	Eric Rodriguez	Ernie Macias
2006	NA	NA	Todd Guevara	Gonzalo Quiddam, Ernie Macias
2007	2-5	6-9	John Alcala	Ernie Gonzales, Ernie Macias
2008	1-6	1-6	John Alcala	
2009	3-3	8-10	Gerry Abas	Ernie Gonzales, Jon Martinez, Vincent Rodriguez
2010	4-4	8-12	Gerry Abas	Ernie Macias
2011	4-4	4-4	Jon Martinez	Fernando Garcia, Cory Valov, Andrew Rodriguez, Sonny Silva, Amandeep Singh
2012	3-5	3-5	Jon Martinez	David Avita, Ryan Robles, Frankie Mendoza
2013	3-2	5-2	Jon Martinez	Andrew Rodrigues, Sonny Silva, Pete Noble, Ryan Robles, David Avita, Christian Heredia, Lance Wankum, Alan Manriquez
2014	1-4	1-4	Jon Martinez	Andrew Rodriguez, Sonny Silva, Pete Noble, Ryan Robles, C. Rubio, Christian Heredia, K. Cabal, S. Bonita
2015	1-4	3-4	Jon Martinez	Andrew Rodriguez, Sonny Silva, C. Rubio, Pete Noble, Christian Heredia
2016	2-3	3-4	Jon Martinez	Christian Heredia, Sonny Silva, Alex Nava, Pete Noble, Steven Contreras, C. Rubio,
2017	2-3	3-4	Jon Martinez	Christian Heredia, Alex Nava, Sonny Silva, Steven Contreras
2018	0-5	2-5	Jon Martinez	Christian Heredia, Alex Nava, Daniel Nunez
2019	0-2	1-4	Jon Martinez	Alex Nava, Angel Nava, Angel Mariscal, Fred Valov
2020	0-2	1-4	Jon Martinez	Alex Nava, Angel Mariscal, Angel Nava, Pablo Alonso

East Bakersfield High School

Year	League Record	Season	Head Coach	Assistant Coaches
1957	NA	5-1	Kay Dalton	
1958	NA	NA	Kay Dalton	Grover Rains
1959	6-2	NA	Grover Rains	Bob Aston
1960	4-3-1	NA	Leon Tedder	Bob Aston
1961	8-0	NA	Leon Tedder	Bob Aston
1962	7-0	NA	Leon Tedder	Bob Aston
1963	10-0	NA	Leon Tedder	Bob Aston
1964	5-4-1	8-4-1	Leon Tedder	Bob Aston
1965	4-6	8-8	Leon Tedder	Bob Aston
1966	4-4	NA	Leon Tedder	Jim Nuanez
1967	4-4	4-5	Leon Tedder	Jim Nuanez
1968	7-2-1	NA	Leon Tedder	Jim Nuanez
1969	5-5	8-7	Leon Tedder	Jim Nuanez
1970	8-2	8-4	Jim Nuanez	Quinn Morgan
1971	8-2	NA	Jim Nuanez	Quinn Morgan
1972	8-4	NA	Jim Nuanez	Bill Pineda
1973	6-6	NA	Leon Tedder	Bill Pineda
1974	0-6	NA	Leon Tedder	Bill Pineda
1975	0-12	NA	Leon Tedder	Rudy Gonzalez
1976	0-6	NA	Rudy Gonzalez	Jim Groves
1977	0-5-1	NA	Rudy Gonzalez	Jim Groves
1978	1-5	NA	Rudy Gonzales	Jim Groves
1979	1-5	NA	Rudy Gonzalez	Jim Groves
1980	NA	NA	Rudy Gonzalez	Abe Olivras
1981	0-7	NA	Rudy Gonzalez	Carl Cruz
1982	1-6	NA	Rudy Gonzalez	Leon Tedder
1983	1-6	NA	Rudy Gonzalez	Leon Tedder
1984	2-5	NA	Rudy Gonzalez	Steve Nickell
1985	2-4	NA	Rudy Gonzalez	Anthony Padilla
1986	3-7	NA	Rudy Gonzalez	Anthony Padilla
1987	NA	NA	Rudy Gonzalez	Anthony Padilla, Mike Gonzalez
1988	5-2	NA	Rudy Gonzalez	Mike Gonzalez
1989	2-5	NA	Rudy Gonzalez	Mike Gonzalez
1990	5-2	NA	Rudy Gonzalez	Mike Gonzalez, Joe Triggs
1991	5-1	NA	Rudy Gonzalez	Joe Triggs
1992	6-0	NA	Joe Triggs	Rudy Gonzalez
1993	NA	NA	Joe Triggs	Rudy Gonzalez, Tony Levario
1994	6-1	NA	Joe Triggs	Tony Levario, Rudy Gonzalez, Saul Mesa
1995	2-2	11-3	Joe Triggs	Tony Levario
1996	2-2	NA	Joe Triggs	Tony Levario
1997	NA	NA	Joe Triggs	Brian Nava
1998	NA	NA	Joe Triggs	Brian Nava
1999	NA	NA	Joe Triggs	
2000	3-1	NA	Joe Triggs	Cirilo Reyes

East Bakersfield High School

Year	League Record	Season	Head Coach	Assistant Coaches
2001	NA	NA	Joe Triggs	David Gardner, Ken Gabin
2002	NA	NA	Joe Triggs	David Gardner, Ken Gabin
2003	NA	NA	Joe Triggs	Ken Gabin, David Gardner
2004	NA	NA	Joe Triggs	Ken Gabin
2005	NA	NA	Joe Triggs	Ken Gabin, Chris Felix
2006	NA	NA	Joe Triggs	Ken Gabin, Pete Gonzalez
2007	3-2	7-5	Joe Triggs	Ken Gabin, Pete Gonzalez, F. Gonzalez, Andrew Stuebbe
2008	3-2	3-2	Joe Triggs	Ken Gabin, Pete Gonzalez, Fred Gonzalez, Henry Gonzalez
2009	3-2	3-2	Joe Triggs	Ken Gabin, Pete Gonzalez, Cruz Hernandez, Henry Gonzalez
2010	2-2	2-2	Pat Huych	David Gardner, Ken Gabin, Pete Gonzalez, Henry Gonzalez, Cirilo Reyes, Fred Gonzalez
2011	1-2	1-2	Pat Huych	D. Gardner, P. Gonzalez, F. Gonzalez, Gabe Tackett, Michael Gonzalez, Brady Gomez, Antonio Hernandez, John Sanchez
2012	1-2	1-2	David Gardner	Pete Gonzalez, Gabe Tackett, Tony Pena, Fred Gonzalez, Henry Gonzalez, Brady Gomez, Freddy Gonzalez Jr.
2013	3-1	3-1	Pete Gonzalez	Freddy Gonzalez Jr., Fred Gonzalez Henry Gonzalez
2014	0-4	0-4	Pete Gonzalez	Freddy Gonzalez Jr., Fred Gonzalez Sr.
2015	2-3	4-3	Pete Gonzalez	Freddy Gonzalez Jr., Fred Gonzalez Sr., Fred Lomas
2016	2-3	4-4	Freddy Gonzalez	Pete Gonzalez, Fred Gonzalez, Fred Lomas, Martin Lopez, Nick Gonzalez, David Gardner, Peter Gonzalez
2017	2-3	2-3	Freddy Gonzalez	Jared Armijo, Pete Gonzalez, Peter Gonzalez, Fred Gonzalez
2018	2-3	2-3	Freddy Gonzalez	Pete Gonzalez, Peter Gonzalez, Fred Gonzalez, Jared Armijo, Gabby Pelayo
2019	0-5	0-5	Freddy Gonzalez	Peter Gonzalez, Pete Gonzalez, Fred Gonzalez, Jared Armijo
2020	0-1	0-1	Freddy Gonzalez	Pete Gonzalez, Peter Gonzalez, Niko Gonzalez, Fred Gonzalez, Dave Gardner

Foothill High School

Year	League Record	Season	Head Coach	Assistant Coaches
1963	NA	NA	Doug Collins	Harvel Pollard
1964	2-8	6-9	Doug Collins	Ray Juhl
1965	2-8	8-8	Doug Collins	Ray Juhl
1966	2-6	2-6-1	Grover Rains	Steve Powers
1967	NA	7-3	Grover Ranis	Dennis Tangeman
1968	3-7	NA	Grover Rains	Dennis Tangeman
1969	5-5	NA	Grover Rains	Lee Hammet
1970	1-9	NA	Grover Rains	Lee Hammet
1971	0-10	NA	Frank Sousa	Dave Edmondson
1972	5-11	5-15	Frank Sousa	Dave Olds
1973	3-5	9-11	Frank Sousa	Dave Olds
1974	3-3	NA	Frank Sousa	Dave Edmondson
1975	6-6	NA	Frank Sousa	Dave Edmondson
1976	4-2	NA	Frank Sousa	Dave Edmondson
1977	4-2	NA	Dave Edmondson	Karl Herrera
1978	2-4	NA	Dave Edmondson	Karl Herrera
1979	0-6	NA	Dave Edmondson	Karl Herrera
1980	NA	1-13	Karl Herrera	Lloyd Dickey
1981	1-6	3-13	Karl Herrera	Lloyd Dickey, Chris Kirby
1982	4-3	8-3	Seymour Nerove	Frank Ramos
1983	7-0	NA	Seymour Nerove	Frank Ramos, Scott Chambers
1984	6-1	NA	Seymour Nerove	Scott Chambers, Richie Sinnott
1985	7-0	NA	Seymour Nerove	Lee Noble
1986	5-2	NA	Mark Loomis	Jeff Caputo
1987	NA	NA	Mark Loomis	Jeff Caputo
1988	1-6	NA	Mark Loomis	Jeff Caputo
1989	1-6	NA	Mark Loomis	Jeff Caputo
1990	0-7	NA	Mark Loomis	Pat Zimmerman
1991	0-6	NA	Mike Dallas	Dennis Reed
1992	0-6	NA	Alan Paradise	Matt Smith
1993	NA	NA	Alan Paradise	Tom Osendorf, Pat Higa
1994	1-5-1	NA	Alan Paradise	Pat Higa
1995	3-1	16-1	Alan Paradise	Bo Steinbach, George Anderson
1996	3-1	NA	Alan Paradise	Bo Steinbach, George Anderson, Bobby Soto
1997	3-1	5-2	Alan Paradise	Bo Steinbach, George Anderson, Craig Noble, Richie Sinnett
1998	NA	NA	Alan Paradise	Bo Steinbach, Craig Nobel, Kirk Moore
1999	NA	NA	Bobby Soto	Kirk Moore, Craig Nobel, Bo Steinbach
2000	2-2	4-6	Bo Steinbach	George Anderson, Kirk Moore
2001	NA	NA	Brad Hull	Pete Hernandez, Phillip Marquez
2002	0-4	1-6-1	Brad Hull	Phillip Marquez, Steve Hernandez, Carlos Sanchez

Foothill High School

Year	League Record	Season	Head Coach	Assistant Coaches
2003	3-2	5-2	Brad Hull	Phillip Marquez, Thomas Juarez, Carlos Medina
2004	4-1	7-1	Brad Hull	Phillip Marquez, Thomas Juarez
2005	3-1	11-2	Brad Hull	Thomas Juarez, John Wren, Robert Pfeifle
2006	4-0	7-0	Brad Hull	Thomas Juarez, John Wren, Robert Pfeifle
2007	3-2	5-2	Brad Hull	Robert Pfeifle, Brian Hull, Todd Guevara, Addison Hay
2008	3-2	9-2	Brad Hull	Robert Pfeifle, Brian Hull, Addison Hay, Daniel Sanchez
2009	4-1	7-1	Brad Hull	Robert Pfeifle, Addison Hay, Brian Hull, Joe Flores
2010	3-2	3-2	Brad Hull	Brian Hull, Robert Pfeifle, Addison Hay, Joe Flores
2011	3-0	7-0	Brad Hull	Addison Hay, Robert Pfeifle, Joe Flores
2012	3-0	7-0	Brad Hull	Addison Hay, Brian Hull, Robert Pfeifle, O J Martinez, Juan Lopez, Teddy Villaobos, Joe Flores
2013	4-0	10-0	Brad Hull	Brian Hull, Robert Pfeifle, Addison Hay, O J Martinez, Nathan Wren, Joe Flores
2014	4-0	12-1	Brad Hull	Brian Hull, Robert Pfeifle, Addison Hay, O J Martinez, Angel Posadas, Joe Flores, Daniel Sanchez, Diego Lopez
2015	3-1	7-1	Brad Hull	O J Martinez, Brian Hull, Addison Hay, Angel Posadas, Robert Pfeifle, Joe Flores
2016	4-0	11-0	Addison Hay	Brian Hull, Angle Posadas, Anthony Marquez, O J Martinez, Diego Lopez, Joe Flores
2017	3-1	3-2	Addison Hay	Charles Hay, Angel Posadas
2018	2-3	3-4	Anthony Marquez	Phillip Marquez, Joe Flores, George Gardoni, Martha Marquez
2019	3-2	3-2	Anthony Marquez	Phillip Marquez, Joe Flores, Doug Booth, Keenen Booth, Abraham Herrera
2020	2-1	7-2	Anthony Marquez	Phillip Marquez, Joe Flores, Willie Dallas, Kenan Booth, Doug Booth

Frontier High School

Year	League Record	Season	Head Coach	Assistant Coaches
2007	4-2	10-21	Kirk Moore	Ray Mooney, Andy Jeffrey, Greg Torres, Alex Herrera
2008	6-0	17-3	Kirk Moore	R Mooney, A Jeffrey, G Torres, Sean Sheets, Carlo Franciotti
2009	6-0	14-0	Kirk Moore	R Mooney, S Sheets, Bob Collins, Rex Davis, Jordan Bryan, Dustin Odom, Greg Torres
2010	6-0	6-0	Kirk Moore	R Mooney, Daniel Chapman, R Davis, S Sheets, D Odom, Matt Machado, B Collins, Jordan Kecker
2011	4-1	9-2	Kirk Moore	R Mooney, R Davis, Bob Collins, Blain Paregian, D Chapman, Anthony Griffin, Carlo Franciotti
2012	4-1	9-1	Kirk Moore	Daniel Chapman, Rob Tracy, Carlo Franciotti, Rex Davis
2013	4-1	8-1	Kirk Moore	D Chapman, R Tracy, R.Davis Carlo Franciotti, Chad Troxler, David Fletcher, Ray Mooney
2014	4-1	9-1	Kirk Moore	Rex Davis, Daniel Chapman, Carlo Franciotti, Rob Tracy, David Fletcher
2015	3-1	7-1	Kirk Moore	Carlo Franciotti, Rex Davis, Daniel Chapman, Rob Tracy, Joe Appleton, David Fletcher
2016	3-1	8-1	Kirk Moore	Carlo Franciotti, Rex Davis, Robert Rios, Robert Appleton
2017	4-1	7-2	Kirk Moore Carlo Franciotti	Joe Appleton, Rex Davis Calloway Morphis, Robert Rios
2018	4-1	4-1	Carlo Franciotti	Joey Granada, David Fletcher, Matt Gonzalez, Isaiah Ozuna
2019	5-0	7-1	Carlo Franciotti	J Granada, D Fletcher, Jose Landin, Pete Sarabia, Josh Davis, Joe Appleton, Kirk Moore, Tommy Wahi, Rex Davis, Rick Rios, Brett Clark
2020	1-1	6-4	Carlo Franciotti	Josh Davis, Torie Casper, David Fletcher, Joe Appleton, Rick Rios, Kirk Moore

Garces Memorial High School

Year	League Record	Season	Head Coach	Assistant Coaches
2015	0-5	4-17	Robert Flower	Raymond Saldana, Fernando Cholometes
2016	0-5	3-17	Robert Fowler	Raymond Saldana, Alex Gomez
2017	0-5	2-8	Robert Fowler	Fernando Cholometes, Brian Cobb, Ray Yocum
2018	0-5	0-5	Robert Fowler	Fernando Cholometes, Ray Yocum, Brian Cobb
2019	1-4	1-4	Robert Fowler	Fernando Cholometes, DeAndre Beldo, Marc Caputo, Roman Flores
2020	0-0	0-6	Robert Fowler	Matt Monterio, Floyd Reading, Fernando Cholometes, Jordan Cooper, Isaiah Martin

Golden Valley High School

Year	League Record	Season	Head Coach	Assistant Coaches
2005	1-4	1-5	Arron Wherry	Elizar Ceballos, Dan Mundanke
2006	3-2	3-3	Aaron Wherry	Elizar Ceballos, Dan Mundanke
2007	1-4	2-4	Aaron Wherry	Dan Mundhenke, Antonio Jones, Gabriel Acosta Tackett
2008	1-4	2-4	Aaron Wherry	Dan Mundhenke, Antonio Jones, Juan Olmos
2009	2-3	5-6	Aaron Wherry	Nick Rasmussen, Juan Olmos, Efren Cisneros
2010	2-3	7-3	Aaron Wherry	Efren Cisneros, Juan Olmos, Brandon Silva, Nick Rasmussen
2011	1-3	10-3	Aaron Wherry	Joe Rojas, Jim Poteete, Juan David Gamino, Efren Cisneros, Brandon Silva
2012	2-2	7-3	Aaron Wherry	Joe Rojas, Jim Poteet, Manuel Perrea, Efren Cisneros, Jose Leandro, Michael Lopez, Juan David Gamino
2013	4-0	8-1	Aaron Wherry	Joe Rojas, Jim Poteet, Efren Cisneros
2014	4-0	NA	Aaron Wherry	Joe Rojas, Jim Poteete, Efren Cisneros, Kendal Banducci, Jose Hernandez
2015	5-0	5-0	Aaron Wherry	Joe Rojas, Jim Poteete, Efren Cisneros, Miguel Trejo, Juan David Gamino, Jose Hernandez
2016	4-1	4-1	Aaron Wherry	Joe Rojas, Jim Poteete, Jason Duran, Juan Valdivinos, Juan David Gamino, Bryn Brund, Alivia Llanes
2017	5-0	5-0	Aaron Wherry	Jose Rojas, Paul Gonzales, Jose Leandro, Bryn Bruno, Juan David Gamino, Alicia Llanes
2018	4-1	4-1	Aaron Wherry	Joe Rojas, Andrew Stanley, Juan David Gamino, Jose Leandro, Nimrod Quintanilla
2019	5-0	5-0	Aaron Wherry	Joe Rojas, Alex Herrera, Juan David Gamino, Joe Leandro, Jonathan Hunter, Valeria Sanchez
2020	1-0	1-0	Joe Rojas	Alex Herrera, Jose Leandro, Joe Hernandez, Jonathan Hunter

Highland High School

Year	League Record	Season	Head Coach	Assistant Coaches
1972	7-5	NA	Joe Barton	J R Williams
1973	9-3	NA	Joe Barton	Jim Kliewer
1974	4-2	NA	Joe Barton	Jim Kliewer
1975	10-2	12-2	Joe Barton	Jim Kliewer
1976	5-1	NA	Joe Barton	Jim Kliewer
1977	4-2	NA	Joe Barton	Mike Spensko
1978	4-2	NA	Joe Barton	Mike Spensko, Jim Kliewer
1979	2-4	NA	Jim Seay	Dick Molina
1980	NA	NA	Jim Seay	Chris Kirby, Dick Molina
1981	2-5	NA	Jim Seay	Dick Molina
1982	1-7	NA	John Gonzales	Kevin Finnel
1983	2-5	NA	Bob Thisle	Charlie Chaney
1984	2-5	NA	Bob Thisle	Charlie Chaney
1985	NA	NA	Joe Vega	Don Richards
1986	6-1	NA	Ted Hunter	Steve Tucker
1987	NA	NA	Bob Thisle	Dennis Reed
1988	0-7	NA	Todd Owens	
1989	0-7	NA	Jim Norsworthy	Dan Willis
1990	3-4	NA	Dan Willis	Brian Neufeld
1991	1-5	NA	Dan Willis	Brian Neufeld
1992	4-2	NA	Dan Willis	Brian Neufeld
1993	NA	NA	Dan Willis	Brian Neufeld
1994	3-3-1	NA	Dan Willis	Pete Cortez
1995	0-4	0-6	Dan Willis	Eric Williams
1996	0-4	NA	Ernie Geronimo	Frank Ramos
1997	NA	NA	Ernie Geronimo	Carlos Marquez
1998	NA	2-8	Carlos Marquez	Steve Montano
1999	NA	NA	Carlos Marquez	Steve Montano
2000	1-3	NA	Carlos Marquez	Richard Eaton
2001	3-1	10-2	Carlos Marquez	Chris Felix
2002	NA	NA	Carlos Marquez	
2003	1-4	3-4	Carlos Marquez	Jess Ortega
2004	1-5	1-7	Carlos Marquez	Chris Felix
2005	1-3	2-4	Ann Miller	Brian March
2006	0-5	1-9	Anthony Gonzalez Paul Gonzales	Juan Lopez
2007	NA	NA	Paul Gonzales	
2008	0-5	1-5	Paul Gonzales	Joe Rojas, Ray Moroyoqui, Fernando Arreola, O J Martinez, Steve Franco
2009	1-4	2-4	Paul Gonzales	Joe Rojas, Steve Franco, Ray Moroyoqui, Nick Burnett
2010	0-5	0-6	Paul Gonzales Joe Rojas	Robert Rivera, Steve Franco, Victor Torres, Oscar Martinez, Ernesto Ancona, Ray Moroyoqui

Highland High School

Year	League Record	Season	Head Coach	Assistant Coaches
2011	NA	NA	Paul Gonzales	Oscar Martinez, Victor Torres, Ernesto Ancona, Eric Martinez
2012	0-3	1-3	Paul Gonzales	Tony Gonzales, Richie Ramirez, Jeff March, Richie Takington
2013	0-4	1-4	Paul Gonzales	Tony Gonzales, Fred Lomas, Fernando Bocanegra, Josh Burnett
2014	3-1	6-1	Paul Gonzales	Tony Gonzales, Joe Corona Fernando Bocanegra, Josh Burnett, Jordan Olgin, Moses Delfin
2015	2-2	6-2	Paul Gonzales	Fernando Bocanegra, Josh Barnett, Juan Lopez, Art Santore, James Phillips
2016	2-2	3-3	Joseph Kuntz	Fernando Bocanegra, Billy Pitcher
2017	2-2	9-3	Joseph Kuntz	Fernando Bocanegra, Kris Kohls
2018	4-0	7-0	Joseph Kuntz	Addison Hay, Angel Posadas, Kris Kohls
2019	3-2	8-4	Joseph Kuntz	Addison Hay, Angel Posadas, Charlie Hay
2020	2-1	3-2	Addison Hay	Angel Posadas, Robert Pfeifle, Michael Aguirre, Charlie Hay

Independence High School

Year	League Record	Season	Head Coach	Assistant Coaches
2009	5-1	12-2	Dante Borradori	Richard Tarkington
2010	4-2	2-1	Dante Borradori	Richard Tarkington, Hugo Teague, Quinn Moore, Chris Alfonso
2011	1-4	1-4	Dante Borradori	Caleb Smith, Quinn Moore, Brent Fulce
2012	2-3	10-8	Dante Borradori	Caleb Smith, Jawayne Fambrough
2013	0-5	0-5	Julie Walker	Tom Miralez, Geoffrey Demalade
2014	1-4	1-4	Garth Wara	Julie Walker, Juan Gutierrez, Tom Mirelez
2015	1-4	1-5	Tom Mirelez	Julie Walker, James Carrillo, Tony Webber
2016	4-1	4-2	James Carrillo	Peter Corona
2017	3-2	4-2	James Carrillo	Peter Corona, Albert Deval, Esteban Drew Schilhabel, Julie Walker
2018	3-2	3-2	James Carrillo	Jacob Hall, Nick Enriquez, Albert Deval
2019	3-2	4-3	James Carrillo	Gage Viss, Nick Enriquez, Albert Deval, Junior Layman
2020	1-0	2-1	Gage Viss	James Carrillo, Shawn Hendrix, Vincent Carrillo, Albert Debal

Robert F. Kennedy High School

Year	League Record	Season	Head Coach	Assistant Coaches
2009	NA	NA	Aaron Garza	Sean Gonzales, Jesse Flores
2010	0-6	NA	Aaron Garza	Sean Gonzales
2011	2-6	4-8	Miguel Sanchez	Ivan Sanchez, Chris Alfoso
2012	5-3	9-4	Miguel Sanchez	Ivan Sanchez, Chris Alfoso, Johnathon English
2013	4-2	2-3	Miguel Sanchez	Ivan Sanchez, Chris Alfoso
2014	3-3	8-4	Miguel Sanchez	Ivan Sanchez, Chris Alfoso
2015	3-3	8-4	Miguel Sanchez	Ivan Sanchez, Chris Alfoso
2016	5-1	10-2	Miguel Sanchez	Ivan Sanchez, Chris Alfoso
2017	4-2	5-5	Miguel Sanchez	Ivan Sanchez, Chris Alfoso
2018	5-1	5-4	Miguel Sanchez	Ivan Sanchez, Chris Alfoso
2019	4-1	5-3	Miguel Sanchez	Ivan Sanchez, Chris Alfoso
2020	1-4	4-8	John Alcala	Ivan Sanchez

Kern Valley High School

Year	League Record	Season	Head Coach	Assistant Coaches
1980	NA	NA	Denny Knight	
1981	NA	NA	Denny Knight	
1982	NA	NA	Denny Knight	
1983	NA	NA	Denny Knight	
1984	NA	NA	Denny Knight	
1985	NA	NA	Denny Knight	Marty Maciel
1986	NA	NA	Denny Knight	
1987	NA	NA	Denny Knight	
1988	NA	NA	Denny Knight	
1989	NA	NA	Denny Knight	John Arcurio
1990	NA	NA	Denny Knight	John Arcurio
1991	NA	NA	Denny Knight	John Arcurio
1992	NA	NA	Denny Knight	Eric Allison
1993	NA	NA	Denny Knight	
1994	NA	NA	Denny Knight	
1995	NA	NA	Denny Knight	
1996	NA	NA	Denny Knight	
1997	NA	NA	Denny Knight	
1998	NA	NA	Denny Knight	
2000	NA	NA	Denny Knight	Josh Factor
2001	NA	NA	Denny Knight	Josh Factor
2002	NA	NA	Denny Knight	Josh Factor
2003	NA	NA	Denny Knight	Josh Factor, Mike Bull
2004	NA	NA	Denny Knight	Josh Factor
2005	NA	NA	Denny Knight	
2006	NA	NA	Denny Knight	Cody Cunningham, Josh McCartney
2007	NA	1-9	Denny Knight	Cody Cunningham
2008	NA	NA	Denny Knight	Robert Swan, Jim Uribe
2009	3-1	3-3	Robert Swan	Wes Woody
2010	3-0	4-0	Wes Woody	Jim Uribe, Kyler Robinson, Frank Woody
2011	1-2	2-2	Wes Woody	J Uribe, K Robinson, F Woody
2012	0-0	4-3	Wes Woody	Jim Uribe, Kyler Robinson, Frank Woody
2013	4-0	4-4	Wes Woody	Jim Uribe, Kyler Robinson, Frank Woody
2014	4-0	8-5	Wes Woody	Jim Uribe, Kyler Robinson, Frank Woody, Weston Williams
2015	4-0	5-4	Wes Woody	Jim Uribe, Frank Woody
2016	4-0	6-2	Wes Woody	Jim Uribe, Frank Woody
2017	5-0	5-0	Wes Woody	Jim Uribe, Frank Woody
2018	5-1	5-1	Wes Woody	Jim Uribe, Frank Woody
2019	5-1	5-1	Wes Woody	Jim Uribe, Frank Woody
2020	6-0	6-0	Wes Woody	Jim Uribe, Frank Woody, Jamie Woody

Liberty High School

Year	League Record	Season	Head Coach	Assistant Coaches
2000	NA	NA	John Eisel	
2001	NA	NA	Joe Vega	Steve Elisondo
2002	NA	NA	Joe Vega	Coach Williams, Coach Genaro, Richard Gutierrez
2003	NA	NA	Jay Curtis	Ernie Lindley, Coach Williams
2004	NA	NA	Ernie Lindley	Rick Christensen, Doug Booth, Sean Ponce
2005	NA	NA	Ernie Lindley	Ron Rodgers, Dean Brown, Doug Klinchurch
2006	NA	NA	Ron Rodgers	David East
2007	3-2	10-3	Ron Rogers	David East, Phil Kapler
2008	3-2	4-2	Ron Rodgers	Joe Seay
2009	0-5	0-4	Ron Rogers	John Sizemore, Phil Kapler
2010	3-2	3-2	Ron Rogers	John Sizemore, Kail Rogers, Martin Cueto, Robert Rios, Vance Rivera, Keith Mioni
2011	0-5	0-5	John Sizemore	Chuck Hartsfield, Martin Cueto, Nick Childers, Jeff Lanier
2012	1-4	3-4	John Sizemore	Chuck Hartsfield, Martin Cueto, Jeremiah Bridges, Ryan Stieber, Ruben Guerra, Robert Candeleria
2013	2-3	2-3	John Sizemore	Chuck Hartsfield, Martin Cueto, Jeremiah Brides, Ryan Stieber, Chris Sizemore, Tyler Hartsfield
2014	3-2	3-2	Kyle Plummer	Chuck Hartsfield
2015	2-2	2-2	Kyle Plummer	Glen Campbell, Paul Garcia, John Conley, Ryan Meleoche
2016	2-2	2-2	Kyle Plummer	Glen Campbell, Paul Garcia, Fernando Flores, Ryan Meleoche
2017	2-3	5-3	Kyle Plummer	Glen Campbell, Ryan Meloche, Paul Garcia, Dylan Bolinger
2018	2-3	4-3	Kyle Plummer	Bryan Bruno, Paul Garcia, Brandon Silva, Ryan Meloche, Glen Campbell
2019	2-3	5-5	Kyle Plummer	Glen Campbell, Paul Garcia, Brandon Silva, Kris Kohls
2020	1-0	4-0	Kyle Plummer	Paul Garcia, Glenn Campbell

McFarland High School

Year	League Record	Season	Head Coach	Assistant Coaches
1968	NA	NA	Bob Miller	
1969	NA	NA	Bob Miller	David Kistler
1970	NA	NA	Lisle Gates	Coach Karr
1971	NA	NA	Lisle Gates	
1972	NA	8-5	Lisle Gates	
1973	NA	6-5	Lisle Gates	
1974	NA	NA	Lisle Gates	
1975	NA	7-6	Lisle Gates	
1976	NA	NA	Lisle Gates	
1977	4-4	NA	Lisle Gates	
1978	NA	NA	Lisle Gates	Jim Robesky
1979	NA	NA	Ed Levenson	
1980	NA	NA	Ed Levenson	
1981	NA	NA	Ed Levenson	
1982	NA	2-9	Ed Levenson	
1983	NA	NA	Ed Levenson	
1984	NA	7-1	Ed Levenson	
1985	NA	NA	Ed Levenson	
1986	NA	NA	Ed Levenson	
1987	NA	NA	Ed Levenson	
1988	4-0	NA	Ed Levenson	
1989	NA	NA	Ed Levenson	Martin Davidson
1990	NA	NA	Ed Levenson	Martin Davidson
1991	NA	NA	Ed Levenson	Martin Davidson
1992	NA	NA	Ed Levenson	Jeff Nichols, Rick Sparks
1993	NA	NA	Ed Levenson	Rick Sparks
1994	NA	NA	Ed Levenson	Rick Sparks
1995	NA	NA	Ed Levenson	Rick Sparks
1996	0-4	0-4	Ed Levenson	
1997	NA	NA	Ed Levenson	
1998	NA	NA	Ed Levenson	Javier Holguin
1999	NA	NA	Ed Levenson	Javier Holguin
2000	NA	NA	Ed Levenson	Javier Holguin
2001	0-5	NA	Ed Levenson	Javier Holguin
2002	NA	NA	Ed Levenson	Javier Holguin
2003	NA	NA	Ed Levenson	Javier Holguin,
2004	NA	NA	Ed Levenson	Javier Holguin, Jose Navajar, Danny Camacho, Coach Cardoza
2005	1-5	4-12	Ed Levenson	Javier Holguin, Branden McFarland, Jose Ramos, Danny Camacho
2006	1-4	4-9	Ed Levenson	Javier Holguin, Joey Ramos Branden McFarland, George Silva
2007	1-5	2-8	Ed Levenson	Javier Holguin, George Silva, Sean Fiser

McFarland High School

Year	League Record	Season	Head Coach	Assistant Coaches
2008	0-5	1-10	Ed Levenson	Javier Holguin,
2009	1-4	7-4	Ed Levenson	Javier Holguin, Ernie Gonzales, Fernando Soto
2010	2-3	2-3	Ed Levenson	Ernie Gonzales, Javier Holguin, Jorge Silva, Fernando Soto,
2011	2-3	6-6	Ed Levenson	Ernie Gonzales, Fernando Soto, John Alcala, Javier Holguin
2012	2-3	3-12	Ed Levenson	Ernie Gonzales, John Alcala
2013	3-3	9-5	Ed Levenson	Javier Holguin
2014	2-4	2-8	Ed Levenson	Javier Holguin
2015	1-5	3-8	Ed Levenson	Javier Holguin
2016	NA	12-4	Javier Holguin	Fernando Ramirez
2017	0-6	0-7	Javier Holguin Roman Ozuna	
2018	2-4	2-4	Javier Holguin	Fernando Ramirez, Ernie Gonzales, Casey Quinn
2019	1-5	1-5	Javier Holguin	Ernie Gonzales, Fernando Ramirez
2020	1-4	1-4	Javier Holguin	Fernando Ramirez, Ernie Gonzales

Mira Monte High School

Year	League Record	Season	Head Coach	Assistant Coaches
2009	NA	NA	Matt Olejnik	Chris Felix, Miguel Gutierrez
2010	4-2	4-4	Matt Olejnik	Chris Felix
2011	0-4	0-5	Matt Olejnik	Brett Clark, Chris Felix
2012	1-3	1-3	Brett Clark	Kyle Plummer, Mark Austin
2013	1-3	1-4	Brett Clark	Kyle Plummer, Jeremy Adan, Jawayne Fambrough
2014	1-3	1-3	Brett Clark	Jawayne Fambrough
2015	0-4	2-4	Rafael Ruiz	Oscar Garza, Josh Villarreal, Angelica Llanes
2016	0-4	0-5	Efren Cisneros	Rafael Ruiz, Juan Lopez, Mark Rodriguez, Anthony O'Hara
2017	0-4	0-5	Efren Cisneros	Julio Fentes
2018	0-4	0-5	Efren Cisneros	Hector Sanchez
2019	1-4	2-4	Efren Cisneros	Hector Sanchez, Avila Reyes, Lance Castaneda
2020	0-1	0-1	Mario Gomez	Cirilo Reyes, Vincente Gomez, Hector Sanchez

North High School

Year	League Record	Season	Head Coach	Assistant Coaches
1957	NA	NA	Dick Westbay	
1958	NA	3-3	Dick Westbay	
1959	3-5	4-6	Win Bootman	
1960	0-8	NA	Win Bootman	
1961	0-8	NA	Win Bootman	
1962	2-6	4-9	Win Bootman	
1963	3-7	4-9	Win Bootman	Ken Kiefer
1964	6-4	12-4	Win Bootman	Gil Roberts
1965	6-4	10-4	Win Bootman	Gil Roberts
1966	2-6	8-6	Win Bootman	Roger Kelly
1967	6-2	9-2	Win Bootman	Bob Spencer
1968	3-7	5-7	Win Bootman	Bob Spencer
1969	1-9	5-9	Gary Kuster	Charles Lovell
1970	3-7	NA	Gary Kuster	Charles Lovell
1971	4-6	8-6	Gary Kuster	Jack O'Brien
1972	3-9	3-10	Gary Kuster	Jeff Tuculett
1973	1-11	6-14	Gary Kuster	Jeff Tuculett
1974	1-5	7-12	Gary Kuster	Rick Harvick
1975	2-10	3-13	Gary Kuster	Ron Shearer
1976	4-2	13-8	Gary Kuster	Ron Shearer
1977	3-3	NA	Gary Kuster	Ron Shearer
1978	6-0	14-1	Gary Kuster	Ron Shearer
1979	5-1	9-3	Gary Kuster	Jack O'Brien
1980	2-5	4-9	Gary Kuster	Bob Gamboa
1981	3-4	3-10	Richard Alvarez	Bob Gamboa
1982	2-5	NA	Mark Hall	Kevin Duggan
1983	0-7	NA	Ted Hunter	Darrin Lindsey
1984	0-7	NA	Craig Shoene	Lewis McNabb
1985	2-4	NA	Tim Maestas	Rick Contreras
1986	0-7	NA	Tim Maestas	Rick Contreras
1987	NA	NA	Rick McKinney	Armand Medina
1988	3-4	NA	Rick McKinney	Jordan Holt, Rocky Churchman
1989	6-1	NA	Rick McKinney	John Branch
1990	4-3	NA	Rick McKinney	Bill Thomas
1991	5-1	NA	Rick McKinney	Bill Thomas
1992	6-0	NA	Rick McKinney	Bill Thomas
1993		10-2	Rick McKinney	Bill Thomas, Rocky Churchman, Brian Malavar
1994	3-2-1	NA	Pat Huych	Bill Thomas, Rocky Churchman, Jeff Heberle
1995	3-1	15-9	Pat Huych	Rocky Churchman, Jeff Heberle, Travis Spears
1996	3-1	8-8	Rocky Churchman	Roman Aguilar, Bobby Sherrill, Chad Hobbs
1997	NA	NA	Rocky Churchman	Roman Aguilar, Jake Shirley

North High School

Year	League Record	Season	Head Coach	Assistant Coaches
1998	1-3	5-10	Rocky Churchman	Roman Aguilar, Ted Hunter
1999	NA	NA	Rocky Churchman	Roman Aguilar
2000	0-4	5-10	Ty Stricker	Parris Whitley
2001	NA	NA	Ty Stricker	Parris Whitley
2002	2-2	2-3	Ty Stricker	Parris Whitley, Billy Pitcher, Jeff Tensley
2003	0-4	0-5	Ty Stricker	Billy Pitcher, Jeff Tensley
2004	1-3	2-3	Ty Stricker	Billy Pitcher, Jeff Tensley, Dusi Terrell, Mike Stricker, Derrick Hunter
2005	3-2	4-2	Ty Stricker	Billy Pitcher, Jeff Tensley, Mike Stricker
2006	3-2	3-3	Ty Stricker	Billy Pitcher, Brad Heinman, Jeff Tensley, Mike Stricker
2007	3-2	3-2	Billy Pitcher	Brad Heineman, Tyler Grady, Christian Hernandez
2008	3-3	3-3	Billy Pitcher	Jim Maricich
2009	0-6	0-6	Billy Pitcher	Jim Maricich, Casey Ray, Christian Hernandez
2010	2-4	2-4	Billy Pitcher	Jim Maricich, Tyler Grady, Christian Hernandez
2011	3-1	11-4	Billy Pitcher	Jim Maricich, Chris Lucas, Dan Farley
2012	2-1	9-3	Billy Pitcher	Jim Masicich, Chris Lucas, Caleb Smith
2013	1-3	6-5	Brady Garner	Ryan Schmehr
2014	2-2	9-4	Brady Garner	Fred Wong, Chris Lucas, Aaron Garza
2015	2-2	9-3	Brady Garner	Jon Quijada, Chris Lucas, Fred Wong, Oren Dramen
2016	1-3	5-5	Brady Garner	Jacob Lucas, John Mello, Jon Quijada
2017	4-0	9-3	Brady Garner	Jacob Lucas, David Chavez, Andrew Binger, Jessica Findley
2018	3-1	5-1	Brady Garner	Andrew Binger, David Chavez, Will Scheer
2019	4-1	12-4	Brady Garner	Andrew Binger, David Chavez, Will Scheer, Logan Creel, Chris Lucas
2020	1-0	2-1	Brady Garner	Chris Lucas, Calloway Morphis, David Chavez, Billy Sherer, Kevin Mello, Blake Hieneman, Brian Hossman, Andrew Binger

Ridgeview High School

Year	League Record	Season	Head Coach	Assistant Coaches
1994	NA	NA	Brad Case	Roman Aguilar
1995	NA	NA	Brad Case	Craig Oliver
1996	1-4	1-4	Brad Case	Craig Oliver
1997	NA	NA	Lee Ramos	Steve Montano
1998	2-2	3-2	Lee Ramos	Steve Montano
1999	NA	NA	Lee Ramos	John Paredez
2000	NA	NA	Lee Ramos	John Paradez, Chris Hertzog
2001	NA	NA	Lee Ramos	Paul Gonzales, Craig Oliver, Tony Gonzalez
2002	NA	NA	Lee Ramos	Craig Oliver, Paul Gonzales, Tony Gonzalez
2003	NA	NA	Lee Ramos	Tony Gonzalez, Sony Mord
2004	NA	NA	Lee Ramos	Tony Gonzalez, Bobby Sherriel, Eric Coleman
2005	2-3	5-8	Lee Ramos	Seba Wright, Calvin Cox, Anthony Gonzalez, Eric Coleman
2006	1-4	2-4	Adam Setser	Seba Wright, Calvin Cox, Jarred Cox
2007	3-2	3-3	Tony Gonzalez	Juan Lopez, Carlos Gonzalez, Calvin Cox
2008	2-4	3-4	Tony Gonzalez	Carlos Gonzalez, Juan Lopez
2009	1-5	1-6	Tony Gonzalez	Carlos Gonzalez, Calvin Cox, Juan Lopez
2010	0-6	0-6	Tony Gonzalez	Juan Lopez
2011	3-1	4-2	Tony Gonzalez	Juan Lopez, Carlos Gonzalez
2012	2-2	3-4	Fred Wong	Aaron Garza, Dani Kamad
2013	2-2	4-4	Fred Wong	Aaron Garza, Mark Narvaez, Renee Garcia, Sal Garcia, Jose Santos
2014	0-5	0-7	Adam Setser	Mark Narvarez
2015	4-1	4-1	Aaron Garza	Mark Narvarez, Albert Urias
2016	4-1	4-1	Aaron Garza	Mark Navarez, Albert Urias, Jose Santos
2017	4-1	7-2	Aaron Garza Albert Urias	Manuel Perea
2018	5-0	5-0	Aaron Garza	Albert Urias
2019	4-1	9-3	Aaron Garza	Albert Urias
2020	0-1	2-1	Aaron Garza	

Shafter High School

Year	League Record	Season	Head Coach	Assistant Coaches
1966	NA	NA	Bill Hatcher	Darrell Fletcher
1967	2-4	4-8	Bill Hatcher	Darrell Fletcher, Bill Dauphin
1968	NA	NA	Bill Dauphin	Darrell Fletcher
1969	NA	NA	Bill Dauphin	Darrell Fletcher
1970	8-0	NA	Darrell Fletcher	Kalmon Matis
1971	NA	NA	Darrell Fletcher	Kalmon Matis
1972	2-4	NA	Darrell Fletcher	Kalmon Matis, Arlie Smith
1973	4-2	5-0-1	Darrell Fletcher	Kalmon Matis, Arlie Smith
1974	NA	NA	Darrell Fletcher	
1975	NA	NA	Darrell Fletcher	Mike Spensko
1976	6-2	NA	Darrell Fletcher	Ben Ansolabhere, Tom Williams
1977	8-0	NA	Darrell Fletcher	Tom Williams
1978	6-0	7-1	Darrell Fletcher	Tom Williams
1979	5-1	NA	Don Burns	Tom Williams
1980	6-0	8-1-1	Lisle Gates	Dana Ellison
1981	6-0	NA	Lisle Gates	Joe Lopez
1982	6-0	NA	Lisle Gates	Joe Lopez
1983	NA	NA	Joe Lopez	Lisle Gates
1984	NA	NA	Joe Lopez	Roger Giovannetti
1985	NA	NA	Steve Nickell	
1986	NA	NA	Rick McKinney	Rick Sparks
1987	4-0	7-9	Gary Pederson	Rick Sparks
1988	3-1	7-8	Gary Pederson	Rick Sparks
1989	3-1	9-6	Gary Pederson	Allen Salazar
1990	NA	NA	Gary Pederson	Allen Salazar
1991	2-4	3-5	Gary Pederson	Rick Gabin, Pat Hyuck
1992	3-2	3-3	Gary Pederson	Joe Lopez, Rick Gabin, Pat Hyuch
1993	3-1	8-5	Gary Pederson	Rick Gabin
1994	NA	NA	Gary Pederson	Rick Gabin, Ken Gabin
1995	NA	NA	Gary Pederson	Rick Gabin, Ken Gabin, Julian Irigoyen
1996	4-1	5-3	Gary Pederson	Rick Gabin, Ken Gabin, Julian Irigoyen
1997	4-2	6-3	Gary Pederson	Julian Irigoyen
1998	2-1	6-1	Gary Pederson	John Paredez, Joe Jolley, Kevin Kellior
1999	5-0	7-1	Gary Pederson	Ray Organ, Joe Jolley, Kevin Kellior
2000	3-1	6-3	Gary Pederson	Ray Organ, Joe Jolley, Kevin Kellior
2001	5-0	6-1	Gary Pederson	Juan Gallardo, Kevin Kellior
2002	5-0	9-2	Gary Pederson	Juan Gallardo, Aaron Wherry
2003	4-0	10-1	Gary Pederson	Juan Gallardo, Aaron Wherry
2004	4-0	11-13	Gary Pederson	Jacob Prendez, Pat Hyuck
2005	3-2	10-4	Gary Pederson	Pat Hyuch, Rick Gabin, Andrew Stuebbe
2006	2-2-1	6-3-1	Gary Pederson	Rick Gabin, Juan Gallardo, Pat Hyuch, Andrew Stuebbe

Shafter High School

Year	League Record	Season	Head Coach	Assistant Coaches
2007	3-3	5-3	Gary Pederson	Rick Gabin, Pat Huych
2008	4-1	5-2	Rick Gabin	Pat Huych, Roy Delarosa, Vincent Navarro, Cain Maldonado
2009	4-1	4-1	Rick Gabin	Pat Huych, Dave Mack, Dave Jackson, Charles Wilson, Eli Espercutea, Roy Delarosa, Cain Maldonado
2010	4-1	4-1	Rick Gabin	Steve Nickell, Dave Mack, Julian Irigoyen, Chris Bailey, Gary Mouser, Clint Parrish, Roy Delarosa, Pat Coyle, Eli Espericueta, Cain Maldonado, Charles Wilson
2011	3-2	7-4	Rick Gabin	Dave Mack, Gary Mouser, Julian Irigoyen, Roy Delarosa, Matt Maldonado
2012	4-1	7-7	Rick Gabin	Dave Mack, Ed Vega, Roy Delarosa, Charles Wilson, Pat Coyle, Eli Espericutea, Lucas Espericutea, Pat Huych, Matt Maldonado
2013	4-2	4-2	Rick Gabin	Dave Mack, Julian Irigoyen, Ed Vega, Rick Ishida, Pat Coyle, Roy Delarosa, Eli Espericueta, Lucas Espericutea, Pat Huych, Matt Maldonado
2014	5-1	11-10	Rick Gabin	Dave Mack, Julian Irgoyen, Pat Huych, Rick Ishida, Roy Delarosa, Matt Maldonado, Pat Coyle, Eli Espericueta, Eric Gutierrez
2015	5-1	9-2	Rick Gabin	Pat Huych, Teddy Villalobos, Eric Gutierrez, Eric Munoz, J T Watson, Roy Delarosa, Pat Coyle, Eli Espericueta, Matt Maldonado, Wade Wilson, Clint Parrish
2016	3-2	3-2	Rick Gabin	Spencer Hill, Pat Huych, Eric Gutierrez, Teddy Villalobos, Matt Maldonado, Eli Espericueta
2017	6-0	10-2	Rick Gabin	Spencer Hill, George Portillo, Sergio Camacho, Eric Gutierrez, Pat Huych
2018	??	??	Rick Gabin	Spencer Hill, George Portillo, Sergio Camacho, Xavier Garcia, Pat Huych
2019	4-1	4-2	Rick Gabin / Spencer Hill	George Portillo, Xavier Garcia, Eli Espericueta, Melisa Espericueta, Kalina Dominguez-Smiley
2020	3-2	6-13	Spencer Hill	George Portillo

South High School

Year	League Record	Season	Head Coach	Assistant Coaches
1958	NA	4-2-1	Bruce Pfutzenreuter	
1959	7-2-1	11-2-1	Bruce Pfutzenreuter	
1960	7-0-1	11-0-1	Bruce Pfutzenreuter	Ed Hageman
1961	4-4	9-4	Bruce Pfutzenreuter	Doug Collins
1962	4-3	9-3	Bruce Pfutzenreuter	Doug Collins
1963	7-3	13-3	Bruce Pfutzenreuter	Bob Lathrop, Rod O'Meara
1964	9-0-1	16-0-1	Bruce Pfutzenreuter	Bob Lathrop
1965	9-0-1	15-0-1	Joe Seay	Bob Lathrop
1966	7-1	11-1	Joe Seay	Bob Lathrop
1967	6-2	7-3	Joe Seay	Bob Lathrop
1968	8-1-1	12-1-1	Joe Seay	Bob Lathrop
1969	10-0	15-0	Joe Seay	Bob Lathrop, Bill Bruce
1970	8-2	20-3	Joe Seat	Bob Lathrop
1971	8-2	15-2	Joe Seay	Bob Lathrop
1972	10-2	NA	Joe Seay	Bob Lathrop
1973	10-2	NA	Art Chavez	Bob Lathrop, Mike Stricker
1974	3-3	NA	Art Chavez	Bob Lathrop, Mike Stricker
1975	6-6	NA	Bob Lathrop	Eugene Walker
1976	2-4	NA	Bob Lathrop	Eugene Walker
1977	3-3	NA	Bob Lathrop	Eugene Walker
1978	2-4	5-8-1	Eugene Walker	Art Chavez
1979	5-1	14-1	Eugene Walker	Mike Stricker
1980	6-1	10-3	Eugene Walker	Mike Stricker
1981	7-0	12-6	Eugene Walker	Mike Stricker
1982	6-1	11-8	Eugene Walker	Mike Stricker, Jim Poteete
1983	4-3	8-11-1	Eugene Walker	Jim Poteete
1984	5-2	6-12	Eugene Walker	Mike Stricker, Jim Poteete
1985	5-2	11-6	Eugene Walker	Mike Stricker, Jim Poteete
1986	7-0	15-1	Eugene Walker	Mike Stricker, Jim Poteete
1987	7-0	20-3-1	Eugene Walker	Mike Stricker, Jim Poteete
1988	7-5	9-13	Eugene Walker	Mike Stricker
1989	3-4	8-14-1	Eugene Walker	Mike Stricker
1990	3-4	11-14	Eugene Walker	Mike Stricker
1991	2-4	5-10	Eugene Walker	Ramon Hendrix, Brian Henderson
1992	3-3	NA	Eugen Walker	Brian Henderson, Ramon Hendrix
1993	NA	NA	Brian Henderson	Cary Mills
1994	2-5	NA	Brian Henderson	Cary Mills
1995	1-3	NA	Brian Henderson	Cary Mills
1996	4-0	5-3	Brian Henderson	Cary Mills
1997	4-0	18-7	Brian Henderson	Cary Mills
1998	2-2-1	18-7	Brian Henderson	Cary Mills, Andy Silvestro
1999	NA	NA	Brian Henderson	Cary Mills, Ted Hunter, Andy Silvestro

South High School

Year	League Record	Season	Head Coach	Assistant Coaches
2000	3-1	14-7	Brian Henderson	Cary Mills, Ted Hunter, Andy Silvestro
2001	NA	NA	Brian Henderson	Cary Mills, Andy Silvestro
2002	1-3	6-7	Brian Henderson	Cary Mills, Derrick Hembree
2003	3-0-1	4-0-1	Brian Henderson	Cary Mills
2004	3-1	8-5	Brian Henderson	Cary Mills, John Wren, Ric Cox
2005	4-1	20-1	Brian Henderson	Cary Mills, Tyson Jones
2006	4-1	11-1	Brian Henderson	Cary Mills
2007	2-3	3-4	Brian Henderson	Cary Mills, Tyson Jones, David Davenport
2008	3-3	3-4	Brian Henderson	Cary Mills, Manuel Vasquez, David Davenport
2009	3-3	NA	Brian Henderson	Cary Mills, Manuel Vasquez, David Davenport, David Martinez
2010	3-3	3-3	Brian Henderson	Cary Mills, Manuel Vasquez, David Davenport, David Martinez
2011	3-1	3-2	Brian Henderson	Cary Mills, David Martinez
2012	4-0	4-1	Brian Henderson	Cary Mills, David Martinez, Tyson Pinon
2013	3-1	3-2	Brian Henderson	Cary Mills, Manuel Vasquez, David Martinez, Tyson Pinon
2014	2-2	2-3	Brian Henderson	Cary Mills, Manuel Vasquez, David Martinez
2015	3-1	3-1	Brian Henderson	Cary Mills. Manuel Vasquez, Quinn Moore
2016	3-1	12-2	Manuel Vasquez	Cary Mills, Quinn Moore, Ramon Perez
2017	1-3	1-3	Manuel Vasquez	Cary Mills, Quinn Moore, Andrea Price
2018	1-3	3-7	Manuel Vasquez	Cary Mills, Levi Garcia
2019	4-1	6-1	Manuel Vasquez	Cary Mills, Stephen Battisto
2020	1-1	12-4	Manuel Vasquez	Cary Mills, Stephen Battisto, Bryan Battisto

Stockdale High School

Year	League Record	Season	Head Coach	Assistant Coaches
1992	NA	NA	Craig Shoene	
1993	1-3	NA	Craig Shoene	Bill Graham, Tim Martin
1994	NA	NA	Craig Schoene	Bill Graham, Tim Martin
1995	4-0	21-9	Craig Schoene	Bill Graham, Chris McFadden
1996	0-4	0-7	Louis Chiparelli	Danny Castaneda
1997	NA	NA	Craig Schoene	Pat Zimmerman, Ric Cox
1998	3-1	6-10	Craig Schoene	Pat Zimmerman, Paul Garcia
1999	NA	NA	Craig Schoene	Pat Zimmerman, Paul Garcia
2000	2-2	11-4	Craig Schoene	Pat Zimerman, Paul Garcia
2001	NA	NA	Craig Schoene	Paul Garcia
2002	3-1	13-4-1	Craig Schoene	Jason Mesa, Sean Ponce, Ric Cox, Joe Lopez
2003	2-2	4-2	Paul Garcia	Jason Armijo, Joe Espejo, Joe Martinez, Elizar Ceballos
2004	3-1	4-2	Paul Garcia	Jason Armijo, Elizar Ceballos, Paul Carrillo
2005	2-5	5-9	Paul Garcia	Jason Armijo, Travis Marchant, Jose Morales, Lalo Celedon
2006	2-3	2-5	Paul Garcia	Dante Borradoni, Jose Morales, Joey Martinez, Lalo Celedon
2007	3-2	6-6	Paul Garcia	Dante Borradori, Jose Morales, Lala Celedon
2008	3-3	10-6	Paul Garcia	Dante Borradori, Marcus Austin, Joe Espejo, Joe Aguilar
2009	4-2	10-4	Paul Garcia	Joe Espejo, Marcus Austin, Matt Tamandong, Brian Cobb, Rudy Flores, Joe Aguilar
2010	5-1	7-5	Robert Fowler	Fred Wong, Averil Morales, Donnie Lynd
2011	2-3	7-16	Robert Fowler	Fred Wong, Averil Morales, Doug Booth
2012	0-5	2-9	Robert Fowler	Averil Morales, Doug Booth
2013	1-4	5-5	Robert Fowler	Doug Booth, Averil Morales, Christian Martinez
2014	0-5	0-5	Troy Goodban	Doug Booth, Aviril Morales, Darren Burkhart, Chris Braten
2015	2-2	2-6	Andrew Clifton	Doug Booth, Averil Morales, Brady Maiden, Darren Burkhart
2016	1-3	3-8	Andrew Clifton	Doug Booth, Averil Morales, Darren Burkhart, Brady Maiden
2017	1-3	1-4	Lalo Celedon	Doug Booth, Averil Morales, Brady Maiden, Darren Burkhart
2018	1-4	1-6	Lalo Celedon	Doug Booth, Averil Morales, Brady Maidin, Frank Lara, Ashley Ortega
2019	0-5	0-8	David Orozco	Raymond Menchaca, Juan Herrera
2020	0-1	0-1	David Orozco	Ray Menchaca, Juan Herrera, Kevin Madding

Tehachapi High School

Year	League Record	Season	Head Coach	Assistant Coaches
1988	na	na	John Caminitti	Coach McGrath
1989	na	na	John Caminitti	Coach McGrath
1990	na	na	John Caminitti	
1991	na	na	John Caminitti	Coach Victor
1992	4-0	6-1	John Caminitti	
1993	na	na	John Caminitti	Robert Bjerknes
1994	na	na	John Caminitti	Robert Bjerknes
1995	na	na	Pat Snyder	Jeff Gentry
1996	2-3	2-3	Pat Snyder	
1997	3-0	3-0	Pat Snyder	
1998	na	na	Pat Snyder	Jeff Gentry
1999	2-1	2-1	Coach Maxwell	Coach Hale
2000	3-0	3-0	John Jeans	Coach Hale
2001	3-2	3-2	Coach Maxwell	Coach Hale
2002	2-3	3-3	Tony Keller	
2003	3-1	3-1	Tony Keller	Desi Lovenguth
2004	na	5-2	Tony Keller	Desi Lovenguth
2005	na	9-2	Tony Keller	Desi Lovenguth, Coach Wilson
2006	na	5-0	Tony Keller	Desi Lovenguth
2007	5-0	5-0	Tony Keller	Bo Steinbach, Charlie Waltz, Desi Lovenguth
2008	5-0	5-0	Tony Keller	Desi Lovenguth, Charlie Waltz, Joe Smith, BO Steinbach, Sean Hilman, Evan McBride
2009	5-0	5-0	Desi Lovenguth	Bo Steinbach, Joe Smith David Liebman, Roger Mesa Evan McBride, Mike Hail Josh Thompson, Doug Stone, Sergio Martinez
2010	4-2	4-2	Desi Lovenguth	Bo Steinbach, R Mesa, J Smith Josh Thompson, Mike Hail,
2011	4-1	4-1	Desi Lovenguth	J. Smith, M. Hail, R. Mesa Bo Steinbach, David East, Charlie Walz, Will Avery, Doug Stone, Curtis Nelson
2012	2-3	2-4	Charlie Walz	Benny Esquivel, Evan McBride, Adam Moreno,
2013	2-2	2-2	Charlie Walz	Benny Esquivel
2014	2-4	3-7	Charlie Walz	Benny Esquivel
2015	0-5	0-7	Desi Lovenguth	Benny Esquivel, Hector Mesa, Bryan Lindsey, Jason Hail
2016	0-5	1-5	Desi Lovenguth	B. Lindsey, H. Mesa, Ted Meek Tom Fredrick, Destiny Rendon,
2017	1-4	1-4	Desi Lovenguth	Benny Esquivel, Bryan Lindsey, Hector Mesa, Eric Parker
2018	1-4	1-4	Desi Lovenguth	Benny Esquivel
2019	0-5	0-5	Desi Lovenguth	Benny Esquivel
2020	0-5	0-5	Desi Lovenguth	Benny Esquivel

Wasco High School

Year	League Record	Season	Head Coach	Assistant Coaches
1965	NA	NA	Dale Dillingham	
1966	NA	NA	Dale Dillingham	
1967	NA	NA	Ted Hammack	
1968	NA	NA	Ted Hammack	
1969	NA	NA	Ted Hammack	
1970	NA	6-5	Ted Hammack	Michael Worley
1971	NA	2-10	Ted Hammack	Michael Worley
1972	5-1	NA	Gerald Branden	Ken Gladden
1973	NA	7-1-1	Gerald Branden	Keith Smith
1974	NA	14-0	Gerald Brandan	
1975	NA	NA	Gerald Branden	Larry Pearson
1976	8-0	NA	Gerald Branden	Larry Pearson
1977	6-2	NA	Gerald Branden	Larry Pearson
1978	NA	NA	Gerald Branden	Larry Pearson
1979	5-1	NA	Rodney Balch	Randy Horton
1980	NA	NA	Jim Wooster	
1981	NA	NA	Jim Wooster	
1982	NA	NA	Lloyd Dickey	Jerry Kerns, Al Soto
1983	NA	NA	Rodney Balch	Jerry Kerns, Al Soto
1984	NA	NA	Jerry Kerns	Al Soto
1985	NA	NA	Mark Kelly	Vincent Moreno
1986	NA	NA	Vincent Moreno	George Moreno
1987	1-3	NA	Vincent Moreno	George Moreno
1988	NA	NA	Phillip Sullivan	George Moreno
1989	NA	NA	Dennis Reed	Craig Nobel
1990	NA	NA	Rocky Bridges	
1991	NA	NA	Rocky Bridges	
1992	NA	NA	Rocky Bridges	Mark Loomis, Brett Clark
1994	NA	NA	Mark Loomis	
1995	NA	NA	Brett Clark	
1996	2-2	3-3	Brett Clark	
1997	NA	NA	Brett Clark	Joe Blanchard, Juan Gallardo
1998	NA	NA	Brett Clark	Joe Blanchard, Juan Gallardo
1999	NA	NA	Joe Blanchard	Juan Gallardo
2000	NA	NA	Joe Blanchard	Juan Gallardo
2001	3-1	5-1-1	Joe Blanchard	
2002	0-5	NA	Stacy Hoffman	Cleo Johnson, Jose Landin
2003	NA	NA	Joe Vega	Alex Gallardo, Coach Acosta
2004	NA	NA	Alex Gallardo	Nacho Martinez
2005	2-3	5-3	Nacho Martinez	Orlando Landois, Alex Gallardo
2006	0-6	0-10	Nacho Martinez	Alex Gallardo, George Romero
2007	3-2	3-3	Jose Landin	Alex Gallardo, George Romero, Juan Gallardo, Nacho Martinez
2008	1-5	1-6	Jose Landin	George Romero, Phillip Solorio, Nacho Martinez

Wasco High School

Year	League Record	Season	Head Coach	Assistant Coaches
2009	NA	NA	Jose Landin	
2010	5-0	5-0	Juan Gallardo	Russell Prado, Seth Hokit, Donny Johnson
2011	5-0	5-0	Juan Gallardo	Russell Prado, Seth Hokit, Donny Johnson
2012	5-0	5-0	Juan Gallardo	Seth Hokit, Donny Johnson, Eric Soto
2013	6-0	12-1	Juan Gallardo	Seth Hokit, Donny Johnson
2014	6-0	9-2	Juan Gallardo	Joe Blanchard, Jared Johnson
2015	6-0	13-3	Juan Gallardo	Garth Wara, Joe Blanchard
2016	3-2	9-3	Juan Gallardo	Garth Wara, Joe Blanchard, Danny Arellano, Russell Prado, Cody Stone
2017	5-1	9-1	Juan Gallardo	Garth Wara, Joe Blanchard, Danny Arellano
2018	3-3	7-3	Juan Gallardo	Garth Wara, Joe Blanchard, Matt Maldonado, Danny Arellano
2019	4-1	4-1	Garth Wara	Juan Gallardo, Joe Blanchard, Danny Arellano, Jason Dibble, Michael Martinez, Rigo Lopez
2020	5-0	13-3	Garth Wara	Juan Galardo, Joe Blanchard

West High School

Year	League Record	Season	Head Coach	Assistant Coaches
1966	NA	NA	Ray Juhl	Floyd Thionett
1967	6-0	11-3	Ray Juhl	Gary Monji
1968	0-10	NA	Ray Juhl	Gary Monji
1969	1-9	NA	Ray Juhl	Ted Cano
1970	NA	NA	Ray juhl	Dallas Grider
1971	2-8	NA	Ray juhl	Dallas Grider
1972	1-11	NA	Ray Juhl	Dallas Grider
1973	2-10	NA	Ray Juhl	Dallas Grider
1974	6-0	NA	Ray Juhl	Dallas Grider
1975	10-2	NA	Ray Juhl	Rick Varner
1976	2-4	NA	Ray Juhl	Rick Varner
1977	3-3	NA	Ray Juhl	Bill Kalivas
1978	1-5	NA	Bill Kalivas	Ray Yocum
1979	3-3	4-4	Darrell Fletcher	Randy Shaw
1980	6-1	NA	Darrell Fletcher	Mike Johnson
1981	3-2	NA	Darrell Fletcher	Mike Johnson
1982	5-2	NA	David East	Glen McCollough
1983	6-1	NA	David East	Glen McCollough
1984	2-5	NA	Don Lundgren	Darrell Fletcher
1985	0-7	NA	Don Lundgren	Darrell Fletcher
1986	1-6	NA	Don Lundgren	Darrell Fletcher
1987	NA	NA	Don Lundgren	Darrell Fletcher
1988	4-3	NA	Joe Barton	Darrell Fletcher, Don Lundgren, Mike Harvey
1989	5-2	NA	Joe Barton	Darrell Fletcher, Mike Harvey
1990	5-2	NA	Joe Barton	Darrell Fletcher, Ric Cox
1991	3-3	NA	Don Lundgren	Bill Richardson, Ric Cox
1992	2-4	NA	Ric Cox	Bill Richardson, Rich Bailey
1993	NA	NA	Ric Cox	Bill Richardson, Troy Beavers
1994	2-4-1	NA	Steve Lawson	Bill Richardson, Matt Smith
1995	2-2	NA	Ric Cox	
1996	2-2	4-12	Ric Cox	
1997	NA	NA	Ty Stricker	Mario Gonzales
1998	0-4	4-12	Ty Stricker	Parris Whitley
1999	NA	NA	Ty Stricker	Parris Whitley
2000	1-3	2-5	Terry Tabbytosavit	Trent Fussel,
2001	NA	NA	Terry Tabbytosavit	Trent Fussel
2002	0-4	1-5	Ben Sherley	Scott DeGough, Trent Fussel, Anthony Tobin
2003	1-3	3-2	Ben Sherley	Scott DeGough, Trent Fussel, Anthony Tobin
2004	0-4	1-6	Ben Sherley	Scott DeGough, Trent Fussel
2005	0-5	06	Ben Sherley	Scott Degough, Trent Fussel
2006	0-5	0-6	Ben Sherley	

West High School

Year	League Record	Season	Head Coach	Assistant Coaches
2007	0-5	1-6	Ben Sherley	Robert Rivera, Matt Lugo, Andy Heironymous, Albert Holguin
2008	0-6	0-7	Ben Sherley	Albert Holguin, Matt Lugo, Manuel Perea
2009	2-4	2-4	Carlo Franciotti	Anthony Griffith, Michael Morrison
2010	1-5	1-5	Carlo Franciotti	Anthony Griffith, James Herrera, Matt Lugo
2011	3-1	3-2	James Herrera	Alex Herrera, Matt Lugo, Jose Santos
2012	1-3	NA	James Herrera	Alex Herrera, Matt Lugo, Johnny Garcia
2013	0-4	0-8	James Herrera	Johnny Garcia, Alex Herrera, Joseph Kuntz
2014	3-1	3-3	Joseph Kuntz	Billy Pitcher
2015	3-2	3-4	Joseph Kuntz	Billy Pitcher
2016	1-4	1-4	Miguel Trejo	Phillip Garcia
2017	0-6	0-6	Miguel Trejo	Phillip Garcia, Alex Herrera
2018	0-4	0-6	Alex Herrera	Phillip Garcia, Jacob Chairez, Mathew Lugo
2019	0-5	0-5	Mathew Lugo	Chris Salazar, Vincent Morantes
2020	1-1	3-3	Mathew Lugo	Brandon Wright, Brian Galindo

Taft High School

Year	League Record	Season	Head Coach	Assistant Coaches
1969	NA	NA	Joe Garrett	
1970	1-7	3-9	Joe Garrett	Ken Anderson
1971	2-8	2-9	Joe Garrett	Ken Anderson
1972	0-6	NA	Joe Garrett	
1973	NA	NA	Joe Garrett	Ray Newton
1974				
1991	NA	NA		
1992	NA	NA	Coach Cummings	Coach Graham
1993	NA	0-4	Matt Smith	

Maricopa High School

Year	League Record	Season	Head Coach	Assistant Coaches
1966	NA	NA	Terry Cummings	
1967	NA	NA	Terry Cummings	
1968	NA	NA	Terry Cummings	
1969	NA	3-4	Terry Cummings	
1975	NA	NA	Mike Rucks	
1976	NA	NA	David East	
1977	NA	NA	David East	
1978	NA	NA	David East	
1979	NA	NA	David East	
1980	NA	NA	David East	

COACH/WRESTLER PROFILES

Franc Affenntranger
2X South Sequoia League Champion, Sierra-Sequoia Divisional second and first, sixth and third in the section for Shafter High. Bakersfield College State, Regional and Conference Champion and a third in JC – record 62-7. CSUB he was 89-7-2 2X Division I third place, Division II Champion and named Most Outstanding Wrestler and Division II second place.

Jimmy Aguirre
Clovis High 2X League, 3X Section and 3X State Champion, seventh and first in the Junior Nationals. Stanford University Pac 10 Champion and Most Outstanding Wrestler In 1993 and a 3X NCAA qualifier.

Robert Arballo
Placed second in the section for Madera High. A 2X State JC Champion for Fresno City College. Then, he wrestled at Fresno State. Assistant Coach at Porterville High, Fresno City College, and named Assistant Coach of the Year 1989, 1994, and 1998, at Martin Luther King Middle School, Madera South High. Head Coach at Delano High, Madera High, Madera South, and Fresno City College State Champions in 1998 and named Coach of the Year. He Coached a total of 34 years.

Dennis Bardsley
A league Champion placed 2X in the CIF NCS and won the CIF North Coast Section. At Santa Rosa JC he was a Conference, Regional, and State Champion. Named the Most Outstanding Wrestler in the State Championships – JC record 59-1 with 40 falls. At Cal Poly he placed second in the Far Western Regionals, AAU Junior World Champion, Greco Title, Sambo Title and an alternate on 1978 Greco World Team. Coach for 35 years, 19 as a Head Coach. His teams won 216 Dual Meets. He served as director of the Central Valley Wrestling Association for 12 years, served on the CIF Wrestling Advisory Committee, Board Member, and inductee in the California Wrestling Hall of Fame.

Florencio (Flo) Rocha A 2X League Champion, second and third place in the section third in the state. Record at Bakersfield High 76-7. Bakersfield College - named the Most Outstanding Wrestler in the conference, 2X Regional Champion, State Champion 1974, and second in 1975. JC record 63-4. CSUB 1976 NCAA Division II Fourth, 1977 Division II Champion, 1977 Division I fourth. Wrestled in the NWCA All Star Classic. Record at CSUB 63-4

Ray Hernandez
At Corcoran High he was a 2X League Champion, 2X Sierra-Sequoia Division Champion. College of The Sequoia 2X League Champion, Regional Champion, and placed Fifth in the state JC. He was the San Francisco State Far Western Conference Champion, placed second in the NCAA Division II Championships. He coached for 26 years with 16 at Mt. Whitney High. Inducted into The San Francisco State Athletic Hall of Fame.

Rick McKinney
At Livermore High he was 4x League Champion, and a Section Champion, coached wrestling for 25 years, Coached 76 League Champions, 47 Valley placers, 36 Masters placers, 21 Valley Champion, 11 Master Champions, 40 state qualifiers, 10 state medalists. He coached The California National Teams from 1982-1997, World Team Coach 1987, 1988 and 1994. Since 2006 Rick has been rated as one of the top Wrestling Officials in the state and national level. Inductee in the California Wrestling Hall of Fame and the USA Wrestling Hall of Fame California Chapter.

Nathan Morgan
At Bakersfield High, 4X League Champion, Divisional second, and 3X Champion, CIF Section second and 3X State Champion – in 2004 named the Most Outstanding Wrestler in the Section Tournaments. Named the Most Outstanding Wrestler in the State Tournament. Dapper Dan Classic, Amateur Wrestling News 3X All American, 3X Asics All-American, Dream Team. Oklahoma State University 3X All American, 3X Big 12 Champion, 2X NWCA All-Academic Team wrestled In NWCA All Star Classic, OSU Male Athletic of the year.

Kent Olsen
Wrestled at Royal Oak High, Mt. Sac, Cal State Fullerton. Head Wrestling Coach at five Different High Schools with a record and still counting 451-65-2 – Now coaching at Pioneer High. At Lemoore, his teams have won 16 League Titles, 102 Individuals League Titles, 90 CIF Divisional medals, 13 Champions, 67 CIF Sections

COACH/WRESTLER PROFILES

placers with 16 CIF Section Champions. He was named League Coach of the Year nine times. At West Hills College his teams won three Conference Titles, two Regional Titles, teams placed in the top ten three times, eleven of his athletes earned All-American honors. Coach Olsen is still active with California USA Wrestling. Inducted into the California Wrestling Hall of Fame.

Gary Pederson
Wrestled for Yuba College and San Jose State. He was the Head Coach at Yuba College 1973-1979 coaching two Conference Titles and five state placers. Holtville High 1976-1986 his teams won three Conference Titles. Shafter High 1986-2007 dual record 157-38-2 with a league record of 84-19-2, eight South Sequoia League Championship Teams, named The 2003 Bakersfield Californian Coach of the Year, He served for 26 years as the South Sequoia League reprehensive to the CIF. 84 of his wrestlers were League Champions, 60 Sierra-Sequoia placers, 29 Masters placers, 5 State Placers. Coached the California USA Wrestling Team for 2 years. Inducted into California Hall of Fame and USA Wrestling Hall of Fame California Chapter.

Chris Pendleton
Lemoore High Yosemite Divisional second and first, Section second and first, State fourth and first. Most Outstanding Wrestler Award in the Divisional, Section and State Tournaments. Record 178-15 with 104 falls. Wrestling USA All American. University Nationals second, first, University World tenth. Oklahoma State University 2x Big 12 Champion, 2X NCAA Champion and third place – record 115-11, wrestled in the NWCA All Star Classic 3 times. US Open fourth, seventh, and second, Currently Head Coach at Oregon State University.

Nick Quintana
Wrestled at Selma High, Fresno City College, and Fresno State. Coached Selma High for thirty years winning eight Sierra-Sequoia Divisional II Titles and a 1989 CIF Section Championship. Inducted into the California Wrestling Hall of Fame

Jim Seay
Was a 2X runner up in the state of Kansas, wrestled at Oklahoma State University and the University of Oklahoma. Head Coach at Northwest Classen High in Oklahoma, Highland High, Bakersfield High, San Luis Obispo High, Head Coach and Assistant Coach at Paso Robles High for a total of 29 years. Coached 12 state medalist. Founder/Director Paso Robles Tournament for eleven years, Co-Founder/Board Member Kern County Wrestling Association, Co-Founder/Coach Paso Youth Wrestling, Youth Coach for 27 years, High School, JC and College Referee for over five years

Adam Tirapelle
4X CIF Champion Hiram Johnson, Buchanan SAC-Joaquin Section 1993,94,95, Buchanan 1996, State Tournament Second In 1994, first 1995, first 1996 Central Section first Yosemite Divisional and first in Central Section record 214-7. Junior National fifth in Greco, fourth in Freestyle. Nation High School Championships first, Amateur Wrestling News All-American, Wrestling USA All-American, ASICS All-American. University of Illinois 1997 FILA. National Champion, FILA Junior World Championships fifth, NCAA Championships third, second, and first, Big 10 Champion, record 127-21, Midlands Championships placed third twice, Wrestled in the NWCA All Star Classic, US Open seventh. Currently Assistant at Clovis High. Inducted into the California Wrestling Hall of Fame

Steve Tirapelle
Wrestled at Ponderosa High School and American River College. Coached at Hiram Johnson High School and Clovis High School. 28 years of coaching, 21 League Championship Teams, 68 State Medalist, 8 CIF Section Championship Teams, Coach of the year 2003, 2008 and 2011 Clovis High – NCAA Division II All-American Placing fifth at Humboldt State. Inducted into the California Wrestling Hall of Fame and the USA Wrestling Hall of Fame California Chapter.

Steve Varner
A SYL and Central Section Champion his junior year at Bakersfield High. A severe neck injury hampered his senior year. He wrestled at Bakersfield College, and San Francisco State. Two-year Assistant Coach to Olan Polite at Bakersfield High. He was the Driller Head Coach for 10 years coaching four SYL titles, 27 wrestlers that won a League titles, nine Divisional Champions, Nine

COACH/WRESTLER PROFILES

CIF Section Champions and two State Champions. Board Member of the Coyote Club, and Kern County Wrestling Association, SYL and SEYL Representative to the CIF. Inducted into the California Wrestling Hall of Fame.

Jake Varner
Bakersfield High 4X League, Divisional, CIF Section Champion, Most Outstanding Wrestler Awards in League 2005, Divisional 2003, 2005, CIF Section 2005. 2X Reno Champion, Brut National Most Outstanding Wrestler, State Placer fourth, second, first, first State Most Outstanding Wrestler Award 2004, Wade Schalles Award. Record 157-10 – 132 falls NHSCA second, Amateur Wrestling News All-American, Wrestling USA All-American, Asics All-American, Junior Nationals Greco third, Freestyle Third, FILA Nationals fourth, FILA Junior World injured. Iowa State University-Amateur Wrestling News All Rookie Team, Big 12 first, second, first, second NCAA second, second, first, first. Midlands Tournament third, first, second, first. Harold Nichols Tournament 4X Champion, selected three times to wrestle in the NWCA All Star Classic. Record 121-10 - 42 falls. University Nationals Third, US Open eighth, seventh, first, second, first, first, second, second Pan-Am Games First, - World Championships ninth, third. Yarygan third, fifth Canada Cup first, World Cup Team 2015, 2016. 2012 OLYMPIC GOLD MEDALIST.
Currently Assistant Coach at Penn State University.

Darrell Vasquez
Wrestled at Bakersfield High with a record of 204-7, 3X League, 4X Divisional, 3X CIF Section Champion – 4X State Champion, Most Outstanding Wrestler Award Divisional 2000, 2002, CIF Section 2002, State 2001, 2002,4X five Counties, 4X Morro Bay, 2X Reno Tournaments Championships - Most Outstanding Wrestler Reno. 3X Junior National Freestyle All-American, Dapper Dan Classic, 3X Asics All- American, Wrestling News All American, Wrestling USA All-American. Cal Poly Record 82-15 Pac-10 placer third, second, first – NCAA 2X All-American Fourth, Fifth, Reno Champion and Most Outstanding Wrestler Award, 2005 NWCA All Star Classic. Coached 2 years at Harvard.

Eugene Walker
An outstanding Three Sport Athlete at South Bakersfield High SYL –third, first - Divisional second, fourth CIF Section third, first, third. First in the AAU Junior World Championships in California. Bakersfield College 2X Conference Champion and Most Outstanding Wrestler Award 1970 State JC Third 1969, Third 1970, Record 58-9 Idaho State University, Big Sky Champion, MIWA Champion, NCAA Qualifier. Coaching – Head Assistant under Joe Seay at CSUB – one-year, Assistant Coach at South Bakersfield -two years, 1977-1993 Head Wrestling Coach at South Bakersfield, Two CIF Central Section Championship Teams, Two Divisional Championship Teams, Five South Yosemite League Champions. 1979 team placed Fourth in the State, the 1990 Team placed Ninth in the State.1997-2003 Head Coach Fremont Middle School Roseburg, Oregon, Five District Championships, 58-0 in Dual Meets. 2004-2008 California State Tournament Weigh-in Director, Inducted into the South Bakersfield Hall of Fame.

Rodney Balch
Was a State Champion at Clovis High. State Community College Champion at Fresno City College. At Cal State Bakersfield he was three-time CCAA Conference Champion. Placed second in and fifth in the D-II Championships, with a record of 96-24-2. He coached Wasco High from 1979-1980. Assistant coach at Clovis High in 1980-1981 and Head Coach 1982 to 1995. At Clovis he led his teams to eight league, seven divisional, and seven CIF Championships. He coached six State Championship Teams, 28 CIF Champions, 29 State placers. He was voted the California State Coach of the Year. Record at Clovis 238-20-3. Career record 248-21-3. He was an Assistant at Buchanan for seven years after Clovis. Inducted into the California Hall of Fame.

Fred Bohna
Placed second and first in the CIF at Clovis. At UCLA, was NCAA Champion, PAC 10 Wrestler of the Year, wrestled in NWCA All-Star Classic, was a National Champion in Freestyle, placed second in World Cup, Pan-American Champion, placed third AAU Nationals. Inducted into the

COACH/WRESTLER PROFILES

California Wrestling Hall of Fame.

Vern Brooks
High School: Will Rodgers High School, Tulsa, Oklahoma-College: Northwestern State College. Coaching Springs, Wyoming 1953 Wyoming State Wrestling Champions, Madera 1954-1965. At Madera, his teams won two Northern California Invitationals, five CIF Championships, and coached 27 individual CIF Central Section Champions. Inducted into the California Wrestling Hall of Fame and the USA Wrestling Hall of Fame California Chapter.

Mike Bull
At South High he won the Sam Lynn Award as the Most Outstanding Athlete in Kern County. Placed third, third and first in the CIF. State Champion with a record of 44-0. National Junior Greco Roman Champion, he placed fourth in the Olympic Trials as a 17-year-old. He was named the California Wrestler of the Year in 1973. At Bakersfield College, he was the California Community College State Champion with a 30-2 record. At Cal State Bakersfield, he wrestled in the NWCA All Star Classic, was a three-time D-II All-American, placed fourth, first and second. Record 85-10-1. Inducted into the California Wrestling Hall of Fame and the South High Hall of Fame.

Bruce Burnett
At North High School, he was a two-time league champion, placing in CIF first, second and third. At Bakersfield College, his record was 55-3. He was a two-time State Community College champion and won the 1970 Outstanding Wrestler Award in the state championships. At Idaho State University, he was a two-time Big Sky Conference Champion. He never lost a dual match in college. Coaching at Meridian High School in Idaho, he attained a 14-year record of 154-13-2, along with four state championships. He was Idaho Coach of the Year six times and a five-time runner-up. He was assistant at Oklahoma State University from 1987 until 1990 and coached for USA Wrestling from 1990-2000. He served as the developmental and national freestyle coach, coaching national teams, world teams, and Olympic teams. He was named Freestyle Wrestling Coach of the Year in 1995 and 1996 and named Olympic Committee Elite Coach of the Year in 1996 and 2000. He became the head wrestling coach at US Naval Academy for 10 years. Inducted into Meridian Hall of Fame, Idaho State Athletic Hall of Fame, California Wrestling Hall of Fame, Bob Elias Kern County Hall of Fame, and the National Wrestling Hall of Fame.

Art Chavez
In high school, he was a CIF champion at South High. At Bakersfield College he placed second in the State Community College meet. At San Francisco State, he won the Far Western Conference and named the Outstanding Wrestler. He placed fifth in the NCAA D-II Tournament. He earned first at San Jose, San Francisco State Mare Island Tournaments and third at the UCLA Tournament. Internationally, he was seventh in World Greco Roman Championships And won both National AAU Freestyle and Greco Roman Championships the same year. He wrestled for the San Francisco Olympic Club, winning the Olympic Trials in Freestyle in 1968. He coached two individual state champions at Gonzales High and South High and officiated the State High School Championships. Inducted into the San Francisco State Hall of Fame.

Joe Conley
Joe attended high school in Chicago and Loras College in Dubuque, Iowa. He became coach at Exeter High in 1965 and coached for 30 years. His teams won more than 500 dual meets, 10 league championships and boasted seven undefeated seasons. He was member of the Central Section Wrestling Advisory Committee for 10 years. Inducted into the California Wrestling Hall of Fame.

Lennis Cowell
In high school he placed first, second and third in the Northern California Championships at Pleasant Hills High School and was undefeated his senior year. At Diablo Valley College, he placed third in the State Community College Championships. At Cal Poly he was a two-time CCAA champion and placed third and fourth in NCAA D-II Championships. He coached at Allan Hancock College, Cuesta College, San Luis Obispo High School, and Clovis West High School. At Clovis West, his record was

COACH/WRESTLER PROFILES

97-5. He coached four league, three divisional, three CIF, and two state championship teams. His teams won 85 straight duals in a row. He was the Southern Regional Coach of the Year in 1983 and National High School Coach of the Year in 1984. At Cal Poly, he had a 18 year record of 167-147-8. He coached 14 PAC-10 Champions and eight NCAA D-I All-Americans. His overall record is 300-165-9. Inducted into the Cal Poly Hall of Fame and California Wrestling Hall of Fame.

Sam Crandall
Joining the coaching staff at Kingsburg High School. Crandall coached wrestling for more than 40 years. In 1973, he was voted Central Sequoia League Coach of the Year. His 27-year coaching record was 260-82-9. Inducted into the California Wrestling Hall of Fame.

Dennis Deliddo
He wrestled at Bullard High School and Fresno City College placing fifth in the State Committee College Championships. At Fresno State University, he was he was a two-time conference runner-up. He was an assistant coach at Fresno City College before becoming the coach at Clovis High School from 1971-1981. His record was 147-7-1. He led his teams to eight league, six divisional, five CIF, and five state championship. In 1974,1975 and 1976 his teams placed second and third in 1981. He was named (Valley) CIF Coach of the Year five times. At Fresno State University from 1981-2005, he coached 27 All-Americans, and 58 conference champions. He was a four-time WAC Coach of the Year and twice named PCAA Coach of the Year. His teams won seven consecutive WAC titles, nine conference titles, and 11 top 25 finishes in the NCAA Tournament. He was a runner-up for the 1993 NCAA Coach of the Year. Record at Fresno State 314-171-4. He was a long-time coach for the Sunkist Kids Wrestling Club Team. Inducted into Fresno County Hall of Fame, California Wrestling Hall of Fame and the USA Wrestling Hall of Fame California Chapter.

Dennis Downing
At bell Gardens High School, he placed third in the CIF. At Cerritos College two-time runner-up in the State Junior College Championships. At Cal Poly he was a NCAA D-II Champion. He was assistant coach at Cal Poly for one year. He was head coach at San Luis High School one year, at Merced High School for three years, at Sierra High School for 27 years and coached one year at Heidelberg High School in Germany.

David East
At Bakersfield High he was a CIF Champion. He attended Bakersfield College, two-time Conference champion, J.C. All-American- record 53-11. At Cal State Bakersfield he boasted a two-year record of 75-17. He coached at Maricopa High School for five years before coaching at West Bakersfield High and then as assistant coach at Bakersfield High. He was head coach at Bakersfield High for 24 years. His varsity record at Bakersfield High was 204-12. He coached 14 League, two divisional, three CIF and one state championship teams with seven state champions, and 31 state place winners. He was named National High School Coaches Association Co-High School Coach of the Year. Inducted into the California Wrestling Hall of Fame.

Dick Francis
At Orange Coast College and then San Jose State University, he was undefeated for three years. He was the P.I.C. champion in 1953 and 1955, second in 1954. He was a Far Western AAU Champion in 1955, 1956, and 1958 and third in 1954, 1955 and 1957 at the National AAU Championships in Freestyle. He placed third in 1956 and forth in 1957 in the National AAU Greco Roman Championships. He coached at Fresno High from 1956-1959, McLane High from 1959-1964 and Fresno State University from 1964-1981. He coached two conference championship teams, and 39 individual conference champions. Inducted into the California Wrestling Hall of Fame and the USA Wrestling Hall of Fame California Chapter.

Sam Gollmyer
At Bakersfield High he was a CIF Champion. He wrestled at Bakersfield College and Humboldt State College. He coached at Victor Valley High School from 1975-1993 with a 306-73 record, 14 league championships and one CIF championship. His teams placed second two times and third one time. He coached one state championship team

COACH/WRESTLER PROFILES

in 1987, three individual state champions and 10 state placers. He coached the unofficial Masters Champions – Southern Section three times. Inducted into the California Wrestling Hall of Fame.

Al Kiddy
An outstanding three-sport athlete in high school, he lettered in three sports at the University of Oklahoma, where he wrestled for Port Robertson and played football for Bud Wilkerson. His coaching record is 237-15-2. He coached three Trans Valley Championships teams at Hughson High School from 1960-1964. He coached at McLane High in 1965. At Madera High, he coached six league, two divisional, and two CIF championship teams. He was assistant coach at Fresno City College from 1976-1984. Inducted California Wrestling Hall of Fame.

Webber Lawson
At Cal Poly, he wrestled for Los Angeles Athletic Club and was the 1948 U S Western Regional Olympic Trials Champion and named Outstanding Wrestler, a three-time Far Western Champion, a six-time Southern Pacific AAU Champion, a U S Western Pan-Am Champion and Senior Open AAU Champion. He coached at Inglewood High, Tulare Western High and Fremont of Sunnyvale. At Fremont High, his teams Won 52 dual meets in a row and four Central Coast titles in a row. His teams won the Northern California Invitation in 1967 and 1968, placing second in 1966. He served as president of the National High School Wrestling Association and coached for 25 years in three different CIF sections. Inducted into the California Wrestling Hall of Fame.

Vern McCoy
At the University of Iowa, he wrestled varsity four years and was the team captain in 1948. He coached at Roosevelt High School from 1957-1966 and at McLane High. Inducted into the USA Wrestling Hall of Fame California Chapter

Bill Musick
At Madera High School, he was a CIF finalist. He was an outstanding football player in high school, Bakersfield College and Fresno State University. He was head football and wrestling at Fresno City College for 19 years in wrestling. He coached 17 league championship teams, 12 Northern California Championship teams and won four California Community College titles. He was a four-time Coach of the Year for Community Colleges with a record of 247-50-5. Inducted into the California Wrestling Hall of Fame and the USA Wrestling Hall of Fame California Chapter.

Larry Morgan
At East Bakersfield High School, he was 82-2 his two years. He was a two-time National High School Champion and Junior World Champion. In college his record at Cal Poly was 112-21-1. He placed second in 1972 and 1973 – first in 1973 and named Outstanding Wrestler in the NCAA D-I Tournament. He placed fifth in the D-I Tournament in 1973. He wrestled in the East-West All Star Classic. Internationally, he was first in the Olympic trials in 1973, fourth in the World Championships, first in the AAU Greco Roman Nationals in 1976, US Federation National Freestyle, US Federation Greco Roman. He spent two years as assistant at the University of Iowa and was an assistant coach at Cal State Bakersfield from 1979-1981. Then he was an assistant at Bakersfield High. Inducted into the Cal Poly Hall of Fame, Bob Elias Kern County Hall of Fame, California Wrestling Hall of Fame, Division II Wrestling Hall of Fame.

Corky Napier
Napier wrestled at Madera High, Fresno City College and Fresno State University. He was assistant coach at Madera High where his Junior Varsity record was 55-5. He was the head coach at University High School from 1976-1980 where his record was 33-3, coaching one State Champion and three CIF Champions. He was the head coach at Madera High from 1980-2004 with 208 wins in the Central Section and 10 team championships. He was a six-time League Coach of the Year. He coached the CIF team champions in 1990, and runner-up in 1982, 1985, and 1991. He coached six individual State Champions and 28 CIF Champions. Madera was second in the state in 1984. His overall coaching record 314-48. Inducted into the California Wrestling Hall of Fame.

Lorenzo Neal
At Lemoore High School, Neal was the CIF football

323

COACH/WRESTLER PROFILES

player of the year, a High School All-American, and Cal-Hi Athlete of the Year. In wrestling, a three-time Divisional and CIF Champion, a runner-up for Divisional and CIF his freshman year and fourth, second and first at the State Championships. At the Junior Nationals he placed third in both Freestyle and Greco Roman. At Fresno State University in football, he was All Big West champion and the MVP in the Freedom Bowl. In wrestling, he was Espoir Champion in both styles, two-time WAC Champion, and placed seventh in the NCAA Tournament. Neal has played 14 years in the NFL with New Orleans, New York Jets, Tampa Bay, Tennessee, Cincinnati, and San Diego. He is a three-time Pro Bowl selection, a four-time Pro Bowl alternate and four-time USA Today All-Joe Team.

Joe Nigos
At Delano High School, Nigos was an outstanding football player and a CIF wrestling champion. At Bakersfield College an outstanding running back and a two-time Community State Champion with a record of 52-1. At Cal Poly he played football and wrestled. He wrestled for the USA at the World Greco Roman Championships. Head wrestling Coach at Oak Grove High in San Jose. High School and College wrestling official. Officiated the State Championships.

Chuck Patton
Patton wrestled at East Waterloo High School in Iowa and Northern Iowa University. He coached Exeter High from 1962-1963, Reedsport High School in Oregon. He was the head coach at Northern Iowa University for 18 years with a record of 217-87-8. He coached 10 conference championship teams, placed second four times, coached NCAA II championship teams in 1975 and 1978 and placed 17 times in the top 12. He was the NCAA II Coach of the Year in 1969 and 1978. Inducted into the Division II Hall of Fame.

Bruce Pfutzenreuter
Pfutzenreuter coached two league championship teams at South Bakersfield High from 1957-1964. His record was 74-14-3. He coached football, wrestling and was the head track coach. At Bakersfield College his coaching record was 264-81-2. He coached a State Community College Championship team in 1968-1969 season. His teams placed second three times, third three times, fourth twice, and ninth twice. He coached 32 tournament championship teams, 66 state placers, 16 state champions, 47 All-Americans and named Coach of the Year 1n 1969. His 28-year coaching record: 338-95-5 Inducted into the Bob Elias Kern County Hall of Fame, The South High Hall of Fame, California Wrestling Hall of Fame, USA Wrestling Hall of Fame California Chapter.

Olan Polite
At Bolder High School in Colorado, Polite placed fourth in the 1949 Colorado State High Championships at 127 pounds. He coached at Arvin High from 1957-1959, and at Bakersfield High School from 1959-1977. He coached four league, two Divisional, and two CIF championship teams.

He was named California Coach of the Year, District 8 (13 states) Coach of the Year in 1979, and he was nominated for National High School Wrestling Coach of the Year. His career records 189-37-2

Grover Rains
Rains was an NCAA champion at Oklahoma State University. He coached at Stillwater High School in Oklahoma, East Bakersfield and Foothill High in California. He was a long-time wrestling official in high school and college. Oklahoma State Gallagher Award in 2004 and inducted into the USA Wrestling Hall of Fame Oklahoma Chapter.

Rocky Rasley
At South Bakersfield High School, Rasley was an outstanding three-sport athlete. He placed second in the CIF in wrestling. At Bakersfield College, he was again a three-sport athlete, Named a Community College Football All-American and two-time Regional Wrestling Champion. He placed second and third in the State Community College Championships. At Oregon State he played football and wrestled placing fifth in the World Wrestling Freestyle Championships. He played eight years in the NFL for Detroit and San Francisco Inducted into the Bob Elias Kern County Hall of Fame, South High Hall of Fame, and Oregon State University Hall of Fame.

Jessie Reyes
At Bakersfield High School, Reyes was a two-time league champion, a divisional champion and third in the

COACH/WRESTLER PROFILES

CIF, His record was 32-0 his senior year until an injury ended his season. At Cal State Bakersfield, he was 151-22-1, a two-time NCAA Division II and NCAA Division I Champion. 1983 named Outstanding Wrestler D-II Tournament, 1984 wrestled in East-West All-Star Classic. Reyes was assistant at Cal State Bakersfield, Oklahoma State University, Arizona State, Cal Poly and Michigan State University. Head coach at Purdue University for fifteen years in the Big 10. Record 179-120-3, four Big 10 Champions, 16 All-Americans. He coached the USA Junior World Team to a third place. Inducted into the Bob Elias Kern County Hall of Fame and the California Wrestling Hall of Fame.

Chuck Seal
At Redmond High School in Oregon, Seal was a three-time Oregon State Champion at Portland State, he was 110-14-1, placing first, second and first in the NCAA D-II and third and sixth in the D-I tournaments. Inducted into the NCAA D-II Wrestling Hall of Fame. He coached at Reedley High School.

Joe Seay
Attending Kansas State University, Seay was a three-time Greco Roman National Champion, a two-time runner-up Freestyle and placed second in the 1964 and 1972 Olympic Trials. He placed third in the 1968 trials. He coached at South Bakersfield High from 1964-1977 with a 117-13-2 record, coaching six league and four CIF championship teams. At Cal State Bakersfield he coached for 12 years with a 189-56-2 record. His teams won seven NCAA D-II titles, 24 individual titles and placed second twice. At Oklahoma State University, he coached seven years with a 114-18-2 record. He coached five Big 8 Team Champion, 31 All-Americans two NCAA - I Champions and five National Champions, he was the D- I Coach of the Year in 1989 and 1990. He was assistant coach at University of Virginia and head coach at University of Tennessee at Chattanooga where he was named Southern Conference Coach of the Year with a record of 16-8-1. Internationally, he was the head coach of the Sunkist Kids and 1971 Junior World Team, head coach of the 1976 All-Star Classic, World Cup 1985, 1986 and 1991 and the Pan-American Games in 1995. He coached the World Team in 1993, 1995, and 2005, the Olympic Games 1996 and an assistant Olympic coach in 1992 and 2000. He was named Man of the Year in 1991. His record during 22 years of college coaching was 319-82-5. His record during 30 years of high school and college was 436-95-7. Inducted into the Kansas State University Hall of Fame, Bob Elias Kern County Hall of Fame, National Wrestling Hall of Fame, South High Hall of Fame, California Wrestling Hall of Fame, and USA Wrestling Hall of Fame California Chapter.

Phil Sullivan
At Tulare Western High School, Sullivan was a two-time CIF champion. At Cal Poly, he was an NCAA D- II Champion. He placed fifth in the National AAU Greco Roman championships. He coached at Wasco High School and coached numerous youth teams in the Central Section. He was named Southern Coach of the Year 1n 1974 and 1976.

Leon Tedder
Tedder was a four-year Letterman at Oklahoma State University and undefeated in dual meets all four years. At East Bakersfield High School his team won three league championships and two CIF championships. He was a long-time high school and college official. Inducted into the Kern County Officials Association, East High Hall of Fame, and the California Wrestling Hall of Fame.

Tim Vanni
At Monache High School, Vanni was a three-time league, two-time Divisional, And two-time CIF champion. He placed second in 1979 and sixth in 1978 in the State Championships. He was 70-3 his last two seasons.
At Cal State Bakersfield, he was a four-year letterman. Internationally, he was a five-time national Freestyle Champion, placing sixth in 1982, sixth in 1986, and fifth in 1987, fifth in 1989, ninth in 1994. He was on seven World Teams. He placed fourth in 1988 Olympic Games and fifth in 1992 he was a 1996 alternate. On the Pan-Am Team he placed second in1987, second 1990, third in 1991 and second in 1992. From 1981 until 1996, Vanni won or placed in many freestyle tournaments all over the world, including World Cup, Canada Cup, Nation Sports Festival, Club Cup, and World University Trials. Currently head coach at Porterville High School. He was assistant at Cal State

COACH/WRESTLER PROFILES

Bakersfield for three years, and Arizona State for five years. First Head Coaching job Einsiedeln, Switzerland. Inducted into the Bob Elias Kern County Hall of Fame and California Wrestling Hall of Fame, USA Wrestling Hall of Fame California Chapter, Monache High Hall of Fame.

Bill Van Worth
At South Bakersfield High School, he was an outstanding football player and two-time league, two-time Divisional champion, placing first and second in the CIF. His wrestling record was 91-7 with 74 falls. At Bakersfield College he played football and wrestled with a 47-5 record and placed second twice in the Community College Tournament.
At Humboldt State he placed second in the NCAA D - II Tournament. At Cal State Bakersfield he won the NCAA D -II with a record of 40-2. Internationally, he was a member of the Greco Roman World Team and a Gold Medalist on the Pan-American Team. At Dos Palos he coached nine league championship teams and amassed a 126-31-1 record in 13 years.

Yero Washington
At Porterville High School, Washington was sixth in 1990 and a CIF and State Champion in 1992. At Fresno City College he was second in 1993 and a State Community College Champion in 1994. At Fresno State University he placed sixth in 1996 and third in 1997 at the NCAA Tournament. In 1998, he was second in U.S. Open and second in the World Team Trials. In 1999, he was a World Cup Team member, he placed fourth in the World Team Trials and was a Sunkist International Open Champion. Washington placed fifth in the Olympic Team trials in 2000, fourth in the U.S. Open in 2003, fifth in the U.S. Open 2004 and the top eight at the Olympic Team Trials. He was an assistant coach at Columbia University. He is currently a Director of Streets of L.A.

Han Wiedenhoefer
At San Jose State, Wiedenhoefer was a two-time PCAA Champion and a Far Western Champion. He coached at Fresno City College from 1959-1965, coaching five league, two Regional and two State Community College Championships Teams. His teams placed second and twice placed third in the State. Inducted into the California Wrestling Hall of Fame and the USA Wrestling Hall of Fame California Chapter.

Drew Williams
At Paradise High School, Williams was a three-time Northern Section CIF Champion. He wrestled at Yuba City College and Chico State. He coached at Los Plumas High School, Brawley High School 13-0-1, Desert League Title, and Monache High School for 26 years. His career record 401-76-4. His teams won 18 league titles, three Yosemite Divisional, and one CIF Championships. He coached four runner-up teams, 17 CIF Champions, 14 State medal winner and 60 State qualifiers. Served on both the CIF and State Advisory committees. Inducted into the Ponderosa, Monache, California Wrestling Hall of Fame and USA Wrestling Hall of Fame California Chapter.

Floyd Winter
After wrestling all four years at Porterville High School, Winter became 13-time Armed Forces Champion for the U.S. Army. He was a 1972 World Military Greco Roman Champion, a 1977 National Greco Roman Champion, a three-time runner-up at the Greco Roman Nationals and a four-time placer in the World Military Championships. In the U.S. Army, he was an assistant Olympic Greco Roman coach in 1984 and 1988, a World Cup Greco Roman coach in 1985 and 1989, and a 1990 Olympic Festival Greco Roman coach. He was a member of the National Coaching Staff for 10 years. Inducted into the California Wrestling Hall of Fame.

John Woods
At Redwood High School in Visalia, he placed first and second in the CIF with a record of 68-8. At Cal Poly he was a three-time NCAA D-II All-American, an NCAA D-II champion in 1968, and NCAA D-I runner-up. He wrestled in the East-West All Stat Classic. He coached at Orange Glen High School, where his four-year record was 45-9-2. At Palomar Community College, his 15-year record was 179-19-3. His teams won five State Community College Championships and Woods was named the State Coach of the Year four times. He is the former Athletic Director at Palomar Community College.

COACH/WRESTLER PROFILES

Inducted into the Redwood High Hall of Fame, USA Wrestling Hall of Fame California Chapter, and the California Wrestling Hall of Fame.

Howard Zink
Wrestled at North Salinas High School, a conference champion at Hartnell Junior College and a Former Cal Poly Wrestler, Zink coached at Washington Union High School for 26 years, with a record of 328-113-2. He coached 13 league, six Sequoia-Sierra Divisional Championship Teams. 96 individual league champions, 53 Divisional champions, 13 CIF champions, 10 state medalist and one National Champion. Served as assistant at West Valley College. League representative to the CIF for 18 years, served on the CIF State Advisory Committee, Inducted into the California Wrestling Hall of Fame.

L to R – Jacob Good, Adam Tirapelle and Gabe Schaefer
Clovis High School

Rick McKinney

Yero Washington – Porterville High

www.ingramcontent.com/pod-product-compliance
Lightning Source LLC
Chambersburg PA
CBHW060418300426
44111CB00018B/2890